Media Planning & Buying in the 21st Century

Media Planning & Buying in the 21st Century

Ronald D. Geskey

2020:MARKETING COMMUNICATIONS LLC

2020:MARKETING COMMUNICATIONS LLC
Media Planning and Buying
For the 21st Century

Author: Ronald D. Geskey, Sr.,

COPYRIGHT © 2011 BY RONALD D. GESKEY
Publisher: 2020:MARKETING COMMUNICATIONS LLC

ISBN-13: 978-1456505301
ISBN-10: 1456505300

Disclaimer

This publication is designed to provide accurate and authoritative information, recognizing that content is based on opinion. This book is sold with the understanding that the publisher is not engaged in rendering legal, accounting, or other professional services. If legal advice or other expert assistance is required, the services of a competent professional should be sought.

DEDICATION

This book is dedicated to my fantastic wife of 40 years.
Thank you for your patience and support during our marriage, and for your encouragement to write this book. Without your support and patience with my nonsense, this book could not have been completed. Without your belief that sharing some of what I have learned could help others, this book would not even exist.

I also thank my sons, Ron, Jr. and Stephen, for their encouragement and support. I am very proud of both of you for what you have accomplished and especially for the fine young men you have become.

My good fortune is the gift of some great mentors, without whom it's hard to know what might have happened to me. Dr. Don Hileman and Dr. George Brown nurtured me through college and helped me land my first big job. Then Linc Bumba mentored me and put me on a career success track in my first real job at Leo Burnett in Chicago. Lou Schultz, who came at many issues from a different place than I did, nonetheless hired me into Campbell Ewald and inspired me to think out of the box more than I did. I thank all of those who have mentored and influenced me over the years.

I also want to thank Billy I. Ross and the late Jon Wardrip for their confidence in me as a college professor. Their enthusiasm and deep caring for students still brings tears to my eyes.

To these colleagues and the many others who have taught me and mentored me over the years, I offer my deep appreciation.

TABLE OF CONTENTS

Dedication iii
Table of Contents v
List of Figures xi
List of Tables xiii
Foreword 17
Preface xix

SECTION I: INTRODUCTION   1

1. Welcome to the Future 3
   Messages & Media 4
   Media Categories 6
   Media Roles 10
   Professional Media Functions 11
   Why Media Decisions Matter 15
   Let the Buyer Beware 17
   Summary 18
2. The Business of Media 19
   Size & Composition of the Industry 19
   Profitability 25
   Participants 26
   Positions 35
   Summary 39
3. The Revolution 41
   The Revolution 42
   Media Planning for the 21st Century 67
   Summary 70

SECTION II: MEDIA BASICS   71

4. Media Math 73
   Percentages 73
   Averages 76
   Indexing 77
   Weighting 79
   Formulas 80
   Summary 81
5. Audience Concepts 83
   Multi Media Audience Concepts 84
   Broadcast Media Audience Concepts 89

Print Media Audience Concepts 98
Out-of-Home Audience Concepts 101
Internet Audience Concepts 101
Audience Measurement Concepts 104
Summary 113

6. Media Costs **115**
Why Cost is No Expense 115
Media Pricing 116
Media: A Commodities Market? 123
Cost Efficiency: the Better Measure 124
Summary 125

7. Media Impact **127**
Advertising: Medium or Message? 127
Media Effectiveness 128
Media Effectiveness Research 130
Summary 134

SECTION III: MEDIA PLANNING 137

8. Media in Marketing **139**
The Marketing Concept 139
The Strategic Marketing Plan 140
From Marketing Plans to Media Plans 147
Summary 150

9. How Do Media Work? **153**
ARF Response Model 154
Effective Reach 158
Recency 168
Share of Voice 173
Purchase Funnel 176
Engagement 180
Summary 186

10. Target Audience **187**
Defining the Target Audience 187
Summary 201

11. Geographic Problems & Opportunities **203**
Geographic Marketing Philosophies 204
Geographic Market Definitions 207
Retail Trading Areas 210
National vs. Local Media 213
Geographic Market Analysis 215
Geographic Spending Strategies 220
Summary 224

12. Timing & Scheduling...**225**

Media Timing Considerations 225

Summary.. 231

13. A Budget to Grow By **233**

Determining the Budget 233

Allocating the Budget 236

Summary.. 237

14. The Tools of IMC **239**

Advertising... 240

Sales Promotion 242

Product Placement 243

Direct Marketing 245

Word-of-Mouth Marketing................................... 255

Publicity 257

Media Integration 262

Task Matching: an IMC Planning Process................. 263

Summary.. 266

15. Traditional Media...**269**

Television 271

Radio.. 277

Newspapers 282

Magazines 286

Out of Home 290

Summary.. 298

16. Internet Marketing...**299**

Introduction 300

Case Histories... 300

About Websites.. 302

Types of Websites 303

Internet Marketing Tools...................................... 313

Summary.. 322

17. Free Marketing in Social Media **323**

Introduction 323

Social Media in Marketing 325

Blogs & Blogging.. 331

Social Networking Sites 336

Social News Sites... 342

Publishing Platforms & Communities 343

Social Bookmarking Sites 345

Video Sharing 346

Summary.. 349

18. Strategic Media Planning **351**

Introduction 352

Step 1. Marketing Situation Analysis 353
Step 2. Statement of the Problem 355
Step 3. Task Definition 356
Step 4. Media Model Selection 358
Step 5. Establish Media Objectives 359
Step 6. Develop Media Strategies 369
Step 7. Devise Tactical Plan 386
Step 8. Test the Plan 388
Step 9. Obtain Authorizations 390
Summary 391

SECTION IV: MEDIA BUYING 393

19. Media Negotiations 395
    Introduction 396
    The Art of Negotiation 397
    Successful Media Negotiations 399
    Summary 402
20. Broadcast Media Buying 405
    The Broadcast Marketplace 405
    The Buying Process 409
    How to Buy Television 412
    How to Buy Radio 429
    A Media Negotiation Example 442
    Summary 444
21. Buying Print Media 445
    Buying Newspapers 445
    Buying Magazines 449
    Print Negotiating Tips 452
    Out of Home 455
    Summary 456
22. Buying Internet Advertising 459
    Forms of Internet Advertising 459
    Methods of Targeting Internet Ads 460
    Buying Keyword Search Advertising 464
    Creative—the Ads 467
    Buying Banners & Display Ads 469
    Test, Test, Test 473
    Summary 473
23. GUERILLA MEDIA BUYING 475
    Cross Platform Buys 475
    Media Remnants 476
    Online Media Auctions & Bidding Platforms 478

Table of Contents

Novel Payment Models..479
Sponsor a Call for Proposals...482
Summary...483

SECTION V: FUTURE MEDIA   485

24. The Future...487
The Future..487
Why the Future of Advertising Is Now..488
Summary...496
Glossary..497
Web Media Resources 503
Bibliography...505
Index...509

TABLE OF FIGURES

Figure 1-1.—Sample Media Plan 13
Figure 2-1.—Organization for Media Transactions 27
Figure 2-2.—Typical Agency Media Department Organization 29
Figure 3-1.—IMC Problem Solving 45
Figure 3-2.— Experiential IMC event 48
Figure 3-3.—Advertising results on Google and Yahoo search 53
Figure 5-1.—Media Evaluation Triangle 83
Figure 5-2.—Audience Generation Sequence 85
Figure 5-3.—Rating: Universe Percentage Reached by Media Vehicle ... 91
Figure 5-4.—Share of Audience Example in Television 92
Figure 5-5.—Percentage of Homes/Persons Watching or Listening 93
Figure 8-1.—Examples of Mission Statements 141
Figure 9-1.—New ARF Response Model 154
Figure 9-2.—Exponential Decay of Learning 161
Figure 9-3.—Repetition & Reinforcement for Awareness & Recall 162
Figure 9-4.—Effective Frequency Response Curve 165
Figure 9-5.—Total Exposure vs. Effective Exposure 166
Figure 9-6.—Effective Reach Comparisons of Alternative Plans 167
Figure 9-7.—Media Scheduling Options 169
Figure 9-8.—Share of Voice vs. Share of Market 174
Figure 9-9.—Typical Purchase Funnel 177
Figure 9-10.—Experian-Simmons Dimensions of Engagement 183
Figure 11-1.—U.S. High Potential Markets 208
Figure 11-2.—Designated Market Areas 209
Figure 11-3.—Trading Area 212
Figure 12-1.—New Product Introduction Timing of TRPS 228
Figure 12-2.—Promotion Ad Timing 229
Figure 12-3.—Seasonal Products with Heavy-ups 230
Figure 14-1.—Task Matching: IMC Planning Process 265
Figure 14-2.—IMC Task Matching Model: Example 266
Figure 15-1.—Top Ten Radio Station Formats 279
Figure 15-2.—A 30-Sheet Poster 291
Figure 15-3.—A Creative Billboard 293
Figure 15-4.—Truck Wrap 295
Figure 16-1.—Brochure Website 304
Figure 16-2.—A McDonald's Website 305
Figure 16-3.—Example of Banner Advertisement 315
Figure 17-1.—MacDonald's Facebook Page 324

Figure 17-2.—Dave's Cupboard Blog Page 331
Figure 17-3.—WordPress Landing Page 335
Figure 17-4.—Rocket Moms' Squidoo Lens 344
Figure 18-1.—Task Matching: Information/Involvement 371
Figure 18-2.—Hypothetical MARCOM Budget Allocations 372
Figure 18-3.—Example of Flighted Schedule 384
Figure 18-4.—Example of Pulsing Schedule 385
Figure 18-5.—Tactical Flow Chart 387
Figure 18-6.—Last Page of Tactical Plan: Sample 391
Figure 19-1.—Deciding What to Buy 396
Figure 19-2.—Buying Myths 397
Figure 20-1.—Contrasting Media Buying Philosophies 413
Figure 20-2.—US Broadcast & Cable Television Outlets 415
Figure 20-3.—Sample TV Audience Profile 418
Figure 20-4.—Supplemental Audience Data: Sample 419
Figure 20-5.—Commercial Recall by Position in Pod 424
Figure 20-6.—Recall vs. Clutter in Commercial Break 425
Figure 20-7.—Cost as a Function of Supply & Demand 427
Figure 20-8.—CPP for Network vs. Local Spot TV 427
Figure 20-9.—Cost of Prime Time Spots 428
Figure 20-10.—2008 Radio Ad Expenditures 429
Figure 20-11.—Radio Formats 433
Figure 21-1.—Rate Card Sample 446
Figure 22-1.—First Page Search Results 461
Figure 22-2.—Strategic Use of Keywords in Internet Ad 467

LIST OF TABLES

Table 1-1.—Number of Media Outlets 6
Table 2-1.—Marketing Communications Expenditures by Medium 20
Table 2-2.—Media Expenditures ($Billions) 24
Table 3-1.—Association of National Advertisers Top 10 Issues.............. 43
Table 3-2.—Primetime Average % Households Viewing 56
Table 3-3.—Newspaper Advertising Expenditures ($Billions)............... 57
Table 3-4.—Changes in the Media Mix... 68
Table 3-5.—Marketing & Media Revolution: Summary 70
Table 4-1.—Audience Measurement Math 73
Table 4-2.—Analysis of Sales Potential by Market 80
Table 5-1.—Calculating Share of Audience.. 92
Table 5-2.—GRPS = Sum of Ratings 95
Table 5-3.—GRPS vs. TRPS... 96
Table 5-4.—Quick Reach & Frequency Estimator 97
Table 5-5.—Cost Per Click Analysis 104
Table 6-1.—Examples of 2010 Upfront Network TV Costs 117
Table 6-2.—Example of 2010 Spot TV Costs by Market 117
Table 6-3.—Estimated 2010 Cost of 100 GRPS by Daypart 118
Table 6-4.—Estimated 2010 Spot Radio Costs 120
Table 6-5.—Sample Comparison of Magazine Costs 121
Table 6-6.—Comparison of Cost Efficiency of Media Vehicles 125
Table 7-1.—Estimated 2009 Local Advertising Expenditures 131
Table 7-2.—Advertising Effectiveness by Medium 132
Table 7-3.—Effectiveness of Radio in the Media Mix 133
Table 7-4.—US Online Advertising Spending*, by Format, 2008-2013 134
Table 8-1.—Example of Marketing Analysis.. 142
Table 9-1.—Comparison of Effective Reach vs. Recency Plans............ 169
Table 9-2. —Media Planning Implications 170
Table 9-3.—Tracking Purchase Funnel Measures (%) for Brand X 179
Table 9-4.—Comparison of Engagement Ratings* by Medium............. 184
Table 9-5.—Engagement Ratings for Specific Media: Examples 185
Table 10-1.—Demographics of Blimpo's Brand Users 189
Table 10-2.—Comparison of Lifestyles by DMA Index........................ 190
Table 10-3.—Product Category Users vs. Usage 192
Table 10-4.—The Changing Face of America 198
Table 10-5.—Size of Gay vs. Ethnic Market Segments........................ 198
Table 11-1.—Geographic Market Comparisons..................................... 205

Table 11-2.—County Size 210
Table 11-3.—Geographic Media Availabilities 214
Table 11-4.—Cost of Heavy Up Plan: Example 220
Table 11-5.—Spend in Relation to Sales: Example 221
Table 11-6.—Spend in Relation to Sales Potential: Example 221
Table 11-7.—Example-Based Reach & Frequency Goals 222
Table 12-1.—Advertising Expenditures vs. Industry Sales by Quarter .. 226
Table 12-2.—Brand Sales by Quarter vs. Advertising Expenditures 226
Table 12-3.—Seasonality of Competitive Activity, Spending or TRPS . 227
Table 12-4.—Avg. 4-Week Reach & Frequency Goals 227
Table 13-1.—Advertising/Sales Ratios in Selected Sectors 234
Table 13-2.—Industry Expenditures vs. Share of Voice 236
Table 15-1.—Relative Strength of Media Task Performance 270
Table 15-2.— Radio Daypart Availabilities 280
Table 15-3.—Newspaper Readership by Section of Paper 284
Table 16-1.—Internet/Digital Marketing Tools 313
Table 17-1.—Social Media versus Google AdWords Cost per Visit 328
Table 18-1.—Situation Analysis: Factors Affecting Media Planning 355
Table 18-2.—Audience Weighting 361
Table 18-3.—Reach vs. Frequency: The Media Planner's Dilemma 362
Table 18-4.—Support the Current Business 365
Table 18-5.—Spend in Relation to Sales Potential 366
Table 18-6.—Media Genres Within Media Types 374
Table 18-7.—Hypothetical $1 Million Budget: Target Women 25-54 ... 375
Table 18-8.—$10 Million Media Mix Analysis 378
Table 18-9.—Geographic Flexibility of Media Types 379
Table 18-10.—Determination of National vs. Local Budgets 381
Table 18-11.—Key Market Summary FY 2011 387
Table 18-12.—Comparison of Business Magazines 388
Table 18-13—Quarterly Budget Recap by Medium 388
Table 18-14.—Plan Performance 388
Table 18-15.—Media Plan Construction Process: Summary 391
Table 20-1.—2009 TV Advertising Expenditures 414
Table 20-2.—Influence on Purchasing Decisions 414
Table 20-3.—Finding Undervalued Programs 419
Table 20-4.—Index of Commercial Recall by Rating Size 423
Table 20-5.—Viewer Response by Program Involvement 424
Table 20-6.—Recall Index vs. Commercial Length 426
Table 20-7.—Total Radio Audience Size by Daypart 431
Table 20-8.—Share of Audience by Format 436
Table 20-9.—Total Cume Ratings % 437

Table 20-10.—Comparison of Radio Plans.. 438

Table 20-11.—CPP for Top 10 Radio Markets (:60s, Top 10 Markets). 442

Table 21-1.—Weekday Newspaper Readership by Section by Gender.. 447

Table 21-2.—Index of Magazine Ad Recall by Type of Unit................. 451

Table 22-1.—Internet Spending Trends by Type 460

Table 22-2.—Search Page Result vs. Website Visits 462

Table 22-3.—Puzzle of Buying Keywords, May 2011 466

Table 22-4.—Hypothetical Ad Group Scheme...................................... 468

Table 22-5.—Ad Impressions by Most Popular Pixel Sizes 469

FOREWORD

Is Media the "New Creative"?

When a repentant Cannes Advertising Festival awarded BMW Films a Titanium Lion a year after it was originally entered, something changed. The award shifted the center of gravity of the advertising industry from the creative department and put it into the hands of media visionaries. Now it is easy to confuse the statement above and think that it is media planners who are calling the shots just now. Media is not about which channel, what time and the likes, but about the distribution (across an extremely fragmented world of touch points), relevance, and timing of a marketing message, as it is about the creative idea and execution.

In the case of BMW Films, while the execution, idea, and everything "typically creative" about the work was superlative, the fact that the idea put branded entertainment at centre stage and gambled with the web as a no-cost distribution model that makes any new piece of web-enabled, long format film-making a BMW Films clone.

Media as creative has spawned a new breed of advertising thinker, the communications or transmedia planner. His job is not to take the existing creative ideas and find ways to put them out in as many places as possible, but to help the creative and the client find new expressions of the brand's POV and spread these views.

One of the most interesting examples of media as creative thinking came from Adidas in the form of the Adicolor sneaker. Even the product was conceived to tell a story. The all-white shoe, originally released in 1983, was re-released in a kit that included the original plain white shoes, paints, brushes, and a wooden palette. The ensuing campaign was a masterpiece of New Age storytelling: a simple interactive billboard with a white sheet pasted on it, inviting scrawlers and graffiti artists. A few days later, a layer would be added to the board to reveal the shoe with custom created graffiti under it. The idea was taken into film where filmmakers explored different colours, with little or no reference to the product and its benefits.

One of the problems with using a media idea as the creative itself is that once a brand uses a format successfully, it becomes very difficult for some other brand to use a similar format and do it well. While there are many examples of using YouTube as a TV channel to create a miniseries, *LonelyGirl15* will always be the benchmark that will be difficult to beat.

At a time when consumer attention to advertising is flagging and technology is spawning new ideas, there is a need for thinkers who can understand the possibilities of science and the needs of brands to help create ideas to solve marketing problems.

–R. Nishad, VP, IContract
Mumbai, India

PREFACE

This is a different kind of media book. First, my opinions—based on 30 years of media and marketing experience with blue chip agencies and clients—are liberally reflected throughout the book. Second, the book has a practical orientation that is intended to stimulate interest and learning about media, traditionally one of the most important subjects in advertising and certain to be even more important in the future.

The book is written for students and beginning professionals. The early stages of your careers coincide with the early stages of a marketing and media revolution. Consumers are gaining more and more control over access to product information and media consumption—getting the information they want when it is relevant. The emergence of new media like the Internet, DVRs, iPods, mobile phones, and iPads is empowering consumers and creating new communications opportunities for brands.

In the next decade, while traditional media like television, radio, newspapers, and magazines will continue to play a major role for advertisers, digital and interactive media will become increasingly important. We also see media professionals beginning to grow into new roles where they are entrusted with planning, managing, and coordinating all of the multitudes of brand contacts—advertising, promotion, publicity, and interactive communication—via the Internet or iTV.

Recognizing that we are in the early stages of a marketing-media revolution, we must separate the new-media hype from new-media reality. Spending in new media had been increasing 8-30% per year before the economic downturn of 2008/2009, compared to a flatter market for most other media. Despite their relatively rapid growth, however, new media still represent less than 10 per cent of the total ad spend and less than five per cent of total marketing communications spending. This is not to say that new and digital media are not extremely important; they are crucial now and they are opening the door to an even more amazing future.

Caveat Emptor

The doctrines of *Caveat Emptor* and *Caveat Venditor* sum up the nature of the media buying and selling process. *Caveat Emptor* (Latin) means *Let the buyer beware.* This is the principle that, in commerce the buyer alone is responsible for assessing the viability of a purchase before buying. *Caveat Emptor* is the principle that allows advertisers to use puffery in their ads ("This is the greatest product ever!").

Like advertisers, media sellers use puffery to sell advertising in their media. So long as media sales persons don't grossly misrepresent the facts or lie, they are not liable for a buyer's poor or uninformed decisions—or for buyer remorse. The buyer is entrusted with the responsibility to be prudent and to make the most effective buying decisions possible.

In most media buyer-seller transactions, sellers give buyers carefully selected information, consisting of pounds and pounds of facts about their media opportunities and alleged benefits—conveniently omitting unfavorable data. Buyers evaluate sellers' information as it fits with their clients' communications strategies. In exchange, buyers provide sellers with equally obtuse information about their own objectives and needs.

Whether buying a new home, car, or financial investment, an intelligent negotiator is always skeptical. You know that the other party is putting the best foot forward. You know that the other party is not going to be sharing information that would be detrimental to a deal. In other words, *Caveat Emptor*.

On the other hand, *Caveat Venditor* is Latin for *Let the seller beware*. It is the other side of the *caveat emptor* coin, warning that sellers too can be deceived in a market transaction. For example, a buyer may overstate the budget available in order to gain concessions from the seller. *Caveat Venditor* places the burden on the seller to take responsibility for evaluating transactions with eyes wide open.

There are 50,000 or more media vehicles trying to sell advertising time and space. Many media, like signage on a golf course or on a semi-truck trailer, are created solely for earning revenue through advertising. Those responsible for purchasing (or influencing the purchase of) media are barraged with requests for meetings and presentations that contain dozens of pages of facts and figures, graphics, pictures, videos, computer analyses, and occasionally some creative ideas to consider.

You must understand that the sole mission of media sellers is to sell time or space at the highest possible price. Sellers are paid according to their ability to persuade buyers to buy. After learning something about an advertiser's needs, sellers present their proposals with as much rationale and support as possible, sometimes with pages and pages of statistics and analysis, sometimes with images and emotion. Buyers must be able to separate the wheat from the chaff to judge proposals objectively from the standpoint of the advertiser's strategy and needs.

Both buyers and sellers must do their homework. Media decisions are part art, part science. The parties must have and understand the mountains of marketing and media information they need to make buying and selling decisions intelligently and generate new ideas.

This is NOT to suggest that most buyers and sellers are incompetent or dishonest. Marketing is a business where millions of dollars are committed with a phone call or a handshake—with the legal paperwork coming much later. Promises must be honored. Mutual trust is essential.

The Stakes are High

Why are media decisions so important?

In 2009, nearly $800 billion was spent by companies on advertising time, space, clicks, promotions, and other forms of marketing communications. The largest advertisers, like General Motors and Proctor & Gamble, have budgets well in excess of a billion dollars. The financial importance of spending these dollars wisely is enormous.

Uniform errors of only 10 per cent in media decision-making could have a cumulative economic value of $80 billion; errors of 30 percent could add up to $240 billion, in addition to the even greater devastation of lost customers, sales, and profits. The stakes are just as high—or higher—for a company with a small budget, where every marketing dollar needs to do the work of two (or three) dollars.

Which Half of Ad Spending Is Wasted?

Would you pay $100 per share for a stock trading at or valued at $25 per share? Of course not. So why do advertisers sometimes consciously pay too much for advertising time and space?

John Wanamaker, who operated the late-1800s counterpart of Nordstrom's, was once in a meeting with his banker, a Rockefeller. During the meeting, Wanamaker uttered his now famous quote, "I know that half of my advertising is wasted, I just don't know which half."

There are hundreds, maybe thousands, of ways that bad media decisions can waste an advertising budget or diminish its ability to achieve a company's marketing and advertising objectives. Waste can result from naïve decisions made by uninformed or incompetent buyers, the absence of a sound strategy, inadequate analysis, poor negotiation, or simply selecting media based on emotion or the gut rather than facts.

Who Wants a Piece of the Brooklyn Bridge?

Advertisers and media representatives with large budgets are inundated with media sales reps who want a piece of the action. Here is an example of what can happen to a naïve buyer with a substantial budget and insufficient knowledge.

A major radio station sold an extensive drive-time schedule of :60 spots to a small auto dealer located in a small town in the northern part of a large media market of 3 million. The station persuaded the dealer that the station's wide coverage area—nearly 100 miles in every direction would bring the dealer a lot of new customers. However, this dealer's trading area was within a five-mile radius of the dealership. Over 95 per cent of the radio advertising investment was wasted, and a positive return investment was impossible.

More Money than Brains?

Buying media purely on the basis of emotion—with or without the facts—is a sure road to wasting ad dollars and reducing ROI.

Take another case: this is the (true) story of the board of directors of a large automotive dealer group in a major market. Emotionally, the dealers felt connected to a local pro sports team that they had sponsored for years. When their sponsorship was up for renewal, their advertising agency evaluated the audience and promotional value of the station's $550,000 proposal and found the actual dollar value to be about $150,000. Since the station had to pay huge rights fees to the team (and knowing that the dealers would pay almost any price), the station would not go below the $550,000 price for the sponsorship.

Against the agency's recommendation, the board decided to buy the sponsorship anyway, valued at $150,000, for $550,000. It could be argued that, in effect, this purchase wasted $400,000 of the dealers' money, 70% of the total—money that could have been used instead to produce another $3.2 million in gross profit. If the wasted $400,000 had been reinvested in more or better media, it is likely that all the dealers in the association, not just the board members, would have sold more vehicles, and generated more profit for all of them.

Due Diligence

I hope it is becoming apparent that media investments must be made carefully. Just as an individual's investment decisions in the stock market or money markets affect the investor's equity (net worth), media decisions also represent important financial investments in short- and long-term brand equity.

Advertisers and media decision-makers must exercise the same kind of due diligence that others in financial services use. Banks and venture capitalists don't usually lend money without due diligence. Stockbrokers don't usually buy stocks without due diligence. New home or car buyers don't usually make purchase decisions without doing their homework first.

So making uninformed or emotional media decisions will probably result in squandered budgets, lower sales, and lower profits. It is easy to get excited by an idea sold to you by an enthusiastic media seller whose interest is not the same as yours. You must do your own due diligence or you will end up with the short end of the stick! *Caveat Emptor.*

Purpose of Book

My experience as a large agency media director, account manager, and college professor motivated me to write this book, for five reasons.

First, many media books are severely out of date. The marketplace is changing. Media and technology are changing. Clients are changing. Many agencies are not changing.

Second, media will be on the leading edge of the advertising industry for some time to come. An increasing share of jobs in advertising will be in media, and the majority of these will be different from yesterday's jobs. Anyone serious about a career in advertising has to "get" media. Period.

Third, although media planning and media buying are of equal importance, media buying is barely even mentioned in other media books.

Fourth, many media professionals have lost sight of what really matters. Media was, is, and always will be an extension of marketing. However, reading the trade press and blogs would lead you to believe that media is mostly about text messages on cell phones. The excitement of new media has distorted our perspective on what our mission really is.

Fourth, media needs to be more interesting to students and professionals alike. My experience has been that many students find media difficult, and maybe even boring (gasp!), especially when it is compared to the (perceived) fun on the creative side of the business. Many instructors find media a challenge to teach in a way that allows students to get it.

Fifth, I want to throw my hard-won experience—thoughts and conclusions derived from years of contemplating and struggling with marketing and media problems and issues—into the mix. I hope they will make a difference.

The purpose of this book, therefore, is to provide a practical guide into the 21st century, covering both theory and practice of media planning and buying. The book reflects my philosophy of learning by doing and by actively engaging the material. Because it is for students and early career professionals, a workbook and the Thumbnail Media Planner reference are included as a part of the textbook package. The Planner will be a reference and a platform for student exercises and discussion. I hope you find the package useful.

SECTION I: INTRODUCTION

The advertising media business—media planning, media buying, and media selling—is leaping to the forefront of marketing, integrated communications, and advertising. Why? The exponential change that is taking place in markets and media has left many scrambling to catch up. The hype has caused others to scratch their heads, not knowing what to do.

This book presents media conversation in the context of the 21st century. What you learn here will continue to evolve as the future gradually continues to unveil itself.

Section I includes three introductory chapters:

Chapter 1   Welcome to the Future
Chapter 2   The Business of Media
Chapter 3   The Revolution

1. WELCOME TO THE FUTURE

The best way to cope with change is to help create it.

–Lou Schultz, former CEO of Initiative Media

Have you ever wondered how all those ads and commercials got into the media and what they're doing there? How did they get airtime on those TV programs or radio stations? How did they get published in those magazines? Why would you use Time rather than Newsweek? Google rather than Yahoo? How do you choose among YouTube and Twitter and Facebook? When do you use ethnic media? Why do you decide to place double the advertising in Dallas of another advertiser with a similar total budget? Will television even matter in the future?

As you will discover in this book, media is about marketing, and marketing is often about media. Media is about marketing because its role is to help address marketing problems and opportunities. Marketing can be about media when a cornerstone of the marketing plan rests on a big media idea-- such as an integrated advertising, promotion, and buzz marketing program leveraging the assets of the Super Bowl, the network carrying the Super Bowl, as well as other promotional partners.

The purpose of Chapter 1 is to introduce the strategic media planning and buying processes of the 21st century. After reading Chapter 1, you should begin to understand:

- *What media are*
- *What media is about*
- *How the media are classified*
- *What roles media play*
- *Professional media functions*
- *Why media decisions are important*
- *Caveat Emptor*

We'll begin the conversation with where media fits into the overall plan.

MESSAGES & MEDIA

Every advertising or marketing communications plan—past, present, and future—consists of two basic parts: the message (the *creative*) and the medium. As an advertising professional, you will make decisions that depend upon knowledge of both.

Messages: The Creative

Advertising and marketing communications *messages* are usually referred to as the *creative*. Creative are the ads and commercials that we see on television, in magazines and newspapers, on the Internet or on park benches. For larger companies, messages are normally created and produced by an advertising agency's creative department. Smaller businesses, however, may develop their own creative, often with the assistance of the local newspaper, TV, or radio station. Creative may be developed for use in mass media or in targeted media such as direct mail or the Internet.

Creative development is a three-stage process:

1. *Creative strategy* defines the target audience, the basic selling message, reasons to believe the message, and the brand character.
2. Writers and art directors develop *executions of the strategy* in rough ads, scripts, or storyboards.
3. Finally, the *creative is produced* ready to run in the designated media.

To perform its magic, the creative has to come to the consumer's attention; it has to reach eyes or ears. Not only that, but the messages must be delivered to the *right consumers*—those most likely to be purchase the product or service. Delivering the message is the job of media.

Media: The Messenger

Media are the messengers. They deliver creative messages to target audiences. In other words, *media are the channels of communication* by which advertisers deliver marketing messages to target audiences of prospective customers. Media can take almost any form—from television or radio stations, to Google, to the Iowa State Fair, to word of mouth.

4

Definition of Media

Media is a generic term. It means all forms of communications media. Media may refer to a class of media—television, radio, magazines, newspapers, direct mail, and the Internet are all advertising *media*.

Medium, on the other hand, refers to a single class of media—television is an advertising *medium*; radio is an advertising *medium*. It is not correct to say that radio is an advertising media.

Media Vehicles

Media vehicles are the specific media carriers that deliver your creative messages. For example, *60 Minutes* and *The Today Show* are specific media carriers within the medium of television. Radio station WXYZ-FM is also a media vehicle within the media class of radio. *Time* and *Newsweek* are vehicles within the magazine class. Individual websites with banner ads are media vehicles within the Internet medium.

Media vehicles deliver all kinds of messages, not just advertising. *The Today Show* delivers news, entertainment, and weather (as well as the necessary evil of TV commercials). AOL does the same thing on its website, which also provides hard news, entertainment, and a plethora of advertising on the Home Page and every other category page.

Media Overload

Most of us are bombarded daily with hundreds or even thousands of advertising messages. Research estimates vary from 850-5000+ daily exposures in all forms of media—television, radio, magazines, newspapers; on park benches and buses and taxis; at the train station and airport and Yankee Stadium; in our mail boxes and shopping carts; on Internet blogs, games, and information pages; on store shelves and cash register receipts and mobile phones. Just reading that list is overwhelming, isn't it?

Considering the proliferation of media, nobody even knows how many media vehicles there are. You may already have discovered new ones. It is possible to estimate numbers for traditional media, however. Remember that a media outlet can offer hundreds or thousands of individual vehicles, e.g., every TV show on every TV station. Counting only the outlets, not all their individual vehicles, here are the most recent estimates, according to each medium's trade association.

Table 1-1.—Number of Media Outlets

Medium	Outlets
Television Stations	800
Radio	10,000
Consumer Magazines	7,383
Business Publications	13,200
Billboard Locations	450,000+
Websites	43,000,000
Cable Networks	535
Newspapers	6,700

Media: a Creative Product

Creative is usually thought of as ads and commercials and visuals, but some notable media visionaries like Lou Schultz, former CEO of IPG's Initiative Media unit, believe that media is no longer just a communications channel but a creative product in its own right. The creation and blending of cross-media and multimedia opportunities can influence consumers at different levels of their purchase consideration or buying process.

The well-endowed auto company that bought spots in the 2011 Super Bowl pre-game show, introduced its spokesperson during the game, gave away a hot vehicle in the post-game show, and created millions of dollars worth of buzz through cross-promotions with the network and other sponsors was treating media as a creative product.

MEDIA CATEGORIES

Before advertisers select specific media vehicles to carry their ads, they first determine which media categories will best communicate their messages. While experts differ on how to classify media, in this book you will note that this book does not classify media into traditional and new media but into four different categories: (1) traditional media, (2) digital media, (3) alternative media, and (4) marketing services media, also sometimes known as below-the-line media, because of the way its costs are budgeted.

The practice of classifying media as Traditional or New should be banished. The lines between them have blurred as media types converge. Television, for example, now offers a choice of three screens to watch—TV, PC, and handheld. In this reality, should television be classified as a traditional or new medium? Are magazines, which can be read in print editions, e-books, or online, old media or new media?

Traditional Media and New Media are categories currently in use, however, and you can expect to encounter the vernacular as you build your marketing practice. In this book, therefore, you will continue to see the distinction observed, as it is in the real world.

Traditional Media

Before 1995, media relied primarily upon the print and analog broadcast models that were all we had before the advent of the Internet. These traditional media included television, newspapers, consumer and trade publications, outdoor sites, direct mail, movie and music studios, and books.

These media were largely impersonal, engaging in one-way communications with their audiences. Television commercials ran. Radio commercials ran. Magazine ads ran.

Through the 1980s and well into the 1990s, *cable television* was considered new media. Cable's method of distribution was different, but ratings were low, cable penetration was still low in many markets, and cable offered little in terms of original programming. Nonetheless, cable was successful selling more targeted audiences at lower prices vs. the networks—ABC, CBS, NBC.

Beginning in the 1990s, the Internet (previously reserved for government use) began to be commercialized. Now, for twenty years, digital media promoters have been predicting the death of the traditional media devils, especially television.

If you ardently read the trade press, you might be forgiven for believing that television and magazines have already been replaced by social media, Twitter and Facebook, devoured by cell phones, or otherwise overtaken by stealthy new digital media. However, as traditional media evolve into new and interactive forms, they can share Mark Twain's grim comfort: the rumors of their death too have been greatly exaggerated.

The recent rate of Internet spending growth may be up 9-30% annually (though it dropped 6% during the recession), but spending in traditional media was also growing prior to the recession, albeit at a slower rate. Traditional media still account for over 90% of total media expenditures and 97% of total marketing communications expenditures.

Obviously, new media hype can be far greater than the reality...for today. Tomorrow will be a different story.

Digital Media

The Internet (now thirty years old) and all of its digital applications are still considered by some to be *new media*. The last twenty-five years have seen increasingly rapid transformation of media consequent to the use of digital technology. Old media also have felt the impact of computers, changing in response to the effects of digital television and the opportunities of online publication. Even media forms such as the printing press have evolved with digital processes that permit personal image manipulation and desktop publishing.

Digital media therefore encompass the convergence of traditional media with the Internet. Online editions of major newspapers and magazines are new-media publications. So are the movies and television programs that you watch on Internet sites such as Hulu.com. The explosion of digital media includes:

- Websites
- Internet search engines
- Social networks
- Wiki projects
- Email and attachments
- Electronic kiosks
- Interactive television
- Mobile handheld devices
- Podcasts
- Video games and virtual worlds
- Multimedia CD-ROMs
- Blogs
- Social Media
- Skype

Alternative Media

Alternative media are also referred to as *ambient media* or *non-traditional media*. The *alternative media* segment includes innovative concepts and products that are changing the face of the industry. There are thousands of alternative media, as you will be able to imagine when you look at the following examples.

- Gas Station TV that you can watch while you pump gas
- Blimps and skywriting
- QVC & HSN cable-television shopping networks
- In-store (videos, shopping carts, register receipts, POS)
- Buzz marketing campaigns
- Interactive kiosks in shopping centers
- Truck and taxi exteriors
- Signage & displays in sports & entertainment venues (golf courses, stadia, bowling alleys, concerts, fairs)

Media entrepreneurs obviously recognize no boundaries when they're looking for lucrative investments involving the sale of advertising!

Marketing Services Media

Marketing services (as distinct from classic advertising) is a kind advertising communication known as *below-the-line media*. For budgeting and tracking expenditures, many companies have historically defined advertising as an above-the line item, while most other forms of marketing communication are recorded below the line.

The distinction between above- and below-the-line advertising budgets is based on which corporate department is responsible. Above the line you may find the advertising budget for which the Advertising Director is responsible. Below the line, other managers may be responsible for budgets that have a more measurable impact on sales results. Interestingly, below-the-line budgets can be twice the size of above-the-line budgets.

Marketers spend most of their marketing communications budgets in below the line media such those listed below. These forms were not usually always thought of as media, but they are extremely important forms of communication and consumer influence, which gives them legitimacy as a class of media options on a par with traditional, new, or alternative media.

Here are the major forms of below-the-line marketing communications:

- Direct mail (the largest ad medium of all)
- Trade promotion, such as trade allowances and slotting allowances
- Consumer promotion offers and incentives
- Experiential marketing at on-site events, such as sports and entertainment marketing venues
- Product placement in movies and TV shows

MEDIA ROLES

Media's job is to produce maximum communications impact and return on investment (ROI) for the advertiser. This requires connecting with target audiences in the right media, at the right time, in the right place, in the right context, with the right creative messages. You might use traditional media like television and magazines to create awareness, or you might use Internet search engines like Google to drive traffic to the advertiser's website. Whatever your strategy, your media objectives must extend marketing and communications impact.

Key Marketing Function

It can be said that "media is marketing" and "marketing is media" because of media's importance as an element of the strategic marketing plan. Media connects brands and markets.

As you will see in chapter 8, every element of the marketing strategy and plan can impact media strategy. For example, a brand's distribution (bricks and mortar and/or e-commerce) can affect to whom, where, when, and how a brand should communicate. If a brand has low distribution in a geographic area, advertising levels may be reduced because the potential sales rate and ROI are so low. On the other hand, if a brand's objective is to increase distribution in certain channels or geographic areas, more media may be utilized to help convince the trade that the brand will sell the product they have ordered.

Or a particular target audience may be key to accomplishing the company's future growth objectives. If, for example, a client wants to sell very expensive jewelry to an upscale audience by promoting snob appeal in the creative, perhaps the selected media should reinforce that snob appeal. ***Can you think of some media that would lend some snob appeal to the message?***

Can marketing also be media? Marketers frequently build integrated plans around a media platform like the Super Bowl or the Academy Awards or a holiday. The integrated marketing communications plan could include media elements such as multi-media advertising, public relations, consumer and trade promotion, buzz marketing campaigns, and much more. (See chapter 14, IMC Tools).

Communications Function

In order to perform its marketing role of building brand equity, media also performs a communications function when it links the brand with the consumer. See if you recognize these media communications functions:

- **Connect** the brand's marketing messages with its target markets— the right consumers in the right place at the right time.
- **Engage** consumers with the brand's messages.
- **Reach** target consumers often enough to be memorable
- **Reach** consumers just prior to the purchase decision
- **Manage and coordinate** brand contacts—advertising, product placement, direct marketing, new media, and promotion.
- **Address specific marketing problems and opportunities**. For example, if a Brand suffers from low top of mind awareness or low trial, media may play a key role in solving the problem.

PROFESSIONAL MEDIA FUNCTIONS

There are three basic functions media professionals perform to connect ad messages with target markets: media planning, media buying, and media selling.

Media Planning

Media planning is the process of developing an effective media strategy and action plan. The media planning process begins with an analysis of the marketing situation. Then, based on marketing priorities, media objectives are formulated that detail exactly what the media plan is supposed to accomplish, for example, including the definition and prioritization of target audiences the media plan must reach.

Third, media strategies are formulated which will most effectively accomplish the media objectives. Finally, based on the media strategies, a detailed tactical plan is developed.

The media strategy and action plan incorporate the right media classes, the right media vehicles, the right geographic markets, the right timing, the right budget, the right number of advertising exposures, in the right media contexts, and so on. In so doing, media planning contemplates how traditional, digital, alternative, and marketing services media can help best address marketing problems or capitalize on marketing opportunities.

The result of media planning is a *media plan*, often called the *tactical plan*. The media plan provides recommendations and detailed rationale for all media activities and spending. For example, the plan may propose the use of magazines as the important medium for some particular advertising. The recommendation would include how much money should be spent in magazines vs. other media, in which months or weeks ads should be scheduled, and, of course, which specific magazines are most cost effective and best meet the magazine selection criteria.

Of course, media plans must also include other proposed media/marketing activities such as geographic market areas which should receive supplemental media spending, how often the consumer should be reached with advertising, as well as how the advertising should be scheduled throughout the year or planning period.

The example shown in Figure 1 is a calendar of all proposed media activities including details of media vehicles, markets, and timing. Such calendars are usually called *Flow Charts*. Every media plan includes a flow chart, which makes it easier for team members to understand quickly what the plan is at a particular time.

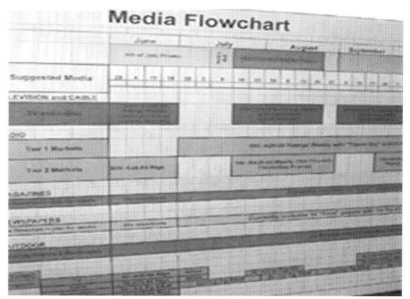

Figure 1-1.—Sample Media Plan

The media plan flowchart will list the media and marketing activities down the first column and a scheduling timeline across the top that takes in your entire planning period, usually a quarter or a year or the duration of a specific campaign. Flow charts can be confusing, so it is important to construct them carefully.

A *media planner* is someone who develops or supervises the development of media plans through a rigorous media planning process. The media planner may occupy any level in the organization; responsibility, not title, defines the job. A media planner was responsible for development of the plan and flow chart in Figure 1-1.

Now, imagine that you are a media planner. You have $3 million to market your product to male beer drinkers. An analysis of media alternatives for reaching this audience suggests these three potential strategies.

1. If you bought one :30 spot in the Super Bowl for $3 million, you would reach almost 33% of male beer drinkers all at the same time.

2. If you bought fifteen :30 spots on male-oriented, primetime, network TV programs, you could reach 65% of male beer drinkers more than once with 35% of them reached at least twice.

3. If you spent half your budget for display ads on male-oriented websites and the other half in men's magazines, you would reach 63% of males twice each, on average, but in different media contexts.

Question: Which option would you choose? Why?

Media Buying

After the media plan has been approved by the client, the media vehicles included in the plan must be purchased from the media sellers. Media buying is the process of identifying the preferred vehicles and negotiating with selling media to reach a satisfactory price and other important terms and conditions. The transaction is called a *media buy*, and the person who negotiated the transaction with the seller is called a *media buyer*.

You might be a media buyer with a budget and instructions to buy a specific display ad on the home page of a major search engine, for example. You find that the budget is sufficient to buy an ad on the home page of either AOL or Yahoo but not both. You therefore ask each of the sellers to submit a proposal, and you negotiate with both of them until one offers you desirable inventory at an acceptable price. After negotiating with the sellers, you may then select the seller with the lowest price or the best additional enticements. When you have completed the transaction, you have done a media buy!

Media Sales

Media selling is obviously the third leg of the professional media triangle. Persuading the media buyer(s) and media-buying influencers to purchase a medium's inventory of time, space, or clicks, media selling involves negotiating with buyers to reach agreement on price, content of the media package (e.g., which programs or times), positioning of the advertiser's spots, and free promotions.

If you were the media seller for AOL in the example above, you might propose a media package consisting of X number of clicks for the one-time-only price of $5 million. But the Yahoo sales rep would be doing the same thing! Your job would be to come up with an offer better than Yahoo's, including a final price and any other terms and conditions that would induce the media buyer to keep negotiating with you until you can reach a contract.

Media sales persons are usually called media representatives or sales reps. Sales reps may work for the medium (e.g., AOL) or for an independent firm that represents several non-competing media. Sellers communicate with buyers by phone, face-to-face in person or videoconference, by mail and email.

Chapter 2 discusses media planning, buying, and selling in more detail. Here, let's consider the importance of media decision making.

WHY MEDIA DECISIONS MATTER

It's the money, stupid!

In the preface, we cited the famous Wannamaker quote: "I know that half of my advertising dollars are wasted, I just don't know which half."

> ### Questions: What was JohnWanamaker saying about the
> ### state of the advertising industry in his day?
> ### What do you think has changed?

It is possible that waste in ad spending is even higher today than 50%. Regardless of the percentage, and despite mountains of research and technology, waste still occurs because of bad marketing strategy, ineffective creative, and inefficient media planning and buying. Perhaps more importantly, waste likely occurs because of the industry's uncertainty about *how advertising works*.

Scientifically speaking, does anyone know how advertising works? Do we know how to create ads that work as intended? Do we know how to develop media plans that maximize ROI? No. Scientifically speaking, it isn't all science.

The smartest media decisions usually reflect a combination of art and science. Although media decisions can reflect quantitative data and analysis, they also can and should be highly creative ways of engaging consumers with messages.

Media is an Art (Isn't it?)

Some believe that *media is the new creative*. Media planning, buying, and selling is an art, because decisions are often generated by creative thinking and ideas. For example, the decision to use a local radio personality to drive a new car and brag about the vehicle on air might be hard to justify with numbers. A different approach is more quantifiable but justification is still artful.

Suppose the radio personality broadcasts from a dealer sales event, calling for listeners to visit the dealer, test-drive a car, and take advantage of a special $2500 cash-back incentive for immediate purchase. The media buyer should be asking a couple of questions. Numbers after the fact will answer whether the profit on cars sold exceeded the cost of the media buy. They will not answer whether car sales increased more than they would have done with a different buy.

Here's an out of the box creative media idea for an ice cream manufacturer. This out of home media idea involved the use of a smile-activated vending machine placed in malls. Passers-by were drawn to an interactive kiosk by an "attractor screen" that superimposed their faces onto the heads of cute illustrated characters. Then, they just had to smile at the vending machine to receive free ice cream. Using facial recognition, the "smile-o-meter" measured smiles and took pictures, which were uploaded to Facebook. Users could browse the menu and select their ice cream via a touch screen. (Mediapost, *2010 Creative Media Awards*)

Finally, here is an example of how creative thinking affected a media plan for Dunkin' Donuts. When you have a brand that quite literally starts many of its consumers' days, the best media strategy is built around the first media that communicates with them each day. That is effectively what Hill Holliday did with its 2009-10 media plan for client Dunkin' Donuts. Leveraging research indicating that consumers of the brand were already predisposed to receiving the Dunkin' Donuts message at the start of their days, Hill Holliday developed a plan to "own" as many of them as possible, including TV morning news and weather reports, radio ("Rush Hour Runs On Dunkin'"), and key digital day-starters (Yahoo, Facebook, Pandora, Weather Channel), as well as digital out-of-home locations where people tend to start their days. (Source: Mediapost, 2010 Creative Media Awards)

Media is a Science (Isn't it?)

Media is perceived as having a scientific component because of the huge amount of research data available, the many computer models, and systems analysis that are available to media planners, buyers, and sellers. Using the available information resources, then, how can you fail to maximize media effectiveness and ROI?

For example, you can find audience sizes and demographics for almost any media vehicle. In addition, there are sophisticated computer models to simulate media exposure of almost any target audience and different budget levels. Media planners often use computer models (given various assumptions) to help them determine what percentage of the budget should be in television, radio, magazines, online, etc. Yet, since the data, models, and assumptions are not perfect, messages may still be delivered to the wrong audience in the wrong place at the wrong timeand without sufficient impact.

Finally, media and creative must work together. You are spending your clients' advertising dollars to get maximum returns on investment. Great creative commercials and ads delivered carelessly waste the client's budget. On the other hand, a great media plan can't make weak creative better. Media decisions matter to your client, your firm, and your career.

LET THE BUYER BEWARE

You would not buy a new car or house without researching the options. Most employers would not hire a new executive without checking references and credentials. Venture capitalists usually do not invest in a business without conducting due diligence. Media decisions also require due diligence.

Media planners and buyers always need to understand market conditions, for example, in order to know when to buy. Consider the ad agency that failed in due diligence on market timing. A large corporation purchased a schedule of primetime spots on several TV stations in the New York market. A few days later, the corporation decided that it needed an even heavier TV schedule in New York. The advertising agency's New York media buyer contacted the stations included on the original schedule and asked for additional spots in the same primetime programs at the same price. However, there was a problem. Demand for TV time had increased suddenly owing to new TV buys from competitors. This resulted in a 100 percent price increase for the same primetime spots *in just one week*.

Timing can be everything. This was not a failure of art or science. It was a simple *lack of information about the media market in New York*. Had the advertiser or agency been educated about market conditions and encouraged to plan accordingly, the entire buy could have been made earlier at a significant cost savings.

Advertisers and others making media decisions must exercise the same kind of due diligence that investors and financial services companies are expected to use (before the deals that led to the mortgage meltdown). Uninformed or emotional media decisions may squander budgets, depress sales, and impair profits. It is easy to get excited by an idea sold to you by an enthusiastic media sales rep that does not have your interest in mind. You must do your own due diligence to keep from finding yourself with the short end of the stick!

SUMMARY

Chapter 1 introduced the terms medium and media and the segmentation of the media into traditional, digital, alternative, and below-the-line classes. You learned that media has both a marketing function and a communications function, and that you yourself can play one of three roles in the triangle of professional media functions—media planner, media buyer, media seller.

You should have gained an appreciation for the significance of the media decisions that you will make and their inevitable blend of art and science. Finally, having been introduced to the principles of caveat emptor and caveat venditor in the preface to this book, you came full circle in this chapter, returning to the imperative of due diligence in whatever part you play in the wonderful world of media.

That wonderful world will be the focus of Chapter 2. How big is it? How do agencies or media services make money? How do the media make money? What, exactly, do media professionals do? What kinds of job opportunities will you find in the wonderful world of media? The answers are in Chapter 2.

2. The Business of Media

Advertising is the art and sole of capitalism…

–Jef Richards

Media has been called the business side of advertising. Media itself is also a business, which specializes in putting advertising at the fingertips, eyes, nose, or ears of consumers.

This chapter is an overview of the marketing communications and media business: how it is organized to conduct media buying and selling, its size, composition, and trends. You will see what media professionals do and what kinds of jobs they have.

This chapter should raise a lot of questions in your mind about interesting aspects of the business. For example, why have traditional broadcast television networks (ABC, CBS, NBC) fallen at the feet of cable TV, which now enjoys more total revenue than broadcast does?

This chapter you will show you:

- Size and composition of the marketing communications and advertising media industry
- Basic economics of the media business
- Industry organization for media buying and selling transactions
- Media professional responsibilities and tasks
- Examples of job opportunities

Size & Composition of the Industry

Marketing communications is a huge industry. In 2009, total expenditures in media and marketing services exceeded $776 billion. Traditional media represented only about one-quarter of that, with the other three-quarters composed of direct marketing and consumer/trade promotions and other forms of marketing communications.

Table 2-1 shows estimated expenditures for these various forms of marketing communications. Numbers vary from study to study, due to different methodologies and sources of information, but the general proportions of these figures are probably about right.

Table 2-1.—Marketing Communications Expenditures by Medium

Medium	2006	2008	2009	Per cent Total*	Per cent Change**
Traditional Media	$184.0	$190.0	$188.0	24.0	–1
Direct Marketing	156.0	168.0	174.0	22.4	–1
Trade Promotion	170.0	177.0	162.0	20.9	–1
Consumer Promo.	137.0	140.0	141.0	18.2	<1
Online	14.0	21.0	27.0	10.5	29
Custom Publishing	17.0	23.0	24.0	9.5	1
Event Marketing	14.0	20.0	21.0	2.5	1
Video Games	0.3	1.0	2.0	.7	100
Product Placement	5.0	10.0	12.0	4.9	20
Movie Screens	0.7	1.0	1.0	—	—
Public Relations	0.4	4.0	5.0	0.6	25
Other	26.0	21.0	19.0	2.5	–1
Total	$728.0	$775.0	$776.0	100.0	1

Source: Jack Myers Associates & 2020:Marketing Communication LLC   *Percent of 2009 total
**Percent change 2009 vs. 2008

Traditional Advertising

Traditional advertising by means of television, radio, newspapers, and magazines, has maintained its number one position, leading all other communications expenditures as of 2009. According to Jack Myers and 2020 Marketing, traditional media represented approximately one quarter of all marketing communications spend. However, the rate of spending growth in traditional media was an anemic 1%, while some other forms of marketing communications have enjoyed more than 25% growth.

Direct Marketing

The second largest spending category for all three years was direct marketing, with an estimated $174 billion in spending. In this report, direct marketing was mostly direct mail (including production). The $174 billion does not include direct marketing expenditures in television, print media, or the Internet. When those are considered, direct marketing becomes by far the largest form of marketing communications.

Direct marketing is a *method* of marketing, not a medium. Any medium can be used to elicit direct response in the form of sales or inquiries from prospective customers. Television and radio commercials often include toll-free numbers, and magazines contain ads designed to elicit immediate response. Online search attracts visitors to websites that offer opportunities to purchase something or to request information. Google and Yahoo search advertising that drives traffic to e-commerce websites is also form of direct marketing. Most companies place their URLs in all of their ads.

Trade Promotion

The third largest expenditure category is trade promotion, which typically involves providing cash incentives or allowances to the wholesale or retail trade in exchange for some form of special treatment—in-ad coupons (like a product/price feature in a supermarket ad), more shelf space or better shelf positioning, in-store product displays, and especially end-aisle displays. When manufacturers offer retail chains *slotting allowances* just to get their products into stores, that's also trade promotion. When auto manufacturers offer cash allowances that dealers may pocket or pass, that's also trade promotion. Trade promotion can be visible to consumers at the point of purchase. Trade promotion is popular with many brand and marketing managers because it typically provides more predictable *sales lift* than advertising does.

Consumer Promotion

The fourth ranking category of spending on marketing communications is consumer promotion. Unlike trade promotion, which focuses on distribution channels, consumer promotion focuses on is the purchaser. Consumer promotion typically offers some form of purchase or trial incentive, such as cents-off coupons, sweepstakes, product sampling, and next-purchase coupons communicated on packages, on the shelf or even on cash register tapes. Besides the consumer promotion expenditures counted in Table 2-1's figures, billions of media dollars are used to tell consumers about these promotions.

Custom Publishing

Custom publishing includes newsletters or magazines published by companies for their customers or subscribers. Examples are *Westways,* the AAA travel magazine for Southern California, and *GEICO Now*, a re-

21

launched magazine for GEICO Insurance customers. Companies believe that their magazines are a Customer Relationship Management (CRM) tool because they can help maintain positive customer relationships. It is easy to forget about custom publishing as a form of marketing communications; however, by attracting an expenditure of $24 billion (in 2009), custom publishing was almost as important as online advertising.

Online

Online advertising is the fastest growing major media form, increasing 29% in 2009 vs. 2008. Of the $27 billion in ad spend for Internet advertising, almost half is for paid ads on search engines, especially Google, Yahoo, and Bing. The rest includes email, social networks, Internet video, mobile, banner and display ads on websites, and the variety of other online applications.

Event Marketing

After online, event marketing is the next largest category, attracting about $21 billion in 2009. Companies sponsor events like auto shows, fairs, races, sports, concerts and other venues where a lot of targeted consumers visit. For example, a sponsor of an NHL hockey game might receive the rights to extensive signage inside the venue and on the scoreboard, product displays within the venue, and backboard signage, as well as media coverage.

Product Placement

As Table 2-1 shows, product placement expenditures more than doubled in just three years. Product placement is what it sounds like—getting a product placed in a movie or television show. In exchange for receiving product exposure, the marketer pays a fee to the promoter. This is a popular technique used by auto companies to show how fast and tough their cars are as they hurtle through chase scenes!

Advertising Media Expenditures

Advertising expenditures support a variety of marketing tasks such as brand building, communication of promotions and offers, and retail traffic building. Table 2-2 shows ad spending estimates by medium and calendar year. Total advertising expenditures in 2009 were estimated at $279 billion, down about 2% from 2007 but up 17.6% from 2002.

Television

Contrary to the impression created in the trade press, the television business is up, not down, even though the broadcast networks have lost share of market at the stealthy hands of the cable networks.

According to competitive reporting sources, the big losers (growth rates below total television average) were syndicated television, the broadcast networks and national spot television, and local/regional cable. With an increase of 77%, cable television showed the strongest growth. Clearly, advertisers still want to advertise on television, but they are migrating to cable, where ads often are targeted better and cost less than on broadcast networks.

Radio

The radio advertising business has been flat since 2002, and Internet advertising has overtaken it as the third largest medium. Small volume radio networks lost sales, because radio continues to rely primarily on local advertisers, whose spending was down.

Newspapers

Historically, newspapers were the largest advertising medium in the United States in dollar volume. However, as circulation declines and news alternatives spring up, spending in newspapers continues to decline significantly even among the local retailer base. As Table 2-2 shows, ad spending in newspapers is roughly half of the 2000 baseline.

Table 2-2.—Media Expenditures ($Billions)

Medium	2000	2005	2009 Est.	% Change*
Television	$45.0	$61.9	$61.8	37.3
Network	13.6	15.5	16.0	11.8
National Spot	9.0	13.5	12.7	14.1
Local Spot	8.0	12.0	11.2	40.0
Cable Network	9.7	15.3	17.2	77.3
Local/Regional Cable	2.5	3.4	2.9	11.6
Syndication	2.2	2.2	1.8	−18.2
Radio	19.9	20.2	14.1	− 29.2
Network	1.1	1.3	1.1	—
National Spot	3.6	3.7	2.6	36.0
Local Spot	15.2	15.2	10.4	− 31.5
Newspapers	48.7	47.4	25.8	−47.0
National	6.9	7.1	3.6	−47.8
Local	41.8	40.3	22.2	− 46.9
Magazines	21.6	21.3	15.5	−28.2
Directories	12.4	13.5	10.7	−13.7
Internet	8.1	12.6	22.8	28.2
Out of Home	5.2	6.3	6.1	17.3
Direct Mail	16.6	20.6	19.2	15.7
TOTAL	$178.2	$196.0	$162.1	−8.9
Source: Kantar, Jack Myers, 2020				*2009 vs. 2000

Magazines

Ad spending in consumer and business magazines has been in long-term decline. In 2009, magazine spending sank again, down 28% vs. 2000. This has caused many magazine publishers to look at ways to get readers pay more for magazines by offering fewer deep discounts to entice subscribers. Longer term, while the flagship will likely continue to be the print version of the magazine, increasingly revenues from digital magazines must make up the gap.

Internet

In 2009, the Internet became the third largest ad medium, and could overtake newspapers in 2010-2011, as spending on the Internet continues to grow. Internet ad spending is dominated by paid search, while spending on banners and display ads decreased in 2009 and 2010. Social media, mobile, digital video, and games will ensure Internet ad growth well beyond the bread-and-butter search.

Outdoor

With the assistance of growing demand for digital outdoor locations and a new audience measurement methodology, out-of-home advertising posted an increase of 10% between 2000 and 2009.

PROFITABILITY

Historically, media have been profitable, except for some large newspapers. Recently, until the economic downturn of 2009, media companies enjoyed average pretax profit margins around 7%. This means that many media companies—including some independent media buying companies—had margins of 15% or more. Advertising agency profit margins in good times could average around 9%.

Media companies often have multiple revenue streams. For example, magazines and newspapers generate income from subscriptions, advertising, and, increasingly from advertising on their websites. Google's business model has a plethora of online businesses generating revenue, from paid search to YouTube and targeted cable TV advertising.

Beginning with the establishment of advertising agencies in the early 20th century, the agency compensation model was to take a commission paid by the media from the dollars placed for its clients, the advertisers they represented. Today, most media still pay advertising or media agencies a 15% commission on the gross cost of time or space. For example, if the time or space cost $100,000, the agency's commission would be $15,000 ($100,000 x 15%). In this example, the agency would bill the client $100,000, pay the medium $85,000, and keep $15,000 as its commission.

Recently, however, some clients have reduced agency compensation in order to cut costs or because they felt that their agencies were simply profiting too much. Many agencies are now compensated with a commission of less than 15%, with the client pocketing the savings. If the media still paid 15%, the client would leave only two-thirds of that with the agency and keep the other third. Some clients pay their agency a flat fee or an hourly rate, based on the agency's cost to service the account plus a reasonable profit.

Some leading agency global networks are now calling for a pay-for-performance compensation system. This makes sense in view of the pressure on agencies to provide integrated marketing communications services. On the other hand, it is difficult to measure performance because of the number of variables affecting marketing outcomes.

PARTICIPANTS

Buying and selling goods and services drive a capitalist economy. In the advertising media business, everyone is either a buyer or a seller. Buyers of advertising media represent the demand side of the equation. Buyers are typically the advertisers or agencies (agents for advertisers) who are seeking the best and most cost effective media vehicles to deliver their advertising messages to consumers.

Buyers ⟺ Sellers

Sellers represent the supply side of the equation; they control the supply of media inventory. Sellers include global, national, and local media such as television networks and stations, radio networks and stations, magazines, Internet sales representatives, event promoters, or any other media seeking to sell time, space, or clicks to advertisers with budgets to spend.

Buyers and sellers of media time and space continuously interact with each other in individual and group meetings and by telephone and email. Buyers are usually looking for new ideas and information, especially about media costs. Sellers are prospecting for new clients and looking for ways to increase sales to existing clients. Organizationally, buyers of media time and space include advertiser companies, advertising agency media departments, and media planning and buying firms as Figure 2.1 illustrates.

Buying & Selling Media

Figure 2-1.—Organization for Media Transactions

The Advertisers

Regardless of whether an advertiser company (agency *client*) ever deals with media sellers, clients are always considered buyers because they have final approval over media plans and buys, and they pay the bills.

Advertisers vary widely in their management of media investments. Some large companies—General Motors, Ford, and Proctor & Gamble—have their own media departments that work with and manage their agencies or media agency. These client media specialists want to ensure that the advertiser's money is being spent optimally and that the media activities for all of the company's brands, often handled by several different agencies, are well coordinated.

In companies that do not have their own teams of media specialists on staff, the advertising manager, marketing manager, or brand manager will provide the agency with direction, provide plan and budget approvals, and oversight. Regardless of the internal organization for managing media functions, an authorized manager formally approves all the client's media expenditures before the agency executes the media plan and places orders. This ensures that the client company—the advertiser—rather than the agency, is legally responsible for paying the bills.

The agency typically presents the media plan, revising it as necessary until the client approves it and signs a Budget Authorization for the agency to execute the media buys as planned. Until the client signs the authorization to spend the money, a responsible agency does not commit what often amounts to millions of dollars.

The Agency

Except for the smallest of small advertising agencies, every agency has a media department responsible for media planning and media buying for the agency's clients. Large agencies have hundreds of employees in the media department; smaller agencies have few media personnel.

The Agency Media Department

Large media departments are subspecialized to handle specific responsibilities, with some teams having direct client responsibilities, and others providing support. In larger agencies there are usually *planning groups* that develop media plans for one or more of the agency's clients. The agency will also have specialized support personnel to execute the client's plans. If the agency's clients use broadcast media, for example, the agency may have specialized *buying groups*, e.g., for network TV, spot (local market) television or radio, outdoor, newspapers, Internet. A larger agency may also have a *media research group* and other *media specialists*.

Figure 2.2 shows how the organization of a large agency might look. In this example, a media director oversees agency services that comprise media planning groups, buying groups, a new media group, and a media research group. In another agency, different or additional specialized services may be offered, such as programming for clients who are especially interested in developing and sponsoring their own TV specials.

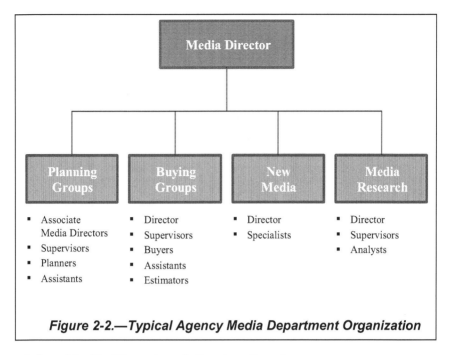

Figure 2-2.—Typical Agency Media Department Organization

Other Media Planning & Buying Services

In addition to agency media departments, many large and small agencies specialize in media planning and media buying. In fact, hundreds of specialized agencies and freelancers, sometimes just one or two persons, function as media boutiques, each providing part of the full range of media support services needed by clients who may also use a traditional advertising agency for overall strategic planning and creative.

At the other end of the spectrum are the big global networks that have formed mega-media service companies. Interpublic Group of Companies operates Initiative Media; Publicis operates Starcom. These and other mega-shops have offices all over the world and can do anything required for the interface between advertiser and media.

There are good reasons why a company might prefer to have one agency for its creative work and another for its media planning or buying. An agency that provides a good or even great creative product won't always be the strongest agency in media. Many smaller agencies are creative boutiques that were founded by talented persons whose forte was not managing media planning and buying. On the other side, the business wizards who so skillfully managed media likewise may have underdeveloped creative talents.

The Media

The lion's share of media revenues are produced not by subscriptions but by the sale of advertising (though subscriptions can affect advertising rates). A top priority of media companies therefore is to sell consumer access—time, space, clicks—to media buyers. ABC Television Network does it. Google does it. *Fortune Magazine* does it. WKBD does it. Media want your ad dollars!

Almost every magazine ad, TV commercial, or park bench message has been sold to a media planner or buyer by a media sales rep. All the television and radio networks, television and radio stations, cable TV networks and systems, magazines, newspapers, outdoor companies, Internet service providers and website networks, and other media employ sales organizations that solicit advertisers and advertising agencies to try to buy advertising.

At the media property, sales staff responsibilities may be national, regional, or local. Sales representatives are typically assigned to a list of clients in a defined geographic area. They make sales calls on these clients and provide sales-support services to them. A small medium may have a few sales representatives who must cover a large geographic area, while a large medium may have a sales staff in each of the major markets.

Some media use a direct sales force (employees), while others hire a media representative firm to represent and sell advertising on their behalf. Some media companies do both, employing their own sales force in certain markets and contracting with rep firms to represent them in other markets.

Direct Sales Force

Larger media usually have sales staff calling on advertiser companies and agencies. The sale reps typically works out of a small office, at home or in a regional office located in a major market, especially in New York, Los Angeles, Chicago, Detroit, and San Francisco. Each of the television networks—ABC, CBS, NBC, and FOX—has its own sales force with offices in the largest markets.

On the other hand, a newspaper or local TV or radio station usually has only a *local sales force* working with local accounts in its home market. These media often hire rep firms to work with planners and buyers in other markets.

Media Rep Firms

Sales representative firms are usually hired to work with accounts that the medium can't cover cost effectively with its own sales staff. Like advertising agencies do, media rep firms will normally work with a large number of non-competitive media clients—newspapers, magazines, television or radio stations, outdoor companies, or Internet. A media rep firm would not represent two competitive stations or newspapers within a market.

Independent sales reps function as the medium's own sales persons would. They conduct sales prospecting, prepare sales presentations, and meet potential buyers to try and sell them advertising time or space. Such firms may work for commissions, fees, or both.

What do Media Professionals Do?

Media professionals have a myriad of responsibilities and assignments determined by the firm size, nature, organization, and client roster. Advertising and media agencies represent the best cross section of jobs, so this discussion will focus on those environments.

In a larger agency, the media department is managed by a *Media Director* who is responsible for the quality and timeliness of all of the agency's media planning and buying.

Reporting to the media director there usually are several media group heads, often with titles like *Associate Media Director* or *Media Supervisor*. These managers will have day-to-day responsibility for media planning for a certain client or group of clients. The media group managers and staff work closely with the agency's account and creative groups and often with the client. On the group manager's staff, there will be personnel with titles like *Media Supervisor, Senior Planner, Media Planner,* and *Media Assistant.*

Media Planners

Media planners can have titles like Media Director, Department Heads, Group Heads, Media Supervisors, Media Planners, or Assistant Media Planners, depending on what job titles a particular agency has. The following discussion will use the term *media planner* as a functional description of job responsibilities that may be performed in any of those positions.

Media planners are like investment advisors to their clients because they develop recommendations about how clients' communications budgets should be spent. The main aim of a media planner is to help the client achieve advertising communications objectives by making the best possible use of available media platforms. Planners' analyze target audiences, keep abreast of media developments, study market trends, and understand consumer motivations, including the contributions of psychology and neuroscience.

Traditionally, the role of the media planner was quite similar to that of the media buyer, the obvious distinction being that the planner would devise with the client a plan for how to reach the target audience, and the buyer would negotiate with the media on implementation and costs. The role of the modern media planner is more wide reaching.

Media planning has been elevated in importance and complexity because of technology advances, fragmentation of media audiences, and a more complex and evolving marketing and media environment. Media planners are increasingly assuming responsibilities for coordinating and managing the communications touch points on a brand. Many agencies are eschewing the role of *media planner* in favor of more expansive roles such as *communications planner*, or *strategist*.

This more holistic approach requires planners to consider both above-the-line and below-the-line channels, as well as alternative and new media opportunities, to ensure that the client's advertising budget is effectively spent to implement the overall marketing strategy devised by marketing consultants or the client.

Media planners used to be able to count on a more relaxed working environment, but their expanded job scope has now placed them in the immensely pressured situations faced by their creative counterparts, copywriters, and art directors.

Many media planners are housed within advertising firms; others work for stand-alone global media planning agencies such as Initiative Worldwide, Carat, ZeniOptimedia, Starcom, Mindshare, and OMD. In either situation, media planners work closely with clients' marketing departments and creative advertising agency to develop media recommendations.

Media Buyers

The media planners and buyers may be the same in a smaller agency, but a larger agency is more likely to have a separate group to negotiate contracts for media buys.

There may be a *senior media executive,* reporting to the *media director, responsible* for all media buying. Media buyers negotiate the terms for the purchase of time and space called for in the media plan.

Media buying is often the job of media specialists. Buyers may specialize by medium, functioning as network television negotiators, spot (local market) TV buyers, spot radio buyers, magazine or newspaper buyers, outdoor buyers, interactive digital specialists, or Internet media specialists. Other agencies prefer to use a market specialist system where buyers are expected to be experts on all media but focus on a particular local market.

Question: Is it more important to understand a medium in depth without in-depth knowledge of the market, or is it better to understand a market in depth without in-depth understanding of media?

Communications Planners

Rather than asking their media planners to manage all their brand communications, some agencies employ *communications planners,* experts in many forms of marketing communications, who can facilitate the development and execution of integrated marketing communications plans. Communications planners typically have experience in both advertising and marketing communications disciplines such as digital media, direct marketing, and sales promotion.

Media Researchers

Other department heads reporting to the media director usually include a *director of media research*. The media researchers conduct and interpret media research for planners and buyers. The media research group's responsibilities include audience measurement, computer modeling, measurement of competitive activity, media effectiveness evaluation, and digital media research.

Media Specialists

Many larger agencies employ a variety of other specialists with expertise in a particular aspect of media planning or buying. Some of their specialties are described here.

Emerging Media

The agency's *emerging media experts* are expected to be on the leading edge of current and future technologies and advertising media applications.

Network TV Negotiators

Some large agencies have a staff of senior, savvy *Network TV negotiators* to buy network TV for their clients. The stakes are huge. Network television buys for large clients can be in the neighborhood of $100 million, where a 10 percent difference is worth $10 million. Furthermore, in order to receive any special consideration requires the cultivation of personal relationships with network executives. To play in this league, an agency is well advised to hire or retain a skilled negotiator with established connections and credentials.

Programming

When clients' media strategies include original TV or radio specials, agencies need *programming professionals* to work with the networks, producers, directors, and talent to create and place these specials or program series. Agencies representing, or hoping to represent, such clients my include programming professionals on staff.

Outdoor Buying

Buying outdoor billboards, posters, and spectaculars requires specialized knowledge and implementation skills. Many agencies have *outdoor buyers* that negotiate out-of-home buys, paying careful attention to precise location of outdoor boards (assuring visibility, traffic, and weather-resistance), audience potential, and, of course, price.

Direct Marketing

Direct marketing is a highly specialized service which many clients need. *Direct marketing specialists* must be knowledgeable about database development and analysis and about all the creative and media aspects of direct marketing, including such subspecialties as promotion and telemarketing.

Social Media

Social media specialist is an emerging position that helps clients leverage their participation with social networks and media. Some advertiser companies like Ford, and agencies like Campbell Ewald, have hired social media specialists to serve existing clients and help pave the way into the future.

Custom Publishing

Custom publishing specialists may be required to produce and oversee distribution of the company magazine a client sends to its customers. Custom publishing specialists provide may editorial content and art direction, and the agency may even have a special sales force to sell ads in the publication.

Event Marketing

Many integrated communications agencies and *event-marketing specialists* offer expertise in event marketing and sponsorship. Sports and entertainment events are an alternative way to reach and interact with target consumers and effective production and management requires special expertise.

Website Development & Internet Marketing

Virtually all major agencies and hundreds of boutique agencies employ *website development and marketing specialists*.

POSITIONS

The media revolution is defining the future of advertising. If media—the leading edge of advertising—is where you find your heart lies, you will be interested in how you might be able to make a living and how likely you are to succeed.

Job Opportunities

Looking at classified ads can provide some insight into what is occurring in the advertising business, where media will be the career of the 21st century. Here are some of listings in a major media trade publication in 2010. Job opportunities are generally classified as planning, buying, research, or sales, often with a specialization such as broadcast or interactive. See if you can spot a common thread that runs through these ads.

Advertising Media Director

Full service agency seeking a strategic thinking media planner with 3-5 years experience to translate client's marketing and advertising objectives into fully integrated media strategies. We offer excellent benefits, competitive salary, 401(k) plan, paid vacation. To apply, please email resume...

Media Assistant

Looking for a smart, media focused individual with at least 1-year experience to work with account team to ensure media plan is executed flawlessly. Facilitate booking of insertions and insertion order creation & assist Senior Media Planner. Develop and maintain Account specific Hot/Status sheets. Ensure that ads appear as specified and obtain tear sheets...Send resume and cover letter...

SVP Director, Local Buying

(Major agency) looking to add local media buying function to Los Angeles office...responsible for establishing negotiation strategy, maintain Media Partner relationships, embrace nuances in local markets, cultivate staff...

"Media Professionals"

*(Agency) is a recognized leader in **digital media planning** and buying. We are currently looking for Media Supervisors and Associate Media Directors with digital experience...*

Interactive Media Planner/Buyer

Fast growing interactive agency seeks a smart analytically oriented media planner/buyer to help implement an exciting mix of solutions for our expanding client base. Email CV...

Assistant Media Planner

Entry-level position in media department within full service advertising agency. Req. College graduate, knowledge of Microsoft's programs and excellent math skills. Competitive salary, standard medical benefits, 401-K, etc.

Sales Associate

The Sales Associate position is an excellent opportunity for a dedicated, professional, and experienced sales associate to liaison between sales account managers, TWC Marketing, and customers. This person will be the "pre-call" sales strategist and partner with weather.com account managers on client presentation development. Also assist with the day to day account management including campaign assessment and stewardship. The Sales Associate is a developmental role for the next level of sales, Account Manager.

Media Planner

The Media Planner provides research and strategic media planning recommendations. Knowledge on all forms of media, including interactive and alternative media expected. Professional communication, presentation and organizational skills will contribute to success. Bachelor's degree and 3+ years experience required. Send resume & salary requirements to...

Connection Planner

The Boston...office is looking for a Connection Planner. The ideal candidate has 7 to 10 years experience in developing and applying breakthrough customer insight in a general or interactive agency account planning group, brand consulting firm or strategy consulting firm. Exceptional thinking, communication and influence skills are required.

Sales Director

Prospect, negotiate & close advertising sales partnerships within assigned territory. Qualifications: 1) Bachelors' degree, 2) 5+ years experience in sales, including prospecting, negotiating & closing deals. 3) Demonstrated success in consistently meeting and exceeding sales goals. 4) Skilled in analyzing potential.

Web Analytics

Gather info about how visitors use the website/emails/mobile products to impact web consumption; analyze this info to educate the team, improve usability and drive revenues. This position will work with the Marketing, Creative, and Technical teams to optimize the customer experience.

Job Qualifications

Succeeding in a media career is not a matter of luck. My observations as a large-agency media director indicate that you need to have or develop the following, sometimes paradoxical, qualities.

Passion & Knowledge

The advertising industry has no place for employees who are not passionate about what they do. You must love marketing, advertising, and integrated marketing communications. The best media professionals are really marketing experts, who happen know a lot about communicating with consumers via media. Candidates who demonstrate superior knowledge of all aspects of marketing and media are more promotable.

A Media Mind

The best media professionals use both sides of their brain. They are highly *creative*, yet *analytical*. Media professionals must be able to make sense of data, ideas, and an array of seeming contradictions. Yet, creativity is and always will be the lifeblood of advertising and marketing communications. The better you can think outside the box and develop creative new solutions to stubborn old problems, the more likely you will be to excel in media.

Moreover, with so many media choices available, the most successful media professionals must be *global* thinkers who also pay attention to all the *details* (not that many are good at both). You must understand the client's marketing situation, objectives, problems, and opportunities almost as well as your client does.

At the same time, media planning, buying, and sales are rich with details, including complicated budgets and timelines measured in days as well as years. Miss a deadline, and you'll blow the budget (or the campaign). Overspend the budget, and you'll probably be outta there!

Great Communications Skills

To be successful, media planners must be great communicators, both in writing and oral presentation. Be prepared to present your ideas in person, in written documents, and in Power Point, using a computer projector. Media buyers and sales personnel especially must have great oral communications, because they are constantly communicating and negotiating with one another.

Teamwork

The advertising business has little tolerance for the Lone Ranger. Teams are interdependent: you have to work with peers, account managers, clients, suppliers, and media representatives, and you have to be able to synthesize the results.

Hard Work

Do you like to work hard? Yes? Then you'll love working in media. Few jobs require longer hours and more hard work than media. You will always feel overwhelmed with work that must be completed on time— because others are dependent on you. Which means you will always feel that the work you are doing matters, because great client service is your priority!

SUMMARY

If you are excited by new ideas and new ways of doing things, there has never been a more exciting time to be involved in marketing and media planning or buying. The 21st Century is a time of marketing/media renaissance, with the media world changing at light speed.

In Chapter 2, The Business of Media, you explored the marketing communications and advertising industry. You saw how it is configured, how it operates, what it produces, where you might fit into it, and how you *qualify to enter it. You now have the basic structure to understanding media planning and buying for the 21st Century.*

Chapter 3 will try to prepare you for what you can expect to encounter when you join the marketing and media revolution that is getting underway. You will be part of the change in client priorities, market, and media that are reshaping what we do.

3. THE REVOLUTION
If this be treason, make the most of it!

–Patrick Henry

Media planning and buying used to be far simpler. Advertisers sought mass audiences, and advertising agencies and media delivered them.

It was a convenient truth that television audiences were large, and networks had comparatively little competition for viewers. In the 1970s, the three television networks garnered at least a 90% share of the primetime viewing audience; today their share is less than 50%. In the '70s, mass magazines such as Life, Look, Saturday Evening Post, and Readers Digest were the strongest contenders for magazine advertising budgets; today, only two of those remain. Readers Digest survives with dramatically downsized circulation and ad rates; and Saturday Evening Post, despite its title, publishes bi-monthly.

In the '70s and '80s, there was no Internet advertising. There were no blogs, no Twitter, no digital outdoor, no gas station TV. Brand managers favored trade promotion (giving money to chains or stores in exchange for distribution in the stores, end aisles, or other preferential shelf treatment), because they could predict sales results while giving the trade what they most wanted—cash.

Historically then, media planning and buying, though not simple by any means, was much simpler than it is today and much simpler than it will be tomorrow, because there were far fewer media choices and issues to consider. The 21st Century begins with a marketing and media revolution spelled c-h-a-n-g-e.

Think about it. Clients want agencies that can deliver integrated marketing communications. Clients want accountability and maximum return on their investment. They want to know how to deal with issues arising from increased consumer control over media and advertising consumption. Given all the new digital media, clients want to know what their new media mix should be.

Clients want to know the strategic implications of changes in population demographics. They want to know how they can expand their business in a global economy. Clients who provide products or services to consumers have to identify and satisfy the wants and needs of their consumers. It is no different for an agency or marketing services company or for an advertising or marketing department within a company. Satisfy

41

the wants and needs of your customers better than your competitors do or you will lose their business, or you will lose your job, or both.

Clients want integrated marketing. In order to survive, agencies must give them integrated marketing communications (IMC) better than anyone else does. The changes occurring in the marketing environment require smarter, more creative integrated solutions. In this chapter, you will meet the six mega-trends that are driving the IMC revolution. After studying Chapter 3, you should understand:

- Integrated marketing
- Accountability
- Consumer control
- Media proliferation
- Multicultural markets
- Globalization

THE REVOLUTION

Media and marketing are changing at warp speed. As expenditures for advertising media and other forms of marketing communications begin to approach $1 trillion, we are also witnessing dramatic changes in the population and markets, media technologies and convergence, and advertiser needs and demands, . The effects of these changes are magnified by audience fragmentation and an explosion of media choices, with consumers taking more and more control of their media consumption.

Regarding the magnitude and speed of change, one new-media expert recently quipped, "We are in the beginning of the beginning." The role and importance of media planning and buying are being redefined.

Perhaps the best way to begin a discussion of the marketing/media revolution is to examine the priority concerns of our clients and bosses, the Association of National Advertisers (ANA). Table 3-1 identifies, in rank order, how a sample of ANA members prioritized their concerns in April 2007.

Six of the 10 top issues are media related—IMC, Accountability & ROI, media proliferation, consumers taking control, globalization, and growth of multicultural markets.

Table 3-1.—Association of National Advertisers Top 10 Issues

Top 10 ANA Issues	Rank 2007	Rank 2006
Integrated Marketing Communications	1	4
Accountability & ROI	2	1
Aligning Marketing Org with Innovation	3	2
Building Strong Brands	4	2
Media Proliferation	5	5
Consumer Taking Control of Viewing Ads	6	8
Globalization of Marketing	7	10
Growth of Multicultural Consumer	8	6
Advertising Creative that Gets Results	9	9
Attracting & Retaining Top Talent	10	7

Source: Media Post, 2009   *italic = media related issues*

Integrated Marketing Communications (IMC)

In a 1950 speech at an ANA conference, advertising legend Leo Burnett said,

When you are planning an advertising campaign, the people involved in the planning must be able to mentally integrate, in the thought and structure of the advertising itself, the things that should take place in the store, at the service station, in the showroom, at the ticket window, or when the salesman calls.

This advice may have introduced the concept of integrated marketing communications (IMC).

Almost 60 years later, the ANA rates Integrated Marketing Communications as the number one issue among marketers. An online survey of nearly 200 senior marketers was conducted in April 2007 by CoActive Marketing Group. The results show that a large majority (74%) of marketers by then employed IMC campaigns for most or all of their brands. Yet challenges remained, with only one-quarter of marketers giving their company's integrated marketing efforts a rating of very good or excellent. Clearly, clients and potential clients (marketers/advertisers) are struggling with effective implementation of IMC.

What is IMC?

Integrated Marketing Communications (IMC) has been defined by the American Marketing Association as:

> *...a planning process designed to assure that all brand contacts received by a customer or prospect for a product, service, or organization are relevant to that person and consistent over time.*

IMC takes into account (at least as much as possible) every single possible imaginable way that brands and customers (and prospects) interact with each other—whether in traditional, digital, non-traditional, and marketing services media, online and offline. For example, if a brand's marketing communications included television and magazine advertising, direct mail and telemarketing, banner ads on the Internet, and a major sales promotion, the creative for all of those elements should be consistent in theme, message, and brand character.

Sometimes in pursuit of immediate sales, a brand normally committed to quality resorts to down-and-dirty promotional tactics inconsistent with its desired image. On the one hand, the brand is desperate for sales; on the other hand, the brand wants a best-in-class image. Its campaigns disintegrate as promotions go in one direction and advertising in another.

> **Question: Faced with a real world conflict such as the one described above, between sales and image, how would you resolve the conflict?**

Tools of IMC

Integrated marketing communications includes all the tools or methods used to communicate with consumers: advertising, sales promotions, public relations, direct marketing, websites, Internet search, and many more. Chapter 14 examines each of the major tools of IMC. For now, it is important for you to know that the selection of IMC tools should be determined by the marketing problem you have to solve.

KIDS EAT FREE!

terms & conditions apply

Objective: Trial

This restaurant is trying to generate trial by offering a purchase incentive for families.

Problem: *What media could be used to communicate this offer?*

Figure 3-1.—IMC Problem Solving

Benefits of IMC

Why are advertisers concerned about integrated marketing? The benefits of IMC to the company or brand include the following:

- Advertising alone may not be sufficient to solve the client's marketing problem. For example, if a client suffers from low awareness and low trial or repurchase, promotion may be a needed supplement to advertising. When the right forms of communication are selected to address specific marketing problems, the resulting integrated campaigns are better able to solve those problems.

- Not surprisingly, there is actual evidence that IMC improves sales results and ROI.

- IMC produces *synergistic* effects greater than the sum of the individual communications, producing more bang for the buck.

- By presenting a cohesive view of what the brand represents, IMC contributes to branding objectives.

- When all stakeholders—consumers, employees, and trade—receive one common message, shared understanding is enhanced.

Barriers to IMC

As desirable as IMC may be to clients, it isn't growing as rapidly as you might expect. Among the barriers cited by respondents to the 2007 ANA survey described above were these:

- Insufficient marketing budget (36%)
- Lack of a standard measurement process (36%)

- Lack of needed skill sets among marketing staff (33%)
- Difficulty developing the big creative idea that can be leveraged across different media disciplines (32%).

In addition, some advertising agencies have been slow to respond to the call for IMC because they haven't found it profitable. On the other hand, agencies like the WPP Group have long recognized the need for non-advertising marketing services and worked to develop them.

IMC can be organizationally difficult to implement due to differences of opinion within the client organization and/or between the client and the agency. For example, an agency may be the agency of record for advertising but not for sales promotion or other communications. This practice disrupts integration and sometimes results in the agency's IMC ideas being bid out to other suppliers for production and implementation, leaving the agency without compensation for its work. This is a disincentive for the agency to try to implement IMC.

IMC and Media: Do or Die

Nonetheless, clients want IMC and agencies have to learn how to deliver it. But what does Integrated Marketing Communications have to do with media planning and buying?

IMC is not limited to ensuring that the creative is consistent across media forms. The stewards of IMC must also ensure that the right mix of communications and media forms are utilized to address the client's marketing needs. Despite its challenges, integrated marketing communications is necessary for agency survival and success.

As media planners transform themselves into communications planners, you should be prepared to take on IMC planning responsibilities. Here are examples of an agency—Campbell Ewald—and an event— Seattle Sea Fair—that demonstrate how IMC can look.

Campbell Ewald Agency

Campbell Ewald is an agency that provides most forms of marketing communications for its clients: advertising, sales promotion, magazine publishing, direct marketing, web development, social media, point of sale, catalogues, and more. Planners at Campbell Ewald work across media platforms to formulate the most effective marketing communications solutions for their clients. When the agency presents a new campaign, its goal is to present advertising, sales promotion, direct marketing, and online ideas together *as an integrated campaign*. The Seattle Sea Fair episode shows how the agency went beyond advertising and promotion to address a major marketing problem.

Problem: A client's vehicles had improved dramatically over the past 10 years, but consumers still regarded the products as inferior to competitive products. The problem was not one of awareness but one of perceptions, which were out of line with reality.

Challenge: How can ingrained misperceptions be changed for this considered purchase?

Event marketing is one way to familiarize consumers with products by allowing them to touch, feel, smell, taste, and learn about a product. Even the best advertising cannot do all these things. If the marketing problem is to overcome consumers' misperceptions, an experiential approach like event marketing can prove product quality to consumers while effectively complementing the advertising.

Experiential Marketing Event: Seattle Sea Fair (Boat Races)

The Seattle Sea Fair presented an opportunity to better align product perceptions with reality for vehicles that were still carrying no-longer-justified quality image baggage.

The boat races and entertainment at the venue attract more than 500,000 upscale visitors over a long weekend. Sponsorship included multiple onsite product displays, kiosks, onsite product specialists, opportunities for product interactions, games, prizes, and fun. Figure 3-2 shows one of the vehicles on display.

Visitors were able to get inside the vehicles, ask questions of the product specialists, play with the technology, and win prizes for correctly answering questions about the products. Entertainment included music and photos with Batman or the Navy's Blue Angels pilots. (Test drives are even possible at some venues.)

A form of marketing communications other than advertising addressed directly a problem that advertising could not solve.

A vehicle display at an event venue where visitors can inspect the vehicles and ask questions of the product specialists present on site

Figure 3-2.— Experiential IMC event

Accountability & ROI

ANA members identified their second concern as *accountability and ROI* (Return on Investment).

ROI = Cost / Results

How many sales does a particular expenditure generate? How much profit is created from the investment? Who knows?

Advertiser frustration is easy to understand. The difficulty of quantifying ROI means they don't know what they got for the millions and even billions of dollars they spent in media and other forms of marketing communications.

This question is probably as germane and as alarming today as it was for John Wanamaker. Are we smarter today about advertising's impact on sales? The relationship between advertising and sales is inevitably difficult to measure because of changing economic and competitive situations, brand marketing—the product itself, pricing, distribution, sales, marketing communications, and budgets—and all the other factors that play a role in business results. This ambiguity may explain the difficulty of accounting for ROI; it does not reassure advertisers that they are getting their money's worth.

Metrics

The metrics most commonly used to measure marketing effectiveness include (source: www.brandamplitude.com):

1. Changes in brand awareness (81%)
2. Changes in market share (79%)
3. Changes in consumer attitude toward the brand (73%)
4. Changes in purchase intent (59%)
5. Return on objective (36%)
6. Lifetime customer value (23%)
7. Changes in the financial value of brand equity (20%).

Effectiveness

Discussions of effectiveness often focus on the metrics (numbers) used to measure marketing performance. It may be obvious, but metrics and effectiveness are two different things.

On the one hand, it is extremely difficult for traditional media to measure accurately the ROI of advertising. The objectives of traditional advertising are often conceptual, even ethereal, and there just aren't meaningful response metrics. Television commercials run, but most advertisers do not measure results and fewer are rigorously measuring the ancillary results of website visits, inquiries, or online sales.

On the other hand, digital media generate metrics, including website visits and sales data, which can be analyzed to calculate ROI. Since results measurement is a good thing, digital media may be seen as more effective than traditional media. This is careless, however; quantitative data don't show that digital media are better, only that its results are more measurable.

When trying to sell advertising on the basis of branding effectiveness rather than website traffic generation, digital media encounter similar sales problems to those of traditional media—trying to prove their value.

- The problem of quantitatively measuring the marketing effects of advertising on brand related measures is imprecise and difficult to isolate for both traditional and digital media.
- Advertising affects brand awareness, but so do other elements of the marketing mix.
- Advertising affects market share, but do other elements of the marketing mix.

As measurement methods are improved, you can expect the future effectiveness of advertising media, especially traditional advertising media, to become increasingly subject to quantitative scrutiny.

Consumer Control

Sixth on the ANA's list of issues is consumer control over the advertising to which they are exposed. Chris Vollmer, partner in consulting company, Booz Allen & Company, explored today's rapidly shifting media landscape in his book, *Always On: Advertising, Marketing, and Media in an Era of Consumer Control.* Vollmer suggests that we are at the beginning of a consumer-centric digital age where traditional ways of marketing products and services are no longer viable because of consumer control.

Consumers are in control, he says, because they have greater access to information and more command over media consumption (including advertising). Emergence of new media—the Internet, DVRs, iPods, mobile phones, and other devices have reduced marketers' ability to use traditional media effectively to create brands and influence purchasing.

Consumers are taking control partly because they are drowning in ad messages that are irrelevant to them (if you don't have a baby, baby food  commercials are irrelevant). In fact, the amount of exposure is staggering. Daniel Yankelovich's research shows that advertising exposure has increased to the point where the number of advertising messages to which the average person in a city is exposed was about 2000 per day in the late 1970s; today it's over 5000—about 3 messages per minute!

Believing that they need to reach time-constrained consumers whenever and wherever they can, some marketers have gone to extremes to make their messages unavoidable. For example, these media were reported in 2007 in the *New York Times*:

- CBS-TV program names stamped on supermarket eggs
- GEICO ads on subway (train) turn-styles
- Airline ads on Chinese food cartons

Nevertheless, consumers are in control; their increased access to information and increased freedom of choice through digital communications have created a sharp decline in the efficacy of analog media (TV, radio, and print) to shape brand preferences and consumer behavior. Corporate demand for marketing accountability and return on investment has reached a crescendo. The previous exclusive relationships between marketers and ad agencies are weakening.

On-demand video is a good example of increased consumer control. From TiVo to iPods, an estimated 27 million consumers owned one or more on-demand media devices as of January 2008, according to a study by Arbitron and Edison Media Research.

The study, based on interviews with 1,855 participants, found that 10 percent of consumers had watched video-on-demand via cable or satellite in the prior 30 days; 11 percent had accessed news online; and 37 million had listened to Web radio.

"The study shows that consumers, while still using traditional media, have great enthusiasm and passion for on-demand media," says Bill Rose, senior vice president for marketing and U.S. media services at Arbitron. His belief is supported by the Arbitron and Edison data:

- Twenty-seven percent of 12- to-17-year-olds own iPods or other portable MP3 players;
- An estimated 43 million Americans record TV programming, either with VCRs or TiVo/DVRs, so that they can watch it at their convenience rather than the broadcasters';
- Seventy-six percent of consumers own at least one DVD; and 39 percent own 20 or more DVDs in their personal collections.

On-demand programming (usually commercial free), DVRs, and TiVo-type devices that permit consumers to view programs when they choose—with the option of zapping or fast-forwarding through commercials, and Internet search all give surfers complete control over content.

Not only new media but also new technology is enabling consumers to control their access to content, ever since the remote control introduced viewers to channel surfing. Consumers by now can control not only what they see but also when they see it and how they see it. They can strip portions of content out—such as ads—and they can share content with others.

It's common for viewers to watch TV, movies, and sporting events that they have downloaded from file-sharing services. At a recent party, someone suggested going to see the new Spider-Man movie. Another guest objected, saying, "Oh, I've got that at home." He'd downloaded a pirated copy from a file-sharing service.

Revolution in Media Options

Bill Gates recently said, "The future of advertising is digital." This may or may not be an overstatement, but there is little question that digital media and digital advertising will continue to increase in importance.

Media Proliferation

Media proliferation has occurred as the media have learned better how to serve specialized consumer needs. Media used to be almost exclusively produced for mass or general interest. Televisions programs were intended for a large, homogenous audience.

For example, as mentioned previously, the magazines that enjoyed the highest circulation in the 1970s and 1980s—like *Life, Look, the Saturday Evening Post* and *Reader's Digest*—addressed the interests of a mass market. Today, only the *Readers' Digest* still exists in its original form, but at a small percentage of its previous circulation. The Internet and countless new media forms, digital and non-digital, are springing up almost daily. Many new media offer advertising opportunities, and mobile media, digital outdoor, and many others provide a smorgasbord of media choices—television on the Internet, blogging, social media, podcasts, and video games. Figure 3-3 gives you an idea of the advertising choices the Internet offers.

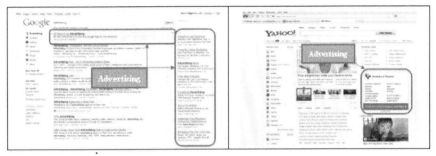

Figure 3-3.—Advertising results on Google and Yahoo search

In a world with so many more media choices, marketers must understand how the various media, especially those in digital form, can effectively communicate their brand or action messages to consumers. If agencies and media planners are going to thrive or survive in this new age, they must become conversant with all their media/communications options, know the right questions to ask, and be able to challenge their partners when necessary.

Experimentation with new media ideas is often the key to learning about those that could increase effectiveness, ROI, or time to market, e.g., online video, social networks, or even coupon advertising on mobile phones.

Fragmentation of Audiences

Media proliferation has led to increasingly fragmented media audiences. Audience fragmentation refers to dividing consumers into smaller and smaller groups, each with its preferred media options.

As the number of media vehicles has increased, the average media vehicle's share of the available audience has decreased. This means that the individual audiences of media vehicles purchased for advertising are getting smaller and smaller, while costs are not.

Consequently, a media plan developed in 1980 may have had 100 ads in popular media vehicles intended to reach the desired number of consumers. Today, to reach the same number of consumers, 200-300 or more ad insertions may be required.

Look at the following examples.

Television

The television-viewing universe has been fragmented with the growth of cable television and the Internet. In 1970, there were no specialized cable channels for entertainment, news, sports, food, or home shopping. Today, there are well over 100 cable networks delivering both reruns and, increasingly, original programming. Cable has now captured half of the total prime-time viewing audience and generates more advertising revenues than the over-the-air broadcast networks (ABC, CBS, NBC, FOX, CW, and UPN).

Radio

There are over 10,000 radio stations, large and small, in the U.S. If 25% of consumers are listening to one of 10,000 stations during radio's prime listening times, what percentage are listening to the average station? Answer: 0.000025 of consumers would be tuned to the average radio station. Obviously, many stations generate comparatively large audiences, while other stations do not.

Now let's complicate things a little more. Today's listeners can also go online, they can tune in to satellite radio (XM or Sirius), or they can listen to mobile devices. These listening options are good for consumer choice, but they further fragment and reduce the advertising audience available from radio stations.

Magazines

The growth of special interest magazines over the last several decades also has fragmented the magazine reading audience. There are typically over 1000 new consumer magazines introduced each year, and online editions further divide the magazine reading audience.

Internet

The Internet now commands a significant percentage of the available media audience, with billions of searches, millions of websites, and billions of ads around the world. This will be discussed more fully in Chapter 16.

Non-Traditional Media

Added to the proliferation of new Internet-related media is the growth of non-traditional media such as Gas Station TV, a plethora of in-store advertising opportunities, advertising on product packages, (including

Starbucks coffee sleeves), posters in student dorms, and thousands of other targeted ads in unexpected places.

Declining Effectiveness of Television

In 2008, the Association of National Advertisers (ANA) encouraged its members to move ad dollars out of traditional television into digital and non-traditional media, where they could theoretically get more bang for the buck. The ANA cited as support for their recommendation the declining effectiveness of television, exacerbated by its escalating costs.

ANA Concerns about Television

ANA cited evidence that television, the perennial favorite for mass-market national advertisers, has declined in effectiveness. The ANA's advice rested on several observations.

- Decreased TV audience sizes due to fragmentation
- Poorer cost efficiencies because costs have continued to rise
- Increased clutter caused by putting more commercials in or between programs
- Commercial zapping—devices like DVR or TiVo allow consumers to block or fast-forward through commercials had reduced the number of impressions, which reduced their value to the advertiser
- Declining long-term commercial recall

Despite smaller audiences and perceived lower effectiveness, television's advertising costs have continued to soar. During difficult economic times, moreover, advertisers take an even closer look at costs vs. value.

On the positive side, television continues to dominate all other media in terms of time spent (8.7 hours per day). In addition, the popular perception that young viewers are going entirely to the Internet for free viewing is exaggerated. While they view less than they used to, they still watch traditional television; online viewing is still a small percentage of their total television time.

Finally, in discussing television, two stories must be told: one for the broadcast networks and one for the cable networks. The traditional broadcast networks (over the air) include ABC, CBS, NBC, FOX, CW, and UPN. The cable networks are transmitted via cable or satellite and include over 100 different channels—A&E, ESPN, CNN, Discover, Fox News, History Channel, SciFi Channel, Lifetime, and many, many others.

The Minnow Ate the Alligator

In the 1980s, when cable was in its infancy and advertising revenues were almost nonexistent, Ted Turner was on the road personally trying to sell advertising on his first cable venture, Superstation WTBS (Atlanta). WTBS was the largest of the three TV stations broadcast by satellite able to provide national coverage via cable. (The other two were WGN/Chicago and WOR/New York.) Cable TV, even WTBS, was such a minnow in the alligator-filled media pond that the great Ted Turner was doing his own media sales.

How things change! The minnow has grown up and is eating the alligator.

As Table 3-2 shows, viewing of over-the-air broadcast network stations has declined substantially (from 45% to 27%) since 1984, while ad supported cable network viewing has grown by leaps and bounds, increasing from <4% to 35% of households viewing on average during primetime.

Viewing of independent stations has also plunged, as most of these stations are affiliated with one of the broadcast networks like Fox or Warner. Public TV has also lost viewers, while pay cable (HBO, Showtime, etc.) increased for ten years then returned to its 1984 baseline.

Table 3-2.—Primetime Average % Households Viewing

	1984-85	1996-97	2007-08
Network Affiliates	44.8%	33.2%	26.9%
Independents	9.7	6.7	1.0
Public Stations	2.6	2.1	1.2
Pay Cable	2.6	3.7	2.6
Ad Supported Cable	3.6	19.8	35.1
Other Cable*	NA	NA	3.0

Source: Nielsen Media Research
*Other cable includes pay per view, shopping networks, music, etc.

Armed with better targeting abilities, an increasing amount of original programming, and lower costs, the cable networks have also widened the advertising sales gap vs. the broadcast networks. In 2008, syndicated sources estimated that the broadcast networks received approximately $16 billion in ad revenues compared to $21 billion flowing to the cable networks.

An Interactive Future?

While it is always risky to speculate, it may be safe to predict that the trends in television viewing and advertising will continue, with two significant modifications. First, you can look for interactive television finally to make its debut as a serious medium. Second, you can expect further convergence of television and the Internet, which has already begun.

Newspapers in Free Fall

Newspapers were historically the largest advertising medium in the United States, thanks to heavy usage by local and retail advertisers. However, recent declines in newspaper circulation and sales revenues have put newspapers into a distant second place now behind television.

Reported annual newspaper advertising expenditures totaled approximately $48 billion in 2002 and only $40 billion in 2008, a decrease of nearly 20%, compared to an approximate 20% increase in total measured media.

Table 3-3.—Newspaper Advertising Expenditures ($Billions)

Advertising	2002	2007	2008 Est.
National	$7.6	$6.6	$6.3
Local	40.0	35.5	33.7
Total	$47.6	$42.1	$40.0

Source: 2009 Thumbnail Media Planner

However, the long-term decline in newspaper circulation, combined with the aging of the newspaper audience, continues to cause steep sales declines. Newspaper circulation fell about 2 percent annually for years (until it began to accelerate in 2007-2008). Some individual newspaper circulation numbers have fallen even faster, according to the reports filed with the Audit Bureau of Circulation (ABC). For example, the *Houston Chronicle, Boston Globe, Star-Ledger of Newark, Philadelphia Inquirer, Orange County Register,* and *Detroit News* fell 10 percent or more. Even the *New York Times* and *Los Angeles Times* have experienced above-average circulation decreases, and both have been near bankruptcy

On the other hand, there were exceptions among the nation's biggest newspapers. *USA Today* and the *Wall Street Journal*, two national papers and the two largest in circulation, were virtually unchanged, at 2.3 million for USA Today and 2 million for Journal on weekdays. Neither paper publishes on Sundays. Among more than 100 papers with weekday circulation above 100,000, none had more than a fractional increase.

The trend of sharper declines on Sundays is also troubling for the newspaper industry, because Sunday has represented the largest share of advertising and circulation revenue for most newspapers. Furthermore, online newspaper revenues have not made up for the sales deficit on the print side of the business.

Declining sales revenues have created a profitability crisis for the newspaper industry, which is plagued by high fixed costs in equipment and plant as well as by high labor costs. Consequently, newspapers have been desperately trying to cut costs by reducing labor and distribution costs, despite analysts' warnings that by offering steadily less in the print product, they were inviting readers to stop buying.

Most papers have sharply reduced their physical size—fewer and smaller pages, with fewer articles—and the newsroom staffs that produce them. Some papers—like the *Detroit Free Press* and the *Detroit News* have reduced content (eliminating writers), and while they continue to print a paper daily, it is delivered to customers only three days a week.

Newspapers are clearly in a downward circulation and revenue spiral, partly driven by the changing marketplace and partly driven by the newspapers themselves. The paradox newspapers face is that they need to reduce costs in order to avoid bankruptcy, but their cost cutting just makes their situation worse.

Reasons cited for the decline of newspapers included:

- News is available free online and in broadcast media.
- Newspapers with shrinking revenues have to resort to reducing costs by eliminating reporters, columnists, and editors, resulting in a less desirable, lower quality product.
- As quality deteriorates, revenue declines; as revenue goes down, the paper gets thinner and thinner.
- Newspapers attract an older and aging audience.
- Newspapers are perceived as a retail-advertising medium, not suitable for building brands.
- Newspapers have experienced big reductions in their cash cow—classified ads.

Newspapers may or may not have a future. Had newspapers focused on news rather than papers, they probably would have invested heavily in digital ventures. Is it too late for newspapers?

Convergence

Convergence is the occurrence of two or more things coming together, and it is an important media trend still in its early stages. As today's media forms continue to converge, they are creating new hybrid media forms that combine the advantages of their parent forms.

Many newspapers and magazines now publish both print and online editions. Television and radio stations also have websites for news and entertainment. Online extensions of traditional media are no longer to be just a copy-and-paste presentation of the print version.

There is also growth in Internet television and radio. Check out www.Hulu.com, where you can watch certain television programs free on demand. The NBC/FOX joint venture provides some free, on-demand viewing of their television programs. (Commercials are integrated into Hulu presentations, of course.)

Mobile phones are another good example of media convergence. These devices increasingly include digital cameras, camcorders, MP3 players, and voice recorders. Phones can be used to conduct Internet searches and to watch downloaded videos or live sports. Advertising messages are being sent via text message, which has been reported (*caveat emptor*) to be more effective than search.

Most important, perhaps, will be the convergence of the Internet and television. This convergence will be complete when: (1) computers and televisions are content interchangeable—computers are able to view TV content, and televisions are able to view Internet content and (2) it is commercially feasible—viewers are sufficiently interested to pay for the service. (WiFi enabled television is already a reality.)

In thinking about Internet-TV convergence, remember that television is both a medium and a transmission system. That is, *television* refers to the screen you watch and to what you see on that screen. The Internet on the other hand, is just a system for transmitting bits of data, and it is different from the device that receives those bits and converts them for you, the computer.

Therefore, when we say that the media will converge, we mean that current television shows will merge into a hybrid with World Wide Web style content. (You do not have to struggle here with the technology needed to make it happen!)

Television programs for Internet viewing will include other types of media like text, and World Wide Web pages will begin to be temporal entities that tell a story. Another way of looking at this convergence is to realize that both your television and your computer will be running a similar super browser that will allow the same content to be viewed on both devices. To say that the two will converge, then, it is not enough simply to say that you will be able to watch television on your computer.

Here is some of the content that consumers will be able to see both on television and online.

Content from Television:
- Television programs
- Movies
- Sports
- Commercials

Content from Internet:
- Media Presentations (text, 3D graphics, audio & video)
- Games
- Information blocks to browse

What Kind of Hardware Will Prevail?

As convergence between television and the Internet continues, what kind of hardware will prevail—the television or the personal computer? There are two views.

The first view is that to facilitate convergence, there will likely be a merger of television and computer hardware. There won't be televisions and PCs, but some new device that combines the capabilities of both. Just like today's television screens and computer monitors, the new viewing device will come in different sizes no doubt, but it will be thought of as a single piece of hardware.

The second view is that, although TVs may take on some computer-like functionality and vice versa, fundamentally the two will be thought of as different devices. For research and browsing the web, you will want a PC; for watching shows and movies, you will want a television.

Engagement

Historical media planning models have been based primarily on exposing consumers to various media that carry ad messages. Advertisers' questions included: how much of the target audience do we need to reach? How often do we need to reach them? When and where should we reach them?

Now, however, there is growing interest in how effectively consumers are reached by media. Some leading professionals, including the Advertising Research Foundation (ARF) are working on a new communications model that emphasizes audience engagement with the advertising message. Are consumers paying attention? Are they interested in the product? Are they engaged with the message? How can media help engage the audience with the message? What is the importance of media context? These issues will be discussed in Chapter 9.

Each media industry conducts research claiming to show that their medium is the most effective. For example, a recent study conducted for the TVB found that television is much more engaging and effective because it arouses emotions that can't be duplicated on the handheld device's small screen, especially on mobile phones.

Addressable Media

At the heart of traditional media planning has been an assumption about the ability to target a particular audience precisely with an advertising message. In the real world, however, any medium's audience will include a few members who are part of the target audience and a lot more who are not.

For example, if you define your target simply as all adults 18-34 years old with a dog or cat in the household, you would seek media vehicles which really zero in on these consumers. What you may find, however, is that 70-80% of the best media vehicles' audiences are NOT in the target audience. They are under 18, over 34, and/or do not live with a dog or cat!

Wouldn't it be cool to deliver targeted commercials to 18- to 34-year-olds who DO live with cats or dogs? Well, Project Canoe intends to make that happen.

The cable industry's hush-hush Project Canoe initiative is developing addressable media featuring advanced set-top boxes that will, the cable biz hopes, deliver on its long-touted promise of precisely targeting ads to individuals, based on taste and lifestyle, just like Internet advertising does.

Google, the pacesetter, is pushing the addressable media envelope. Based largely on its extraordinary ability to tie Internet search to targeted text-based ads, Google expected to generate $16.6 billion in revenue in 2011, potentially representing the majority of the total online advertising market.

In 2009, Google teamed up with a technology company to combine Google's Internet search technology with the partner's software that creates multiple versions of an ad. Google hopes to be able to send tailored TV commercials to audiences of shows that best reach an advertiser's target. For example, for a program, the audience could be split to .send a minivan ad to households with children and a sports car ad to single, childless households.

Seeking to adapt its targeted, automated approach to television, Google partnered with Dish Network operator, EchoStar, on a program built around the online auctioning of :15, :30, and :60 TV commercials. Advertisers uploaded their own spots, then purchased inventory on the Dish Network feed of cable channels such as Nickelodeon, the Game Show Network, and Current TV. This automated, revolutionary approach may be a long way away from mainstream adoption, but it may also be a clue to the future.

Most of the addressability dream is yet to come. When Google's system is debugged, however, addressable media that permit the targeting of specific commercials to the precisely selected audiences will be a major breakthrough in media targeting and engagement through relevance.

Interactive Media

For at least 20 years, we have dreamed about being able to order a pizza or request additional information from our TV remote control device. We talk about interactive media as if it were something brand new. It isn't. You can already order a pizza over the Internet.

The truth is, in a variety of response-need-driven ways, we have already created many forms of interactive media. Toll-free numbers and web addresses appear in print ads and on TV or radio commercials. Most importantly, the Internet has brought unprecedented interactivity with audiences, particularly through email, search, and social media, where the consumer can easily have a conversation with an advertiser.

Interactive media isn't just television, but interactive television, which has been available for years on a limited number of cable systems, is perhaps getting much closer to a real debut.

In February 2010, a joint ANA and Forrester Research survey of more than 100 national advertisers, representing nearly $14 billion in measured media budgets, found that 75% of respondents believed interactive TV would be an effective source of lead generation and could become a multi-billion dollar industry. (Annual advertising expenditures in the US are currently around $70 million.)

Media Multi-Tasking

In an age when emails, text messages, phone calls, and instant messaging are always available, multi-tasking almost seems to be necessary for media survival.

The proliferation of media choices has created a great propensity for multi-tasking, watching or using more than one medium at the same time. According to one study, more than 80% of adults with online capabilities simultaneously listen to radio, read magazines, or newspapers, or watch TV (Big Research, 2007).

Mediamark Research (MRI) reported that 45% of newspaper reading, 46% of Internet usage, and 47% of magazine reading takes place in front of the TV. The other side of the coin, of course, is that a little over half of the above media usage occurs individually (MRI, 2008).

According to a recent study conducted by a UCLA professor, there is strong evidence that multi-tasking decreases efficiency and learning, compared to focusing on one task at a time. Further, not only is learning inhibited by multi-tasking, but time-efficiency is hampered as well.

On balance, while media multi-tasking increases total media consumption and audiences, multi-tasking reduces the attention paid to any particular medium, dilutes its effect, and makes it even more difficult to engage audience members who are consuming multiple media.

The Changing Face of America

Besides changes in media technologies, media options, and audience fragmentation, the changing Face of America will increasingly affect target audience priorities and media decisions. Chapter 10 will examine more extensively the effects of changing population demographics. What follows is your introduction.

Baby Boomers

About 76 million Baby Boomers (born after World War II: 1946-1964) are either beginning to retire or competing with younger adults for jobs. *AARP Magazine* (American Association of Retired People) has by far the largest circulation, at 23 million copies per month, of any magazine in America.

The abrupt emergence of the massive Baby Boomer population increases competition in the job market, is beginning to place what will become dire economic pressure on Social Security and Medicare, and is over-stressing the healthcare system.

On the other hand, representing over 30% of the population, Baby Boomers own an even greater share of disposable income and constitute a huge market opportunity. In addition to healthcare services, Boomers' product and service choices distinguish them from younger adults. Ever notice who's driving those new, bright red, Corvette convertibles?

As you are developing your media plans, evaluate the Boomer Market as a special target of your marketing communications programs.

Ethnic Minorities

By 2050, nearly half the total population will consist of ethnic minorities. They already constitute majority populations in many local market areas.

Hispanics

Hispanics are now the largest and a fast-growing minority group in the U.S. accounting for over 13% of the total USA population. Hispanic-Americans include U.S. residents of several different origins: Cuba, Puerto Rico, Central and South American countries, and Mexico.

Language is a major consideration in advertising to Hispanics in the U.S. Should you try to reach them in Spanish or English? Many Spanish language media available in the U.S., including Hispanic television networks (Univision & Telemundo)), cable systems, radio, magazines, and newspapers. Other Hispanic media (e.g., Hispanic Business) are published in English.

African Americans

African Americans represent about 12% of the U.S. population, projected to grow to 13% by 2025. Nielsen Media Research estimated that advertising expenditure targeting African Americans exceeds $2.3 billion per year (based on period 10/06-7/07). Of that total, about 35% was spent in local radio, followed by magazines with 30%, cable TV networks like the Black Entertainment Network (BET) with 15%, and the balance mostly in other television.

Asian Americans

The *fastest growing* ethnic group in the U.S. is a diverse Asian population from China, Japan, Vietnam, East India, and a few other countries of origin. The Asian-American market is a particularly complex market with which to communicate because of the variety of languages and cultures it encompasses.

Asian Americans are also the best-educated and wealthiest minority group, surpassing European Americans in both categories. Although Asians represent only 4.5% of the population now, they are projected to grow to 7.5% by 2025.

Change in Traditional Family Units

Traditional family units (father, mother, and children) have been decreasing—from 81% of households in 1970 to 68% today. In fact, only 7% of contemporary families represent the Ozzie-&-Harriet model with a never divorced father and stay-at-home mother. Almost 80% of U.S. households include either dual-income or single parent families. On the positive side, dual-income households have created a higher standard of living for most families. On the negative side, the rise in single-parent families has resulted in rising child poverty rates.

Geographic Migration

Migration south and west from the Central United States is another factor that has changed the face of America. Clearly, all these changes will require marketing and media decision makers to consider new marketing and media segmentations. Not only are you going to be using new media but you also will be targeting newly defined audiences for present and future geographic market development.

Globalization

Most large corporations are already global players. Some of these companies operate under a global strategy with a uniform strategic focus applied across international boundaries. Other companies use a multinational strategy, with individualized objectives and plans for the countries where they operate.

Today, going global is not a business development strategy restricted only to the largest corporations. The Internet has created an opportunity for medium-sized and smaller-sized companies to expand globally without necessarily having to navigate the complexities of traditional media in every country.

Since the Internet offers global reach at low cost, e-marketing opens new avenues for accessing potential customers all over the world. Even smaller companies can use the Internet to generate direct sales, create sales leads, and provide customer service and public relations.

It is unlikely that most medium or small business owners or managers would have extensive knowledge of markets and consumers in foreign countries, but the Internet can reach almost any interested consumer anywhere. Furthermore, the interactive nature of the Internet opens up a two-way channel of communication that can help build business relationships with potential foreign customers, as well as obtain valuable feedback on marketing and operations.

Finally, regardless of a customer's time zone, the Internet provides 24/7 access and response. So, globalization will have a significant impact on media usage, not only for large corporations doing business all over the world, but also for smaller firms who, because of the global reach of Internet, are able to become global players.

MEDIA PLANNING FOR THE 21ST CENTURY

As you have seen even in this brief discussion, change is occurring everywhere. Our mission is changing. Media are changing. The market is changing. We are being challenged by our clients. No wonder our heads are spinning!

In the 21st Century, media planning and buying will continue to be influenced by the kinds of media megatrends reviewed in this chapter. The old media-planning paradigm is giving way to New Media Planning.

What is the New Media Planning?

Media Planning, old or new, is the process of developing a strategic media plan to help solve marketing problems that inhibit business growth. Any plan must deliver a brand's marketing messages (what) to the right target audiences (who) at the right geographic location (where), at the right time (when), often enough and with enough impact (how) to accomplish the media objectives (or capitalize on an opportunity) to influence purchasing decisions.

The old media planning was comparatively simple. Target audiences were most often defined by their basic demographics. Media audiences were huge. There were only three television networks, and one primetime spot reached over 20% of the households (compared to less than 8% today). General-interest magazines with circulations above 6 million had big general audiences.

Now, there is a marketing and media revolution going on that gives the media planner many new options. In choosing the right combination of media, new media planning must embrace four principles: (1) marketing focus, (2) integration, (3) emerging markets, and (4) increasing communications effectiveness.

Marketing Focus

Media planning and buying must go back to the future, back to its traditional *marketing* focus. Media is first and foremost a marketing tool for addressing clients' marketing problems and opportunities, some of them identified by the media planner. The excitement of the new digital age must not obscure our vision of the job.

Integrated Marketing Communications

The ANA's number one priority, according to a survey of its members, is planning and implementing IMC programs more effectively. The number two priority is maximizing ROI and accountability. As advertisers blur the lines around marketing communications disciplines (e.g., media advertising vs. product placement vs. social network media), agencies must move away from traditional advertising and become more responsive to clients' wants and needs for integrated marketing communications.

Emerging Markets

A part of their target audience analysis, media planners should consider whether clients are addressing the market segments that are emerging with the changing face of the country: Baby Boomers, Hispanics, African Americans, Asian Americans, and the changing population and demographics of certain geographic market areas. Media plans directed to specialized market segments may consider the use of targeted media such as English-language Hispanic media and Spanish-language television, radio, print, and web.

Changing Communications Mixes

In the past, media planners may have considered a few hundred media options. Now decision-making is much more complex, with perhaps hundreds of thousands of potential media choices.

Table 3-4.—Changes in the Media Mix

Medium	% Current Spend*	% Future Spend**
Television	44	15
Radio	10	3
Print	33	25
Outdoor	4	3
Search	9	22
Interactive	–	30
Mobile	<1	2

*Source: 2010 Thumbnail Media Planner
**Kellogg on Advertising & Media

According to Kellogg's book, it is expected that more dollars will shift into digital media, especially into search, as consumers increasingly look online for information. Kellogg also believes that the role of print in the media mix, especially magazines, will decline further, although at some point newspapers will stabilize. Television is harder to predict. On the one hand, network audiences continue to decline and prices continue to rise, and the ANA is recommending to its members that they seek alternatives. On the other hand, if interactive television succeeds and if there is a convergence with the Internet, television actually could grow. Finally, some growth in outdoor advertizing is also possible, facilitated by new digital platforms.

Changing Role of Media Planners

Chapter 1 began with this quote from Lou Schultz, former CEO of Initiative Media, one of the largest media planning and buying services in the world: "The best way to cope with change is to help create it." That's a good summary of your position in marketing. There has never been a more exciting time to be in media, to help write the future.

The role of media planners has already begun to change from traditional media planners to marketing communications planners. Media planners must become conversant not only with traditional and new media but also with marketing services media and non-traditional media.

New media planning will require new knowledge and skills:

- **Engagement.** The emerging communications model is about engaging consumers. Media plays a role in consumer engagement by providing the appropriate context for messages.
- **New Metrics.** The ANA's second most important issue is accountability and ROI. This requires that the right metrics be available to make these determinations. Planners must learn about and even develop new metrics for both traditional and new media plans.
- **Optimization.** New models will be needed to help planners optimize and synergize media mixes that include both traditional and new media, combined with other forms of marketing communications as needed.

SUMMARY

Chapter 3 has described a marketing and media revolution in six dimensions that will have a profound impact on media planning and buying in the 21st century.

All of the key media planning and buying considerations are and will be in the midst of dramatic change— from media's role in marketing and ROI to identifying and addressing new target markets with new media.

Table 3-5 summarizes this multi-faceted analysis.

Table 3-5.—Marketing & Media Revolution: Summary

IMC	◆ #1 issue among larger advertisers ◆ Expands role of media planners ◆ You must get with the program!
Accountability & ROI	◆ Close #2 issue among ANA members ◆ Measurement & metrics crucial ◆ Traditional media metrics are poor ◆ Digital media metrics are better
Consumers Taking Control	◆ Consumers taking more control of media and ad consumption ◆ Must find ways to engage and retain this consumer's attention
Changing Face of America	◆ U.S. population undergoing historic demographic change ◆ Apply market learning to selection of target audiences
Globalization	◆ Global expansion no longer the purview of only the largest corporations ◆ The Internet can take you there!

You must understand these changes and their effect on decision-making about media planning and buying, so that you can help create and cope with the future.

Since advertising agencies and other marketing services companies serve at the pleasure their clients, it is critical to provide the services they want at the highest level of quality.

SECTION II: MEDIA BASICS

Now that you have finished Section I, you should understand the basic nature and role of media; the media business, planning, and buying; and what to expect as the future brings continued change. Section II will make sure you are equipped with the arithmetic you will need to analyze markets and media and the concepts that will allow you to understand media audiences, costs, and impact.

Section II explores the foundational strategic media planning and buying concepts of audience, cost, and impact, after first providing instruction in the basic media math skills required for media and marketing analysis, Section 2 includes four chapters to prepare you for the analyses that follow:

Chapter 4	Media Math
Chapter 5	Media Audiences
Chapter 6	Media Costs
Chapter 7	Media Impact

4. MEDIA MATH
An Inconvenient Truth

–Al Gore (movie)

Here's an inconvenient truth: you will have to be able to use math for the analyses that underlie good media decisions and media plans. Media planners routinely use math to analyze marketing information, media audiences, media costs, and media plans.

The purpose of Chapter 4 is to give you a refresher on these basic math skills—percentages, decimals and fractions, averages, indexing, weighting, and formulas. For real mastery, you might put to good use the exercises in Chapter 4 of the Media Planning & Buying Workbook. Lucky you, if you're the rare adult whose math doesn't need to be refreshed!

PERCENTAGES

Marketing and media audience information rely on percentages; e.g., the *Times* covers 44.5% of Oakland County households, or *Time Magazine* is read by 20.1% of males aged 18-34 in the USA, or the network television program *Crime Drama* reaches 9.6% of women aged 25-54 in the Pacific Region of the United States. Percentages vs. Decimals vs. Fractions

Percentages may be expressed as fractions or decimals. Table 4-1 converts each of the percentages in the above paragraph to its corresponding decimal or fraction.

Table 4-1.—Audience Measurement Math

Media Vehicle	Audience Measure		
	Percentage	Fraction	Decimal
Times Newspaper	44.5	4/10	0.445
Time Magazine	20.1	1/5	0.201
Crime Drama (TV)	9.6	1/10	0.096

Manipulating Decimals

Percentages, decimals, or fractions may be manipulated mathematically in their decimal forms. To convert percentages to decimals, you just move the decimal point. To convert fractions to decimals, divide the numerator by the denominator. Here are the basic decimal math formulas at work.

- Addition: 0.15 + 0.10 = 0.25
- Subtraction: 0.15 - 0.10 = 0.05
- Multiplication: 0.15 x 0.10 = 0.0150
- Division: 0.15 / 0.10 = 1.50

Beware of Mixing Apples & Oranges

Percentages, decimals, or fractions may be added when their base or universe is the same. They may not be added if their bases are different. If you add three apples and three oranges, what is the mathematical result? The answer is six fruits. Three apples and three oranges cannot be added because they represent entirely different universes.

In the audience-measurement example above, the figures in Table 4-1 for the three media types cannot be added or even compared in any way that makes sense because they represent disparate universes. The base or universe for the *Times* newspaper figure is coverage of households in a particular county. The universe for the *Time* magazine figure is men of a certain age in the United States. The universe for the *Crime Drama* figure is women of another age in a single region of the United States. The three universes are completely different—apples, oranges, and watermelons— because the underlying population sizes, demographics, and locations are different.

Calculating Percentages from Raw Numbers

Media planners and buyers often have to calculate percentages from a set of raw numbers. For example, if you knew that there were 1,000,000 adult viewers for a television program (universe) and that 650,000 of those viewers were adult women (sample), you could calculate that 65% of the adult viewers were women. This calculation is accomplished by dividing the population subset (sample) by the universe: 650,000 / 1,000,000 = 0.65 or 65%. Planners perform similar calculations to determine percentage of sales by market, by time of year, by medium, or any other percentage where you know the size of the universe and the size of the sample.

Calculating Raw Numbers from Percentages

A buyer or planner may need to calculate in the opposite direction, as well, to determine a whole number from a percentage. For example, if there are 1,000,000 adult viewers and 65% of them are adult women, you could calculate that the number of adult women was 650,000. This calculation is performed by multiplying the percentage times the total universe: 0.65 x 1,000,000 = 650,000.

Calculating Agency Commissions

Chapter 2 reviewed the variety of ways in which advertising agencies are paid for their services, with commission on gross billings being one of the most common. The commission is paid by the media, and the client determines what part of it to retain and how much to pay the agency.

While agency commissions as a percentage of gross billings have declined over time, the traditional standard has been 15%. Therefore, if an agency had $1,000,000 in billings, its commission would have been 15%, yielding $150,000 income: 0.15 x $1,000,000 = $150,000.

Another common media math problem is to determine total billing when the commission and the commission percentage are known. For example, if an advertising agency receives a 15% commission on its billings for a particular client, and you know the dollar commission is $10,000, you can calculate the total billings by dividing the commission dollars ($10,000) by the percentage commission in decimal form (0.15). $10,000/0.15 = $66,667 in billings.

Sometimes a media vehicle doesn't pay commission, so the net cost of the ad has to be grossed up to what the amount would be if the commission had been included in the price. The higher amount is then billed to the client so that the agency can receive its compensation. This is done by multiplying the net amount (without commission) by 1.1765 to determine the gross amount that would include agency commission.

For example, if a magazine charges $1,000 for an ad but doesn't pay the agency a commission, the agency grosses up the $1,000 by multiplying it by 1.1765. This brings the gross figure to $1,176.50 with the agency commission at $176.50. Double-check the math by multiplying the $1176 by 15% commission. This yields roughly $176 commission with $1,000 net to the magazine.

AVERAGES

Everybody uses averages. When the U.S. Census reports the age or income of the population, the government reports the averages because it would be impossible and highly impractical to report the age or income of every individual in the population. Even if they did, how would you use all that data if you had it? Averages make a mountain of data manageable. They are heavily used in media analyses—e.g., average audiences, average cost, etc. An average is simply a number that is typical of a larger set of numbers.

Averages give information about what is typical in a data set. Statisticians define averages as *measures of central tendency*.

The term *average* often refers to an intuitive central tendency without reference to a specific measurement, or it is used as part of a term such as "the average person." However, the phrase "there's no such thing as an average citizen" emphasizes that the average is a number, not a person or object. The average is calculated from several individual measurements that may not even include the average.

There are three types of averages: the mean, the median, and the mode. You should always clarify which average you are using.

Mean

The first and most commonly used type of average is the *mean*. The mean is the sum of all the quantities divided by the number of quantities (e.g., 1+1+2 divided by 3 = 1.3). The mean is the arithmetic average of a set of numbers.

While the mean is used most often, there may be occasions when other types of averages should be used. For example, if there is a highly skewed distribution, the mean is not necessarily the same as the middle value (median) or the most likely (mode). Mean income may be skewed upwards by a small number of earners with very large incomes, when in reality the majority has an income lower than the mean.

The biggest potential problem with using the mean to describe the group is that extreme values may *skew* the results so dramatically that the average is completely atypical. For example, what is the average of 1+50+50+100,000? The mean is 25,025.25. Does that represent ANY of those quantities? Is it typical of the distribution?

Median

The *median* is the level at which the set is divided in half, the number that occupies the middle position when the numbers or measures are arrayed in order (1-2-**3**-4-5). The difference between the median and the mean is illustrated in this simple example:

Suppose 19 paupers and 1 billionaire are in a room. Everyone's pockets are emptied and the money placed on a table. Each pauper puts $5 on the table; the billionaire puts $1 billion on the table. The total on the table is $1,000,000,095.

If that money were divided equally among the 20 persons in the room, each would receive $50,000,004.75, the mean amount of money that the 20 persons brought into the room. The median amount would be $5: you can divide the group into two groups of 10 and say that everyone in the first group brought in no more than $5, and everyone in the second group brought in no less than $5. The median is the amount that the typical person brought in. By contrast, the mean is not at all typical, since nobody in the room brought in an amount approximating $50,000,004.75.

Mode

The *mode* is the number that occurs most frequently in the distribution (1-**2-2**-3-4). The mode of the list 1-2-2-3-3-3-4 is 3. The mode is not necessarily well defined. The list 1-2-2-3-3-5 has two modes, 2 and 3. The mode can be understood as setting each member of the list equal to the most common value in the list if there is a most common value. This list is then equated to the resulting list with all values replaced by the same value. Since they are already all the same, this does not require any change. What is the mode in the pauper/billionaire example above? It is actually a good description of this group's cash value, $5 failing to be an accurate measure for only one of the 20 members.

INDEXING

Media planners frequently *index* certain numbers to other base numbers. This is a convenient way to determine quickly how far a number is above or below some benchmark. Indexing is really nothing more than a percentage of the base number formulated without the percent sign or decimal. Index numbers are shown as whole numbers, and the base number is always indexed at 100.

Example 1.—Suppose 30% of 18- to 34-year-old adults used chili sauce in the past six months, and 20% of all U.S. adults used chili sauce. If you wanted to know how much more likely 18-34s were to use chili sauce, you could index the two numbers by dividing the subset percentage (18-34s, 30%) by the base percentage (all adults, 20%).

Calculating 30/20 = 150, you learn that the incidence of chili sauce use is 50% higher among the younger adults than it is in the general adult population. You might conclude therefore that young adults are a high potential target market for chili sauce!

Example 2.—Indexes can also be benchmarked against any number in the sequence. The following example indexes each year's sales to sales in 1985, the year with the Index shown at 100.

Year	Sales	Index
2010	$50,000	250
2000	40,000	200
1995	35,000	175
1985	20,000	100

Here's how you read this table: *1995 sales were 175% of 1985 sales, and 2010 sales were 250% of 1985 sales (or 2.5 times higher than 1985 sales).*

Example 3.—Indexes can also be developed against an average. The following table indexes actual quarterly sales to the quarterly average:

Quarter	Sales	Index
JFM	2500	76
AMJ	2250	68
JAS	3500	106
OND	5000	141
Average	3300	100

This type of analysis might help schedule media weight through the year. You read it this way: *Sales of 2500 units in the JFM quarter were 76% as high as the average quarter, while sales in OND were 141% of the average, i.e. 41% higher than the average quarter's sales of 3300 units.*

Media planners will often scan pages of marketing or media data to identify quickly which demographics or media vehicles are most selective, i.e., have the highest vs. lowest index numbers. Index numbers can be misleading, however, when they result in an irrational choice.

For example, if a group has an extremely high index number but represents a miniscule percentage of the target market, it may not be wise or cost effective to target the group. Conversely, a group may have a somewhat below-average index, but may represent such a large percentage of the user group, that it must be targeted in order to ensure high reach of the user group.

Here's an example. A demographic group is five times more likely than the general population to use a particular product category. The group represents less than 1% of the user population. Would you use your limited resources to target the group? Probably not.

Here's another example: A group represents 55% of all users. It has a below-average index to the general population. Would you target that group? Probably. Think about it: a smaller proportion of a larger segment still represents more consumers.

WEIGHTING

When conducting media analyses, it is often necessary to weight or adjust the raw numbers so that the numbers you are working with more accurately represent true media/marketing values on which to make decisions or recommendations. This is called *weighting*.

The applied weights can be percentages, indices, fractions, or ratios. The weight is multiplied times the raw number in order to obtain a weighted number that then can be compared to other weighted numbers.

Example. A magazine reaches 1,000,000 women and 1,000,000 men. Women are five times more likely to buy your product. Simply adding the male and female audiences does not yield a good measure of the value of that magazine's audience compared to the value of other magazines' audiences.

If women are five times more important than men are, men are 20% as important as women are when it comes to buying this product. In order to compare the value of alternative media audiences, the female audience could be weighted at 100% (1,000,000) and the male audience could be weighted at 20% (200,000). The total weighted audience would equal 1,200,000, which could then be compared to the weighted audience delivered by other magazines.

	Unweighted Audience	Weighted Audience
Magazine A	2,000,000*	1,200,000
Magazine B	3,000,000**	1,050,000

*50% women, 50% men
**80 % men, 20% women

You should consider weighting whenever the raw numbers don't provide an accurate and realistic estimate of the value you are trying to measure. Here are some situations where weighting is appropriate:

- Media audiences, as in the above example
- Target audience segments
- Geographic market areas
- Seasonal periods
- Qualitative media considerations beyond audience

The media planner's best friend can be an Excel spreadsheet created for a specific analysis. Spreadsheets frequently contain weights for the data to guide a more intelligent solution. For example, in the following table, the planner examined what percentage of the client's sales occurred by market (33.3% per market). Knowing that the sales potential was much higher in Market A and much lower in Market C, the planner applied sales potential weights to each market. If the advertising budget had been allocated to each market in relation to sales, each market would have received 33.3% of the budget. However, after sales potential weights were factored in, it was found that Market A should receive 57% of the budget, not 33%, and Market C should receive only 14% of the budget, not 33%.

Weighting Data

Table 4-2.—Analysis of Sales Potential by Market

Market	Sales	% Sales		Index	Adj. Sales	% Adj. Sales
A	1000	33.3	X	200	2000	57
B	1000	33.3	X	100	1000	29
C	1000	33.3	X	50	500	14
Total	3000	100.0		100	3500	100

FORMULAS

You will frequently use several simple formulas or equations, all of which are solved in exactly the same way you learned in junior high school. It wasn't too much for you then; you can handle it now.

$$A = B \times C \qquad B = A/C \qquad C = A/B$$

If you know any two elements of an equation, you can solve it for the other element by selecting the applicable version of the formula above. For example:

> If $B = 6$ and $C = 4$, then you can find A: $6 \times 4 = 24$. A = 24.
> If $A = 24$ and $B = 12$, then you can find C. $24/12 = 2$. C = 2.

The most important media formulas will be introduced in the next two chapters:

CPM = Cost/Audience x 1000
GRPS = Reach x Frequency
Rating = Share x HUTS

You will find yourself creating your own formulas, as well, to weight variables, to solve problems, and to gain insight. Don't be afraid of math. Make it your ally.

SUMMARY

Chapter 4 reviewed the basic math skills you need for media analysis—including percentages, decimals, and fractions; averages; indexing; weighting; and formulas. The practice exercises in Chapter 4 of the companion Workbook will help you make much better sense of this as you put it to use and make it your own.

5. AUDIENCE CONCEPTS
GRPS spoken here...What are GRPS, anyway?

–Anonymous

Audience is the number of homes, eyes, or ears exposed to (given the opportunity to see/hear) an advertising medium or vehicle at a given time. Audience is the primary commodity that media sellers sell and buyers buy.

Planners, advertisers, and media reps can often be heard discussing who a particular medium reaches, how much money the audience makes, how many kids they have, what their occupation is, or how much beer they drink. In reality, audience is but one factor in making decisions about media selection. Other equally important factors compose the triangle of media evaluation: audience, cost, and impact.

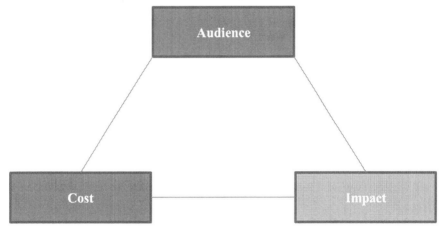

Figure 5-1.—Media Evaluation Triangle

Media planners and buyers always want to know what audience a media vehicle reaches, how many and who. Simple enough—if you have defined exactly what your subject is.

*Press headlines the day after the 2011 Super Bowl game announced, **SUPER BOWL RATING TOPPED 106 MILLION VIEWERS**. What, exactly, did the headline mean by* viewers? *(The media don't always use numbers precisely.)*

Here are some questions a media planner might ask the reporter:

"Uh, is that 110 million viewers a global or USA-only audience?"

83

"Why are you referring to a numerical audience projection as a rating, since ratings are usually expressed as percentages?"

"Are you talking about <u>all</u> viewers (total men, women, and children)? Or are you just reporting the adult audience?"

"When you cite a rating of 110 million viewers, are you talking about an <u>average</u> audience rating, viewers during the average minute? ...or are you talking about the cumulative audience, counting everyone who viewed for at least five minutes?"

"Of that 110 million, how many were really paying attention?"

"Was that rating based on the overnight report or the full report?"

"What was the rating for my specific commercial?"

"Does the rating include DVR views?"

Here's what the reporter might have answered—to any question!

"Oh, duh! I have no idea what that number means!"

Here's what's going through the mind of the advertiser, your client:

"110 million what? When? Where?"

"How many men aged 25-54 were tuned during whatever is the average minute?"

"What were the demographics of whoever those viewers were?"

"How many of the 106 million were tuned at the time my commercial came on? How attentive were viewers to the commercials in general and my commercial in particular? Shouldn't we know at least that for $3 million a :30 spot?"

"What is the difference between being tuned in and watching? Did viewers who recorded the Super Bowl on their DVRs fast forward through my commercials when they replayed the game.

Are you getting the idea? Media planners and buyers have to understand clearly what the audience numbers bandied about so casually actually mean!

MULTI MEDIA AUDIENCE CONCEPTS

Advertising is placed in media in order to reach specific, defined target audiences in an environment that will enhance the message effect. It is important that students of media gain a good understanding of the currency of audience. Audience is sequentially generated by the consumer's ability to see a medium, then the ads within. A simplified sequence is shown in Figure 5-2.

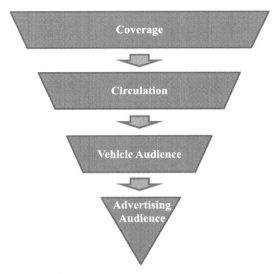

Figure 5-2.—Audience Generation Sequence

Coverage (Potential Audience)

Coverage defines the audience that has an opportunity to view, hear, or read a media vehicle. Coverage is *potential audience*, not actual audience. When a media sales representative talks about his medium's coverage, be aware that the term has different meanings for different media. The universe for measuring coverage also depends on whether you are describing broadcast, newspaper, or magazine audience potential.

Broadcast

In broadcast media, the term *coverage* refers to the geographic area capable of receiving a station's signals. Coverage has absolutely nothing to do with whether anyone is watching or listening! A buyer would never buy time on a TV or radio station purely based on its coverage. You want live audiences to see or hear your spots. Obviously, if they are exposed to your spot they are in the station's coverage area. Some major television and AM radio stations have such a large coverage area that a lot of the audience they do generate actually may be outside the geographic area where your advertiser wants to spend ad dollars.

Newspapers

In newspapers, *coverage* refers to the gross percentage of households in a geographic area that gets the newspaper by subscription or by single copy sales. Newspaper coverage, therefore, is *circulation* (copies distributed) in a defined market area divided by the number of households in the same market area. Newspaper coverage is not a measure of actual readership of the newspaper.

In theory, a free newspaper with a circulation of 100,000 in a market area of 100,000 homes could claim 100% coverage, even though few residents actually may read it. Planners often calculate the gross coverage of several newspapers in a market area. For example, if a planner selected three newspapers with a combined circulation of 100,000 to cover a metro area of 200,000 households, the combined gross coverage would be 50%. (100,000/200,000 = 50%) It is called gross coverage because some of the households may get more than one of the papers.

Magazines

In the magazines world, *coverage* is a more meaningful audience concept because it refers to a magazine's reach (coverage) of a particular target group. For example, if a target audience universe consists of 1,000,000 persons, and 300,000 of them picked up or looked into the average issue of the magazine, the magazine's coverage of the target group is 30% (300,000/1,000,000).

Circulation (Potential Audience)

Circulation is another prerequisite to actual audience generation. Print media such as magazines and newspapers generate audiences from the copies they print and distribute—whether the copies are paid or free. In either case, the number of copies printed/distributed is their *circulation*. Obviously, without circulation, there can be no audience for print media. While circulation is necessary to generate an audience, circulation does not guarantee an audience. Why not?

The *circulation rate base* is the guaranteed circulation on which a publication bases its rates. If the publication falls short of its rate base circulation, it owes the advertiser a pro rata rebate. For example, a magazine's circulation may vary somewhat from month to month, and not all copies printed may be sold, so the magazine guarantees the advertiser that its circulation will be at least 100,000. If the magazine delivers only 90,000 copies (circulation), the advertiser should receive a rebate of at least 10% for the shortfall.

Consumer publications' circulation is audited by the Audit Bureau of Circulation (ABC), and business/trade publications are audited by Business Press Association (BPA). Always ask newspapers and magazines for a copy of their most recent audit reports so that you know exactly what you are paying for.

For outdoor/billboards, *circulation* refers to the traffic passing by a location. You should ask the outdoor sales rep for a copy of the location traffic audits on which they are basing their rates.

In summary, planners and buyers must understand that although circulation is a prerequisite to generating an audience, circulation itself is not audience (actual viewers, readers). For many specialized consumer and business/trade publications, nevertheless, circulation data will be the extent of the audience data available to you. You should be suspicious of media vehicles that do not have their circulation audited. A sworn statement of print runs from the publisher is not an independent audit.

Vehicle Audience (Measured Audience)

You will recall from Chapter 1 that *vehicle audience* refers to the number of persons who are in the average audience of a media vehicle. For example, an average of 6,000,000 adults may pick up and look at the average issue of *Timely Magazine*. Of those, some may browse through some pages; some may actually read certain stories; some may read the majority of the magazine. Advertisers, of course, hope that in the process of looking through a magazine or watching or listening to a program, their target audience will see and read their ads or commercials.

Media reps arm themselves with a lot of data proving vehicle audience superiority in size, demographics, or lifestyle. If college education is an important demographic for your target, the rep might show you data about better audience education, higher median income, larger investment portfolios, or stronger preferences for wine than those of competitive audiences. *Caveat emptor:* Every media vehicle tries to figure out how to present and sell itself as an indispensible element of your media plan based on its ability to present your ad to the consumer group you want to reach.

Advertising Audience (Mostly Unmeasured)

Advertising audience is the number of persons (total or by demographic group) who were in the average vehicle audience <u>and</u> were exposed to the ad or commercial.

There are many reasons (to be examined in Chapter 7) why advertising audience is always lower than vehicle audience is. TV viewers may channel surf, leave the room, or look at a magazine when a commercial comes on. Magazine readers may spend a short amount of time reading and skip over material that is not relevant to them. Radio listeners just may not be paying much attention. Internet surfers are exposed to many search results but click on only a few.

Further, does the media environment enhance or diminish exposure to different ads? How relevant is a Corvette ad in Good Housekeeping Magazine?

If *Newswork* reaches 2,500,000 target persons (vehicle audience), and 40% are exposed to the average ad, average advertising audience would equal 1,000,000, recognizing that some advertisers would receive higher audiences, some lower. For network television, Nielsen Media Research, which measures network TV audiences, now provides commercial audience ratings called *C3 ratings*. These are based on the numbers in the audience when a particular commercial aired. Even C3 ratings, however, fail to account for those who are simply not viewing or paying attention because of distractions like bathroom breaks, family discussions, and media multi-tasking.

Gross Impressions

Impressions are the total number of contacts with one or more media vehicles carrying ads. If 1000 adults pick up and look at *Metro Daily*, however briefly, the paper would theoretically deliver 1000 adult impressions to each of the advertisers inside the paper. Impressions may be based on any demographic such as 1000 women impressions or 1000 men aged 25-54 impressions.

Gross impressions are the sum of the impressions provided by a list of media vehicles carrying an ad. To combine impression numbers, they must be based on the same universe—e.g., adults, men 18-34, etc. You can't add men 18-34 impressions to women 50+ impressions. Can you figure out why not?

Gross impressions don't differentiate between the same 1000 persons exposed ten times or 10,000 different persons exposed one time. They simply define the potential number of potential ad contacts in a group.

Impressions can and should be calculated for your target audience delivery so that you know how many potential ad contacts you had, in total and in each media vehicle, in comparison to other media vehicles.

Impressions are relevant when comparing vehicles of the same type. When media lines are crossed—television vs. magazine impressions, for example—you cannot make legitimate comparisons between or among impressions because impressions mean different things in different media. TV impressions are different from magazine impressions owing to differences in the nature of the message, research methodologies used to measure their audiences, and the different physical characteristics of the media.

The concept of audience and the measurement of audience are different for every medium. In magazines, impressions could refer to the numbers of adults 25-54 who picked up or looked into the average issue of a magazine. Radio impressions, however, could refer to the number of persons whose listening diaries recorded that they were listening to a certain station at a certain time on a certain day. TV program tuning is measured by Nielsen's black box hooked up to TV sets in Nielsen's sample, while outdoor audiences are traffic counts projected to vehicle audience impressions.

BROADCAST MEDIA AUDIENCE CONCEPTS

The multi-media concepts discussed above are universal for all media. However, some audience concepts are more applicable to broadcast media, others to print media, still others to outdoor or the Internet. The following discussion will focus on some important concepts that are exclusive to broadcast media—like ratings. *American Idol*'s ratings are buzz, but have you ever heard anybody refer to *People Magazine*'s rating?

Average Audience Rating (AA)

A rating is the percentage of a defined universe (e.g., households, children, or Native Americans) that is tuned to a program or station during a particular time. In television and radio, the most cited rating is the *average audience rating.*

In addition to gross impressions, broadcast audiences for individual programs or time periods are most often expressed as average audience ratings. The 2010 Super Bowl had a 46.4 average household rating, meaning that 46.4% of all U.S. TV households were tuned to the Super Bowl during the average minute of the telecast. How do we know this? Because Nielsen Media Research measured how many households were tuned to the Super Bowl as well as to all other television programs. (Nielsen's methodology will get more attention later in this chapter.)

Ratings for radio are calculated in the same way as for television. For example, a radio station with a 1.5 rating among adults 18-34 during AM drive time means that an average of 1.5% of 18-34s in the market area were listening during the average quarter hour. How do we know this? Respondents' listening was either electronically recorded by a Personal People Meter or recorded in a diary by Arbitron's recruited sample.

Total Audience Rating (TA)

Total Audience (TA) ratings are the *cumulative* percentage of a universe that watched or listened to some part of the program for at least five minutes. The Super Bowl's 60 TA rating means that while 46% of TV households were tuned during the *average minute*, 60% of the total U.S. homes were tuned in at least for at least a little while (5+ minutes).

That radio station mentioned above with an average rating of 1.5 among adults 18-34 might cumulatively reach 10% of 18-34 adults during the morning drive time period. You may have thought that a 1.5 rating represented a small audience, but a schedule in morning drive time on a particular station might have the potential to reach 10% of the 18-34 target, making the station a more significant factor in the market.

Figure 5.3 suggests a way to visualize ratings in graphic terms. In this example, in a universe of ten homes, the Super Bowl reached four during an average minute—in other words, a 40 rating (4/10).

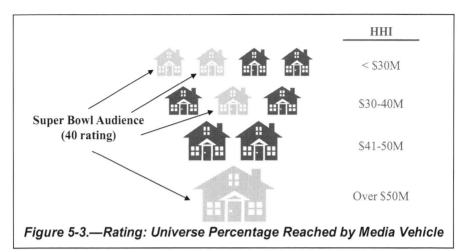

Figure 5-3.—Rating: Universe Percentage Reached by Media Vehicle

Four of the households had incomes under $30K, three had $30-40K, one had $41-50K, and one enjoyed more than $50K. Suppose the gray icons represent households where a TV was tuned to the 2010 Super Bowl. What was the game's average rating among $30-40K households? Over $50K households?

Share of Audience

Share of audience is each viewing/listening alternatives share of the total viewing or listening universe at a given time. If there are 10,000 radio listeners at 6:00 AM, and station WRDG has 1500 of them, WRDG's share of the available audience is 15%. However, if there are only 100 listeners and WRDG's share is 15%, WRDG's audience is only 15 persons.

Some stations will try to sell you share points. Don't fall for it. Although share defines the relative strength of different programs or stations in a particular time period, share is not audience size.

Table 5-1 demonstrates the calculation of three radio stations' audience shares from their ratings. The *total rating* of 10.0 means that 10% of the audience was listening to one of these three stations. Dividing their *individual ratings* by the total rating yields each station's *share*.

Table 5-1.—Calculating Share of Audience

Station	Rating	Share
WAAA	5.0	50%
WBBB	1.5	15%
WCCC	3.5	35%
Total	10.0	100%

In television, share simply defines every channel or program's percentage of the available viewing audience (share total = 100%). Sales representatives, media buyers, and media planners often discuss programming in terms of competitive shares: "We think *Bullets* will get at least 20% share against *Sing Along*, which will get no better than a 12% share."

Everybody with an audience has a slice of the viewing or listening pie and usually wants a bigger slice. Figure 5-4 provides a graphic example of theoretical audience shares achieved by various television channels, with ABC and CBS tied for the largest shares.

Share of Audience Example
October Average, 7 -8 PM

Total Viewing = 100%

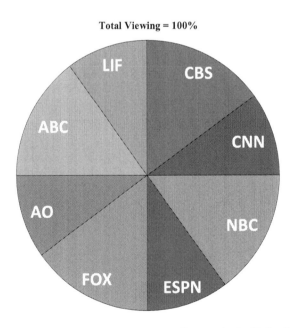

Figure 5-4.—Share of Audience Example in Television

Households/Persons Using TV/Radio (HUTS/PUTS/PUR)

Television and radio viewing/listening levels vary by time of day, day of the week, and season of the year. *Households Using Television (HUTS)* is the percentage of households watching TV at a given point in time. *Persons Using Television (PUTS)* is the percentage *of a group of persons* (e.g., total persons, adults, men/women, demographics) watching television at a particular time. *Persons Using Radio (PUR)* is the percentage of a group of persons listening to radio at a given point in time.

For example, if HUTS are 30% at noon, it means that 30% of *homes with television sets* have their sets on at noon. Another way to think about it is that HUTS or PUTS are the *sum of all program ratings* (whether based on households or persons) at a particular time.

Figure 5.5 provides a graphic example of HUTS and PUTS, where four of ten homes (40%) were watching television at 9:00 PM on a Saturday in March. Examining the data by income level, you will note that HUTS among lower income households (<$30M HHI) was 50%, while HUTS among homes with incomes of $30-40M was 33%.

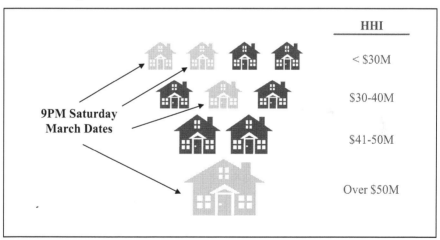

Figure 5-5.—Percentage of Homes/Persons Watching or Listening

Rating = Share x HUTS

Stockbrokers have to determine which stocks to buy based on estimated future performance. Similarly, media buyers have to select networks, stations, time periods, and programs for availabilities that have not yet aired. How do you know which programs are going to deliver the largest or best audience at the best price next January? Since you don't know what the actual audience will be for a future spot, you must *forecast* future audience just like stockbrokers might do for stocks.

The formula, Rating = Share x HUTS, is used to project ratings for programming that has not yet aired. To project future ratings, follow these steps:

1. Determine the historic viewing levels (*HUTS*) for the week/day/time of each program under consideration. These data are available in HUTS reports from Nielsen Media Research.

2. Estimate what *share* of the available viewing audience you believe each show will achieve, considering its historical track record, competitive programs in the time period, and any foreseeable changes in the network's or station's program schedule. (Planners and buyers often ask their bosses or peers for opinions about share projections. ("Bill, I am guessing that the last episode of *Smash* will get a 15 share up against *NCIS* and *Brother, Brother*...what do you think it will do?")

3. Multiply the estimated *share x HUTS*, which will provide estimated ratings for each show. For example, for the primetime program, *Smash*, multiply your projected share of audience for the program (15%) times average HUTS (50%) to arrive at a rating estimate of 7.5. This means that you are betting that 7.5% of the households in the market area will tune to *Smash* during the average minute or quarter hour.

Gross Rating Points (GRPS)

Rarely does someone buy just one spot or one rating point. Rather, an advertiser typically buys a schedule of many programs/spots. As noted above, each spot will have an estimated household or target audience rating. Adding the ratings together for all of the spots tells you how many projected Gross Rating Points (GRPS) you have in your schedule.

Since each *gross rating point* (*GRP*) represents one per cent of the household universe, 100 GRPS is equivalent of reaching 100% of the households in the market one time.

94

Of course, that assumes every household was reached just once, but the laws of chance would tell us that many households were tuned in to more than one of your shows. Thus, there is *duplicated audience* in the GRPS; that's why they are called *gross* rating points. With 100 GRPS, some of the universe will be reached once, some twice, some three times, and the heaviest viewers may be reached even more often.

Looking at Table 5-2, you will see a plan that includes thirty-two 30-second commercials spread throughout four programs. By multiplying the number of spots in a show by the average rating projected for that show, you will arrive at the number of GRPS for that program. Add the GRPS for all programs to determine the total GRPS in the plan. What is the average rating for the whole plan laid out in Table 5-2?

Table 5-2.—GRPS = Sum of Ratings

Program	:30s	AA (HH)	GRPS
Bermuda	4	3.0	12.0
Parenting	10	4.5	45.0
Party Time	8	5.0	40.0
Shark Waters	10	8.5	85.0
Total	32	5.7	182.0

Target Rating Points (TRPS)

GRPS are based on the *households* in a defined geographic universe—whether the total U.S. or an individual market like Lubbock, TX. Households don't buy products and services, though, consumers do. So another measure is needed: *Target Rating Points*, or *TRPS*.

While GRPS relate to a universe of households, TRPS relate to the target audience universe, e.g., cosmetics purchasers or adults 25-54 in the Chicago market or Cadillac owners in the Detroit market. TRPS are consequently the preferred measure of gross media weight, because they represent consumers who buy stuff!

Table 5-3 compares the audience delivery of a media plan in GRPS and TRPS. The greater the concentration of target audience in households reached, the greater the number of TRPS.

Also, note that some GRPS and TRPS are accumulated by running multiple insertions in a media vehicle as well as by using different media vehicles.

Table 5-3.—GRPS vs. TRPS

Media Vehicle	Number of Insertions	GRPS	TRPS	Index
A	5	50	35	70
B	7	30	40	133
C	10	40	20	50
D	3	30	25	83
Total	25	150	120	80

In Table 5-3, you will notice that the lowest concentration for the target audience was in Vehicle C. The 50 index is the result of dividing the TRPS by GRPS.

Question: Which is the most targeted media vehicle in this comparison?

Reach & Frequency

Media planners and marketers want to know to what extent they are exposing their campaign to their target audiences. If a campaign appears not to be generating the desired results, you might ask whether you are reaching enough of the market to achieve your objectives. What percentage of the target audience is even exposed to the campaign?

Other questions might be whether your target audience is being reached often enough to remember or ask for your brand. Are you reaching some too often and others not often enough?

To answer questions like these, media planners and marketers use an analytic tool called Reach & Frequency to understand how a media plan is exposing the target audience to the campaign.

Reach is the net percentage of the target universe reached one or more times by a media schedule. *Frequency* is the average number of times those persons are reached. TRPS will deliver some reach and some frequency as expressed in the following formula:

TRPS = Reach x Frequency

You already know about the building blocks for reach and frequency. You know how to calculate GRPS and TRPS, and you know how to calculate ratings from HUTS x Share. The next step is to reduce the GRPS or TRPS into their component parts of reach and frequency. Here's how you do that.

Let's say you can afford to buy 100 TRPS in television with your budget. Would you prefer to reach 100% of your target once? Half of your target twice? One-third of your target an average of 3.3 times?

Your answer to the above questions will help determine how you construct the media plan and how the media buy is executed. For example, the greater the number of dayparts and media vehicles in the media plan, the higher reach will be. On the other hand, concentrating in one or two programs will increase frequency at the expense of reach.

The following table provides some estimates for TV reach and frequency at different TRP levels and dayparts.

Table 5-4.—Quick Reach & Frequency Estimator

TV Reach & Frequency Example
Based on Equal TRPS

TRPS	100% Prime R/F	50% Prime 50% Late R/F	100% Late/Late R/F
100	56/2	60/2	38/3
200	70/3	75/3	52/4
500	83/6	88/6	55/5
1000	96/10	98/10	60/16

Table Reads: 100 TRPS in a day part mix of 50% prime time and 50% late night should reach 60% of the target an average of two times.

Source: Nielsen Media Research, 2010

Reach and Frequency can help you understand how an audience is being exposed to a media schedule. It is also an important tool for comparing the estimated reach and frequency of alternative media plans, so you can select the option that more nearly delivers the exposure pattern you want.

Effective Reach

Effective reach is based on the theory that message exposure *frequency* is needed to create awareness or to stimulate a purchase. Many advertisers and researchers believe that the first exposure might have little or no effect, and only with multiple exposures can you get the consumer's attention and have an influence. Other researchers believe that one exposure just prior to purchase is all that is needed.

The truth is, nobody knows. There is no simple answer. Planners have to decide on reach and frequency goals based on the marketing and communications situation they are facing.

Some research suggests that 3-10 exposures of the message are optimum. Fewer than three exposures are wasted because the threshold of effectiveness was not reached, and more than 10 exposures produces diminishing returns and reduced ROI.

Note that the effective-reach frequency research is based on actual exposure to the <u>ads</u>, not just exposure to media vehicles.

An alternate theory is called *Recency Planning*. The objective with Recency is to maximize daily or weekly reach, on the assumption that exposure will stimulate immediate purchases. The purpose of this approach is to remind as many consumers as possible to buy Product X when they go shopping today or tomorrow.

PRINT MEDIA AUDIENCE CONCEPTS

Audience concepts for print media, i.e., magazines and newspapers, are different in all respects from those for broadcast media. Print audiences are defined, measured, and estimated differently.

Average Issue Audience

In print media, the vehicle audience is usually described as *average issue audience.* Average issue audience is the estimated number of persons (by demographic) in the average audience of a publication, equivalent to a magazine's coverage. In reality, of course, the audience of a magazine—especially those that rely heavily on newsstand sales—fluctuates from issue to issue (depending on the lead story), week to week, and month to month.

Several large syndicated research companies attempt to measure the number of readers in the average issue audience. Methodologies vary by researcher, but all rely on readers' memories that they at least picked up and looked at a particular issue of a publication.

For some publications, readership is measured, for others it is unmeasured. If a credible media research company has not measured a publication's average issue audience, the advertiser has to rely on circulation figures, with some faith that the publication actually is read.

The number of readers is usually much greater than the publication's circulation, because a copy of the publication is typically seen by more than one person. In fact, the number of *readers per copy* can range as high as 10 for publications like *People*, which has extremely high pass-along readership.

Clearly then, the nature and quality of measured magazine or newspaper audiences can vary significantly depending on issue life, content, and how and where publications are read. To describe the nature of the print audience adequately, therefore, you will need several additional concepts.

Primary Audience

Primary audience is the audience represented by subscribers or newsstand buyers and their families. The *primary audience* is sufficiently interested in the publication to shell out some cash for it. Not surprisingly, therefore, primary readers see a large percentage of an issue's pages, spend more time reading it, are interested in its editorial content, and have the highest probability of ad exposure.

Pass-along Readers

Pass-along readers are those outside the purchaser's family who are exposed to a publication however briefly. Consumers look at publications in hair salons and doctors' offices, in airplanes and train stations, at the library and friends' homes, and anywhere else magazines and newspapers are found. These hitchhikers are called *pass-along readers.*

The distinction between primary and pass-along readers is important, because the latter usually do not read a publication as thoroughly. They see fewer pages and spend less time with the magazine, and the advertising exposure probability is much lower than for primary readers.

Total Audience

Total audience is the combined number of primary and pass-along readers. The syndicated research services report total audience as well as primary audience. Unfortunately, most planners and media reps use total audience data in raw form, which gives equal weight to primary and pass-along readers. That assumes that a subscriber and a reader in a hair salon are equally valuable readers. Are they?

Careful planners often devalue pass-along readers for reasons such as those cited above. Therefore, if a publication had 1000 primary readers and 2000 pass-along readers, total audience would be 3000, but the weighted audience might be 2000 readers (100% of the primary readers and 50% of the pass-alongs). This weighting process probably comes closer to estimating the relative value of print audiences. (Some planners weight pass-alongs at even less than 50%.)

Cume Audience

Because it is common for advertisers to place ads in every issue or every other issue of a publication, average issue audience—average number of readers for a single issue—doesn't provide sufficient information to compare net reach potential among publications that are issued daily, weekly, or monthly.

Syndicated media research companies, which measure magazine audiences, not only measure average issue audience but also provide estimates for *cumulative audience*. They measure how many readers say they read one of four issues, two of four, three of four or four of four issues. To estimate the cumulative number of persons reached by the publication over time, you want to know the publication's *cume audience,* which is available from MRI or Experian-Simmons.

For example, if one issue of a magazine reached 15% of a target group, that could build to 20% with two issues and 23% with three issues. The three-issue cume would be 23%. Therefore, if an advertiser had ads in three issues of the magazine mentioned above, what would be the reach and frequency for that schedule? Let's review:

TRPS = 45 (15% x 3 ads)
Three issue cume = 23%
Frequency = 2.0 (45/23)

OUT-OF-HOME AUDIENCE CONCEPTS

Outdoor advertising shares many of the basic audience concepts with other media: gross impressions, TRPS, reach, and frequency. Where outdoor audience concepts differ dramatically from those of other media is that outdoor audiences are projections from traffic counts passing by outdoor locations.

The historical concept of outdoor audience was based on someone driving by a billboard location or walking by a display of some sort at a train or bus station, on outdoor furniture or even signs on golf courses. Advertisers have always had a problem with the nature of outdoor audiences because of concerns that vehicle or pedestrian traffic counts did not translate to ad exposure by a long shot.

Unlike magazines or newspapers whose circulation is based on the number of copies printed and distributed to readers who want them, outdoor circulation is based on counts of the number of vehicles or pedestrians passing outdoor locations. *The Traffic Audit Bureau (TAB)*, a non-profit organization, independently audits circulation for outdoor locations and aggregates circulation data. Counts are adjusted to an estimate of annual average daily traffic taking into account seasonal variance, weekly changes and other factors.

The outdoor industry has now created an innovative new audience measurement and reporting system called *Eyes On,* which addresses many advertiser concerns. You will learn more about Eyes On later in this chapter, in the section on audience measurement.

INTERNET AUDIENCE CONCEPTS

Several unique Internet audience concepts are required to use the Internet effectively for advertising.

Key Metrics

In its early days, the Internet industry was concerned that competing with traditional media would require Internet audience measurement to include data that would be familiar to planners. Consequently, Internet audiences today are defined in many of the same ways that audiences for traditional media have been defined—ratings, demographics, impressions, product category interest. Many Internet audience measures also go way beyond those for traditional media, however, allowing Internet advertisers to calculate ROI of alternative internet ad plans.`

Impressions

Internet *impressions* represent persons potentially exposed to your search result, ad, or sponsored link visible on a web page, article, or the results page of a search engine. If your ad appears before a user, that counts as an impression. Only a very small percentage of impressions convert to clicks, which are much more important.

Clicks

When a mouse clicks on an ad or a link, it takes the user to a website. When the number of impressions (users exposed to your ad) is divided by the number of *clicks* (users actually clicking on your ad), the result is a *click-through rate (CTR)* that provides a measure of your ad's ability to provoke interest. There is much more to know about Internet metrics, and you will learn it in Chapter 22.

Visitors

Visitors refers to the total number of Internet users who arrive at a website, some of whom may have visited the site more than once. Visitor behavior on a site varies; some stay on the site only very briefly, while others may navigate around the site examining its content, making number of visitors a non-specific piece of information that only hints at audience size.

Unique Visitors

Unique visitors are those who visit a website, counting each person only once during the reporting period. This statistic is relevant to advertisers as a measure of a site's true audience size, similar to reach in other media.

Page Views

Page views are the gross number of times particular pages are accessed—without regard to the number of different individuals accessing the page, from where, or why. For example, if a site earns a major portion of its income through advertisements displayed on it, then page views play a significant role. However, page views are not significant if the site earns most of its revenues from converting visitors to buyers.

Conversion

Conversion is the number or percentage of visitors to a website who go on to take action, a more useful measure than page views. The action could be making a purchase while on the website or filling out a form to request information. In most cases, conversions can be tracked on Google, Yahoo!, and MSN to help determine ROI.

Hits

Hits are easily confused with clicks and website visits. When someone visits a website and clicks on its content—links, graphics, or text—that is a *hit*. Hits are not clicks or visitors! However, analyzing hits might help the publisher assess users' interests, e.g., what content gets a lot of hits?

Reach & Frequency

Does reach and frequency apply to the Internet? Yes. If you want to do reach and frequency analyses of a schedule of display ads appearing on a variety of websites, you can. You will need to work with a supplier who owns a database of Internet audience data for a very large number of websites. Nielsen NetRatings, for example, has audience data on websites accounting for over 90% of global Internet activity. Nielsen can provide online media mix optimizations, demographics, reach and frequency, and other data relevant to Internet advertising.

Analyzing Internet Metrics

Table 5-5 shows a basic analysis of several keywords used for a CPC campaign on a search engine such as Google. You will note differences in the number of impressions for each keyword, click through rates (CTR = Impressions/Clicks), cost per click, conversion rate, and cost per conversion.

Table 5-5.—Cost Per Click Analysis

Keyword	Impressions	CTR %	Clicks	Cost/Click	Total Cost	Conversions	Cost/Conv.
A	10,000	2.50	250	$0.50	$125.00	10	$12.50
B	50,000	1.50	750	0.25	187.50	12	15.62
C	40,000	0.50	200	0.75	150.00	10	20.00
D	15,000	0.25	38	0.30	11.40	2	5.70
Total	115,000	0.96	1238	$0.38	$473.90	34	$13.94

*Question: If you were managing this CPC program,
how would you rate the performance of your keywords?*

AUDIENCE MEASUREMENT CONCEPTS

Media audiences are measured continuously by a variety of research companies. Advertising companies, media organizations, and agencies subscribe to research services, paying fees tailored to the type and size of the subscribing company. If you represent a small company, you can often get the data you need from media sales representatives whose companies subscribe to the studies.

Television Audience Research

Broadcast and cable network television, as well as local market television audiences, are measured by *Nielsen Media Research*.

Nielsen Data Collection

Electronic metering technology is the heart of the Nielsen ratings process. Two types of meters are used: *set meters* capture what channel is being tuned, while *people meters* go a step farther and gather information about who is watching on what channel. *Diaries* are also used to collect viewing information from sample homes in many television markets in the United States, including smaller markets (measured only by paper diaries).

Set Meters

Network, cable, and major market TV viewing is measured by a technologically sophisticated system that uses *set meters*, small devices attached to television sets in the homes in Nielsen's sample. These devices continuously monitor set tuning and transmit the information nightly to Nielsen through a *home unit* connected to a phone line.

The home unit system is meant to allow market researchers to study television-viewing habits on a minute-to-minute basis, seeing the exact moment viewers change channels or turn off TV. Networks and the largest DMAs are measured with electronic set meters in a large sample of households. Nielsen plans to achieve a TV household sample of 37,000, with 100,000 viewers, by 2011.

People Meters

Individual viewer reporting devices, called *people meters*, have allowed the Nielsen Company to separate household viewing information into specific demographic groups. Nielsen so far has refused to refine its distribution of ethnic group data into subgroup data that could give more targeted information to networks and advertisers.

Viewer Diaries

Viewer *diaries*, in which a target audience self-records its viewing or listening practices, are Nielsen's third data collection tool. By targeting various demographics, these diary data are combined with other Nielsen data and assembled into statistical models that render estimates of the audiences for any given show, network, or programming hour.

Nielsen also reports commercial audience measures with the C3 ratings mentioned above, based on the audience tuned in to a program at the time a commercial airs. This has resulted in a slight deflation of the traditional Average Audience ratings, and still does not accurately estimate actual commercial exposure, reflecting attention levels, leaving the room, giving the kids their snack, and so on.

It also must be noted that as of December 2010, Nielsen changed its calculations of average audience ratings to include duplicated viewing from the Internet, PVRs, and even some Video on Demand (VOD). Nielsen says that the effect of this change is miniscule—an increase in ratings of 1% or less. Nielsen argued that there is a very low probability that anyone exposed to program content more than once would also be exposed to commercial content more than once.

However, one agency media director said: "Now it seems like Nielsen is telling us that we can reach a target audience twice with one bullet, so to speak."

Nielsen Reports: Ratings, Shares, Demographics

The most commonly cited Nielsen results are reported in two measurements: *rating points* and *share*, usually reported as ratings points/share. As of September 1, 2009, there were an estimated 114.9 million television households in the United States. A single national ratings point represented one percent of that total number, or 1,149,000 households for the 2009–10 season.

Younger viewers are considered more attractive for some products, whereas older and wealthier audiences are desired for other products, or female audiences are preferred over males. Because advertising rates may be influenced by such factors as age, gender, race, economic class, and location, Nielsen Media Research also provides statistics on specific demographics.

Commercial Ratings

Nielsen also provides viewing data calculated as the average viewership for only the commercial time within programs. *Commercial Ratings,* the official name of *C3*, first became available on May 31, 2007. Nielsen provides different streams of commercial ratings data in order to take into consideration delayed viewing (DVR) data at any interval up to seven days. C3 refers to the ratings for average commercial minutes in live programming plus three days of digital video recorder playback.

Sweeps

Each year Nielsen processes approximately 2 million paper diaries from households across the country for the months of November, February, May, and July—also known as the *sweeps* rating periods. Seven-day diaries (eight-day diaries in homes with DVRs) are mailed to homes with instructions for keeping a tally of what is watched on each television set, when, and by whom.

Over the course of a sweeps period, diaries are mailed to a new panel of homes each week. At the end of the month, all the viewing data from the several weeks are aggregated.

This local viewing information provides a basis for program scheduling and advertising decisions for local television stations, cable systems, and advertisers. In some of the mid-size markets, diaries provide viewer information for up to three additional sweeps months (October, January, and March).

Radio Audience Research

Measurement of network radio and local market radio audiences is the specialty of *Arbitron*, another major media research firm. Arbitron collects data from random samples of populations in more than 300 metro areas throughout the United States.

In larger markets, Arbitron uses a year-round electronic audience measurement device known as a Personal People Meter (PPM). In smaller markets, respondents record their listening in a paper diary two to four times a year.

The radio industry's term for the quarterly ratings based on these data is the *Arbitron Book*, or the *Spring Book*, *Summer Book*, *Fall Book*, or *Winter Book*. Arbitron also releases monthly information twice between the releases of each book. These ratings, called Arbitrends, are commonly referred to as *trends* and are labeled Phase I and Phase II. The Arbitrends, despite being mid-term indicators, reflect the entire three-month block leading up to them.

Arbitron surveys listener habits from six a.m. to midnight, Monday through Sunday, 48 weeks per year. There is a one-week break in data collection following publication of the Spring Book and a three-week break following the Fall Book. Turnaround time for release of a report after the end of survey period is approximately three weeks.

After collection, the data are marketed to radio broadcasters, radio networks, cable companies, advertisers, advertising agencies, out-of-home advertising companies, and the online radio industry. Major ratings products include *cumes* (cumulative number of unique listeners over a period), average quarter hour (*AQH*: average number of listeners every 15 minutes), time spent listening (*TSL*), and market descriptions by gender and age. It is important to understand that cume only counts each listener once, whereas AQH can count the same person multiple times.

Here's how to determine the TSL. Suppose you look into a room and see Fred and Jane listening to the radio. Fifteen minutes later, you look again and see Fred with Sara. The cume would be 3 (Fred, Jane, Sara), and the AQH would be 2 (an average of two persons in the room in that 15-minute period.)

Magazine Audience Research

Magazine audience measures by *Mediamark* (*MRI*) and *Experian-Simmons* (*SMRB*) are the best known. There are methodological differences between the two research companies, and they compete with each other. Both have been successful in selling their research to advertising agencies, some advertisers, and the media. Some users subscribe to only one of the services, while others subscribe to both.

MRI and SMRB provide single-source measurement of purchase behavior, media usage, demographics, psychographics, and more. The data can be cross-tabbed to answer non-standard questions. For example, if you wanted to know how many Cadillac owners are in the audience of both Time Magazine and American Idol TV program, either of these services can answer that for you.

Experian-Simmons's National Consumer Study[1] provides a good example of their methodology. It employs a patented sample design and a two-phase data collection approach: Phase 1 is a telephone placement interview to secure participation in the survey, and Phase 2 is a mailed survey using self-administered questionnaire booklets to query eligible household members. The study generates year-round measurements of major media, including English and Spanish language, yielding in-depth demographic, lifestyle, and psychographic data to produce representative measures of consumer behavior and attitudes toward products, brands, services, and media among all American adults.

Reading the SMRB and MRI research reports can be challenging at first, but it is an important skill. The *Media Planning & Buying Workbook* offers practice exercises that can help shorten your learning curve.

---

[1]Experian Simmons' National Consumer Study is accredited by the Media Rating Council (MRC), a non-profit organization formed in 1964 at the urging of the U.S. Congress, whose goal is to ensure measurement services that are valid, reliable, and effective.

Newspaper Audience Measurement

Local daily newspaper audiences are measured by *Scarborough Research*, the *Media Audit*, or local newspapers themselves. (SMRB and MRI also measure total newspaper readership.) National newspaper audiences for publications like the *Wall Street Journal*, *USA Today*, and the *New York Times* are measured by the syndicated research companies such as SMRB, MRI, The Media Audit, and Scarborough Research.

Accredited by *Media Rating Council* (*MRC*), Scarborough and Media Audit (competitors) are important sources of newspaper and other local media audience information, which can be cross-tabulated with local market consumer lifestyles, shopping patterns, media usage, and demographics.

Out-of-Home Audience Measurement: Eyes On

Out of home audiences for billboards and posters were measured traditionally by traffic audits that counted the amount of traffic passing by the different locations. This form of circulation measurement was problematic because driving or walking by a location had little known relationship to whether an outdoor board was actually seen.

Now the outdoor industry (*Traffic Audit Bureau—TAB*, see Chapter 21) has created an innovative measurement system called *Eyes On* that reports audiences who theoretically see your ads. This makes out-of-home media the first to provide advertisers with a measurement based on *commercial audiences* that notice advertising. (Source: TAB, 2011, and Clear Channel Outdoor)

The Eyes On audience measurement system serves four objectives:

- Report the audience for each of 400,000 outdoor units around the country;

- Report audiences using the same demographics and analytics (like reach & frequency) used by other media;

- Cover over 200 geographic market areas;

- Finally and perhaps most important, report the advertising audience who (theoretically) noticed the outdoor ads

The Eyes On research methodology, rolled out nationally in 2010, involves four basic steps: (1) count traffic, (2) merge with MRI and Census data, (3) make visibility adjustments, and (4) analyze and report.

Traffic Counts

Traffic counts continue to be the foundation of the Eyes On measurement system. National, state, and local traffic counts are collected from the Department of Transportation with some assistance from outside private suppliers for pedestrian traffic counts. Traffic counts are ultimately available for each of 400,000 out of home locations.

Data Merge

The traffic counts are then merged with extensive Mediamark (MRI) data from a travel behavior survey of 50,000 persons, plus U.S. census data for population and demographic characteristics. Ultimately, the merged data provide estimates of travel patterns and demographics of those passing each outdoor display.

Visibility Adjustment

What makes the Eyes On methodology so innovative is application of eye tracking and perceptual data to audience estimates. TAB had contracted with several perceptual and eye tracking research companies to study video simulations of vehicular and pedestrian exposure to various outdoor formats in various environments. The result was a model (Visibility Adjustment Index or VAI) for estimating advertising exposure. Variables affecting VAI include unit format, unit size, which side of the road the board is on, angle to the road, street type, and distance to the road.

Analysis & Reporting

All of the data are brought together, analyzed, and reported by Telmar, a well-known research company that specializes in media modeling. Telmar's output includes all of the audience estimates, demographics, reach, and frequency for campaign/ad exposure by outdoor display in over 200 markets.

Internet Audience Measurement

Several research companies measure Internet audiences, including Nielsen NetRatings, comScore, Jupiter, and Arbitron. These and others measure Internet ratings and cumulative audiences.

Nielsen NetRatings

Nielsen measures audiences on websites, complete with demographics and certain behaviors that are helpful to advertisers who are using banners and display ads to reach targets on the net.

Patented consumer panels enable Nielsen to deliver audience and Internet measurement metrics. Panel recruitment follows proprietary methodology that combines the representativeness of a Random Digit Dial (RDD) panel with the depth provided by an online-recruited panel. The RDD core of this methodology provides a baseline for representative demography and online behavior. This baseline is used to create demographic and behavioral weights for the online-recruited panel.

Nielsen claims that they use an advanced data-mining program to harvest and clean a myriad of data sources, so they can uncover and integrate data-driven insights culled from nearly 100 million blogs, social networks, groups, boards, and other consumer-generated media platforms.

ComScore

ComScore is another major Internet research firm that measures audiences and demographics for websites, mobile media, and search. Here is how they describe themselves:

> *ComScore provides syndicated and custom solutions in online audience measurement, e-commerce, advertising, search, video and mobile and offers dedicated analysts with digital marketing and vertical-specific industry expertise. Advertising agencies, publishers, marketers and financial analysts turn to comScore for the industry-leading solutions needed to craft successful digital, marketing, sales, product development, and trading strategies.*

Unmeasured Audiences

For many media, audience measures simply are not available. These media are too new, too small, or too specialized to fund audience measurement. To make decisions about these media, planners and buyers must attempt to project audiences based on data that might be applicable about similar media and any information that is available about the unmeasured medium.

For example, in the case of a magazine whose audience is unmeasured by Simmons or MRI, you could assess its editorial content and production quality, then project an audience for the publication based on quantitative benchmarks from similar magazines. For example, if the publication in question had an audited circulation of 100,000, you might determine the readers per copy and demographic profiles of similar magazines. If you found that the average competitive magazine had four readers per copy, you could apply that finding to the unmeasured magazine's circulation and extrapolate the demographic profile percentages to estimate audiences—if the publication was of interest on its own merits.

New Research: Coming Soon

Several new research initiatives are underway to address changing advertiser needs. Current research is investigating multi-platform measurement, neuroscience, shopper-based data, and set-top box data.

Multi-Platform Measurements

A lot of television programming is streamed on the World Wide Web, but the Web audience has not been counted in audience measurement. Multi-platform buys including print media, outdoor, books, and other media also have not been aggregated into a composite audience estimate. Nielsen and media companies like ESPN are putting their weight behind an initiative to create multi-platform composite measures.

Neuroscience

Neuroscience measures brainwave activity and eye movement to assess recall and engagement. The A&E cable network has been a strong supporter of this kind of attempt to measure what is in viewers' heads. One question neuroscience might answer is whether appearing first is more effective than being buried in the middle of a large commercial pod.

Shopper Based Data

What marketer wouldn't like to have store-level sales data? One research company, *TRA*, which provides TV measurement software that analyzes set-top box data, has partnered with several media companies and agencies—CBS, MTV Networks, Discovery, Group M, and Publicis—to measure second-by-second viewing data from TiVo compared with sales data from a list of grocery stores.

Set-Top Box Data

Based on concerns that certain networks are under-represented in traditional media sampling, the *Coalition for Innovative Media Measurement* (*CIMM*) is charged with identifying better best practices. One of its priorities is to test a variety of pilot programs using set-top data.

Question: Which of these research initiatives seems most useful? Why?

SUMMARY

Audience analysis and evaluation is typically the starting point for media planning, buying, and selling. In traditional media, vehicle audience measurements are usually available. In digital media, the focus is on counted impressions or behavioral measures such as click-throughs.

Comparing media audiences is a complicated because the nature of each media audience is so different from all the others. For example, how do you compare the number of viewers tuned to a specific TV program on a certain night at a certain time, to average issue audience of a magazine, measured by respondents' saying they picked up or looked into 1, 2, 3, or 4 issues of a magazine title, or to Internet impressions or clicks?

Chapter 5 has helped you understand what makes these questions complicated. You have reviewed basic audience concepts—ratings, coverage, reach and frequency, and effective reach—that are used to evaluate media plan options, and you have examined the most important audience concepts for each media class.

Ultimately, audience definition is determined by the measurements of media research companies. Therefore, you have been introduced in this chapter to audience measurement providers such as Nielsen, Arbitron, MRI, Scarborough, and TAB, and to measurement methodologies for each media class.

Now you are capable of analyzing media audiences!

6. MEDIA COSTS

Cost is no expense!

–Anonymous

Cost is no expense? Price is no cost?

Few things drive advertisers and CFOs crazier than looking at the price tags on their media schedules. Theirs is a world where one average-rated primetime network :30 costs more than $150,000. A four-color page ad in a major magazine may be priced at more than $200,000. One :30 in the Super Bowl can cost advertisers up to $3 million. A light radio schedule in Los Angeles costs $500,000.

As the late Senator Everett Dirkson said, "A billion here, a billion there, pretty soon we'll be talking real money."

Obviously, advertisers are concerned about the cost of media is that costs are a big part of the ROI equation. Lower costs for the same inventory yield a better return on investment. Moreover, advertisers look at costs as something they can control, by telling their agency to "Buy it for less!" It is imperative, therefore, that anyone studying marketing communications or advertising develop an understanding of media pricing, costs, and expense.

WHY COST IS NO EXPENSE

You probably haven't thought much about the important distinctions among the terms *price*, *cost*, and *expense*, especially when they are applied to spending advertising dollars in media. However, the distinctions are essential to understanding the buying and selling of media time and space.

Price

Price is the amount of money or goods, asked for or given in exchange for something else. Media sellers have their rate card prices in mind for their inventories of time and space. Buyers attempt to negotiate a reduced price with sellers, which would require sellers to reduce their price.

115

Cost

Cost is the amount agreed or required in payment for a media purchase, i.e., the amount an advertiser pays the media in exchange for advertising time or space. For example, media sellers may price some inventory at $100. The buyer may pay full price ($100) or something less than $100. If the buyer paid $50, the media cost would be $50. Cost and price are different things.

Expense

Expense is money spent to attain a goal or accomplish a purpose: an expense of time and energy on the project. It is assumed that expenses are good because they accomplish something. Whether or not media costs are legitimate expenses depends upon what they accomplish!

MEDIA PRICING

How are media priced? Price is what sellers ask but it is not necessarily what buyers pay. What do time and space cost the advertiser?

From the seller's perspective, media are priced in time or space units such as a :30 time slot or a half-page black and white ad. Let's examine each medium's pricing principles.

(Note: your *Thumbnail Media Planner* is an excellent source for estimated media costs.)

Television Pricing

Many factors affect sellers' pricing of time slots for TV commercials—geographic coverage, commercial length, time of day, audience size, and supply and demand conditions.

Geographic Coverage

The first factor that affects pricing of TV time is whether the spot runs on a national broadcast or cable network, or whether it is on one of the 800 local-market television stations. Broadcast (over the air) networks like ABC, CBS, NBC, FOX, or CW price their spots based on national coverage. National cable TV networks like TBS, Lifetime, Discover, and Fox News compete for business with the broadcast networks. Table 6-1 shows examples of network television costs paid in the 2010 upfront market.

Table 6-1.—Examples of 2010 Upfront Network TV Costs

Program	Rating	Cost per :30
2010 Super Bowl	46.4	$2,600,000
NCIS	12.7	133,000
Sunday Night NFL	10.9	311,000
Castle	6.8	93,000

Television stations in local markets compete with each other for buys in their local market, pricing their inventory to be competitive. Table 6-2 shows the cost of a 500-GRP schedule that includes a mix of dayparts:

Table 6-2.—Example of 2010 Spot TV Costs by Market

Market/DMA	% US Households	Cost/500 TRPS*
New York	5.7	$550,000
Detroit	1.9	200,000
Austin	0.6	75,000
Toledo	0.4	33,000

*Based on primetime programming/Adults 25-54

Commercial Length

The second factor affecting TV prices is commercial length. The basic commercial unit in television is :30. However, advertisers may buy shorter lengths like :10 or :15, or longer lengths like :60 or :90. Shorter lengths are typically priced at 70% of the :30 rate, while :60s cost twice as much as a :30. If a given spot in a good primetime network show cost $150,000 for a :30, one :60 would cost $300,000.

Time of Day

The third factor affecting television prices is the daypart in which the commercial would run. Primetime commands the highest prices, while lower prices are available during the daytime and late night. The differences in average cost of 100 GRPS in various day parts is shown in Table 6-3.

Table 6-3.—Estimated 2010 Cost of 100 GRPS by Daypart

Daypart	Cost 100 GRPS	Cost per GRP
Primetime	$2,200,000	$22,000
M-F Daytime	500,000	5,000
Late Night	1,570,000	15,700
Early News	902,000	9,020

Audience Size

The fourth television ad-pricing factor is audience or rating size within a daypart. All else equal, a spot during primetime with a 10 rating will likely be priced 100% higher than a 5 rated spot. However, as discussed below, there can be large variations in prices based on the demand for different shows.

Supply & Demand

Television costs result from a process of negotiation between the network or station sales representatives and the buyer. Sellers attempt to price their inventory based on what the market will bear, while buyers attempt to drive the cost down. The effect of supply and demand on media costs is examined later in this chapter.

Here is an example, however, of pricing gone wild. ABC priced the last episode of Lost at $900,000 per :30. (The program sold at an average of about $215,000 for the 2009-2010 season.) At $900,000, considering the program's performance (6.1 rating/$147,500 CPP vs. $73,000 CPP for the Super Bowl), *Lost* is one of the most expensive TV buys of all time.

Question: Would ROI justify that price?

Radio Pricing

Like television, radio commercial inventories are perishable. So pricing and cost factors for radio are similar to those for television.

Geographic Coverage

Like television, radio can also be purchased on a network or local market basis, with pricing influenced by the size of market. Well over 100 radio networks target different demographics with different radio station formats. There are also approximately 10,000 local radio stations competing for local advertising budgets. Network radio generates minor revenue compared to local spot radio, because 80% of radio is purchased by local businesses.

Commercial Length

Unlike television, the basic unit of radio sale is a :60 commercial, which stations prefer to sell in order to reduce clutter and number of commercial interruptions. Shorter or longer commercial lengths may be available; however, you should beware that a station may attempt to charge as much as 80% of the :60 rate for a :30.

Time of Day

Radio dayparts include morning drive time, daytime, evening drive time, night, and weekend. Higher-demand dayparts like morning and afternoon drive times usually command premium prices.

Size of Audience

Like television, the fourth pricing factor in radio is audience size or rating size. Radio time usually costs more in large markets than small markets. All else equal, a :60 spot during morning drive on a station with a 2.0 rating will be priced 100% higher than a 1-rated spot same during the same daypart on another station with the same format.

Supply & Demand

Finally, like television, radio networks and stations attempt to price their inventory based on what the market will bear, while advertisers will attempt to drive the price into the basement. There is an important difference between television and radio, however. The radio market is much more competitive, with 10,000 stations scrapping for declining radio expenditures.

Table 6-4.—Estimated 2010 Spot Radio Costs

Market	Cost 500 TRPS (Adult)	Cost per TRP
Los Angeles	$400,000	$400
Columbus, O	34,000	68
Tulsa	16,000	32
Columbia, SC	13,500	27

Print Pricing

Ads in print publications—magazines and newspapers—are priced based on type of unit, ad size, coloration, circulation, geographic edition, and measured audience.

The Creative Unit

A variety of factors affects the pricing of print ads. What are the characteristics of the ad unit itself: size, shape, coloration, and bleed? Is the ad a special unit such as a supplied insert on heavy, glossy stock? Is it a gatefold off the second or third cover? Does it contain a microencapsulated scent or a product sample?

Size of Ad

The size choices for print ads are almost infinite. An ad may be a full page or a fractional page, a two-page spread or several consecutive pages. Some advertisers also buy gatefolds running on a foldout from the front or back cover. Ads are also sometimes sold in column inches (e.g., one column x 4 inches = four column inches).

Coloration

The cost of a basic ad is based on black and white printing. However, print media charge extra for color, which can be black and one color, or two-color, or full color, or even five-color. Many publications also offer matched colors for advertisers who need a special color.

Bleed

Most magazines try to charge a 10-15% premium for ads that bleed to the edge of the page. Of course, media planners believe this charge is nonsensical, since the publication has no significant incremental cost (except for a little extra ink). Bleed charges have always been controversial with buyers who don't want to pay extra and sellers who are accustomed to the extra profit.

Circulation

Publications usually base their rates on their audited guaranteed circulation. If the rate base were 1,000,000 circulation @ $50 per thousand for a black and white page, their rate card price would be $50,000.

Audience Measurement

Print ad pricing is also influenced by the results of syndicated audience research studies (e.g., MRI and SMRB). The larger the reported audience, in general, the higher the page rate.

Since advertisers compare publications by audience size and cost efficiency, a publication's measured audience (from MRI or SMRB) will play a big role in how a publication prices its ads. Magazines with a large pass-along audience may ask for higher rates. Table 6-5 is a comparison of several magazines' general audience data and cost for a *full-page four-color* (*P4C*) ad.

Table 6-5.—Sample Comparison of Magazine Costs

Magazine	Circulation	Adults	Cost P4C
Business Week	900,000	4,726,000	$112,000
Cooking Light	1,700,000	12,068,000	103,000
National Geographic	5,000,000	32,472,000	205,000
Reader's Digest	8,000,000	35,000,000	228,000
Women's Day	3,800,000	21,250,000	252,000
Source: 2010 Thumbnail Media Planner			

Internet Pricing

There are three models of Internet ad pricing: pay per click, pay per thousand impressions, and pay per action. The first applies to paid search; the other two apply to display ads. You will learn more about all these methods of Internet advertising in Chapter 22. Here you'll review their pricing.

Paid Search

The largest category of Internet advertising is *paid search*, where prices are set per click-through to the advertiser's website. This is called *pay per click* (*PPC*) or *cost per click* (*CPC*), two terms for the same concept. Search engines such as Google, Yahoo, and Bing auction keywords to the highest bidders. For example, a company selling gourmet food on the website might bid $1.00 per click on Google AdWords for the search term *gourmet cheese*. When an Internet surfer searches for *gourmet cheese*, that bidder's ad may appear in the search results. If the surfer clicks the ad and goes to the company's website, the advertiser will pay Google $1.00.

Each time your keyword is clicked, in paid search pricing, you pay the cost that was established in the bidding. If your negotiated cost per click on Google for the keyword *gourmet pasta* was $.50 per click, and it received 1000 clicks redirecting visitors to your website, your total cost would be $500. (Cost = CPC x # Clicks).

Display Ads

When Internet advertisers buy display ads or banners on search pages or on the pages of other users, they have two payment options. The first option is priced on the basis of *impressions*, with rates established at a *cost per thousand* (*CPM*). In a CPM agreement, you pay for *impressions* or potential exposures to the page containing your ad.

Let's say you have a display ad or banner on an AOL page that generates 5,000,000 impressions per day. If you have agreed to pay a CPM price of $5.00, your cost will be $25,000 per day (5000 x $5.00). However, because click-through rates can be extremely low, you should evaluate this purchase by estimating the number of clicks you should generate from the impressions. Which is more cost effective—CPM or CPC pricing?

Some Internet vendors also offer a *cost per action* (*CPA*) option, where you pay only when a visitor driven to your website takes some action, e.g., joins a mailing list, requests information, or makes a purchase. These *conversion rates* are influenced by the effectiveness of your website, selection of the effective keywords to attract the right visitors, and creative ads that will attract them to your site.

In a CPA agreement, you pay only for actions. If you have agreed to pay $5.00 CPA and you get 1000 actions, you will owe the seller $5,000.

MEDIA: A COMMODITIES MARKET?

If you were buying commodities like pork bellies or precious metals or currencies or stocks, you would bid on the commodity. Other investors would also be bidding. If you were buying commodities or stocks, you would hope that if your bid was successful, your investment would eventually return a profit.

Pricing in the media market is a lot like pricing in the commodities market. If you are buying media, you hope that your investment will return the audience and results you anticipated. Prices are a function of what buyers are willing to pay. This is especially true for media with the most perishable inventory—broadcast and the Internet. However, it also spills over into the print media.

In general, when demand rises, as money in the market increases and supply of time and space decreases, prices will rise. You see this play out in vivid color every year in the network upfront market, where the biggest TV advertisers are committing billions for the next year. Supply and demand and perceptions of supply and demand can change quickly. Like the stock market or the commodities market, the media market can be extremely volatile.

Negotiations between buyers and sellers therefore are driven by forecasts of supply and demand—as perceived by buyers and sellers at a particular point in time. Sellers try to sell for the highest possible price, and buyers try to get what they want at the lowest possible price. When they agree on the terms, there is a deal.

The market, especially for television, was strong between 2004 and late 2008, fueled by a strong economy, which caused advertisers to boost spending. Then, beginning in the fall of 2008 when the economy went South, sales declined; especially in key categories like automotive, advertisers began cutting their advertising and marketing communications budgets, which drove media prices down significantly (creating a buyers' market). Television prices continued their decline well into 2010.

COST EFFICIENCY: THE BETTER MEASURE

Let's face it, if a media seller offers you a "good deal" for only $50,000, you don't know that's a good price or a terrible price. You need to calculate the *cost efficiency* of a potential media buy to relate cost to audience delivery. Media efficiency is a better measure of price and cost because it gives you more and better information about the value of the buy.

Even though all media place unit prices on their inventories, the true asking price is reflected in cost efficiency terms like CPM or CPP or CPC. A price of $1500 may seem low for a media vehicle, but the price is NOT low if the vehicle doesn't deliver enough audience to make it a good deal.

In order to measure the relative cost efficiency of a media vehicle or a media schedule, you can calculate how much audience each media vehicle delivers for the money. The measures commonly used are CPM and CPP, calculated as follows:

CPM (Cost per Thousand): Cost/Audience x 1000
CPP (Cost per Point): Cost/GRPS or TRPS

Calculating cost efficiency allows the buyer to select media vehicles that deliver the most audience for the money. Table 6-6 demonstrates a traditional analysis using the above cost efficiency formulas to calculate and compare several CPM and CPP rates.

For example, the asking price for Media Vehicle A is $2500 for one advertising unit (e.g., a :30 commercial). A 10 rating is projected for the spot, so the cost per point calculation is simple: cost of $2500/10 rating = $250 per point, which happens to be the highest priced spot on the list. The CPM for this spot is also the highest on the list.

Table 6-6.—Comparison of Cost Efficiency of Media Vehicles

Media Vehicle	Unit Cost	Rating	CPP	CPM
A	$2500	10	$250	$50.00
B	3000	15	200	40.00
C	5000	30	167	35.00

Vehicle C is the most cost efficient of the three options. Even though the out of pocket cost is the highest, the rating is 2-3 times higher and the CPP and CPM are the lowest (Cost/Rating or Cost/Audience x 1000).

As measures of cost efficiency, CPMs and CPPs may seem to be equivalent efficiency concepts, but there is an important difference. CPP is based on rating points delivered in a specific geographic area, while CPM counts impressions from anywhere.

For example, CPP for a radio station may be based on audience counted only in the metropolitan area. However, some stations with big coverage areas may generate half or more of their total audience outside of the metro area. In this case, CPP would be based only on the audience in the metro area, while CPM would be based the station's total audience, inside and outside the metro area. As a media planner, you must decide whether to base your analysis and decisions on total audience or the audience within a smaller geographic area.

SUMMARY

In media, there are special meanings for the words price, cost, and expense. Sellers price their inventories; buyers incur cost.

Whether you are buying airplane tickets or advertising time or space, cost is an extremely important factor affecting your decision. Along with audience and impact, cost also plays an important role in the return on investment of different options. Planners and buyers want to get the most communication possible for their money.

Chapter 6 has reviewed the basics of cost for each major medium, including the major factors that affect pricing and advertisers' costs. Broadcast and print media have entirely different cost influences, and the Internet is different from both.

Finally, costs to the advertiser for time or space must be viewed from the perspective of out-of-pocket costs and the perspective of cost-efficiency. Which do you believe is the better indicator of real cost?

7. MEDIA IMPACT

The medium is the message.

–Marshall McLuhan

Media impact is a measure of the effect a medium has on its audience. Of equal importance with reaching the target is how effectively or with what impact the message is delivered. If sight, sound, and motion more effectively communicate your message, you want to use television. If your product's benefits need to be explained in detail, you want to use print. These are impact *considerations.*

Chapter 7 will show you how media impact facilitates communication of the advertising message to the intended consumers. Is the audience of one medium more likely to be paying full attention? Does another medium offer an engaging program environment? Do magazines printed in color on high-quality paper more effectively communicate the appetite appeal of your food? Are your target buyers contemplating purchases, like home repairs, about which they're going to seek information on the Internet? Is your target audience searching newspaper ads for the best deal on a product or service they have already decided to buy?

Media types and individual media vehicles not only vary widely in audience size and characteristics, cost and cost efficiencies, they also vary greatly in effectiveness. Media effectiveness is perhaps the most important but least understood variable in selecting the right media. All the major media have conducted extensive research designed to prove their effectiveness, but it has had strangely little impact on the spending behavior of advertisers. No single set of data can measure a medium's impact.

A media planner has to make comparative impact judgments every time a media plan is created or changed. In this chapter, you will consider the inevitable tradeoffs among audience, cost, and impact, discovering that any medium can prove effective in the right situation.

ADVERTISING: MEDIUM OR MESSAGE?

The medium is the message was a phrase coined by Marshall McLuhan that achieved axiomatic status in the mid-1960s. It means that the form of a medium embeds itself in the message, creating a symbiotic relationship by which the medium influences how the message is perceived.

The phrase was introduced in his most widely known book, *Understanding Media: The Extensions of Man*, published in 1964. McLuhan proposed that media itself, not the content it carries, should be the focus of study. He said that a medium affects the society in which it plays a role not only by the content delivered over the medium, but also by the characteristics of the medium itself.

For example, McLuhan claimed in *Understanding Media* that all media engage the viewer in different ways; for instance, a passage in a book could be reread at will, but a movie had to be screened again in its entirety if you wanted to study any individual part of it.

The medium through which a person encountered any piece of content, according to McLuhan, would influence the individual's understanding of it. Some media enhance one single sense, as the movies enhance vision in such a manner that you don't need to exert much effort to fill in the details of a movie image. He contrasted this with TV, which he claimed required more effort from the viewer to determine meaning, and comic strips, which due to their minimal presentation of visual detail required a high degree of effort to supply details that the cartoonist intended but did not portray.

A movie was thus said by McLuhan to be *hot* (intensifying one single sense) and *high definition* (demanding only the viewer's attention), and a comic book to be *cool* and *low definition* (requiring much more conscious participation by the reader to extract value.) This concentration on how the medium conveys information—rather than on the specific content of the information—was the principle underlying *the medium is the message*.

When it comes to advertising, should the medium or the message be selected first? Media planners who are McLuhanites, believing fervently that the medium can be the message, would say to select your medium first. Most advertising professionals at least accept that the context of a message can change consumers' perception of it. Therefore the medium in which a message is delivered matters.

MEDIA EFFECTIVENESS

From the consumer's perspective, is a television commercial more memorable or more persuasive than a radio commercial? Than an ad in a magazine? Or a banner? For a retailer, will radio be more convincing than newspapers? For an appetizing food product, are magazines more enticing than television? These are all effectiveness questions.

Effectiveness in general is defined as the extent to which an activity fulfills its intended function or purpose. Media effectiveness, therefore, is the extent to which media achieve advertising objectives—increasing awareness, generating inquiries, or stimulating direct purchases. Does television generate higher awareness than another media form? Will radio commercials elicit more phone calls for information? Are newspaper ads better at increasing retail sales? We can examine media effectiveness questions like these on several levels: inter-media, intra-media, or media mix.

Inter-Media Effectiveness

Part of the media selection process is choosing classes of media to be included in the media plan. The planner also has to allocate budget resources by media class.

The judgment about the communications impact or effectiveness of each class of media relative to the other contenders is about *inter-media effectiveness*. For example, you may believe that television is more effective than radio but less effective than online banners. You may judge magazines more effective than newspapers but less effective than television. These are evaluations of inter-media effectiveness.

Measuring media effectiveness for a brand can be like trying to hit a moving target. A brand's creative will have a significant impact on measured media effectiveness. A few great radio commercials can cause apparent radio effectiveness to soar, while a feeble television commercial can make the medium appear to perform poorly.

Intra-Media Effectiveness

After selecting a media class, the planner must then consider *intra-media effectiveness*—potential differences important to the effectiveness of individual media options. For example, once you have allocated $200,000 for a schedule in a medium, you must select the most cost effective media vehicles. Are there also differences in impact among the individual vehicles within a media class? For example, if you were selecting business publications, should you give extra weight to buying

Fortune or *Forbes*? Is there an option you should avoid? These are questions of intra-media effectiveness.

Media Mix

Media mix is blending multiple media together in an effort to achieve communications synergy. For example, if a consumer sees or hears a brand's advertising in several media, is the effect stronger than exposure in a single medium would have been? Do media complement each other, for example, getting attention in television then explaining in print? A considerable amount of research has attempted to show that, in general, media mixes are more effective than using a single medium.

Why? A media mix may increase a higher percentage of the target audience, a mix will reach light viewers more often, and a mix may create a synergy not possible with a single medium

There is good evidence that media class and vehicle choices may matter less than McLuhan would have predicted. Gregg Ambnack, managing director of Analytic Partners in Cincinnati, reported in *Advertising Age* that creative strategy and executions play an equally important or more important role (*Advertising Age*, January 2011). Also, Burke Marketing Research has found that the effectiveness of television commercials could range from a low of 0% impact to a high above 70%, leading my agency to conclude that the creative provided the most leverage of any variable they measured (Burke Inc.)

MEDIA EFFECTIVENESS RESEARCH

How do advertisers decide which media are most effective for their situations and needs? One factor you should look at is how your industry as a whole and your individual competitors allocate their advertising budgets among media. In the absence of better criteria—and sometimes even in the presence of evidence to the contrary—advertisers rely on the belief that competitive expenditures reflect a combined wisdom.

Some research is conducted to influence decisions about allocating advertising dollars, and this chapter examines some samples of that. Advertisers and planners may consider these kinds of data, or their own research findings, reflect on their own experience, and examine any results measures they may have tracked.

Some advertises monitor their key business metrics in relation to media activity, and some conduct experiments to evaluate results achieved through various media mixes. All too often, however, media effectiveness decisions are a matter of habit and instinct.

Table 7-1.—Estimated 2009 Local Advertising Expenditures

Medium	Est. 2009 Expenditures (Billions)	% Total
Television	$16	16.7%
Radio	11	11.5
Magazines	<1	<1
Newspapers	29	30.2
Out of Home	4	4.2
Yellow Pages	12	12.5
Internet	<1	<1
Mail	16	16.6
Misc.	8	8.3
Total	$96	100%

Source: 2010 Thumbnail Media Planner

In the absence of any better data, advertising expenditures are often used as the measure of media effectiveness. For example, Table 7-1 indicates that local advertisers believe newspapers are the most effective medium for their local advertising, with television a distant second. Local advertisers reportedly spent $29 billion in newspapers, which is a little over 30% of local ad spending. (Note the contrast to national ad spending priorities reflected in Table 2-2, where advertisers appear to believe that television is the most effective medium for their national needs.)

Question: From Table 7-1, what would conventional wisdom say is the most effective local medium?

Thousands of studies of comparative media effectiveness have been conducted over the past few decades. Every medium, usually through its industry organization, commissions research to prove its value. Every medium wants to prove to advertisers than it communicates advertising more effectively than competitive media—or that using its medium in combination with other media classes is more effective. Every medium wants to convince advertisers not only that it reaches the target audience better but also that its ads are more powerful.

Television Effectiveness Research

The Television Bureau of Advertising, an organization responsible for promoting broadcast television, commissions Nielsen Media Research to measure the public's perceptions of advertising biannually in several major media: television, radio, magazines, newspapers, and the Internet.

Perhaps not surprisingly, since Nielsen's data collection methods favor television households, the TVB's study shows that adults in general perceive television advertising as far more effective than advertising in any other measured medium, and there is not a close second.

Table 7-2.—Advertising Effectiveness by Medium

Medium	% Total Adults				
	Learn Products	Most Persuasive	Most Authoritative	Most Influence	Most Exciting
Television	53	70	49	79	78
Radio	5	6	10	3	5
Newspapers	10	11	22	7	4
Magazines	16	9	12	4	6
Internet	17	5	6	7	7
Total*	101	101	99	100	100

Source: TVB.org/Nielsen Media Research, 2008   *Rounding error results in imprecise totals

It should be noted that that, while these data are based on total adults, there are differences in responses by demographic groups. For example, a higher percentage of young adults select the Internet, but the differences do not change the rankings by medium.

Radio Effectiveness Research

Radio's counterpart of TVB, the Radio Advertising Bureau (RAB), is responsible for promoting advertising uses of radio. RAB also commissions research to prove radio's communications effectiveness. For example, the Radio Ad Lab (www.RadioAdLab.com) published studies in 2004 showing that a media mix including radio was more effective than plans using only TV or newspapers. The results of the study also showed radio delivering 21-49% more profit than television.

Table 7-3.—Effectiveness of Radio in the Media Mix

Media Mix	Unaided Brand Recall	First Choice Brand
TV Only	100	105
TV + Radio	124	108
Newspaper Only	100	99
Newspaper + Radio	286	106

Source: RAB.org

Radio has been trying hard to get a bigger piece of the ad expenditure pie, but to date has not succeeded with national advertisers. Radio advertising revenues continue to decline sharply. So, despite some interesting data, the perception among most national advertisers is that radio is primarily for local advertisers

Magazine Effectiveness Research

Not to be outdone by its competitors, the Magazine Publishers Association (MPA) has conducted a great deal of research to prove the effectiveness of its industry's advertising. In its 2008 Marketing Evolution study, the MPA reported that magazines raised purchase intention more than television or online advertising did and that magazines' cost per impact point was the lowest of all media.

According to that study, magazines also lead in getting consumers to start an online search, producing website traffic that more often leads to purchases.

Newspaper Effectiveness Research

The newspaper industry, through the Newspaper Advertising Association (NAA), conducts research to measure the advertising value of newspapers. Their 2006 study, *Consumer Usage of Newspaper Advertising*, based on a survey of 3000 consumers, found that over 55% of respondents *cited newspapers as the advertising medium they used most often to check for what to purchase.*

Concludes the NAA, This report illustrates empirically something advertisers have known for years. For many consumers, the largest shopping center in the country is not the Mall of America; it's their newspaper.

Internet Effectiveness Research

Online advertising takes many forms—search, display ads, video, rich media, classified, lead generation, mobile, social networks, sponsorships, email, and more. Not all have been studied, and at present, the best measure of effectiveness is usage.

A 2001 study by Morgan Stanley Dean Witter found that banners were competitive with television and magazine exposure, while lagging behind both television and magazines in lifting brand awareness. Social media, of course, were also found to be effective in brand awareness and image, but low in effecting sales.

Since the Internet advertising world is diverse, the following table of projected Internet ad spend provides a gauge of how advertisers and the industry perceive the importance of different Internet advertising forms.

Table 7-4.—US Online Advertising Spending*, by Format, 2008-2013

Format	2008	2009	2010	2011	2012	2013
Search	10,691	12,285	13,880	15,552	17,686	19,530
Display ads	4,629	4,933	5,448	6,182	7,175	7,958
Video	587	850	1,250	1,850	3,000	4,600
Rich media	1,888	2,030	2,252	2,560	2,960	3,360
Classifieds	3,139	2,956	2,936	2,944	2,960	2,982
Lead generation	1,605	1,645	1,682	1,792	1,998	2,268
Sponsorships	590	514	542	576	629	672
Email	472	488	513	544	592	630
Total	23,600	25,700	28,500	32,000	37,000	42,000

Source: eMarketer, November 2008   *$millions

SUMMARY

Marshall McLuhan said, "The medium is the message"; the medium embeds itself in the message. No doubt, that is true, but it has proven difficult to measure, and measurement results have been applied unevenly in practice.

Most advertising professionals who work with consumer products continue to believe that television is more effective than radio, magazines, or newspapers. The evidence is where they spend their ad dollars: television gets the largest share. A retailer, on the other hand, might believe newspapers are most effective because they reach purchasers when they are actually shopping, and of course, the Internet and new media are changing everything.

Chapter 7 has examined the importance of weighing media effectiveness in the decision-making process along with audience and cost, looking at inter-media effectiveness, intra-media effectiveness, and media mix. The communications effectiveness of media is ultimately a matter of professional judgment, because there is seldom a single right answer and because the creative is decisive regardless of media vehicle. Media audiences may be quantifiable, but this chapter has made clear that there is an equally important consideration more difficult to quantify—media communications effectiveness.

SECTION III: MEDIA PLANNING

Section 3 will prepare you to develop a strategic media plan. Each of the major issues is addressed in detail in a separate chapter, in a sequence that will build a foundation for the last chapter in Section III, How to Develop a Strategic Media Plan.

Section 3 includes:

Chapter 8	Media in Marketing
Chapter 9	Media Communication Models
Chapter 10	Defining the Target Audience
Chapter 11	Geographic Problems & Opportunities
Chapter 12	Timing & Scheduling
Chapter 13	Developing a Budget
Chapter 14	Integrated Marketing Communications
Chapter 15	Traditional Media
Chapter 16	Internet Marketing
Chapter 17	Social Media
Chapter 18	Developing a Strategic Media Plan

8. MEDIA IN MARKETING

Creativity can solve almost any problem.
The creative act, the defeat of habit by originality,
overcomes everything.

–George Lois, advertising agency founder

The title of this chapter emphasizes that media communication is first and foremost a marketing strategy intended to capitalize on opportunities and solve problems that stifle sales. Marketing communications often play a major role in effectively executing marketing plans that achieve desired results. That fact may seem to be self evident, but it is easy to become so enamored of cool new technologies and capabilities that you lose sight of your raison d'être.

The media challenge requires you to devote your time and thought to creative, smart solutions to marketing problems, while recognizing and capitalizing on business-building opportunities when you encounter them. Chapter 8 will give you a basic understanding of the marketing plan, which has to be the foundation of your media plan.

You will review the marketing concept, the purpose and elements of the marketing plan, and how each can affect media decisions. At the end of the chapter, you will find examples that simulate the use of media to solve marketing problems.

THE MARKETING CONCEPT

Most successful, growing companies subscribe to a consumer-focused marketing philosophy called the *marketing concept*. The marketing concept means that all business endeavors—from product development to pricing and promotion—are based on in-depth consumer insights. Some advertising agencies brag that their competitive advantage is their breakthrough consumer insights.

Interestingly enough, in 1776, Adam Smith wrote in *The Wealth of Nations* that the needs of producers should be considered only with regard to meeting the needs of consumers. This philosophy is consistent with the marketing concept, but it would not be adopted widely until nearly 200 years later.

Today, the *marketing concept* still means that firms must focus on the needs of their customers and make decisions to satisfy those needs better than the competition. The marketing concept prompts companies to consider marketing issues such as product, price, promotion, and distribution channels from the consumers' point of view.

Proctor & Gamble (P&G) is an example of the marketing concept in action. Few would dispute that, with hundreds of famous brands and $75 billion in global sales, P&G is one of the very best marketing organizations in the world. Their secret? Consumer focus.

One of the ways P&G achieves consumer focus is to invest heavily in consumer research. Since 2001, P&G has invested more than $1 billion per year in consumer research in order to gain consumer insight and understanding. P&G's CEO, A.G. Lafley, (retired 2010) coined a simple but strong message for the organization: *Consumer is Boss.*

THE STRATEGIC MARKETING PLAN

Most quality companies have annual marketing plans that are kept current. A marketing plan is a written document indentifying the marketing actions an organization will take to achieve its goals and objectives. The plan may encompass the entire organization or an individual brand within the company.

A written marketing plan should include five parts:

1. Mission Statement
2. Situation Analysis
3. Marketing Objectives
4. Marketing Strategies
5. Tactical Plan

Media planning and buying considerations will be incorporated in every part of the marketing plan, from the mission statement and situation analysis to the actual elements of the tactical plan.

Mission Statement

A mission statement is a short formal written statement of the purpose of a company or organization. The mission statement articulates an organization's vision, values, and goals. Consequently, it guides the strategies and actions of the organization.

The mission statement provides direction and guides decision-making for all of the stakeholders in the organization. It establishes the framework or context within which the company's business and marketing strategies are formulated. If the organization's mission is to be the leading marketer of high-end widgets, that statement defines the firm's marketing objectives. Following are some examples of mission statements that express the promise, values, and priorities of their organizations.

The Coca-Cola Promise: The Coca-Cola Company exists to benefit and refresh everyone it touches. The basic proposition of our business is simple, solid, and timeless. When we bring refreshment, value, joy and fun to our stakeholders, then we successfully nurture and protect our brands, particularly Coca-Cola. That is the key to fulfilling our ultimate obligation to provide consistently attractive returns to the owners of our business.

****

The mission of the **American Institute of Philanthropy (AIP)**, *a nonprofit charity watchdog and information service, is to maximize the effectiveness of every dollar contributed to charity by providing donors with the information they need to make more informed giving decisions.*

Figure 8-1.—Examples of Mission Statements

Whether simple or detailed, a mission statement must communicate what the organization is all about, including the nature of its business. The marketing plan must be aligned with the mission statement, which has been approved by top management.

Situation Analysis

Your marketing plan begins with a collection and analysis of all of the marketing data pertinent to the business. A typical situation analysis would include data and analyses in at least the following categories:

1. Comparison of company's products vs. competitors' products
2. Total market/industry overview, sales, segmentation, and trends
3. Future market trends
4. Brand's & competitors' sales, market share, trends, & analyses
5. Pricing comparisons and analyses
6. Distribution channels and levels for brand vs. competitors
7. Seasonality of business for brand vs. industry
8. Customer and consumer profiles

9. Consumer decision-making process
10. Brand's vs. competitors' marketing activity—positioning, creative, media expenditures, promotions, public relations, and other marketing communications
11. Review & evaluation of brand's previous marketing activities
12. Measurement evaluation of brand performance in the marketplace, including purchase funnel trends and sales

Analyzing Marketing Information

Table 8-1 is an example of the typical marketing data found in a situation analysis. What are some of the possible implications of this data analysis?

Table 8-1.—Example of Marketing Analysis

Dimension	Industry	Brand	Competition	Implications
2010 Sales	$100,000.0	$10,000.0	$90,000.0	?
% Change	+5.0	–2.5	+6.0	?
Market Share	100.0	10.0	90.0	?
Product Rating (10 = Ex)	8.5	7.0	9.0	?
Median Age	32.0	42.0	29.0	?
Distribution	96%	70%	97%	?
Media Spend	$5000.0	$350.0	$4650.0	?
Chicago CDI	135	—	—	?
Chicago BDI	—	85	140	?

Questions:
How is this Brand performing vs. the competition?
Based on these data, what explains the brand's performance?
What are some of the media implications of this analysis?
Can you fill in the media implications of each dimension?

Assessment of Strengths and Weaknesses

Aside from providing useful information to all stakeholders, the situation analysis must evaluate the company or brand's performance, assess the brand's strengths and weaknesses vs. the competition, and identify what can be improved. A *SWOT* analysis is an excellent tool to get started. SWOT stands for Strengths, Weaknesses, Obstacles, and Threats.

SWOT Analysis

Strengths	Obstacles
Weaknesses	Threats

Strengths include factors like excellent product performance, high consumer awareness, and a favorable brand image. *Weaknesses* might include the brand's inability to attract younger consumers and low budgets. *Obstacles* could include the firm's difficulty get zoning approval for a new plant that would increase production sufficiently to meet consumer demand. *Threats* to a business include things like new competitive product introductions, proposed new government regulations, or lack of working capital.

Marketing Objectives

Based on management expectations, historical performance, and the situation analysis, the company should have some understanding of short- and long-term potential. This is the context for your next step, establishing marketing objectives for top management to approve. Marketing objectives typically address these concerns:

- Sales objectives, short- and long-term
- Market share objectives, short- and long-term
- Trial objectives for existing and new products
- Repurchase objectives
- Distribution objectives
- Market development objectives
- Consumer development
- Profitability objectives, short- and long-term

Question: If one of the marketing objectives
were to increase market share, what are some of the ways

that objective could affect your media planning?
(Hint: where will new customers come from?)

Marketing Strategies

There are two basic parts to any marketing strategy: (1) source of volume and (2) selection of an optimum marketing mix. The first defines where business is expected to come from, i.e., target markets from which the forecasted sales will be generated. The second defines the marketing mix that will address the target market(s). Both are discussed below:

Source of Volume: Target Markets

Your marketing strategy has defined your sales targets for the next year and perhaps for the next five years. Where will you find this business? Either you will increase sales from your *current customers* or you must attract *new customers* who are most likely buying competitive products. Ideally, you will do both, in which case your plan must address both sources of volume.

How much new business will come from current customers? How much incremental business will come from new customers and perhaps new markets? Will there be sufficient growth in the overall market? Are certain competitors' customers vulnerable to recruitment? If so, who are they and how can you reach them? Are there geographic market areas (DMAs) with upward sales potential that you can enter?

Current Customers

A company's current customers are often its single most important asset because they represent a potential ongoing base of sales, market share, and profit. Of course, this assumes that current customers are satisfied with product, price, and customer service. It also assumes that the competition isn't successful in its attempts to steal customers. Incremental business may be gleaned from existing customers by increasing their repurchase rate, frequency of purchase or increasing your share of their purchases.

Finally, putting the customer first is a cliché in firms of all sizes, ranging from giant conglomerates to the corner barbershop. Sadly, for most of them, it's just lip service. Success is most likely for those that dedicate their activities entirely to solving their customers' problems and keeping them happy. For example, a special promotion for customers only is an example of something you might do to solidify your relationship with your customer base.

Creating New Customers

To *grow* a company's customer base, you must first identify and locate prospective customers and convince them to try your product or service. How would you identify good prospects? Would their profiles be similar to the profiles of current customers? Or are you looking at new market segments where consumer profiles differ from customer profiles.

Some companies just blast the airwaves with advertising to a mass audience of everybody and hope that some of them will notice and try their products. Is this as effective as identifying target markets and then trying to engage each one with a relevant message?

Obviously, any marketing program has a better chance of being productive if it is relevant to its audience. Understanding current and prospective customers is so important that large corporations spend billions of dollars on consumer research. Although such formal research is important, a small firm must avoid huge outlays for original research. Typically, the owner or manager of a small concern knows the customers personally, and small to mid-sized businesses can usually access syndicated databases through media reps whose firms subscribe to them.

Business success is based on the ability to build an ever-growing body of satisfied customers. Marketing programs constructed around the marketing concept, which directs managers to focus their efforts on identifying and satisfying customer needs—at a profit—is still the way to go!

Question: Can you think of some recent advertising you've seen that was completely irrelevant to you? Why do you think you received those ad messages?

Selection of a Marketing Mix

Now that the objectives and the target markets are defined, the company must next develop the optimum marketing mix to reach the goals and objectives of the brand. The marketing mix is the toolbox of means by which to influence the target market. It includes the traditional Four P's: Product, Price, Place (distribution), and Promotion. We'll look at each.

Product

Product refers to the service or tangible good that will satisfy your target customers wants or needs. Two effective product strategies are concentrating on a narrow product line or developing a highly specialized product accompanied by an exceptional amount of service.

Place

Place refers to placement of product in the right distribution channels and obtaining good visibility within those channels. Having the product available for purchase where and when consumers easily can buy it is obviously critical.

Promotion

Promotion includes all forms of marketing communications: advertising, PR, event marketing, online marketing, direct marketing, personal selling, channel marketing, and alliances. To determine what marketing communications belong in your marketing mix, ask yourself about each form: *What is its role in accomplishing the objectives?* What is the role of PR? Internet search? Events and sponsorships? Product placement?

Price

Price consists of the whole set of policies regarding competitive upgrades, reseller pricing, discounts, list price, distributor, and street price (actual selling price). Determining price levels and/or pricing policies (including credit policy) is the major factor affecting total revenue. Higher prices generally mean lower volume; lower prices are associated with higher volume. However, small businesses can often command higher prices due to the personalized service they can offer.

***

An effective marketing strategy should not be changed every year just because it seems like time for an update. Great advertising should not be thrown away because somebody is tired of seeing it in the conference room. Good reasons to revise a marketing plan that has been effective are events like a new competitor entering the category, a new technology becoming available or feasible, or evidence of diminishing returns.

The Marketing Plan

The *marketing plan* is the translation of the marketing strategy into an action plan with budgets to implement it. The marketing plan lays everything out on a calendar and spreadsheets. It specifies all marketing actions to be taken, including but not limited to new product introductions, pricing changes, promotions, creative strategy executions, and media plan implementation. The marketing plan also contains detailed rationale and support for all strategic and tactical recommendations.

Monitoring & Measuring Results

Continuous improvement requires a method of tracking results and providing diagnostics. Low-cost market research can be an invaluable tool for understanding what is affecting the business and what can be done about it. Companies must at least track their sales and market share vs. their competition. Many companies use a tracking system like the Purchase Funnel to monitor changes in leading indicators. Awareness, purchase consideration, purchase intention, shopping, and other trends can give valuable insights about forthcoming sales changes.

FROM MARKETING PLANS TO MEDIA PLANS

Studying the entire marketing plan will provide valuable information and insight, but it will not do your thinking for you. Media planners must study the marketing plan and translate its media implications, using imaginative questions and creative thinking.

Do not expect the answers to be obvious or the solutions simple. During your review of the marketing plan, objections and hypothetical questions will arise, many deserving further study and consultation with colleagues and clients. Smart planning is a team effort.

The remainder of this chapter provides examples of marketing issues and opportunities that might affect your planning and thinking as you turn marketing plans into media plans. Since these are taken from live situations, they have no right or wrong answers, only challenges.

Example 1. Marketing Objectives
Suppose you learn that your client wants to increase market share from 10% to 15% over the next five years. You also observe that the client's share is falling like

a rock among Hispanics, one of the fastest growing markets in the US. You wonder if it is possible to achieve a 50% increase in market share even if you do reverse share declines in the Hispanic market. However, that's obviously where you have to start! What are the problems you need to address? Is the product appealing to Hispanics? Are Hispanics aware of the product? Is there adequate distribution in locations and stores where Hispanics shop? Should Hispanics be a specific target market? Possible Action: Get others involved. In order to define problems and opportunities in the Hispanic market, perhaps the brand should conduct industry and brand research among Hispanic consumers.

Example 2. Marketing Strategy

Your brand's premium pricing appears to be out of synch with customers' perceptions of its value. Consumers seem to believe that the brand is not prestigious and not worth its price. Action Challenge: Can media engage the target audience in contexts that will help enhance the brand's image?

Example 3. Geographic Sales Analysis

You have analyzed population, industry, and brand sales by DMA. Unfortunately for the brand, your analysis discovered that the brand was strong in DMAs where the industry was strong but weak in markets of high potential. Why? If the brand could raise its market share to average levels in the large, high-potential markets, sales would grow by 25%. Challenge: Solve the brand's problem of low performance in high-potential markets.

Example 4. Seasonal Budgeting

Nearly 70% of your brand's communications budget is spent in December (as dictated by Santa Claus). But research conducted to shed light on the consumer's decision-making process showed that purchases for the category are planned in advance of purchase. Question: Should 70% of ad spending continue to be in the December budget, or should it lead the brand's sales more than it does?

Example 5. Distribution Problem and Opportunity

A packaged goods brand is having difficulty obtaining distribution in XYZ stores, which account for 40% of category sales. One of your marketing objectives is to gain distribution. So far, however, the marketing and sales organizations have not been able to get in. Action: Think of some highly targeted ideas with sufficient impact to attract the attention of gatekeepers in these stores in order to get appointments for meetings with the sales organization.

Example 6. Integration

Because there are so many different responsibility centers developing and implementing plans for your brand, the media and messages are sometimes all *over the board. On the one hand, there are promotions that make the brand look like a bargain-basement item; on the other hand, the advertising positions the brand for up-scale purchasers. Do you think consumers would be confused about what the brand stands for and who should buy it? <u>Action</u>: Develop an IMC proposal for integrating and synergizing the media and messages.*

Example 7. Creative vs. Media

The creative department wants to use television. The media group believes that the budget could be used more effectively in targeted print and certain Internet sites. What to do? You have a meeting tomorrow with the account and creative teams to resolve the issue. <u>Action</u>: Begin to put together a point of view and facts to support it.

Example 8. Competitive Monitoring

Your major competition is spending most of their budgets in newspapers; your brand is concentrating in local search. Everyone wants immediate sales. Does the competition know something you don't or are you way out in front of them? <u>Action</u>: Develop a plan for research and analysis to measure the ROI for these disparate approaches that focus on the same objective.

Example 9. Relevant Tactical Ideas

Since stopping at one of your restaurants is an impulse rather than a planned purchase, your advertising should remind consumers or offer incentives just prior to mealtime. Question: Would you recommend coupons on mobile phones?

Example 10. Strengthening Customer Relationships

Your company's customer loyalty and repurchase rates are lower than those of your chief competitors. You do not appear to have any kind of a loyalty bond with your customers, and you sell primarily when you are discounted. Why is this? <u>Action</u>: Identify ways that social media could help address this situation.

Example 11. Target Audience Priorities

Baby Boomers account for 45% of the market, but only 30% of your sales. As the Boomer population explodes, your sales to Boomers must increase or your overall market share will decline significantly. <u>Action</u>: Compile a presentation on Boomer market trends for your brand, and schedule a meeting with your client to discuss the issue and possible remedies.

Example 12. Media Mix Out of Synch with Needs

"We want to close more sales faster, but only 5% of our budget is in Internet search." Action: *Evaluate shifting dollars into search and other media that could help generate immediate sales.*

Example 13. Tactical Plan Promotions

Next year you are planning three major sales promotions during the year – in April, July, and November. The success of these promotions will determine whether you meet your sales forecasts for the year. Indicated Action: *Make sure each of these promotions receives sufficient media support and is budgeted appropriately. Figure out where you will find these dollars.*

Example 14. Solving a Problem of Consumer Perceptions

Sometimes products, like domestic U.S. automobiles, dramatically improve their quality while retaining their poor image. When perception lags behind reality, those perceptions can be extremely difficult to change in a highly competitive marketplace where other manufacturers already enjoy high-quality perceptions. Challenge: *figure out how to bring perceptions in line with product reality.*

Example 15. Capitalize on PR Opportunities

With its proprietary technology, XYZ Company has developed some new products with significant energy-savings benefits. The company has a small marketing budget but needs to spread the word. Possible Action: *Develop an economical publicity campaign for business media.*

SUMMARY

Once again, media is about marketing and marketing is often about media. Media is about marketing because marketing information and marketing strategy and marketing plan have a major influence on the media strategy. On the other hand, marketing has often driven media because a big media idea can provide a platform for the marketing plan— such as using the Olympics for a marketing platform, or leveraging a major product placement program in a new blockbuster film.

Because marketing success so often depends on creativity, marketing is a process that never ends. The goal is never reached because the goalposts keep moving back. That's what makes the media business especially attractive and exciting.

Chapter 8 has given you an overview of the relationship between marketing strategy and marketing plan and media planning. Each stage of the marketing plan process has implications for media planning, challenging you to think, explore, and create.

9. How Do Media Work?

If you don't know where you are going,
any road will get you there.

—The Cheshire Cat, Alice in Wonderland

Clients have always had the uncanny ability to ask really good but simple questions that agencies and media planners sometimes find hard to answer.

- *How does our advertising work?*
- *How do we know if it is or isn't working?*
- *What are the minimum number of GRPS we need to do the job? (Client Code for budget.)*
- *How much frequency do we need to break through the clutter? (More Code for budget)*
- *Shouldn't we add...(media)? (Client code for covering all bases.)*
- *How much frequency causes a commercial to wear out? (Client Code for creative.)*
- *How important is media environment for engaging consumers with our ads? (Client code for being on the leading edge.)*

Faced with questions like these, it is important to define your media planning philosophy and the principles that will make it successful in the marketplace. There are a number of theories or philosophies about how media work, but it's difficult to answer the simple question, "How do media work?"

There are many different opinions, philosophies, seemingly conflicting facts, and complex research findings on the subject that combine with a huge number of interacting variables. Yet, anyone responsible for developing or executing media plans must have some guiding principles, beliefs, and logical assumptions that fit the brand's situations. The effectiveness of the creative/message strategy and the creative executions are the most important determinants of results. Remember, a bad ad or campaign cannot be saved by a brilliant media plan.

After studying Chapter 9, you will be acquainted with six leading theories about how advertising media work: (1) ARF Response Model, (2) Effective Reach, (3) Recency, (4) Share of Voice, (5) Purchase Funnel, and (6) Engagement. You should pursue additional investigation of the theories

153

that especially interest you, and see if you can find others that you also find helpful.

ARF RESPONSE MODEL

The first model describing how advertising media work is the ARF Response Model. The Advertising Research Foundation (ARF) published its first advertising/media model, *Toward Better Media Comparisons*, in 1961, creating for the first time a sequential theory about how media work.

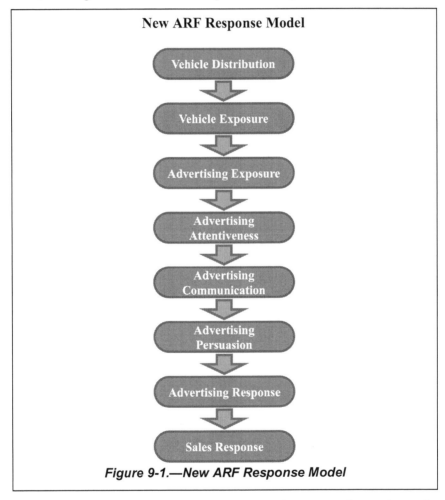

New ARF Response Model

Figure 9-1.—New ARF Response Model

The model emphasized that media comparisons must be made on the basis of apples to apples; that is, you can't compare newspaper circulation to the coverage of broadcast stations. Nor can you make meaningful media comparisons by contrasting TV commercial recall to sales response in a direct mail campaign or clicks from a search campaign.

This is an important perspective for media planners who are deluged with sales pitches. A pitch might say that a medium should be purchased because it generates great sales response. That's a good thing, but since you still don't have comparable measures for other media, how do you whether the sales response rate is excellent, good, fair, or poor?

The 1961 ARF Response Model was subsequently revised in the early 2000s to include new levels of paid media performance—attentiveness, persuasion and response—and to consider new media types, especially online media and Interactive TV. The new model contains eight levels at which media performance can be measured to help marketers plan their advertising campaigns:

1. Vehicle distribution
2. Vehicle exposure
3. Advertising exposure
4. Advertising attentiveness
5. Advertising communication
6. Advertising persuasion
7. Advertising response
8. Sales response

The way advertisers think about media has changed in the last forty years. The Internet, interactive TV, and direct response advertising have expanded media's job from simply exposing a message, to include encouraging and facilitating a response to that message. The concept of *Recency* has focused marketers on advertising's contribution to making the next sale. Media measurement has had no choice but to follow media's newly expanded expectations; increasingly, media are being judged on response.

Figure 9-1 provides a visual representation of the new ARF Response Model. It depicts the first level of every medium's performance as physical distribution—circulation, a cable system carrying a particular network, or a search universe. Physical distribution creates vehicle audiences that are then exposed (Level 2) to advertising to which they are attentive or not (Level 3), that they recall or don't (Levels 4-5), to which they respond or don't (Levels 6-8).

Vehicle Distribution

Vehicle distribution is a measure of a media vehicle's delivery, and it is different for each medium. Print media begin the audience generation process with circulation—physical copies of the publication are made available to consumers. For broadcast media, distribution requires reception of stations' signals before any audience is generated.

Vehicle Exposure

Vehicle distribution generates a <u>potential</u> audience. *Vehicle exposure* is <u>actual</u> contact between vehicle and target consumer. Most audience research reports vehicle exposure data. It is always important to keep in mind when reviewing it that some readers of a magazine or website will spend only a minute with it and don't even see most pages.

Advertising Exposure

Advertising exposure means actual exposure to the ad, not just to the vehicle that carries it. Exposure is a narrow definition that counts persons exposed to the media vehicle who were <u>also</u> exposed to the ad.

In print, this would be the number of readers who picked up and looked into an issue of *Better Homes and Gardens* <u>and</u> were thus exposed to the ABC Furniture ad. In television advertising, exposure is the net number exposed to a commercial after DVR zapping and playbacks. On the Internet, advertising exposure is opening a web page with a banner, display, or text ad. It is important to understand, however, that advertising exposure is not communication but a precondition to communication.

Advertising Attentiveness

Even narrower, *advertising attentiveness* is a measure of how many persons exposed to the ad actually paid attention to it. Both creative and media, of course, play roles in getting attention. For example, news programs in the early morning tend to have low attention levels to begin with—because viewers are using television as a background medium, and a commercial has to break through the background noise. An ad or commercial that is not of interest to the audience receiving it—like a battery ad on a food website—will generate low levels of attention.

Advertising Communication

This measure is most often a recall metric. How well someone can retell the gist of the advertising message is the measure of *advertising communication*. Like attentiveness, recall is a function of both the creative message and the medium. Matching the medium to the message is important to communication because one media type may be able to communicate your creative message better than another can. Which medium do you think could most effectively communicate the mouth-watering appeal of the Red Lobster menu?

Advertising Persuasion

Advertising persuasion is a measure of how advertising influences those who see and remember it. Persuasiveness, of course, is also a function of both creative and media, and again the medium must be well suited to your purpose. For example, a new car ad seeking to improve brand attitudes may find that television does the best job of persuading consumers to change their opinions. However, a new car dealer may find that newspapers most effectively bring shoppers into the dealership.

Advertising Response

Action prompted by advertising—showroom visits, sales leads, inquiries, or click-throughs from small website ads—is *advertising response*. To track this, advertisers often put toll-free numbers and/or website addresses in their ads or commercials. By coding each ad, the advertiser can tally the responses to each ad—requests for more information, coupon redemptions, or sweepstakes entries. Using those data and the cost of each ad, you can calculate and compare digital vehicles' costs per response.

Sales Response

Sales response is a measure of actual product or service purchase by an audience member because of an ad. This most significant metric is also most difficult to determine for traditional advertising. Let's say that a major manufacturer in a highly competitive product category ran an aggressive advertising campaign in order to gain trials of a new product.

The media plan included 500 different traditional media vehicles (television programs, radio stations, magazines, and websites). How could the advertiser know which sales results were from any particular media vehicle? On the other hand, direct marketers and e-commerce companies can easily measure sales response for a large variety of variables.

The ARF's Response Model has made a valuable contribution to understanding how advertising ultimately communicates with consumers. Each of the eight levels the model defines for measurement could potentially represent one of your communications objectives.

EFFECTIVE REACH

The second advertising model is *Effective Reach*, defined as the *percentage of a target audience* that is exposed to a particular ad during a specific period, often enough to effect the purchase of a product or service. Not to be confused with effective reach, *Effective Frequency* is the theoretical *number of times a person must be exposed* to an advertising message before the desired response is achieved (and before too many exposures become wasteful).

The two concepts are easily confused, however, and may even appear to be used interchangeably—or at least, to some extent, inseparably—because one isn't much good without the other. You can reach your entire target audience to no effect if their exposure is insufficient to make an impact. On the other hand, you can guarantee effective frequency (if you can determine what that is) without affecting sales results if you only reach one person effectively. The next sentence shows how the concepts of reach and frequency interact.

Effective Reach is an advertising media theory that attempts to forecast the most effective advertising *frequency*—the number of advertising exposures (advertising audience) needed to achieve a brand or company's communications goals—whether the goals are defined as total or top-of-mind awareness, attitude or opinion change, purchase consideration or sales. Effective Reach contends that multiple exposures to an advertising message are generally necessary in order for the message to have the desired effect.

The mission of the media planner following the Effective Reach Model is to figure out how to maximize the *reach*—exposure of a target audience—with an effective level of *frequency*. To implement the

Effective Reach Model, you have to first define what you mean by *effective frequency*. Do you need one, two, three, five, or 10 exposures to the Mommy Commercial to achieve the desired effect?

The *Mommy Theory of Effective Frequency* describes how Effective Frequency works—in a way that is familiar to most of us (who may not have always responded to our mother's first, second, or even third requests). Envision your mother trying to get you to clean up your room and get ready for dinner.

Impression #1: Mom calls you from the kitchen telling you to turn off the TV and clean your room before dinner. You answer, "OK, Mom," but you continue watching TV. (Mom's message may have reached your subconscious, but you didn't take action.)

Impression #2: After several minutes have passed and noticing that you have not moved, Mom raises her voice and this time speaks using your name: "…I said, turn off the TV, and clean your room…!) You answer again, "OK Mom," but continue watching TV. (This message was relevant to you, but you still weren't ready to act on it.)

Impression #3: After several more minutes, Mom notices that you are still watching TV and haven't cleaned your room. She raises her voice even more and tells you that if you don't do it right now, you will be grounded for a week! (You are now persuaded to do as Mom asks.)

Impressions #4-100: More action messages from Mom, as necessary. Mom will reinforce this new behavior occasionally.

Based on this experience with Mom, you have decided that a frequency of three is what will take to produce action. On that evidence, you build a media plan to *reach* as many of the target audience as possible three times. You would probably computer analyze different media plans to determine which one would deliver the message three times to the most persons in your target audience.

Effective Frequency Research

How much frequency or exposures of the ad message are the right number is one of the most perplexing media planning issues. This is because no two communications are ever the same. Do you think you would need more or less frequency if your ad contained a huge purchase incentive? How about if the product is new? Or what if there is heavy competitive advertising frequency—or, on the other hand, very light levels of competitive advertising exposure? Or does having a superior product or an inferior product affect the need for frequency?

Questions like these have always been around. So, in the 1970s, a period of increasing advertising costs, the Association of National Advertisers (ANA) became interested in studying the effectiveness of advertising exposure frequencies (which, of course, are directly related to advertising costs). In 1979, the ANA published their analysis of the results of their review of scores of studies, including laboratory tests, conducted in both academia and industry in *Effective Frequency,* authored by John Naples.

The ANA's major conclusion was *that three exposures are the minimum necessary to have an effect, and effective frequency was defined as 3-10 exposures within a purchase cycle period.* In other words, according to the ANA's analysis, one or two advertising exposures would have little or no effect and therefore the dollars spent for one or two exposures would be completely wasted. (An exposure was defined as exposure to the ad, not vehicle exposure.)

On the other hand, the research also found evidence that too much frequency is wasteful because the increase in response trailed the increase in frequency (and dollars spent). More than 10 exposures, the ANA said, was beyond the threshold of effectiveness and probably not cost effective.

Since the concept of Effective Frequency was clarified and expanded by the Association of National Advertisers (ANA) in 1979, it quickly became widely accepted in the advertising industry. Of course, in the real world, many factors other than frequency, including the efficacy of the creative, affect communication results.

While the theory is not fully supported by empirical evidence (what theory is?), the majority of the research analysis has supported the Effective Frequency concept. It is important to have some understanding of some of the key studies that led to the theory of Effective Reach. Following are a few of the landmark studies. You can decide whether they shed light or create confusion.

Ebbinghaus, 1885

Hermann Ebbinghaus, an early-learning psychologist, found that initial learning increases quickly, and then decays exponentially and rapidly in a short period, as illustrated in Figure 9-2. (Anyone who has taken or taught a college course knows this to be true!) Ebbinghaus's work eventually stimulated research on exposure frequency and the learning and forgetting of advertising.

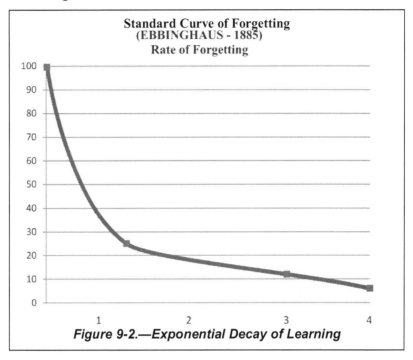

Figure 9-2.—*Exponential Decay of Learning*

Zielske's Famous Study

Another landmark study was Herbert Zielske's famous 1959 study, which was the first to focus on the role of advertising exposure frequency in increasing advertising response, in this case, advertising recall. As shown in Figure 9-3, a concentrated burst of 13 exposures over four weeks provided the highest accumulated ad recall, but when the exposures stopped, recall plummeted (just like old Ebbinghaus would have predicted) based on his learning and forgetting curve presented above.

In a different scheduling pattern of one exposure per week for 13 weeks, recall continued to build; however, recall again fell sharply following each subsequent exposure, also consistent with Ebbinghaus's findings.

Zielskie's research had a great impact on a philosophy of "frequency" which led to scheduling patterns designed to maximize frequency for a short time (a flight), followed by a period of no or low advertising, and then another flight of advertising. Advertisers believed that enough frequency was needed to make a measurable impact on the consumer and were willing to sacrifice periods of no advertising for a period of effective advertising.

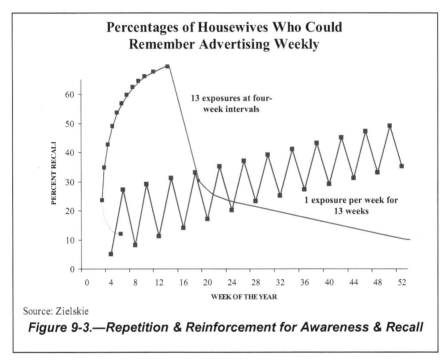

Source: Zielskie

Figure 9-3.—Repetition & Reinforcement for Awareness & Recall

Flighting tends to produce an increased GRP through an increase in frequency, but it reduces the reach, with frequency increasing faster than reach decreases. This narrows the range of the audience receiving the message, based on the assumption that frequency will have a greater impact on the smaller numbers of persons exposed. (You will learn more about scheduling in Chapter 12).

Adstock

Adstock is a term coined by British media researcher Simon Broadbent to describe the prolonged or lagged effect of advertising on consumer purchase behavior. It is also known as *advertising carry-over*. Adstock is an important component of many marketing-mix models.

Adstock advocates say that advertising tries to expand consumption in two ways; it reminds, and it teaches. It reminds in-the-market consumers, in order to influence their immediate brand choice; it teaches to increase brand awareness and salience, making it easier for future advertising to influence brand choice. Adstock is the mathematical manifestation of this behavioral process.

The Adstock theory hinges on the assumption that exposure to television advertising builds awareness in the minds of consumers, influencing their purchase decisions. Each new exposure to advertising builds awareness, and this awareness will be higher if there have been recent exposures and lower if there have not been. In the absence of further exposures, Adstock eventually decays to negligible levels.

There are two important assumptions to adstock: (1) decay or lagged effect and (2) saturation or diminishing returns effect. The lagged or decay component of Adstock can be mathematically modeled and is usually expressed in terms of the half-life of ad copy, modeled with TV Gross Rating Points (GRP). A two-week half-life means that it takes two weeks for the awareness of copy to decay to half its present level. Every piece of creative is assumed to have a unique half-life. Some academic studies have suggested half-life ranges of 7-12 weeks, while some industry practitioners report typical half-lives of 2-5 weeks, with the average for fast-moving consumer goods brands at 2.5 weeks.

Increasing the amount of advertising increases the percent of the audience reached by the advertising, hence, increases demand, but a linear increase in advertising exposure doesn't have a linear effect on demand. Incremental increases in advertising produce progressively smaller effects on demand increases. This is known as advertising *saturation*. Saturation only occurs above a threshold level that can be determined by *adstock analysis*.

Adstock can be transformed to an appropriate nonlinear form like the logistic or negative exponential distribution, depending upon the type of diminishing returns or saturation effect the response function is believed to follow. Saturation will be reached at different times depending on the creative and TRP levels. In one example for particular ad copy, saturation only kicks in above 110 GRPS per week.

In the decades following release of the ANA report on effective frequency, new research as well as reexaminations of previous research suggests that the conclusions on which the expectations of Effective Frequency were based may have been flawed and that there is no accepted frequency threshold for well-known brands. To say that the theory was applied too rigidly, however, is not to discount it.

Media Planning Task

Under the Effective Reach theory, you are faced with the tasks of (1) defining effective frequency parameters and (2) maximizing the delivery of target audience within those parameters.

Using Frequency to Analyze Effective Reach

Your analysis of the *frequency distributions* of alternative plans could guide your media plan selection. Some men drink a lot of beer, others a medium amount, others only occasionally, and some men drink no beer at all. Media consumption is like beer: there are heavy users, medium users, light users, and the rare non-user. In television or any other media class, a minority of the total users account for the majority of usage. A media plan will reach the heaviest users of a medium far more often than it reaches the lightest users of the medium. This can be problematic for advertisers who want to reach as much of the audience as possible, say, between 3 and 10 times—neither too few nor too many exposures to be cost effective.

So agencies and advertisers often analyze the *frequency distribution* of their media schedules. Frequency distribution provides an estimate of the percentage of target audience persons reached one time, two times, three times, 10 times, or ...20+ times.

For example, the following compares two hypothetical media plans in terms of their reach, average frequency, and frequency distribution. Both plans consist of 300 TRPs, but they differ in reach, frequency, and frequency distribution.

	Plan 1	Plan 2
Total Reach	75%	60%
Average Frequency	4.0	5.0
% Reached Once	30	20
% Reached 2 Times	20	10
% Reached 3-10 Times	10	20
% Reached 11+ Times	40	10

Question: If Effective Frequency is 3-10 exposures,
which plan should deliver the highest effective reach? Explain.

164

Question: If your objective were to maximize net reach of the target audience, which plan would win? Explain.

Quintile Analysis

Quintile analysis is another method of analyzing the frequency distribution of media exposures. A quintile is 1/5 or 20%. For example, if 75% of a target group were reached, each viewing quintile would represent 20% of the reached group, or 15% (20% of 75%).

You can then analyze the number of exposures each quintile received, from heaviest to lightest. For example, the heaviest 20% of those reached might be exposed 10 times, while the lightest exposure group may be reached only once.

Your task might be to figure out how to reach a greater percentage of the target audience with *effective frequency.* Since the threshold of effectiveness was defined by the ANA as 3+ exposures, the response curve is S shaped rather than linear, as shown in Figure 9-4. After three exposures, the effect begins to increase until it *levels* off at 10.

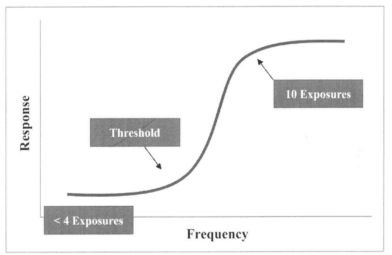

Figure 9-4.—Effective Frequency Response Curve

As shown in Figure 9-4, beyond 10 exposures, the small amount of incremental gain is not sufficient to justify the cost of additional exposures. This is not as clear-cut as it sounds, though. The maximum number of exposures is difficult to quantify, since it depends on a large number of variables such as pre-existing brand awareness, stage in the product lifecycle, and competitive activity.

Figure 9-5 illustrates the potential difference between a schedule planned traditionally vs. one planned for effective frequency. The effective frequency schedule reaches a larger percentage of the target audience 3-10 times, while the traditional media schedule reaches more of the audience but with inadequate or excessive frequency.

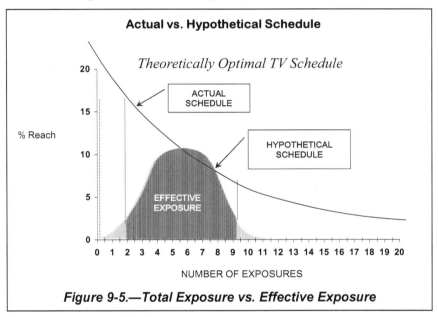

Figure 9-5.—Total Exposure vs. Effective Exposure

There is no doubt that Effective Reach is an important concept, so long as you understand that there are no magic numbers. There will never be one-size-fits-all solution for reach and frequency parameters, because all marketing and communications situations are radically different. For example, do you think a frequency of three would be powerful for a product where the competitor's frequency is 12?

Developing a media plan based on the Effective Frequency model presents challenging questions that research and diagrams cannot answer. For example, what is the optimum budget allocation among media types? Should the plan focus on a few good media vehicles or spread out over many vehicles? To what extent does adding a new medium to the mix flatten out the frequency distribution? How should search or display advertising on the Internet be counted?

What are the audience, cost, and impact differences among the media being considered to supplement other media in the plan? While flattening the frequency distribution might be a wise objective, the cost must be in line. It would not make sense to add an inefficient medium to a plan.

From a media planning perspective, if you are following the theory of Effective Reach, you would attempt to develop a media plan that maximizes your reach of the target audience with a frequency of 3-10 times. Based on a frequency distribution analysis of alternative media plans, Figure 9-6 shows that media plan option I reaches a larger percentage of the target audience 3+ times than Plan II.

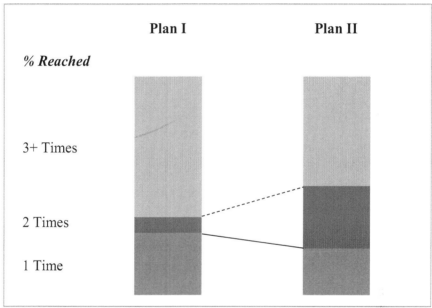

Figure 9-6.—Effective Reach Comparisons of Alternative Plans

A marketer launching a new food product in a highly competitive marketplace is also facing some specific brand realities: consumers are unaware of the product; the grocery trade will be watching to see whether the turnover warrants shelf space; competitors already are achieving high reach and frequency—and the jury is still out on the creative!

Using a database of metrics from new product introductions, new product models typically forecast trial and repurchase rates and sales from the amount of advertising and promotion used to launch the product. Results are strongly affected by message repetitions, but there is no formula to determine how many repetitions are needed or when.

Clearly, certain situations require more or less frequency than others. New product introductions, promotions, and competitive situations may require higher frequencies at least in a particular time frame. On the other hand, if a product is well known and liked, less frequency may be required.

Finally, the Effective Reach model was based entirely on offline media. The model does not account for Internet advertising, where exposure may not be equivalent to exposure in offline media. The media planner must define Effective Reach and Frequency parameters based on each unique marketing situation, problem, or opportunity.

RECENCY

The third important theory of how advertising media work is called *Recency*. This theory has become very popular within the past decade, perhaps replacing Effective Reach as the most cited media planning strategy. In the Recency model, *reach* is the most important parameter, whereas the Effective Reach model gave priority to *frequency*.

What is Recency Planning?

According to Erwin Ephron, the father of Recency Planning:

Recency is based on the idea that advertising messages should "sell" those consumers who are ready to buy. It is as if there is a window of opportunity for the ad message preceding each purchase. Advertising's job is to influence the purchase; media's job is to put the message in the window.   –Ephron on Media, Recency.

Recency theory appears to assume that advertising and communications play a minor role in generating long-term purchase and market share. The primary role of advertising, Recency advocates believe, is to remind buyers, just prior to purchase, to buy the advertiser's widget.

The media planning implications of Recency are that the objective of the media plan is to reach the maximum audience each week just prior to any planned purchase in the product category. While Effective Reach focuses on developing an effective level of frequency, Recency is about maximizing daily or weekly *reach* of the target audience.

For example, an ideal media plan based on Recency might strive to reach 90% of the prospective buyers each week for 52 weeks while minimizing weekly frequency. Table 9-1 provides an example of two media plan structures that require the same expenditure.

Table 9-1.—Comparison of Effective Reach vs. Recency Plans

Media Model	Plan I: Effective Reach	Plan II: Recency
GRPS/Week	100	50
# Weeks	26	52
Weekly Reach	50%	40%
Average Frequency	2.0	1.5
Annual GRPS	2600	2600
Annual Reach Points	1300	2080

While both plans cost the same and deliver equal GRPS, the Effective Frequency approach schedules advertising in a pattern called *flighting,* concentrated blocks of time followed by no advertising. The idea is to generate effective frequency during the advertising schedule. In contrast, a Recency Plan runs regularly every week, shown as the *continuity* schedule in Figure 9-7. You will revisit these scheduling patterns in Chapter 18.

Scheduling Advertising for Maximum Impact
Scheduling Theories

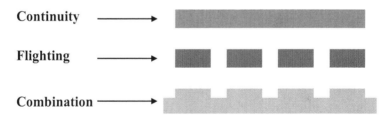

Continuity

Flighting

Combination

Media Planning Implications

Developing media plans based on Effective Reach or Recency requires different media strategies and buying tactics. Table 9-2 summarizes some of the differences involved in planning for Effective Reach or Recency. For example, Effective Reach would emphasize frequency while Recency would emphasize maximum daily reach.

Table 9-2. —Media Planning Implications

Criterion	Effective Reach	Recency
Objective	Frequency	Daily Reach
Media Mix	Focus in Best Media	Diversify media
Cost Efficiency	Important	Super Important
Sponsorships	Yes, creates frequency	No
Audience Duplication	Yes, creates frequency	Minimize
Scheduling	Flights	Continuity

Research Support

Considering the attention that Recency has attracted, the actual amount of research supporting it is surprisingly scant, especially when compared to the number of studies supporting Effective Reach.

John Jones' basic analysis shows that a single exposure in the 7 days before purchase has a far greater effect than anything added by more exposures.

Recency says that continuous advertising is vital because it is critical to reach buyers just prior to purchase. While we don't know what the window is for various products or consumers, we do know that X purchases are made each week. Recency therefore advocates trying to reach as many new target consumers as possible in as many weeks as possible. A pure reach strategy! Plan and buy for continuous short-term reach. Try not to waste money on short-term repetition.

Recency planning is very different from traditional media scheduling. It uses one week as the reach planning period instead of 4+ weeks. It plans for reach, instead of effective frequency. It stresses continuity, rather than flighting. It relies more on dispersion and less on targeting.

In either case, however, one exposure does not do all the work. When John Jones finds that *a single exposure close to purchase can trigger a response*, he is not talking about the first exposure but the most recent in a series of exposures. It is effective because the consumer is *in market.*

The model is said to apply to cars as well as frosted flakes, but does it? A similar concern ties the need for frequency to a product's purchase interval. The argument goes that low frequency might be right for a product that is purchased every week or so, but not for a product that is purchased every four or five years.

Recency planning ignores purchase cycles because it targets the purchase, not the consumer who makes the purchase. As long as there are purchases each week, it doesn't matter how often, or how seldom, the average user buys.

Many writers and art directors are troubled by Recency because it holds that there is little knowledge to be gained about a *brand* through advertising. Furthermore, it implies that advertising itself is not enough to make the consumer pay attention. No wonder creatives are disturbed! They prefer to believe that effective, continuous, creative advertising generates a presence that has branding value.

Recency also contends that consumers screen out advertising except for what interests them and only act upon it when they are ready to buy. That makes it a weak, cost ineffective marketing tool for the public, strong only on individuals who are ripe. In other words, if it is not relevant to consumers in the moment, forget it—they do.

Repetition

Recency says that one good exposure in the 7 days prior to a sale is the effective piece of communication. This last in a series of exposures is really the most important one, the one that sells. A willingness to buy is more important than number of exposures delivered, and willingness is not necessarily triggered by advertising. This seems to imply that one exposure to advertising is enough, replacing Effective Frequency as the modern-day planning model. Effective Frequency, remember, said that that 3+ exposures, in the short-term, were needed to persuade and sell.

The work done by John Philip Jones, using Nielsen Single Source Panel data, is the most often quoted proof of Recency effectiveness. The philosophy of Recency planning has been effectively trumpeted by its father, media consultant, Erwin Ephron for much of the past decade. Ephron calls it, along with *timing,* the organizing principle of media planning. The body of work itself measures STAS (short-term advertising strength). By definition, it measures the effect of advertising on sales mostly during a seven-day short-term period. There is a window of opportunity to sell an individual in the very short term, once s/he is predisposed to buy. The problem is that you never really know, beyond the seasonality of some brands, when that window will appear. It isn't anchored. It floats, depending upon the individual. As a result, you must look to deliver as much short-term reach as possible, over repeated short time intervals. High continuous (redundant) short-term reach sells products. This, in turn, says not to waste money on short-term repetition.

Since many creative professionals like to see their work presented in what they consider the most powerful, repetitious way, they are not happy about Recency. They refuse to believe that their work can be ignored if it is presented frequently, in short bursts. The notion runs counter to all existing logic. They believe that advertising generates awareness, arouses interest, creates desire, and triggers action. Recency holds that in the short term, advertising essentially only performs the last task, and the other three are left to other forces.

Residue

Maybe a misunderstanding shrouds common ground. STAS (the measure used by Recency advocates) does not identify any long-term effect of advertising because it simply doesn't measure it. Recency doesn't say one exposure is enough. It says that in the short-term, added exposures to the ready consumer are wasted. The problem is that for consumers who are not ready, there is no research linking their eventual purchase readiness to whatever it is that prompts their readiness. Is it merely being out of soap or frustrated by a car that continues to break down that readies consumers?

We don't really know what the forces of readiness are. Maybe creatives should feel justifiably free to believe in the value of their cumulative messages, supported by Recency Theory. There is no evidence to dissuade planners from believing that a residue of commercials delivered over time has a value that eventually helps to trigger a readiness to receive that all important last spot that prompts purchase.

Recency Summary

Recency theory is therefore inconsistent with a theory of Effective Frequency because Recency says a single exposure just prior to purchase is all that's needed. In order to maximize weekly reach, the Recency Plan has lower TRP levels and more advertising weeks than other approaches. Guidelines for developing a Recency Plan (Ephron) include planning for:

- Reach, not for frequency
- Continuity, not bursts
- One week rather than four-week planning periods

- Lowest cost per point & :15s to maximize TRPS & reach
- Highly dispersed buys—media, dayparts, and programming; do not concentrate exposures in one selective property

SHARE OF VOICE

A fourth theory of how advertising media work is based on the relationship between *share of voice*, *share of mind*, and *share of market*.

For example, if you were in the market for a new HD television set, what store would you think of (to shop at) first? If you needed a new suit, what store would come to mind first? If you needed some premium, frozen vegetables to serve to your guests on Saturday night, what brand would come to mind first? If you decided to go ahead and buy that new sports car, what model would come to mind first? Which car dealer?

.Your answers to these questions represent the *Share of Mind* (also known as *Top of Mind Awareness*) in its category that each brand or store enjoys with you. It is easy to understand why top of mind awareness is so highly correlated with share of market.

Share of voice (SOV) is simply your brand's percentage (share) of total advertising or communications messages (usually measured as spending) in your primary business category and geographic marketing area and time frame. For example, if you spend $100,000 in your market area on advertising, and your competitors spend another $900,000, then total spending in your category is $1,000,000. Your $100,000 investment represents 10% of the total. Your SOV is determined by the size of your budget compared to the collective ad budgets of your competitors.

SOV vs. Share of Market

Why is SOV important? According to John Davis, author of *Magic Numbers for Consumer Marketing*, SOV is vital. According to Davis:

Advertising does have an influence on perception and a high share of voice can lead to an increased awareness, which ultimately can lead to increased sales and market share.

Today, many large and small companies use "share of voice" to help them understand their competitive situation and to serve as a spending benchmark. Many of the same questions exist for judging effective share of voice as for effective frequency. For example, how does great, memorable creative affect the need for share of voice?

Share of Voice vs. Share of Market

Figure 9-8.—Share of Voice vs. Share of Market

As shown in Figure 9-8, a substantial body of research has found that SOV leads to Share of Mind (Top of Mind Awareness), which in turn leads to Share of Market. In other words, all else being equal, if you increase SOV enough, increased share of market should follow.

How to Measure SOV

Practically speaking the only way to measure Share of Voice is through calculating your spending in relation to competitive media spending. Obviously, it would be preferable to calculate SOV based on TRPs, but the data are not available for competitors.

If your company is large enough, and your ad spending is measured by syndicated media research companies, competitive expenditure research may be used to accumulate measured media expenditures. Information should be gathered for all competitors on a regular (quarterly and/or annual) basis. Each competitor's percentage of the aggregate total is SOV.

If you represent a small company, and there is no existing research report to give you the expenditure data you need, you have to take other measures. Call each of the relevant media and ask them how much each competitor spent in their media vehicle in your marketing area in a certain time frame. Most media are cooperative in responding to such requests.

Don't be afraid to ask. After all, your competitors may be asking the same questions! You may have to guess at some data yourself, nevertheless. When you have compiled all the data, add the total expenditures by competitor by medium and calculate each company's share of the grand total expenditures.

Research Support for SOV/SOM

Historically, there has always been a strong documented relationship between Share of Voice and Share of Market. It is a strong correlation, not a perfect 1:1, but close.

A.C. Nielsen, a large market research company (not the TV ratings division) that tracks sales and share for consumer products, tracks the sales and market share performance of new products in relation to share of voice. Nielsen concluded that SOV most often led the attained Share of Market by 40-100+ percent over an 18-month period. In other words, a new product that achieved a 20% share of market in its category may have accomplished it partly due to a 30-40% SOV during the 18-month introductory period.

Consider also the introduction of Japanese import vehicles into the U.S. market. Initially plagued with product quality problems and negative consumer perceptions, Japanese brands like Toyota greatly improved their product quality and supported an SOV far in excess of their market share as they expanded distribution primarily on the West coast and in the Northeast. Over the years, their strategy paid off; many Americans still perceive Japanese vehicle quality as better than that of American vehicles.

SOV and Share of Market are often very similar numbers, leading to the conclusions that market share will likely be *maintained* when share of voice at least equals share of market and will be *increased* when share of voice significantly leads share of market.

Other companies and advertising agencies have also conducted research on the relationship between SOV and share of market and have found high correlations. Obviously, there are exceptions to the rule—SOV is obviously not the only factor affecting market share. Sometimes the relationship and correlation are not automatic. Although it cannot overcome ineffective creative, price, product, or customer service, SOV has proven an important way to help build market share.

How to Increase SOV

If increased SOV can be a precursor to increased market share, it is important to understand the media options for growing SOV. There are essentially four options:

1. Increase marketing/advertising expenditures sufficient to lead the share of market goal. For example, if current share of market is 10% and the goal is 12%, share of voice would need to be increased to lead the SOM goal. All else equal, achieving 18-20% SOV, may allow the brand to grow to a 12% market share.

2. An alternative or adjunct to the first option would be to increase Effective SOV by eliminating waste in current spending or by increasing effectiveness, while reinvesting savings into more communication.

3. The third option is to improve *Quality of Voice.* This translates to more effective messaging, so it is not directly the media planner's responsibility. In extreme cases, certain advertisers (e.g., like auto dealers) run advertising that conveys a low quality image and is annoying to many.

4. Do all three!

PURCHASE FUNNEL

The fifth model of how advertising media work is based on the purchase funnel concept used by many large advertisers, especially those selling considered purchase products like cars and trucks. The *Purchase Funnel* is a diagnostic model that tracks the consumer decision-making process from the wide-mouth top of the funnel that focuses on attitude formation to the narrow funnel exit that describes the transition from attitudes to purchase behavior.

The Purchase Funnel provides a model for measuring and tracking all the stages leading up to purchase. The model, depicted in Figure 9-9, envisions consumers entering at the top of the funnel and moving downward through it in a predictable sequence.

Definition of Funnel Measures

It is important to understand what each of the Purchase Funnel measures actually represent. The theory is that consumers entering the funnel will move eventually to purchase. Following are definitions of the purchase funnel levels.

Unaware

Unaware consumers are those who say they do not know of a brand's existence. They would respond *No* to the question, "Have you ever heard of the Cadillac CTS?" The object of the Purchase Funnel's first level is to bring unaware consumers to awareness.

Figure 9-9.—Typical Purchase Funnel

Awareness

Total aided awareness is the object of the second level. Total awareness what gets a positive answer to a question like this: "Have you ever heard of Green Giant?" Some awareness is better than no awareness, but your goal is to bring these consumers to familiarity with the brand.

177

Familiarity

Familiarity is like top of mind awareness or share of mind. *When you think of detergents, which brand comes to your mind first?* Familiar consumers think they know a fair amount about the product or brand. The Funnel's object at this level is for consumers to be able to distinguish your brand from competitive brands.

Opinion

Opinion can be positive or negative. Opinion is the degree to which consumers believe a brand is good or bad, high or low performance, tasteful or distasteful, and so on. At this level, your object is consumers who compare your brand vs. the competition.

Consideration

Purchase Consideration is the degree to which consumers planning to make a purchase in your product category consider purchasing your brand. At the level of the Funnel, you want them to be considering you first.

Purchase Intention

To what degree does the consumer actually intend to buy the brand? As a predictor of future sales, how does your brand compare at this level to your competitors in terms of purchase intentions?

Shopping

Did consumers shop for your brand? Did they buy it? How do shopping rates for your brand compare to those of the competition?

Purchase

The mouth of the Funnel represents purchase. In retail or e-commerce situations, it is measured as a closing ratio: the percentage of consumers who were shopping at the store who actually purchased. For example, if 100 shoppers entered a car dealership and 30 of them purchased, the closing ratio would be 30%. Low closing ratios signal problem(s) to be solved—problems with the product, price, salespersons, or sales environment. How do your closing ratios compare to those of the competition?

Tracking Purchase Funnel Measures

One of the important benefits of Purchase Funnel theory is that it involves periodic measurements (usually quarterly) for each level's objectives. These measurements can serve as an early warning system for advertisers who are experiencing declines in funnel measures that if not reversed will lead eventually to sales declines. The measures also can identify competitive vulnerabilities.

By tracking purchase funnel trends, marketers receive a heads-up in time for remedial action to solve problems identified in the Purchase Funnel metrics. For example, if competing brands are increasing their purchase consideration while your brand is static or in decline, what is the problem and how do your address it? Table 9-3 provides a top line example of the kind of diagnostic data that Purchase Funnel tracking can provide.

Table 9-3.—Tracking Purchase Funnel Measures (%) for Brand X

Funnel Level	1st Quarter	2nd Quarter	3rd Quarter	4th Quarter
Awareness	65	62	60	57
Familiarity	30	27	25	20
Opinion	15	14	13	12
Consideration	12	11	12	10
Intention	6	6	5	4
Shopping	5	5	5	4
Purchase	4	4	4	3

The year of funnel tracking data, shown in percentages in Table 9-3 should be arousing the concern of the Brand X product manager, but it is answering an important question. That sharp downward trend on every other funnel measure—awareness, familiarity, opinion, purchase consideration, purchase intention, and closing ratios—surely helps explain the drop in purchase rates.

These data should also be raising questions. What is causing these precipitous and very dangerous drops? Have marketing budgets been cut? Are there new competitors? Can the majority of target consumers recall seeing the ads? Is the new positioning off target?

You can't solve a problem until you know what it is. The Purchase Funnel can help you discover that a problem exists and define what it is.

Does the Purchase Funnel Comprehend Online?

The Purchase Funnel's suitability for the Internet age has been challenged on the ground that it doesn't sufficiently describe the consumer's approach to a considered purchase decision. In the automotive category, for example, the 2004 New Autoshopper.com Study by J.D. Power Associates found that among all new-vehicle buyers, approximately 50% say their make and model decision and the price they paid or offered were influenced by automotive information from the Internet—up from about 40% in 2002.

The Purchase Funnel takes no account of the way consumers use online research to expand their consideration set and to take advantage of the experience of existing owners and users to help guide their choice. Both points have important implications for the purchase funnel. On the other hand, the diagnostics provided in Purchase Funnel reports would likely describe where buyers get their information (recognizing that buyers usually can't do this accurately).

ENGAGEMENT

The newest model of how advertising works is called engagement theory. Of the several definitions of engagement, three are currently prominent:

Engagement measures the extent to which a consumer has a meaningful brand experience when exposed to commercial advertising, sponsorship. Wikipedia)

Here's the definition of engagement presented by Advertising Research Foundation (ARF) Chief Research Officer, Joe Plummer, at the organization's annual conference:

Engagement is turning on a prospect to a brand idea enhanced by the surrounding context.

Finally, here is the definition used by Ted McConnell of Proctor & Gamble:

Engagement is a scale indicating the degree to which a consumer is likely to or has internalized a communication.

Question: Based on these definitions, how would you define engagement?

Advertising Engagement vs. Media Engagement

There is a difference between *advertising engagement* and *media engagement*. The role of an ad or commercial is to engage the consumer creatively in a way that captures attention because it is seen as relevant. "Want more engagement, make a better ad," quips Roger Baron, Director of Media Research at Foote Cone & Belding.

On the other hand, some believe that media play an important role in engaging consumers. Some argue that media with higher attention levels or higher consumer involvement increase engagement with the ads. Others argue that media context is extremely important to engagement.

Concern for engagement and attention to its solutions aren't new; Chapter 7 of this book was devoted entirely to considerations of media effectiveness because professional media planners and buyers have a responsibility to select media which will most effectively communicate the client's message.

Media Context

Advertisers and media planners and buyers have always been concerned with media context—the environment in which their ads were going to run. Any buyer of spot television or radio has heard hundreds of sales pitches based on why a particular station's news program or radio station will confer status on the advertiser.

Years ago, *Fortune Magazine* sold against *Forbes* on the basis of its more credible editorial product. Fortune's sales proposition was that advertisers would benefit from the *halo effect* of *Fortune*'s greater credibility. Fortune argued that its credibility would confer higher status and credibility on advertisers than the competition would. Furthermore, they argued, that status conferral was worth a premium price.

In fact, almost every magazine attempts to sell itself at least partly on the basis of its quality, its editorial, and its engaging environment, audience rapport, trustworthiness, and similar contextual characteristics.

Engaging the consumer's brain and emotions with advertising is at the heart of the marketing communications business. Engagement is perhaps a 70% creative responsibility and a 30% media responsibility. Media planners might say, "Whoa, not my job," but they'd be wrong.

Bobby J. Calder, professor in the Kellogg School of Management, in *Kellogg on Advertising and Media* (2009) takes the position that marketers have not sufficiently taken into account the consumer's engagement with the surrounding media *content*. The medium provides an advertising context that has an influence on ad effectiveness. He further believes that how consumers experience a medium affects their degree of engagement.

Calder cited several studies that demonstrate how media content can affect response to ads. He suggests that it would be smart to adjust the ad to the media content. Perhaps a TV commercial in an action/adventure program would be different from one running in American Idol on a different channel. Calder calls this the *Congruence Hypothesis.*

Another hypothesis is that engagement with the medium leads to engagement with the advertising, where media engagement would be attentive minutes spent and involvement. Using a working definition of advertising engagement as commercial recall, research conducted by Knowledge Networks/SRI found that Unaided Recall is an indicator of engagement. (Rittenberg and Clancy 2006)

Although questions remain about how engagement will be achieved, there's little doubt about the need for new ways to measure it. Media fragmentation has made marketing much more two-way, with consumers capable of engaging in dialogue through interactive media and content they themselves create.

Engagement Metrics

If media context is important to engaging the consumer with relevant advertising messages, what metrics would be used to select media on the that basis?

In 2006, Experian Simmons launched the Multi-Media Engagement Study, in response to the groundswell of advertiser and agency interest in developing media engagement metrics. The study covered a huge array of nationally-aired TV shows and cable channels, magazines and Internet websites, reporting six global engagement indicators for all TV, magazine, and Internet measured vehicles. Respondents claiming recent exposure to any of the TV shows, magazines, or websites were asked to rate the descriptiveness of approximately 40 statements for each of the media they used. From their responses, Experian Simmons derived the engagement dimensions defined in Figure 9-10.

While Simmons's data are very interesting, they raise questions about which audience attitudes are most likely to predict engagement. In addition, there are sometimes seeming contradictions for planners to reconcile. For example, does a high trustworthiness score for a media vehicle mean that its advertising would therefore be more effective?

Question: What conclusions do you draw from the Simmons data?

Dimension	Definition
Inspirational	Media inspire and connect emotionally with consumers
Trustworthy	Media are trusted, media do not sensationalize things
Life Enhancing	Consumers are learning new things from the medium, which helps them make better decisions
Social Interaction	Media give consumers fodder for conversations with family and friends
Personal Timeout	Consumers say the time they spend with the medium is just for them and generally improves their mood
Advertising Receptivity	Ads that run in the medium are of interest and consumer is more likely to purchase products advertised within

Figure 9-10.—Experian-Simmons Dimensions of Engagement

Which media types perform best and worst on each of the six dimensions? As shown in Table 9-4, magazines received the highest ratings on every dimension, including Ad Receptivity. Television's highest rating was on the Personal Timeout dimension, but fared less well on Life Enhancing and Ad Receptivity dimensions. Websites' strength was on the Trustworthy dimension; their weakness was on Inspirational dimension.

Table 9-4.—Comparison of Engagement Ratings* by Medium

Medium	Television	Magazines	Websites
Inspirational	245	273	224
Trustworthy	266	324	308
Life Enhancing	207	302	280
Social Interaction	268	306	283
Personal Timeout	296	308	255
Ad Receptivity	205	288	232
Average	**248**	**300**	**264**

Source: Simmons, Multi Media   *Scale of 100 (Lowest)-500 (Highest)*
Engagement Study, Wave 3, 2007

No doubt, these ratings reflect magazines' strengths of selective editorial content related life enhancement, information to talk about in social interactions, and the like. Websites' ratings, overall, were competitive with television's ratings.

These data represent averages. Individual media vehicles within each media type will deviate above and below the averages. For illustrative purposes, Table 9-5 provides a comparison of several specific media vehicles within each type. Media that engage their audiences are likely to confer superior ad impact benefits upon their advertisers. The question is how to use data like these to develop media plans that engage audiences.

The highest Ad Receptivity ratings typically go to media vehicles that specialize in certain subject matter. Entertainment media or even news media may receive high ratings on Trustworthiness but mediocre ratings on Ad Receptivity. This leads advertisers to place food advertising only on the Food Network or in Cooking Magazine, which may be smart. However, what kinds of products or ads would fit on CSI or O'Reilly on Fox or the majority of websites? Would radio automatically be eliminated from consideration because its content serves the desire for news, opinion, or a zillion genres of music?

Question: How can data like these help media planners select media that will help engage consumers with relevant ad messages?

Table 9-5.—Engagement Ratings for Specific Media: Examples

Media	Inspired	Trust	Life Enhance	Social Interact	Personal Timeout	Ad Receptivity
Today	268	311	284	315	262	208
CSI	250	257	177	263	203	175
24	259	209	161	285	328	190
O'Reilly	305	331	229	367	271	197
Brides	279	319	343	315	321	344
Health	315	359	333	321	293	307
People	245	249	208	279	304	214
Time	288	320	241	316	249	204
Auto	215	314	368	291	245	267
Connect	222	255	216	248	245	289
Jobs	191	301	255	231	179	182
Search	171	294	312	258	205	201

Source: Simmons Multi-Media Engagement Study, Wave 3, 2007

It is curious that the Experian-Simmons data in Tables 9-4 and 9-5 do not include metrics dealing with the pre-requisites to engagement such as advertising exposure, program involvement, or even the positioning of ads in the medium—questions where media selection plays an important role. Doesn't the process of achieving engagement first require exposing the ad?

Engagement Conclusions

Engagement speaks directly to the need to make deeper impressions, not just gross impressions. That's a good thing.

Isn't the real problem *disengagement*? Given that consumers all too often are not engaged in the advertising at all, is it your job to assure engagement or to overcome disengagement?

We do not have metrics adequate to select media on the basis of value added by engagement. Furthermore, engagement with a TV program cannot be expected spill over to all the ads because the frequent and long interruptions tend to break the spell, and because the ads come in sequences that remove most of them very far from program content. Perhaps we need to focus less on trying to define engagement and focus instead on fixing what we know interferes with engagement.

SUMMARY

As the Cheshire cat so wisely said, "If you don't know where you are going, any road will get you there. In order to develop a good media plan, you have to know where you are going, both your marketing objectives and your communications objectives. It isn't unreasonable to build your plan on your best-reasoned theory of how your advertising and media will work to achieve your combined objectives.

In order to develop a professional media plan, you must have some theory about how it will in the marketplace. Are you able to compare media on more than a vehicle-exposure basis? Do you need high frequency or one weekly exposure to the majority of the target? Will share of voice drive your market share? Do you track consumer awareness, attitudes, and behavior? Should you focus on engagement?

Chapter 9 reviewed six media models, each describing a different theory about how media advertising works, or could work, in a perfect world.

1. *ARF Response Model*
2. *Effective Frequency*
3. *Recency*
4. *Share of Voice*
5. *Purchase Funnel*
6. *Engagement*

Your best choice may be to create your own custom model using the best ideas from each, using new discoveries and new data to expand your model so that it continues to work for you.

10. TARGET AUDIENCE

*Deeper Insights...Bigger Ideas...By digging deeper into
consumer values, lifestyles, life stages, belief systems
and decision processes, we create an emotional connection
between the brand and the target to produce the most effective
communications that reach and motivate them....*

–Campbell Ewald Website

A target audience is the specific group (or groups) to whom an advertising and marketing communications campaign is directed. Who are they? What do they do? What do they think? Where do they live? How do they buy?

You cannot develop a media plan without first knowing whom you want to reach with that plan. You cannot develop a good media plan without having the right target audience. You cannot develop a GREAT media plan without having deep consumer insights. In addition, if there are multiple targets, you must prioritize them properly in order to allocate resources effectively among them.

Understanding current and prospective consumers is marketing's Job One. It can be difficult to figure out exactly who your target audience is, but identifying and then relating your messages and media to them is your paramount marketing task. Everything a business does in marketing—from selection of products and services to positioning, location, and pricing—depends on target market definitions and insights.

DEFINING THE TARGET AUDIENCE

The USA constitutes a market area of over 300 million men, women, and children—young and old, rich and poor, Boomers and GenX, Hispanics and Whites and Blacks, Christians and Jews, smart and otherwise. From New York to Los Angeles, the United States is probably the most diverse market in the world.

To begin figuring out to define your target audience well, you must start with some basic homework.

- **Study the marketing plan** and the consumer data contained within it, including all of the consumer research studies that profile the consumer and the consumer's purchase behavior.

- **Study syndicated research reports** such as MRI and SMRB. These provide demographic, behavioral, lifestyle, and media consumption data for almost every product/service category.

- **Study the competition**. A potentially insightful way to identify target audiences is to study what the competition does. Who does their advertising address? What audiences do they target with media? What media channels do they emphasize?

- **Study the trade magazines** that cover your product category. Pay close attention to how those companies sell products or services similar to yours.

- **Conduct your own research** to gain insights into possible targets. If little research has been done in a specific niche, begin with exploratory focus groups, followed by quantitative research.

Target Audience Options

There are many ways to define a target audience. For media selection purposes, your first step in choosing one is to do your research. Few advertisers have only one target audience to reach and persuade. Consequently, in order to maximize media effectiveness and ROI, every advertiser must first define, describe, and prioritize its target groups within the company's marketing area (global, national, regional, DMA, or micro-markets and retail trading areas consisting of selected zip codes). Most of this chapter will review some ways that you can define, describe, and prioritize your target audiences.

Unfortunately, Target Audiences are often used as black and white criteria for deciding who is worth reaching and who isn't. For example, if a brand defines its target as women 18-34, does that really mean that men have NO marketing value or that women 35-49 have no marketing value? Of course not. As discussed in chapter 18, this is why many sophisticated advertisers place marketing importance weights on each segment of the audience.

Demographics

The most common method of defining target audiences is by their demographics. *Demographics* are the basic characteristics of a population—such as gender, age, income, education, ethnicity, marital status, size of household, presence of children by age, and similar descriptive differences. Only gender and age classifications are used for most broadcast media buys, however, primarily because these most basic data are all that is available in the rating reports from Nielsen and Arbitron.

Advertisers require more extensive demographic data than that to understand their consumers. For example, if Heinz Ketchup wanted to develop a profile of the catsup user, they would include the demographics of the total user group as well as the subset that uses catsup most often. The Heinz media planner might begin by asking questions like: What is the gender and age of the purchaser? How many children are present in the household? How old are they? What is the average household income of purchasers? What are the ethnicities of catsup users, and so on?

As an example of demographic data at work, Table 10-1 examines the demographic profile for users of the *Blimpos* brand; 70% of the Blimpo's users are female. However, the highest purchase rates (indices) belong to 18-34s and college graduates. On the other hand, the *least likely* groups to buy Blimpies are males, and adults aged 35+.

Table 10-1.—Demographics of Blimpo's Brand Users

User Category	% Users	Index to US
Male	30	60
Female	70	140
Age 18-24	35	250
25-34	45	200
35+	20	50
College Grad	50	300
HH Income $40M+	40	110

While demographics can add an important level of understanding, demographics tells you nothing about personalities, lifestyles, interests, or desires. Psychographics do.

Psychographics

Psychographics are consumer descriptions based on personality, interests, activities, and opinions. Demographics, however convenient and available, simply do not identify precisely whom a media planner really needs to reach.

For example, if you were constructing a marketing plan for a product designed and geared to those who like gourmet cooking, which would be a better way of describing the real target: women 25-54 (demographic) or men/women who love gourmet cooking (psychographic)?

Nielsen and Arbitron rating reports contain only the basic demographics, such as gender and age, but do not contain the psychographics. However, MRI and SMRB do contain psychographic data, cross-referenced with media audience data. With creativity and common sense, you can use these data to make intelligent targeting decisions. A plethora of magazines for cooking enthusiasts, as well as several cable TV channels and programs devoted to cooking and food preparation, are prime resources.

Psychographics might be expressed as Activity-Interest-Opinion statements like these:

- I go fishing as often as I can. (activity)
- I like to learn about how the Founding Fathers prized liberty and freedom above all. (interest)
- I believe that the incumbent members of Congress need to be replaced. (opinion)

Psychographics often differ by market (DMA). As you can see from Table 10-2, Bible reading is a less frequent activity in Boston and Las Vegas than it is in Mobile, Alabama. Conversely, and equally unsurprisingly, skiing is a Boston favorite, less practiced in Vegas, and of little interest in Mobile. (How to read Table 10-2: *Frequent skiing in Boston is 175% of the U.S. average.*)

Table 10-2.—Comparison of Lifestyles by DMA Index to US

Activity	Boston	Las Vegas	Mobile, AL
Bible Reading	46	70	135
Take Cruises	101	126	111
Fishing	69	79	132
Sewing	93	88	102
Frequently Ski	175	106	49

Source: SRDS Lifestyle Indicator

A lifestyle segmentation tool called *geodemographic* is based loosely on the adage that birds of a feather flock together. Using their *PRIZM* system, Nielsen-Claritas defines every U.S. household in terms of 66 demographically and behaviorally distinct types, or *segments,* to help marketers discern those consumers' likes, dislikes, lifestyles, purchase behaviors, and media preferences. Because PRIZM is linked to the surveys and panels of most major U.S. marketing databases, the segmentation system enables media planners to target virtually any purchasing and media behavior.

Each geodemographic PRIZM cluster is given a clever name—BLUE BLOOD ESTATES, FURS AND STATION WAGONS, SHOTGUNS AND PICKUPS, YOUNG INFLUENTIALS, BACK COUNTRY FOLKS—that characterizes the presumed nature of its members. For example, one of the 66 segments, BLUE BLOOD ESTATES, is described as:

> A family portrait of suburban wealth, a place of million-dollar homes and manicured lawns, high-end cars and exclusive private clubs. The nation's second-wealthiest lifestyle, it is also described as being married couples with children, college degrees, a significant percentage of Asian Americans and six-figure incomes earned by business executives, managers, and professionals (www.claritas.com, 3/7/11).

PRIZM can be a very useful tool to marketers because it provides deeper level of understanding about the target audience. The descriptive labels add a sense of the members' identities (just don't be too literal in interpreting the labels) and simplify somewhat the otherwise-complicated 66-category classification system.

Geo-demographics can also be a useful tool for targeting within a DMA. For example, if a target is defined as a cross section of BLUE BLOOD ESTATES and FURS AND STATION WAGONS, you could identify the zip code locations of the BLUE BLOOD ESTATES and FURS AND STATION WAGONS within a DMA, then saturate those areas with advertising on local cable systems, direct mail, zip-targeted newspaper inserts, or other pinpoint, targetable media.

An auto manufacturer used this method to market a small car that was positioned against small Japanese imports. The vehicle suffered from an extremely low name awareness and familiarity, especially among import buyers, but it did have a well-defined and highly targetable geodemographic profile. The ad agency identified the zip code clusters associated with that profile and saturated those zip clusters with outdoor posters. If you lived in one of these zip codes, you were going to see these posters!

Product Users & Usage

Your next targeting option is to focus not on groups that may include users but on actual, individual users of your product category or particular brand. Product user targeting was conceived in the late 1960s by a forward-thinking research company, Target Group Index (TGI).

Similar to what SMRB and MRI do today, TGI collected product usage data, demographics, and media audience data from the same large sample. For the first time, media planners could directly target product category users as heavy, medium, light, or non-users.

TGI's groundbreaking research gave rise to the *Heavy User* concept. *Heavy users* were found to be an important segmentation because heavy users typically consume a disproportionately high share of a product or service. The underlying concept is that 20% of users typically consume 80% of the product. For example, a family with a new baby will use disproportionately more diapers than a family with a two-year old who doesn't need to be changed as often.

Table 10-3 provides examples of the high concentration of use within a small percentage of total users. For example, in product categories A and C, about 20% of users represent nearly 80% of total usage or purchasing of the categories.

Table 10-3.—Product Category Users vs. Usage

Product Category	% Users	% Usage
(A) Ice Cream	22	78
(B) Shirts	30	65
(C) Beer	20	80

Source: 2020

Referring to Table 10-3, based on the *heavy user* concept, do you think it would be more productive to target heavy beer drinkers directly, or to target men 18-24, 45% of whom are heavy beer drinkers? How about all the other men and women who are heavy beer drinkers but, alas, fall outside the target demographic of men 18-24?

Using the syndicated research studies developed by MRI and SMRB, planners can cross-reference the heavy, medium, or light users of nearly every product category with specific media audiences. Do you want to know how many heavy users of catsup read *Cooking Light Magazine*? Look it up.

Of course, it is still important to describe the heavy user's demographic and psychographic characteristics. The better you understand who your target really is, the better your media decisions will be.

Customers vs. Prospects

Here's an important question: Should you target the company's *current customers* or *potential customers*? Should you target both? Do you have the resources to target both?

One way to look at target audience determination is to consider whether or to what extent a company's target should consist of its current customers. Should you rely solely on the company's current, active customer base? If current customers are at least somewhat brand loyal, and if they tend to influence others to buy from your client, they can be a company's most important asset. How often have you heard about the importance of *word-of-mouth* advertising?

Chevrolet's single most productive target group is the existing Chevrolet owner body, who (if their ownership experience has been good) are the most likely (return) buyers of new Chevrolets. Many companies believe that their number one priority is to maintain the existing customer base that will reliably provide repeat business. For examples of this emphasis, consider the growth in Customer Relationship Management (CRM) programs or the importance that mail order companies place on their customer list to which they mail and mail and mail. Look at the cartons or packaging of many products and you'll likely find a toll-free number for Customer Comments or Questions on the label.

In reality, however, most businesses experience continuous attrition in their customer bases. Some customers discontinue buying—due to retirement, death, changes in lifestyle, dissatisfaction, or discovery of an alternative they prefer. Perhaps they are swayed to a different product or vendor by enticing, targeted advertising. So, alas for the marketing planner, they switch. Macy's Department Stores, for example, estimates that it loses 1.2 million customers every year, which the company measures by the number of active store credit card users.

In the real world, therefore, every business must generate *new customers*—from a pool of good *prospects*—just to replace the ones lost through attrition. Even more customers must be won if the business is to grow and enjoy increased sales, market share, and profits. That's why when you buy something at Macy's (as well as many other department store chains) and don't have their store credit card, you are more than likely to be offered the opportunity to open an in-store credit card account.

In order to grow, companies must attract new customers. The question is what are the best sources of new customers (sales)? A demographic group? A psychographic group? Competitive users? Heavy users? Should the demographic/psychographic profiles of the current customer base be used to target similar new customers? Who should be targeted, and if multiple targets are warranted, what priorities should be followed in allocating resources? How should resources be divided between maintaining the customer base versus attracting some fresh blood into the franchise?

Purchasers vs. Decision Makers

The next consideration is to decide whether to target those who actually make the purchases or those who make the decisions. Purchasers and decision makers: are they the same?

It is important to understand that purchasers and decision makers are not always the same. For example, in the purchase of a new automobile, the married male in the household typically does a lot of the research, physical shopping, and negotiations at the dealership, but that married male is not necessarily the primary decision maker. Traditionally, purchase decisions for new vehicles have been shared between husband and wife, or divided as follows: the husband goes to dealership, negotiates, and signs the papers after the wife has decided on the make, model, color, and trim. In the latter scenario, the wife was the primary *decision maker*. Who would you target—the purchaser husband or the decision maker wife?

Children, while usually not purchasers, may be decision makers for many of the products and services they consume—from foods, toys, and entertainment to cell phones and iPods.

In business-to-business marketing, the roles of purchasers and decision makers can become quite complex. For example, in a small to midsized company, the CEO may be the final decision maker for technology purchases. In a larger company, however, a department head may define the specifications and make recommendations for the department's provision; the Purchasing Department may then refine the specs, obtain bids, analyze value, negotiate with vendors, make recommendations, and conclude the purchase negotiations. In some organizations, the Comptroller has the power to accept or reject the department manager's purchase requests.

194

For other products purchased by the company, particularly commodities, the Purchasing Department may be the sole purchaser and decision maker. The point is that there can be a lot of fingers in the pie, so each finger must be understood. A well-known sales trainer has said that to sell a product you must talk to the person who can say *Yes*.

Life Stage Targeting

Some marketers look closely at defining and describing target audiences in terms of their life stages. Including Pre-Baby Boomers and Baby Boomers, Gen X, Gen Y, and Gen Z are generational groups representing not only different life stages but also different life experiences. Following is a summary describing each of these so-called generations.

Baby Boomers

Demographers, sociologists, and the media define baby boomers as those born during any of the years from 1946 through 1964. In 2010, that would make *Boomers* between 46 and 64 years old. There are about 75 million Boomers in the U.S. representing about 29% of the population. Due to their large population and general affluence in the U.S. and Western Europe, Boomers have dominated marketing since their appearance on the scene. They grew up in the analog era, watching broadcast television and listening to vinyl records, but they readily embraced the digital revolution. In fact, both Bill Gates and Steve Jobs are officially Baby Boomers.

The term Boomers is derived from the boom in births after World War II. Today, Boomers are in their peak earning years and are beginning to enter the retirement ranks. As a group, they will place tremendous pressure on the nation's Social Security and Medicare resources over the next decades.

However, because many Boomers have high incomes and are well educated, they are lucrative targets for the products and services that sell to upscale consumers. Have you ever noticed who is driving all those shiny new Corvette convertibles—or even those big Harley-Davidsons?

Generation X

Gen X is known as the *slacker generation* or the *bof* generation. (*Bof* is French for *whatever*.) Gen X is the generation born after the baby boom ended, with birth dates used by researchers ranging from the mid 1960s to about 1981. The U.S. Census Bureau cites Generation X as statistically achieving and holding the highest education levels in the nation.

Gen X is the first generation to grow up in front of the TV, with Sesame Street, video games, MTV, and PCs. Gen Xers are assuming leadership positions today and taking leading roles in the digital economy. Youthful, educated, energetic, and entrepreneurial, Generation X is also busy having babies and making lots of money.

Why is it, then, that marketing efforts aimed at Generation X don't bring in the sales that everyone has grown to expect? One explanation is Gen X has 40% fewer members than there are in the Baby Boomer generation, according to Ken Gronbach, president of KGA Advertising of Middletown, Connecticut, and nationally known as a generations marketing expert.

Think of the implications for marketers who are used to keeping up with the needs of 80 million Boomers and are now facing 50 million Gen Xers. If you're dealing with a tried and true product aimed at the 18-to-34 year old market, with an infrastructure based upon the consumption rates of the Baby Boomers, you've probably built way past the capacity of this market and focused on the outworn creative. To succeed with Gen X you have to get a larger share of a smaller pie with different tastes.

Generation Y

Generation Y is the children of Gen X. Members of Gen Y are also often referred to as *Millennials* or *Echo Boomers.* Gen Y numbers about 60 million, making it the second largest generational market behind Boomers. As there are no precise dates for when Gen Y starts and ends, social commentators have used birth dates ranging somewhere from the mid 1970s to the early 2000s.

This generation generally represents an increase in births from the 1960s and 70s, not because of a significant increase in birthrates, but because the large cohort of baby boomers began to have children. The 20th century trend toward smaller families in developed countries continued, however, so the relative impact of the baby boom echo was generally less pronounced than the original boom.

Unlike their Gen X parents who grew up in front of the TV, Gen Y consumes every conceivable form of media—television, radio, Internet, cell phone, texting, video games, and all of the new stuff. Gen Y craves interaction, connection, and social validation.

Generation Z

Gen Z represents today's children. Currently under the age of 10, these children are growing up in a world that the rest of us have created—a world of constant, instantaneous media. Gen Z influences many of today's purchase decisions and will become a major market segment in the decades to come.

Purchase Influencers

As noted previously, for some products or services, *Purchase Influencers* are very important in the decision-making process. They play a major, or even the primary, role in deciding what brand is purchased— even though they do not physically make either the purchase or the decision to purchase.

Children, for example, who are the primary consumers of certain kinds of cereals and cookies, exert strong influence on purchasers. That's why cookie companies like Keebler and Nabisco devote a portion of their media budgets to kids' programming. Children exert a large influence over other purchases as well—their apparel, foods, toys, meal deliveries—but adults are usually the decision makers. Although not often the final decision makers, children are powerful and compelling purchase influencers.

Emerging Markets

The demographic face of the USA is changing at breathtaking speed. By 2025, European Americans will shrink to 62% of the population, as Hispanic, Asian, and African American populations continue their rapid growth. In addition, Baby Boomers are not only reaching critical mass but the population also continues its migration to the Sun Belt. Of course, many individual markets (DMAs) already have dominant minorities or older populations. For example, the population of Los Angeles is 48% Hispanic.

Because many of these generational market segments are unique, and differ from the general population in their demographics and economics, culture and values, product preferences and motivations, it is growing late—but not too late—to begin learning how to target and sell to them more effectively.

Sometimes companies decide that they need to target growth markets or market segments where their business is currently weak. Companies that are underperforming in important growth markets may see their market shares decline even further in the future, if remedial action is not taken. Companies' leaders who believe that they need to target emerging markets strategically must understand that it is a long-term proposition that cannot be accomplished with a short-term promotion or a few randomly placed ads.

Table 10-4.—The Changing Face of America

Population Segment	Population (millions)			% Change
	1990	2000	2010E	
<5	19	20	21	+10.5
Age 55+	52	59	78	+50.0
African American	30	36	40	+33.3
Asian/Islands	7	18	23	+228.5
Hispanic Origin	22	36	48	+118.1
White	200	229	245	+22.5
South	85	103	115	+35.3
West	53	66	72	+35.8

Gay Market

Some advertisers choose to target the gay market. According to *Gay Market Advertising Information*, there are about 17 million gay persons in the United States. Gays reportedly spend annually about $485 billion or approximately $28,500 per capita, which is higher than most other market segments, making the gay population one of the highest income and most professional market segments in the country.

Table 10-5.—Size of Gay vs. Ethnic Market Segments

Market	Population (MM)	Spending ($B)	$/Capita ($M)
Gays	17	485	28.5
Hispanics	37	653	17.6
African American	36	485	13.5
Asians	12	344	28.7

The conundrum for advertisers is not whether gays are an important market segment but whether different creative and media are needed to communicate effectively with the gay population. Not surprisingly, the gay media say *yes*, citing research that the majority of gays prefer to buy from advertisers who advertise in gay media. Gay media availabilities are fairly extensive—ranging from gay magazines, radio, websites, and on demand television.

Consumer Behavior

Target audiences can also be defined in terms of *how* they buy products in a particular category. At one end of the spectrum are *impulse purchasers*—at the other end are *considered purchasers*.

Many products are purchased on impulse—chewing gum in a drug store, a can of nuts at the grocery store, a paperback book on an airport layover, or even a new coat noticed in a store window. Impulse purchases usually don't require much thought or analysis or Internet search—in fact, from the seller's perspective, the less thought by the consumer, the better. On the other hand, some consumers are actually capable of making major purchases on impulse.

At the other end of the spectrum are considered purchases, which generally require more research and thought. Deciding on a new vehicle or household appliance or which new phone to get are examples of considered purchases.

In planning media, it is important to understand that purchasers often pay attention to or rely on different media at different stages of their decision making process. The diagram in Figure 10-1 typifies a considered purchase process in which the buyer is interested in different information at different stages.

For new vehicle purchasing, research has shown that seeing television commercials creates initial awareness of a product or brand dealer. Internet search, magazine advertisements or direct mail—perhaps all three—then become more important as purchasers compare and evaluate product alternatives. Finally, when consumers begin actively shopping and visiting stores, they become especially attentive to newspaper ads to learn who has the best prices and product availability.

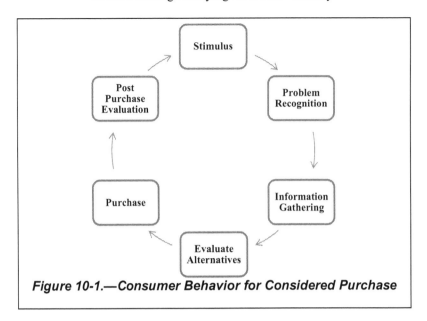

Figure 10-1.—Consumer Behavior for Considered Purchase

Internet Targets

Internet targets can be defined in a variety of ways, including demographic, psychographic, life style, life stage, and all the rest. There are additional important methods of targeting on the Internet with paid search or display ads/banners.

1. *Category targeting* might be based on a subject matter category such as automotive, gourmet foods, dating, or computer interest.

2. *Keyword targeting* focuses on consumers who are searching particular keywords or phrases. If one of your keywords were catnip, then users searching the term catnip would be exposed to your ad, click on it, and link to your website.

3. *Behavioral targeting* uses information collected on an individual's web-browsing behavior, such as the pages they have visited or the searches they have made, to select which advertisements to display to that individual. Practitioners believe this helps them deliver their online advertisements to the users who are most likely to be interested.

4. *Contextual targeting* is an extension of search advertising. Just as users can search for keywords on Google and other search engines and see ads related to those keywords, visitors to content

network sites can see ads related specifically to the content they are viewing on a web page.

Chapter 22 on Internet Media Buying is a fuller examination of targeting opportunities on the Internet.

Business-to-Business Targets

Vertical trade publications covering a particular industry or job function are an invaluable source of information about *B2B* (*business-to-business*) targets and B2B purchasing behavior. If you are a B2B advertiser, call your trade publication reps to see what they have available as well as to give yourself an opportunity to pick their brains.

SUMMARY

The target audience is the foundation upon which a strategic media plan is built. There is nothing more fundamental than really understanding your target audience: who they are, where they live, why they buy. Chapter 10 has emphasized that understanding and showed how focusing on the consumer is vital to marketing success, including developing media plans that reach the right audience at the right time in the right place with enough impact to move them to action.

Media planners are expected to participate in defining target audience priorities. Defining the target audience is not a simple exercise. Target audiences may be multi-dimensional, making it necessary to reach various groups who may be part of the purchase process. You have analyzed targets in ten of the most common ways:

1. *Demographics*
2. *Psychographics & geo-demographics*
3. *Product users & usage*
4. *Current versus prospective customer status*
5. *Purchasers versus decision makers*
6. *Life stages*
7. *Purchase influencers*
8. *Emerging markets*
9. *Gay market*
10. *Consumer behavior*

Internet targets and business-to-business targets offer additional dimensions to consider as you allocate media and resources, figuring out how to reach and communicate with each of your targets most effectively.

11. GEOGRAPHIC PROBLEMS & OPPORTUNITIES

There is no such thing as national advertising.
All advertising is local and personal. It's one man or woman
reading one newspaper in the kitchen or watching TV in the den.

–*Morris Hite,* quoted in
Adman: Morris Hite's Methods for Winning the Ad Game, 1988

National advertisers are those who advertise in national media because their sales occur in all markets. Others are regional or local advertisers, depending on their marketing and sales areas.

Regardless of their specific marketing areas, all advertisers face the challenge of where to advertise. Deciding where to advertise—and how much media weight and budget to place in each geographic area—by communications form, medium, product, and message—is one of your most crucial advertising and marketing recommendations.

Allocating marketing resources to national and local media in a variety of local markets with different marketing situations raises philosophical question: Is the USA one homogeneous market, where one plan fits all? Or is the USA a patchwork of unique geographic market areas, each presenting different problems and opportunities?

Some national advertisers believe that most of their advertising should be placed in national media such as network television or national magazines. Other companies believe that geography is their most important market segmentation because it is so tied to their sales performance and market share.

In one geographic area, where there is high consumer awareness, below average competition, good product distribution, and good trade relations, a brand may enjoy an above average and growing market share. In an adjacent market, competitive activity may be heavier or consumers may buy less of the product category, so that the same brand may have a much lower share of market.

The driving principle behind geography in media planning is that it is most profitable to advertise to customers or prospects that have the greatest likelihood of buying at the lowest cost in customer acquisition. On the other hand, there may be some high volume, high potential markets where the brand is weak. These markets may require significant investment spending and market development efforts. This chapter addresses some of the important issues that determine where to advertise and how to allocate budget dollars to national, regional, and local media.

GEOGRAPHIC MARKETING PHILOSOPHIES

There are different philosophies of how to advertise geographically. Some marketers choose to advertise on a national basis, while others go market by market. Who's right?

Another Inconvenient Truth

An inconvenient truth for some companies and agencies is that the geographic market areas in which they do business may be very different from one another. If they are, this recognition can significantly increase marketing complexity. Should the recognition that markets differ from one another affect the company's approach to marketing and media?

A company's marketing problems and opportunities vary from market to market. Sometimes market performance can be explained by population, demographics and lifestyles, consumption rates of the product category, brand sales rates, competitive activity, brand distribution, trade relationships, or even the cost of doing business. For example, a geographic market with a large Hispanic population may be growing, while sales in an adjacent market may be dropping like a rock due to population declines or growth in competitive activity. Examples of ways in which market areas can differ significantly from one another include all these and many more.

- Size of market and brand sales
- Economic growth or decline, unemployment rates
- Industry and brand sales volume and trends
- Brand distribution/availability
- Consumption rate of the product category
- Consumption rate of the brand
- Competitors & marketing activity
- Demographics of consumers/trends
- Consumer awareness and product preferences
- Lifestyles and activities of consumers
- Effectiveness of brand's sales force or dealer organization

- Trade relationships
- Highly desirable media and promotion availabilities
- Media cost efficiencies (vary significantly by market)

Table 11-1 is a simple depiction of three small to mid-sized market profiles and the USA profile. The comparison demonstrates how markets can differ from one another and from the US average.

Table 11-1.—Geographic Market Comparisons

Characteristic	USA	Bakersfield	Westchester	Syracuse
Adults (000)	200,000.0	432.0	701.8	758.6
% US	100.0	0.2	0.4	0.4
Category Sales (M)	$500,000.0	$1,200.0	$1900.0	$2100.0
Sales Per Capita	$2.50	$2.78	$2.71	$2.77
Index to US	100	111	109	110
Brand Sales (M)	$50,000.0	$150.0	$400.0	$145.0
Sales/Per Capita	$0.25	$0.35	$0.57	$0.19
Index to US	100	140	228	76
Market Share	10%	12.5%	21%	6.9%
Distribution	85%	88%	90%	68%
Awareness	43%	60%	75%	35%
Consideration	20%	30%	40%	15%
Median Age	45	47	51	49
HHI $75K+	26%	20%	48%	23
Hispanic	13%	43%	17%	3%
Bible Reading	25%	33%	12%	15%
Fishing	29%	32%	15%	29%
Share of Voice	15%	20%	25%	12%
Television CPM	$20.00	$15.00	$18.00	$26.00

Note how category sales rates in the three selected markets are somewhat above average, while per capita brand sales rates are high in Bakersfield and Westchester but low in Syracuse. Awareness, consideration, distribution, and share of voice (SOV) are bigger problems in Syracuse than in the other markets. There is also income disparity, with more than twice the percentage of Westchester residents making $75K.

Question: What do these data suggest
for strategic geographic media planning?

Global Philosophy

Some marketers believe in a global communications strategy. The notion of a global strategy is that *one strategy* should be implemented in every country or market. However, if needed, the execution of the strategy could allow tweaks in specifics of language, cultural cues, or media weights. Those who believe in communicating the same way everywhere support the primary use of national media.

Here's an example of a global strategy executed in the United States. A major automotive company heavily advertised full-sized pickup trucks on network television. The commercials featured Texas cowboys and showed the trucks in rugged use in the Texas environment. This advertising aired in New York as well as all other markets in the country. In New York, the incidence of pickup truck buying is about 30 per cent of the national average—and the pickups that are purchased are used by tradesmen (e.g., plumbers, carpenters) in their businesses. The creative director believed that, among truck prospects, the commercial would play as well in New York as in Texas. Do you think this was the right strategy?

Market-by-Market Philosophy

Other marketers believe that the differences in marketing situations from market to market should be addressed individually. In this scenario, each DMA would have its own customized marketing communications plan, taking into account market-by-market differences like market and brand sales rates, trade and dealer organizations, population demographics and lifestyles, and media costs. In addition, a market-by-market approach lends itself to identifying with the community, capitalizing on uniquely local media and promotion opportunities—such as the local news or the high school hockey or basketball tournaments.

Some companies have regional marketing organizations to plan and implement market-by-market regional marketing programs. Regional management makes decisions about the marketing in a region—product mixes, promotions, spending, communications plans—and coordinates the regional marketing plans with local retailers.

The downside of this approach is likely to be some loss in media efficiencies. In addition, market-by-market planning is much more labor intensive than creating one national plan.

Think Global, Act Local

A third philosophy represents a blending of the global and market-by-market philosophies. *Think Global, Act Local* is based on the belief that a company or brand can have a central strategy that still needs to be adapted to local market situations. This philosophy retains a degree of national advertising and spending to improve media efficiencies and presence in selected national media properties. In addition, there is a local market component sufficient to address local marketing issues.

In this approach, it is important that media and creative plans be integrated. In the above truck-advertising example, an alternative could have been to run a different creative execution in New York, one with the same message strategy but executed in a way that would engage New Yorkers.

GEOGRAPHIC MARKET DEFINITIONS

Media cover specific geographic areas, so you'll need to know some of the key *geographic market definitions*. Based on the situation analysis and the marketing objectives and strategy, you must identify the geographic priorities for where you want your advertising messages to be seen and with what frequency in each market. Based on this, you can decide whether to use national, regional, local market, or micro market media to reach the designated target markets.

Global/Worldwide

Marketing strategies and advertising media may be geared to reaching global or worldwide audiences. In addition to international media, the Internet has opened the door for even small businesses to compete in the global marketplace.

National

Many companies and brands consider themselves *national* because they have distribution and sales throughout the country. Those companies may decide that their media should be purchased to provide national exposure. Network or cable television or national magazines are examples of ways an advertiser can achieve national exposure.

The marketing situation of national brands, however, is seldom so simple as to conclude that their advertising should be 100 per cent national. What if there is higher per capita product consumption in certain markets? Or more competition in other markets? Or distribution in stores is high in some markets and low in others? In other words, many national brands may decide that to address their marketing situation appropriately, their media plan needs to include a mix of national media as well as additional marketing support in major markets such as those identified in the following illustration.

Which Geographic Markets?
Identify High Potential Markets Across the Country

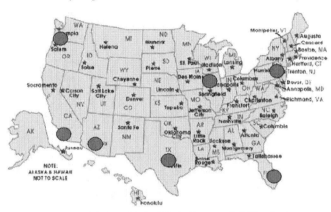

Figure 11-1.—U.S. High Potential Markets

Regional

Some companies do business only in certain regions of the country such as the Northeast or Southwest. Some specialty brands, like salsas, sell and market in only one or two regions of the country. These are known as *regional brands*. Some regional brands, of course, have aspirations to expand their sales and eventually become national brands.

National companies also often organize themselves into sales/marketing regions that are geographically defined by the company. One auto company had six marketing/sales regions: Northeast, North Central, South Central, Southeast, Southwest, and West.

Companies may use state, DMA, or sales territory boundaries for their regions. Each region is likely to be headed by a regional manager, sales manager, or marketing manager. These companies are likely to have a regional sales and/or marketing organization and to track business performance region by region.

Some companies allocate marketing dollars by region. Regional marketing dollars usually target the largest DMAs in the region. Dollars may also be used to motivate the company's sales force and/or retail trade in these markets, or used as *push* to gain distribution.

Advertising, promotion, and/or other marketing communications may be utilized in these regions. Marketing communications decision makers may work in the *central office* or in the regions, depending on the company.

Designated Market Areas (DMAs)

One of the most important local market definitions is the *Designated Market Area (DMA)*. Nielsen Media Research periodically conducts county TV viewing studies to determine which stations the households in a county watch the most. Nielsen then classifies together all the counties that do the majority of their viewing to particular *home market* stations.

For example, all of the counties in the Chicago DMA do the majority of their viewing to Chicago TV stations. Every county in the U.S. is assigned to one of 210 DMAs. DMAs usually include many counties because television stations cover large areas.

Designated Market Areas (DMA)

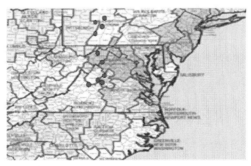

Figure 11-2.—Designated Market Areas

Most consumer goods/services marketers use DMAs as their standard market definition and organize all of their pertinent marketing data by DMA—population statistics, industry and brand sales data, competitive data, budgets,—so that they can perform important market analyses using a single database. Business to business advertisers would not find DMAs of much value unless their customers use DMA market definitions.

Metro Areas (MSAs)

MSAs, or *metropolitan survey areas* (*metro areas*), are often used in media planning, especially for media whose coverage area is smaller than TV's. Radio stations, newspapers, and outdoor advertising are often planned by metro area. This is important because many large DMAs contain more than one MSA.

Other Geographic Concepts

In syndicated research, consumer demographics also describe consumers in other terms that describe where they live. A.C. Nielsen classifies all of the counties in the U.S. by population size. For example, *Size-A* counties are located in the 25 largest *metro areas*, while *Size-C* and *Size-D* counties represent smaller population areas.

Table 11-2.—County Size

County Size	% US	Description
A	42	All counties in 25 largest MSAs
B	27	Other counties with 150,000+ pop.
C	16	Other counties with 40,000+ pop.
D	15	All remaining/smaller towns & rural
Total	100	Entire country

Additional consumer insight is gained by understanding where consumers live within DMAs. In addition to county size, consumers are also described in syndicated research sources according to whether they live in central cities, the suburbs, or outside the metro area.

RETAIL TRADING AREAS

Most retail businesses draw the majority of their customers from a finite geographic area generally called the *Retail Trading Area (RTA)*.

Understanding the geography of a retail trading area is vital to maximizing media effectiveness. Typically, a retail business realizes up to 50% or more of its business from consumers within a 3-5 mile radius of the business.

Almost half of total advertising spending is local, and local retailers account for the majority of local spending. Developing a cost effective media plan for local advertisers can be challenging because, in most cases, small geographic areas surrounding the retailer's business must be targeted, limiting media options.

For example, radio may not be a viable option because it covers MSAs, not RTAs. On the other hand, local cable systems, zoned editions of daily newspapers, suburban newspapers, and direct mail can better zero in on the retailer's trading area at a premium in cost efficiency.

What happens to a retailer's ROI if 80% of the marketing or media expenditure reaches people who are outside the trading area? Unless the retailer's merchandise is unique or highly specialized, it's hard to get people to travel large distances to the store. There is little incentive for a customer to travel 75 miles to a Chevy dealer when there are three other Chevy dealers offering competitive deals within a few miles of the customer's home.

Recall the small-town auto dealer described in the Preface who purchased an extensive schedule on a major radio station, wasting about 95% of the expenditure because 95% of the station's large-market audience was outside the dealer's trading area.

In the example depicted by Figure 11-3, the retailer obtains 50-80% of sales from a small central area surrounding the business, another 15-20% from the next circular layer, and the balance in small amounts from a large area surrounding the business.

Typical Trading Area

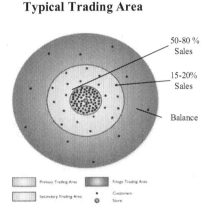

Figure 11-3.—Trading Area

One study estimated the distribution of sales for auto dealerships by traveling distance. It demonstrates the point that even auto buyers (who are willing to travel farther than they might for more routine purchases) primarily purchase close to home.

- 55% of dealership sales occur to consumers within 5 miles
- 83% of dealership sales occur to consumers within 10 miles
- 90% of dealership sales occur to consumers within 15 miles

Clearly, sales performance begins to deteriorate about 5 miles from the dealership.

Trading areas are shrinking as today's consumers are traveling shorter distances to purchase most goods. This means that a retailer's business is becoming more localized and closer to the store. A successful retailer, therefore, may increase market share in the *Primary Trading Area* (inner circle), while losing share in the outer perimeters. Buyers tend to travel further to shop at large regional malls visit or to unique niche businesses with little competition.

The finite, nearby geographic area from which most brick and mortar retailers draw a disproportionate share of their business is defined by customers deciding how far they are willing to travel.

A retail trading area's geography is influenced by several factors:

- Location—the trading area will be larger if the store is in a regional mall than if it is an independent location in an area of lower population
- Uniqueness of business
- Level and location of competition
- Surrounding geography and topography such as mountains, rivers, or railroad tracks
- Compelling short-term reasons to visit the business—great purchase incentives or offers that make it worthwhile for a consumer to travel

To define a particular trading area, the retailer can collect customers' zip codes at check out or purchase. Sales and population can be correlated by zip code.

A costly mistake some retail businesses make is placing their advertising in media that cover areas far beyond where they do business. For example, a local business runs one page per week in the daily newspaper of a large market. The full run cost per page to the advertiser is $15,000 ($780,000 annually). The newspaper has a total circulation of 350,000, of which 70,000 (20% of the total circulation) is distributed within the business' primary trading area ($156,000 worth) and the $600,000 balance falls outside the primary trading area, for all practical purposes, a waste of $444,000.

NATIONAL VS. LOCAL MEDIA

Most media offer a lot of geographic flexibility. Most can be used nationally to cover the entire country, regionally to cover a whole region, or locally to cover individual DMAs or MSAs. Other media focus on micro-markets, geodemographic areas, or zip code clusters within DMAs.

As Table 11-3 shows, broadcast and cable television can be purchased nationally or locally, as can radio and magazines. CPC (cost per click) can target any conceivable geographic area—from worldwide to a single zip code. Newspapers and outdoor can be purchased in whatever and as many markets are desired. Publicity, events, and most other forms of marketing communication can also be conducted in any geographic configuration.

Table 11-3.—Geographic Media Availabilities

Medium	National	Regional	DMA	Zip Codes
Television	Network	Sometimes	Spot/Stations	No
Television	Cable Nets.	No	Interconnects	Cable Systems
Radio	Networks	Regional networks	Spot/Stations	No
Magazines	Natl Edition	Regl. Eds.	DMA edition	No
Newspapers	By market	By market	Dailies/other	Inserts, supplements
Internet	CPC	CPC	CPC	CPC
Outdoor	By market	By market	By market	Neighborhoods
Direct Mail	Yes	Yes	Yes	Yes
PR	Yes	Yes	Yes	Yes

National Media

Here is a general summary of the principal advantages and disadvantages of national media for a national advertiser.

Advantages of National Media

- More cost efficient than local media (lower CPMs)
- Better ad/commercial positioning opportunities
- Easier to execute and monitor (a few media contracts vs. hundreds of local media contracts)
- Greater availability of premium media vehicles

Disadvantages of National Media

- Not targeted: can't reasonably target individual DMAs with different TRP levels, products, or creative
- Uneven media weight delivery by DMA: under delivery (TRPS) in major markets, over delivery in small markets
- Minimal budget flexibility, minimal cancellation options
- Network costs spiraling out of control
- Local media can target DMAs

214

Some advertisers prefer to use national media primarily because it is more cost efficient (lower CPM) than local media. In general, the more targeted a medium is, the higher the general CPM (based on total audience) will be. There is always a tradeoff between cost efficiency and targeting or communications effectiveness. You have to figure out if the higher cost is worth the ability to target.

Local Media

Local media are geographically targetable which permits advertisers to vary media weight levels, product focus, creative/message, and timing. In addition, the cancellation options available in local media usually offer more budget flexibility to the advertiser in case priorities and plans change.

Advantages of Local Media

- Target regions, DMAs, or micro-markets
- Greater message relevance because media, audience, and creative are all targeted
- Potential for increased engagement with the audience
- Greater budgetary flexibility due to more flexible cancellation options (in case an advertiser finds it necessary to cancel a schedule)

Disadvantages of Local Media

- Usually less cost efficient than national media
- More cluttered advertising environment
- Ad/commercial positioning may result in lower recall
- Complexity of many plans and budget allocations
- More work and logistics for agency

GEOGRAPHIC MARKET ANALYSIS

The purpose of geographic media marketing analysis is to identify marketing problems or opportunities on a market-by-market basis. Some marketing problems, like low awareness or negative product perceptions, can be addressed with increased advertising exposure, while a poor product or weak distribution cannot be solved by marketing communications alone. There are at least eleven key dimensions of geographic market analysis:

1. Size of market
2. Market & sales trends
3. Category development
4. Brand development
5. CDI/BDI Matrix
6. Product preferences
7. Consumer profiles
8. Competitive development
9. Competitive activity
10. Trader/dealer considerations
11. Media cost efficiencies by market

Size of Market

The first priority of nearly every marketer is to support and maintain existing sales. Therefore, many companies want to supplement spending in the markets with largest current sales volume. Advertisers may set a minimum size criterion of 0.5-1% of population or brand sales, the rationale being that any market receiving supplemental marketing support should be large enough to make a difference on bottom line sales.

These marketers want to *protect* their customer and sales base. However, focusing only on the largest markets may exclude other DMAs with greater growth potential.

Market and Sales Trends

The second analysis typically looks at long term market and brand trends in each DMA. What is the rate of population and market growth or decline in the DMAs? How do those trends compare to the brand's trends? Momentum is as important to marketers as it is to politicians. Momentum means that you must be doing something right because the trend lines are going in the right directions. Therefore, momentum could be an important criterion for market selection and weighting.

Category Development (CDI)

The *Category Development Index* (*CDI*) is a measure of the per capita purchasing of a product category in a DMA compared to the U.S. average. The formula for calculating the CDI in a market is to divide per capita industry sales in the DMA by per capita industry sales in the total U.S. For example, if sales are $100 per household in the DMA vs. $80 in the total U.S., CDI = 125 (100/80). It can be said that if a product category has an above average CDI (index above 100) in a market, the market potential is higher. For example, if baby food had a CDI of 200 in the Columbus DMA, consumers would be twice as likely to buy baby food in Columbus compared to the US average.

Brand Development (BDI)

The *Brand Development Index* (*BDI*) is a measure of the per capita purchasing of a particular brand in the product category in a DMA compared to the U.S. average. The formula for calculating the BDI is the same as the CDI formula above, except that per capita *brand sales* are used rather than per capita category sales. If a brand's per capita sales in a market is $50 compared to $100 nationally, the BDI = 50 (50/100). Obviously, since this brand is selling in this DMA at half of its national rate, the brand has a marketing problem in this DMA. What could the problem(s) be for this brand?

BDI/CDI Matrix

Once the CDIs and BDIs have been calculated for all markets (Excel spread sheet), you can begin to analyze the market situation facing your client, using a BDI/CDI matrix like this one:

BDI/CDI Matrix

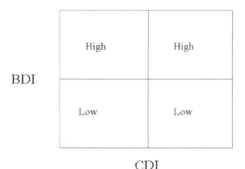

CDI

The BDI/CDI matrix helps you understand which markets may already be maxed out and which may still offer growth potential. For example, how much growth potential exists in high CDI/High BDI markets?

How much growth potential exists in low CDI/Low BDI markets? The brand already has a high market share of a market where per capita consumption is lower.

In contrast, how much growth potential may exist in large markets with a high CDI and a low BDI? What is causing the brand's relatively poor showing in a good market for the market category?

Product Preferences

Sometimes CDIs and BDIs for the total category and brand sales can help to explain a CDI/BDI situation. For example, certain types of cars and trucks, like sportside pickups, sell much better in some markets than others. The right products for the market—including the right flavors, sizes, and price points—must be available and consumers must know about them.

Consumer Profiles

Consumer profiles and brand preferences can differ dramatically by DMA. Consider the high share of market initially achieved by Japanese brand vehicles (like Toyota and Honda) in California markets like Los Angeles and San Francisco compared to the lower market shares they achieved in the Central and South regions.

When you're trying to identify the sales potential of different markets, ask whether the DMAs you're considering have a relatively high incidence of your target audience demographics, interests or activities, and geo-demographics. Do the markets in questions have an above average incidence of likely purchasers?

Competitive Development

The marketing strategy and plan should have defined desired sources of volume. Unless the category is growing, sales increases must come from the sales of competitors. Are there specific competitors who should be targeted by the brand and who are especially vulnerable?

Competitive Activity

Are the brand's marketing and spending levels in a market competitive in each DMA? The brand's share of voice—percentage of marketing messages—vs. the brand's share of market goal in a DMA can help determine whether a brand's spending level is adequate to build or maintain market share. Advertisers usually have to develop these data through surveys of the local media, combining national and local data.

Trade/Dealer Considerations

Are there issues with the retail trade or dealers that make it easier or more difficult to gain market share in a DMA? A brand should be more successful and achieve higher ROI in markets where there is a strong sales force and dealer organization in place. In contrast, it is difficult to build business with incremental marketing if the company's sales or trade organization is weak.

Media Cost Efficiencies by Market

Finally, the cost and efficiency of media in each market will have a significant effect on the plan's ROI. Are media priced cost effectively in the DMAs you have targeted? For example, television CPMs range from $5.00 in Charleston to $35.00 in a high-cost market like San Francisco. Can a sales increase in San Francisco pay out on that media cost?

GEOGRAPHIC SPENDING STRATEGIES

Geographic market analysis forms the basis for development of cost effective geographic spending strategy, often using a mix of national and local media. As you work through the following examples of common geographic spending strategies, you will see that they are defined and shaped by their objectives.

Objective: Protect Key Market Volume
Spending Strategy: Media Heavy Ups in Highest Volume Markets

This strategy places additional marketing communications weight in the brand's highest sales volume markets in order to help protect the brand's current business. Other indicators such as CDI and BDI, competitive and trade situations are secondary to actual sales volume. For example, as illustrated in the following table, a company may decide to place additional TRPS in select DMAs, with the number of TRPS varying by market.

Table 11-4.—Cost of Heavy Up Plan: Example

DMA	% US HH	Sales (000)	% Total	Total TRPS	Local Cost (000)
New York	6.8	1000	8.2	3000	$2250
Boston	2.2	400	3.3	2000	550
Philadelphia	2.7	600	4.9	2000	700
Hartford	0.6	200	1.6	1500	100
AO/Natl Media	87.9	10,000	82.0	1000	—

Table 11-4 assumes a national media base consisting of 1000 TRPS. In New York, an additional 2000 TRPS are added to the national media base, while 1000 additional TRPS were added in Boston and Philadelphia, and 500 TRPS were added in Hartford.

Objective: Spend in Relation to Sales
Spending Strategy: Allocate Resources Proportionate to Sales

As a variation on the first strategy, companies commonly allocate budgets in proportion to sales (or total market sales or other benchmark). In this example, each DMA receives a budget allocation that represents its percentage of total sales. If the total budget were $1,000,000, a market representing 10 per cent of sales would receive a budget of $100,000.

Table 11-5.—Spend in Relation to Sales: Example

DMA	% US HH	Sales (000)	% Total	Total Budget (000)*	% Total
New York	6.8	1000	8.2	$820	8.2
Boston	2.2	400	3.3	330	3.3
Philadelphia	2.7	600	4.9	490	4.9
Hartford	0.6	200	1.6	160	1.6
All Others	87.9	10,000	82.0	8200	82.0

*Based on total $10 million budget, Nat'l/local combined

Objective: Spend in Relation to Sales Potential
Spending Strategy: Weight Sales to Better Reflect Potential

This strategy weights sales by sales potential index. Weighted sales are added and each market's percentage of weighted sales becomes the percentage for determining that market's share of available funds. In the Table 11-6 example, sales potential index is defined as the average of BDI and CDI. Other methodologies may require more sophisticated weighting methodologies and calculations.

Table 11-6.—Spend in Relation to Sales Potential: Example

DMA	% US HH	% Sales	BDI	CDI	Avg. Index	Adj. % Budget	Budget (000)
New York	6.8	8.2	121	200	161	10.9	$1090
Boston	2.2	3.3	150	225	188	4.1	410
Philadelphia	2.7	4.9	182	65	124	3.3	330
Hartford	0.6	1.6	267	100	184	1.1	110
All Others	87.9	82.0	93	92	92	80.6	8060

Note: BDI and CDI averaged together to form hypothetical potential index.   Based on $10 million total budget.

Objective: Achieve Specified Reach and Frequency Goals by DMA
Spending Strategy: Plan TRPS & Media Mix to meet R/F Goals

Essentially, this strategy involves setting reach and frequency goals for target DMAs, then determining the cost of the TRPS in the desired media. This approach assumes that the planner has a rationale for the reach and frequency needed to achieve the communications goals.

Table 11-7.—Example-Based Reach & Frequency Goals

DMA	% US HH	% Sales	Reach Goal %	Freq. Goal	TRPS	Budget(000)
New York	6.8	8.2	95	25.0	2375	$3560
Boston	2.2	3.3	90	20.0	1800	990
Philadelphia	2.7	4.9	85	15.0	1275	895
Hartford	0.6	1.6	80	12.5	1000	200
All Others	87.9	82.0	75	10.0	750	14,550

Objective: Harvest Sales
Spending Strategy: Focus on High BDI/High CDI Markets

Harvesting sales is like fishing where the fish are! Sometimes a marketing objective might be to harvest sales in markets where incremental sales can be generated with minimal cost and effort. Decisions on these markets must be based on whether the markets still offer growth potential or whether they are already maxed out. Here are some criteria for selecting markets that may be harvested:

- Size—large enough to make a difference
- Above average CDI and BDI
- Solid distribution base
- Good trade relations
- Average to below average competitive activity
- Good to excellent media cost efficiencies

Objective: Market Development
Spending Strategy: Major Effort in High CDI/Low BDI Markets

Development markets are high potential markets where the category sells at an above average rate. However, the brand's share of market and BDI is below average. These markets could offer very high growth potential *if* the brand's marketing problems could be solved.

You can calculate how many more sales would be possible if the brand could manage to raise its BDI up to the average CDI. If BDI is 80 and the CDI is 120, the brand would need to increase sales 40 per cent to achieve a 120 BDI. If the brand has sales of 100,000 units and BDI of 80, raising the brand's sales rate to the market average (120) BDI would generate an additional 50,000 units!

When you begin market development efforts it is essential to figure out why the brand's BDI is so low. Is the problem something that marketing communications can address, such as low awareness? Is it consumer perceptions? Price competitiveness? Distribution or trade relations? Competitive share of voice?

Success in market development usually requires a long-term strategy and a heavy investment. Does the brand have the will and the resources to solve the problems that are choking sales growth?

Objective: Maintain Low Potential Markets
Spending Strategy: Minimize Resources in Low Potential Markets

Most brands have a number of markets that are too small to generate much additional volume or are already over performing in a low potential market. While a brand does not want to waste resources in low potential markets, at the same time the brand does not want to lose the book of business it currently enjoys in these markets. Here are two examples of markets—both in Low CDI situations—that do generate sales but may not offer much incremental sales potential.

High BDI/Low CDI Markets

In high BDI/low CDI markets, the brand is already outperforming the market. The brand enjoys a high share of market in a market where consumer demand for the category is below average. Perhaps the brand has unusually high consumer awareness and acceptance or perhaps there is little competition. The market may not offer much opportunity for improving sales, but the brand certainly wants to keep the sales it currently enjoys. It is possible that some markets in this category are very large— like New York, Chicago, and Los Angeles, which need heavier investment spending to help protect the volume.

> *Questions: How important are high BDI/Low CDI*
> *markets to the brand's sales base?*
> *Is there opportunity for growth in these markets?*

Low BDI/Low CDI Markets

These markets (or zip clusters) show below-average purchasing rates for the brand as well as the product category (low BDI/low CDI). Such markets are often called *skinny pigs*! Unless these skinny pigs are very large from a sales volume standpoint, or there are other factors at play that indicate potential for incremental sales, you may decide to recommend minimum spending/media weights necessary to *maintain* the existing business.

SUMMARY

Is the USA one homogeneous market or many heterogeneous markets? This is a core question affecting media planning for every client.

Morris Hite says that all advertising is local. So is every sale local. Every purchase of every product or service takes place at a local store or Internet vendor. Every new car sold is purchased by a person who lives somewhere local, consumes media locally, shops local auto dealerships, and ultimately purchases from a specific local dealor.

Because marketing situations can vary substantially by DMA, it is crucially important for you to understand marketing.

In Chapter 11, you have learned about geography:

- *Geographic market definitions used in media planning*
- *Geography's significance in media planning*
- *Geographic marketing philosophies*
- *Geographic media availabilities*
- *Geographic market analysis*
- *Geographic spending objectives and strategies*

Experience suggests that more marketing problems and opportunities reside in local markets than elsewhere. Unfortunately, retailers—often those who can least afford to be extravagant—are easily convinced to buy advertising that goes outside their trading area, resulting in poor ROI.

Geographic analysis and its strategic implications have meaningful and measurable impact on your client's business. Whether your client is a large national marketer or a small local retailer, the principles of geography are the same and important.

12. TIMING & SCHEDULING

You win battles by knowing the enemy's timing and using a timing which the enemy does not expect.

–*Miyamoto Musashi*, Japanese Martial Arts Master,
One of the world's greatest swordsmen, 1584-1645

Timing is as important to the communications effectiveness of a media plan as Miyamoto Musashi teaches that it is to battle. Timing can surprise. Timing can outflank the competition. Timing can give a brand a head start in awareness. Timing can remind consumers who are ready to buy.

Timing can also be a two edged sword—a strategy used to capture a competitive advantage. It can even lead to a debacle if the entire media budget is spent before a new product has achieved good distribution.

The way the media budget is allocated over the planning period— whether the period is a full year or a quarter—affects how many target consumers have the opportunity to see your advertising messages and how often they are exposed to it.

There are many marketing and media considerations to weigh when determining the optimum allocation of resources by day or by week or by month. This chapter reviews important timing considerations, then reviews scheduling options.

MEDIA TIMING CONSIDERATIONS

When to advertise? There are a number marketing and media factors that you should consider when allocating advertising budgets and exposure throughout your planning period. Timing considerations include industry sales seasonality, brand sales seasonality, competitive activity, and special marketing tasks such as new product introductions or promotions, media opportunities, and efficiencies.

Industry Sales

Some advertisers allocate their advertising budgets *in relation to industry sales* for the product category. Under this advertising spending philosophy, if 25% of industry-wide widget sales occur in the January-March period, 25% of the advertising budget would be allocated during the period. Brands may utilize this allocation philosophy if they believe their own sales do not parallel market potential and if they believe that the purpose of their advertising is to generate an immediate response.

Table 12-1.—Advertising Expenditures vs. Industry Sales by Quarter

Quarter	% Industry Sales	% Ad Spend	Index to Industry Sales
JFM	25	25	100
AMJ	35	25	100
JAS	10	10	100
OND	40	40	100
Total	100	100	100

Brand Sales

Some advertisers prefer to allocate their spending through the year in relation to brand sales or a composite of industry and brand sales. Table 12-2 provides an example of allocating a budget in relation to an average of both industry and brand sales. The brand sells at a rate significantly below average in the first two quarters and at a higher rate in the fourth quarter, showing that this brand's sales patterns are an aberration compared to industry sales patterns. Using a composite of both industry and brand sales will flatten the brand's spending rate somewhat.

Table 12-2.—Brand Sales by Quarter vs. Advertising Expenditures

Quarter	% Industry Sales	% Brand Sales	% Ad Spend	Index to Brand Sales
JFM	25	18	21	111
AMJ	25	17	21	124
JAS	10	5	8	160
OND	40	60	50	83
Total	100	100	100	100

A brand's sales may trail or exceed industry sales rates by month due to competitive or brand advertising and promotional activities or because of other seasonal aberrations.

Competitive Activity

Competitive activity is a third factor affecting timing of advertising media. When does competitive spending historically occur by month, week, or time of day? Are there specific competitors that you need to outflank or at least match? Do you anticipate any atypical competitive spending—such as to support new introductions or promotions? Table 12-3 provides an estimate of competitive TRPS by month. What are the possible implications of these data for Brand X?

Table 12-3.—Seasonality of Competitive Activity, Spending or TRPS

Month	Competitor A	Competitor B	Competitor C	Total
January	100	150	500	750
February	100	250	300	850
March	100	500	600	1200
April	100	300	400	800
May	200	1500	500	2200
June	100	200	300	600
Balance	800	1500	1800	4100

Reach & Frequency Goals

Many advertisers set minimum and maximum reach and frequency goals for different time intervals. The expenditure during a given period would be the amount needed to achieve the GRP goal.

Table 12-4.—Avg. 4-Week Reach & Frequency Goals

Goal	JFM	AMJ	JAS	OND
Reach	70%	80%	60%	90%
Frequency	5.0	6.0	3.3	10.0
TRPS	350	480	200	900

New Product Introductions

New product introductions generally receive heavy, front loaded advertising and marketing support in order to generate initial awareness and trial. A typical new product introduction schedule might look something like Figure 12-1.

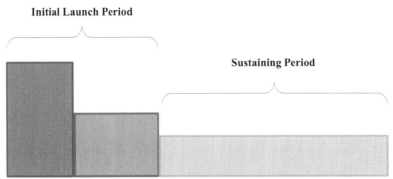

Figure 12-1.—New Product Introduction Timing of TRPS

If the new product has enough availability (distribution), very heavy media weight levels are used at the beginning of the launch period, and then the levels are reduced until they reach *sustaining* TRP levels for the new product. The theory is that the first stage of the launch must create awareness of the new product, trial will follow, and then repurchase must be sustained.

The trickiest timing issue on new product introductions usually relates to availability of the product. Is there enough distribution to have a successful launch? What do we do if media purchase commitments have been made and we are not ready to pull the trigger?

Less important new product launches (like line extensions of existing products) usually do not receive such heavy incremental support.

Promotion Support

Marketers often run special promotions in order to generate a short-term spike in sales. For example, a manufacturer or retailer may offer short-term purchase incentives (e.g., a low sale price, cash back) to motivate new customers to *buy now*, or previous customers to move their purchases forward in order to take advantage of the special offer.

To help ensure that consumers know about the promotion, you can heavy up media weight before and during the promotion. This is diagrammed in Figure 12-2.

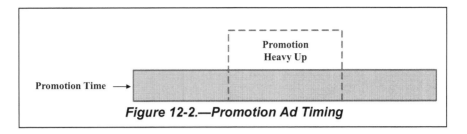

Figure 12-2.—Promotion Ad Timing

Budget Constraints

Budget availability for advertising/communications can affect timing. If the budget is adequate to address the marketing tasks, then sufficient media weight should be available. However, if the budget is inadequate to provide year round effective media support, you may have to focus your spending in the most important months.

Availability & Distribution

Product availability and distribution often pose a dilemma for marketers and media planners alike. It is especially common for product availability or distribution to be delayed for new products. Perhaps there are production problems or shortages of parts or ingredients. Or perhaps the brand has not yet achieved its distribution goals.

If a brand is largely unavailable to consumers, and won't be available for a while, should spending be delayed or used to attempt to build awareness and trade support for later? Sometimes demand exceeds supply or the manufacturer has limited production capacity, which calls into question whether precious dollars should be spent when, short term, there is inadequate supply, but long term, supply may even exceed demand.

Question: You need to build brand awareness
in the face of production and distribution problems.
Would you spend now or wait?

Seasonal Products

Almost all products and brands have seasonality in their sales patterns—higher percentages of consumers buy more at some times than at others. Some brands' sales are highly seasonal. Certain jewelry and gift

229

items may generate upwards of 60% of their annual sales in December (thanks to Santa's generous hand).

Some brands that want to advertise continuously may run heavy-ups in the *colder months* that lead the purchase of seasonal goods and services such as winter tires, summer vacations, or outdoor personal products. Products that are heavily used on weekends may concentrate weight on Thursday and Friday. Shoulders are diagrammed in Figure 12-3.

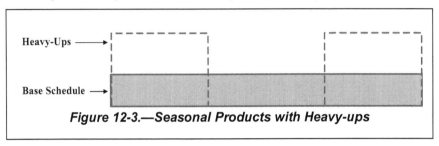

Figure 12-3.—Seasonal Products with Heavy-ups

Should Advertising Lead Sales?

Some advertisers seem to subscribe to the philosophy of *run an ad, get a sale right now.* However, others believe that the timing of their advertising should lead sales because purchase consideration builds over time. Advertisers of considered purchase products and services particularly believe that their advertising needs to lead actual sales. These advertisers typically believe in media models similar to the Purchase Funnel of Chapter 9, where consumer purchases are a result of a process of first acquiring awareness, then gaining purchase consideration, achieving favorable opinion and purchase intention, and then shopping.

> *Question: Now consider the competitive fast food business. Thinking of McDonalds, Burger King, and Hardees, would you say their advertising is intended to generate immediate purchases or trying to build conditions favorable to future purchase?*

Media Cost Efficiency

Broadcast media cost efficiencies fluctuate significantly by time of year due to fluctuations in supply and demand. The first and third quarters are normally the most cost efficient periods—meaning that CPMs and CPPs will normally be much lower. The reason, of course, is that there is lower demand following the conclusion of the holiday shopping season.

Advertisers can capitalize on this pricing opportunity if there is no compelling marketing reason not to.

In contrast, during the second and fourth quarters, prices rise significantly. Therefore, those marketers who advertise a little more heavily in the first and third quarters and a little more lightly in the second and fourth quarters will get more advertising exposure for the money.

Time of Day

In certain marketing situations, tactically, *time of day* to run advertising can also be an important consideration. Consider an interesting Campbell's Soup experience. Campbell's experienced a decline in soup sales and conducted research to discover the cause. They found that, while households had plenty of soup on hand in the pantry, mothers were not serving it to their children for lunch. Soup somehow lost top of mind awareness as a quick nourishing lunch for children.

Campbell's developed radio advertising to remind mothers to serve soup for lunch. The media plan used late-morning radio to reach mothers soon before lunch was prepared, and that problem was quickly solved.

SUMMARY

When you reach your target audience can determine the effectiveness of your media plan. You have learned from this chapter that timing throughout the year, as well as the pattern of scheduling, can have a significant effect on the impact of your media plan.

For timing decisions, you must consider factors including seasonality of industry vs. brand sales, competitive activity, media efficiencies, product availability and distribution, and whether to lead purchasing.

When possible, take advantage of the tactic of surprise! For example, maybe your #1 competitor has established a predictable spending pattern with an October heavy-up promoting a clearance sale.

How might you use timing to pre-empt this advertiser's attempt to pre-empt your own sales efforts?

13. A BUDGET TO GROW BY

If he had been asked how much a company should spend in advertising, what do you think John Wannamaker would have said?

Indeed, how much <u>should</u> a company spend in advertising and/or other marketing communications to maintain or increase market share? If you need a firm answer, you are going to be unsatisfied. It depends.

On the other hand, if you'd like to jump in and try to figure it out, you have an interesting challenge. Unfortunately, budgets are often a function of what was spent last year plus or minus a percentage for next year. This is convenient for financial analysts, but not necessarily good for marketers trying to grow the business.

This chapter will present the conventional wisdom on three ways to develop a budget: based on industry advertising-to-sales ratio, the task method, and share of voice vs. share of market goals

DETERMINING THE BUDGET

Your first budgeting assignment is to establish how much money you have to spend on advertising and marketing communications. There are several ways to do that.

Spending per Unit

Probably the most used method of determining the budget is on the basis of spending per unit. For example, if a company historically spent $5.00 per case on advertising and promotion, and their forecast was for 1,000,000 cases to be sold in 2011, the budget would be $5,000,000 (1,000,000 cases x $5.00). This approach might make sense to the company's accountants, but it doesn't take into account the marketing tasks that must be addressed, the level of competitive activity, budgetary needs for new product launches or promotions, or any of the other factors that actually affect a budget.

Advertising/Sales Ratio (A/S Ratio)

The *Advertising to Sales Ratio* (*A/S Ratio*) is one of the most popular methods of arriving at an advertising budget. The A/S ratio for your industry will help you benchmark your spending against industry norms.

If a particular industry spends on average 5% of sales on advertising, your budget would be 5% of your sales, before any adjustments you might make to that average ratio. (Do you have reasons to be higher or lower than average?) Knowing your A/S ratio can help you spend proportionately to competitors, although your particular situation may call for spending more or less. Recognizing that growth requires investment, the decision is ultimately yours to evaluate.

There are two ways to arrive at a budget using A/S ratios. One is to use current year or last year's sales as the base. The other is to use your projected sales as a base. Assume last year's sales were $500,000 and your category's A/S ratio is 5%. Your budget would be $25,000 ($500,000 x .05). If you were projecting sales to increase to $600,000 with a little help from more advertising, your budget would be $30,000 ($600,000 x .05).

The following table provides some general benchmarks. More detail can be found at www.dnb.com/us

Table 13-1.—Advertising/Sales Ratios in Selected Sectors

Sector	A/S Ratio	% Sales Change
Consumer Products	6.7	3.9
Health Care	4.3	3.8
Retail	1.8	5.4
Financial Services	1.2	7.1
Trans./Travel	2.0	NA
Services	3.6	10.0

Source: Schoenfeld Estimates, 2007

Even if you arrive at a budget by other means, comparing it to what your budget would be if based on your A/S ratio would provide a good logic check.

Task Method

In an ideal world, you would be able to calculate accurately how much it would cost to address each of the marketing or media tasks emanating from your marketing plan. The total cost of the plans needed to address a company's various tasks would constitute the budget. However, to establish a budget using this method, you have to have clearly defined tasks, an accurate method for determining the plan, and an accurate method of estimating the cost of accomplishing each task.

Here are some simplified examples of how you might apply the task method.

Example 1

Assume you sell an impulse purchase product available in grocery and mass merchandising stores. You believe Recency Planning is the correct approach for your business. Therefore, you set a media objective of reaching 50% of your target every weeknight. That projects to 250 TRPS per week, approximately 13,000 TRPS per year. If the cost per TRP in your market averages $20 for the media you want, your budget would total $260,000. How does that budget compare to a budget developed by using the A/S ratio?

Example 2

Assume you sell a considered purchase product such as computers. You believe you need monthly effective reach in traditional media and a heavy search presence on the Internet (CPC). You calculate that you will need about 400 TRPS per month to reach your target audience effectively with traditional media. That totals 4800 TRPS per year at a cost per TRP of $20 in your market. For your media mix, your traditional media budget would be $96,000. In addition, generating 25,000 clicks on Google and Yahoo! will cost another $25,000 at an average of $1.00 per click. Your total budget would be $121,000 ($96,000 +$25,000).

Example 3

Assume you have two key communications objectives and strategies for next year: (1) improve your image by implementing a PR and institutional advertising program, and (2) generate weekly store traffic with sales, offers, and incentives communicated by mail and in the newspaper. The media and PR plan for the image-building program will cost $70,000, and the weekly traffic building mail/newspaper media plan will cost $150,000. The total budget would be $220,000.

Share of Voice vs. Share of Market Goal

The third approach is to set a *Share of Voice (SOV)* goal in relation to your *Share of Market* goal for next year and farther down the road. A great deal of research has found a high correlation between share of voice and share of market (see Chapter 9). You will recall that SOV is the percentage of category ad dollars your product or business represents.

SOV theory says that *to maintain market share, share of voice should equal share of market;* if your share of market is 10%, your share of voice should therefore be 10%.

SOV theory would also say that in order to grow market share next year, share of voice should significantly lead the share of market goal. For example, if your current share of market is 10% , and your objective is to grow it to 12%, your share of voice may need to be 15-20%: in theory, one of every five messages exposed to the target market needs to be one of *yours* in order to get the increased Share of Mind necessary to drive increased market share.

To determine your current SOV, you have to call sales reps from the relevant media vehicles in your geographic trading area and business segment, and have them ask the media how much each of your competitors spent with them during the relevant period. In most cases, the media will cooperate, and you can estimate some dollars to fill in the gaps. Once you have all of the data, you can compile a table similar to this Table 13-2.

Table 13-2.—Industry Expenditures vs. Share of Voice

Competitor	Ad Expenditures	SOV
A	$30,000	30%
B	50,000	50
C	20,000	20
Total	$100,000	100%

ALLOCATING THE BUDGET

Regardless of the method you use to arrive at your total media budget, you will have to decide how to allocate and monitor it most effectively among various forms of marketing communications, products, departments, and weeks or months of the year.

Nobody can anticipate everything that could happen over the course of the year. (Yogi Berra: *We don't know what we don't know.*) We suggest retaining a contingency reserve in your budget to address unforeseen problems or to capitalize on great buying opportunities when they arise.

For the same reason, we also suggest that you maintain flexibility in your budget. You need to be able to reallocate dollars if the marketplace warrants it.

Finally, the ideal budget development process would utilize all of the methods we have briefly outlined so that you can better judge the rationality of the results.

SUMMARY

Chapter 13 has demonstrated that advertising budget development is far from a perfect science, especially when it comes to establishing a budget. You have learned that most budget forecasting methods look backwards—such as spending per unit or A/S ratios—and do not comprehend what budgets should be going forward. That means that historical mistakes in budget setting are simply perpetuated.

Other methods, like the Task Method, look forward but you have seen that they lack good metrics for determining the costs associated with different tasks, e.g., how much it will cost to maintain awareness and consideration among purchase intenders or how much it will cost successfully to launch a new product.

If you use the Share of Voice vs. Share of Market model, you can rely on the proven relationship between SOV and SOM at the brand level. This model, of course, requires you to have accurate metrics for both competitive share of voice and share of market.

Besides some specific budgeting techniques and some perspectives for evaluating budgets, Chapter 13 has taught you that good budgets, like so much of what you're learning, are a matter of informed judgment.

14. THE TOOLS OF IMC
The single biggest problem in communication is the illusion that it has taken place.

–George Bernard Shaw

Businesses use a variety of marketing communications to ensure some form of consistent communication with consumers. Companies use different communications tools to accomplish different purposes. Examples of marketing communications tools this chapter will review include:

- *Advertising*
- *Direct marketing*
- *Sales promotion,*
- *Product placement*
- *Telemarketing*
- *Sponsorships and events*
- *Public relations & publicity*
- *Internet: email, display ads, mobile*
- *Social media*
- *Word of mouth/buzz*
- *Other non media*

The essential process of marketing communication is sending messages intended to bring potential consumers closer to purchase. If the communication is appropriate, there is an enhanced possibility that the potential consumer will buy your product or service.

Integrated marketing communications utilizes the right mix of communications to accomplish your objectives. When traditional advertising is the most cost effective way to promote your business, you use it. When it is not cost-effective, especially if you have a small budget, you choose other tools that better address your needs.

Integrated marketing communication is more than just aggregating the "right" forms of communication or media. It is also, literally, integrating them; assuring that the messages, themes, look and feel, and production values are consistent, coordinated, and synergistic within and across the integrated media. All communications must sing from the same music.

To integrate successfully the best selections from the menu of communication and media forms, you need to command each of the tools you will encounter in Chapter 14, as well as a process we call task matching that evaluates and integrates these tools in IMC strategies.

ADVERTISING

Advertising is paid communication; the sponsor maintains control of its content. In 2007, total advertising expenditures surpassed $300 billion in media such as television, radio, magazines, newspapers, outdoor, Yellow Pages, direct mail, and miscellaneous. Nearly half of advertising spending is local, although the percentage varies greatly by medium. For example, 80% of expenditures in radio are from local businesses, while the majority of TV spending is national.

Advantages of Advertising

Advertising is a communications tool used to communicate messages that the advertiser believes will be beneficial either in the long or short term. Contrary to popular opinion, except for some direct marketing or e-commerce, advertising *does not sell* goods or services. However, advertising combined with the business and product can create conditions for sales to occur. The strengths of advertising are these:

- **Control of message** content and execution
- **Control of media** utilized to deliver the message
- **Control of timing** of communication
- **Reinforcement** of current customers' purchasing behavior
- **Ability to create awareness, familiarity, or purchase consideration** of a product, brand, or business
- **Influential** in shaping consumer attitudes and product image
- **Drives traffic** by communicating a short term incentive

Disadvantages of Advertising

Advertising also has a number of disadvantages for marketers.

- **Expense.** Traditional advertising time, space, and production are expensive and unaffordable; some advertisers may need to consider non-traditional media approaches.

- **Scattershot.** Some advertising media have a limited ability to target audiences or geography in a way that is cost effective to the advertiser.
- **Difficult.** Planning and executing an effective advertising program that positions company/brand against the major advertisers requires considerable expertise.
- **Hard to measure.** Effectiveness of advertising is difficult to measure accurately, if at all.
- **Not scalable.** Effective media planning and buying requires as much expertise for a small business as for a larger business
- **Accountability.** Effectiveness is difficult to measure owing to the number of variables affecting the results.

Best Practices

Here are some criteria to keep in mind when you plan and implement an advertising campaign:

- **Integration** Make sure your advertising plan is based on your marketing strategy and extends it.
- **Specificity** Develop specific objectives. Product placement, or embedded marketing, is a form of advertisement that places branded goods or services in a context usually devoid of ads, such as a movie, the story line of a television show, or a news program.
- **Coordination** Don't expect advertising to sell by itself.
- **Focus** Determine whether your advertising has long-term (awareness, attitude, image, consideration) or short-term objectives (traffic).
- **Communication** Don't expect advertising to drive traffic unless it includes a compelling offer or reason to buy; the job of advertising is to communicate the offer effectively.
- **Precision** Don't confuse advertising with other communications tools, such as publicity.
- **Realistic expectations** Don't expect advertising to offset any deficiencies in the product, store environment, services & customer service, or pricing.

- **Test** Evaluate advertising creative and media to ensure that it is memorable, communicates the intended messages, and projects the desired image for your business.

SALES PROMOTION

While advertising is a long-term marketing tool, the purpose of sales promotion is to generate immediate sales. Sales promotion includes purchase offers and incentives to stimulate purchase, repurchase, or frequency of purchase. More money is spent on sales promotion than on advertising—over $300 billion.

Promotional offers may be communicated to consumers in traditional media, by direct mail, on or in packaging, or in the stores. Promotional incentives usually fall into one of four categories:

- **Price incentives** offer savings such as coupons, rebates, or low-interest rate offers.
- **Product sampling** can be an extremely effective trial device and can be executed in store, by mail, or at events.
- **Merchandise or gifts** may be given as a purchase incentive, like including free airfare with purchase of resort accommodations.
- **Other** incentives include games of chance, such sweepstakes, contests, and drawings.

Cross Promotion involves two or more brands or companies working together to leverage a promotion. For example, one promotional partner may offer to provide 1000 vehicles to be used in a traffic building promotion. The other partner may provide the advertising to create awareness and response to the promotion.

Advantages

Immediate Sales Sales promotion can be a powerful short-term marketing tool for large and small business.

Traffic Generation. Promotion provides an added incentive for someone in the target audience to visit a store or buy a product or service.

Disadvantages

- **High Cost** Promotional incentives can easily exceed the ad budget
- **Value Perceptions** Devalues perceptions of what brand is worth/brand equity
- **Profit Impact** The larger the percentage of product sold on deal, the greater the promotion expense and the lower the profit

Best Practices

Planning and implementing a sales promotion should generally follow a strategy that enhances rather than damages the value of the brand (brand equity).

- **Define your objectives** (trial, repurchase, frequency of purchase, increased transaction size) and design your promotion accordingly, selecting appropriate offers.
- **Make promotions measurable** so you can determine incremental sales and profitability.
- **Keep promotions brief** or a business risks harming its quality image. Do you want consumers to think your products or services are a value at full price? Think about how automotive companies have made financial incentives an expectation among consumers!
- **Use target-specific incentives** that appeal to your particular market.
- **Align promotions** with positioning and image to the greatest extent possible.
- **Coordinate promotions with other elements** of your communications: think about things like advertising to promote the promotion, free publicity, and direct mail.

PRODUCT PLACEMENT

Product placement is just what its name implies: an advertiser pays to place products in movies or television programs or Internet video. Products are *embedded* in an environment usually devoid of advertising. Typically, the product fits into the story line where it is placed. Product placement is a rapidly growing alternative to traditional advertising.

An early example of product placement was Chevy Trucks' sponsorship of a do-it-yourself (DIY) program on PBS. Each episode was devoted to a different DIY project, but Chevy trucks were always there to haul materials, and they were mentioned frequently by the cast.

Recent high profile examples of product placement include embedding FedEx into the movie *Castaway* with Tom Hanks, AOL chirping *You've Got Mail*, James Bond checking his Omega watch, Superman eating Cheerios, and Cadillac's star role in the Matrix movie chase scenes.

TiVo will enhance the role of product placement by providing product integration opportunities within or at the end of programs, where commercial messages can't be zapped!

***Branded Entertainmen*t** is a cousin to product placement. While product placement provides marketers with the opportunity to place their products in a particular production, branded entertainment involves creating an entertainment program built around a product. For example, a television series built around a Camaro that responded to voice commands and retrieved its owner from dangerous situations.

Advantages

- Product placement provides product exposure.
- Viewers cannot skip advertising that is embedded in the program.
- Product placements assure desired contents and contexts.
- Celebrities are seen preferring the product, conferring a halo effect.
- Product placement costs less than traditional advertising.
- Some research has shown positive lifts for embedded products.

Disadvantages

- Huge marketing risk; you cannot predict which productions will be successful.
- Competitor may appear (Coke vs. Pepsi) in same vehicle.
- If improperly executed, product placement could destroy the film/program and reflect poorly on the product.
- Does not address many communications objectives; projecting images of a vehicle is one thing, selling soap is another.

- Results and ROI very difficult to measure

Best Practices

- Secure brand integration first, and then get creative.
- Large brand? Get in on the ground floor and sponsor new shows still in-development.
- Finance a film or event that connects to your audience, and build an integrated marketing program around it.
- Be visible to filmmakers looking to barter for products, services, and locations. According to PQ Media, approximately 60% of product placements (by value) are in-kind (barter) deals.
- Find the right content first: online video distribution is easily scaled. Except for the content served, online video and banner advertising networks work very much the same.
- Marketers strongly prefer professionally produced content to user-generated content. While *user-generated content* (*UGC*) is popular, it has proven unattractive to most advertisers.

DIRECT MARKETING

Direct marketing is a *method of marketing or advertising whose objective is to generate a direct response from the consumer. Direct marketing* is not a medium and should not be associated exclusively with direct mail; any medium can be used for direct marketing For example, advertisers often place toll-free numbers and URLs in their broadcast and print ads to stimulate consumer response. An advertiser in a travel or business publication may utilize the publication's reader service cards to develop leads or inquiries. The Internet is widely used as a direct response medium via e-commerce and product websites.

Direct Mail

Direct mail can be a very important medium for advertisers with highly targeted audiences or customers and for small businesses that need to target relatively small geographic areas. Newcomers sometimes use the terms *direct mail*, *direct marketing*, and *mail order* interchangeably.

Perhaps the best way to distinguish these three similar, yet different, terms is to remember that direct mail is simply an advertising medium, like print or broadcast media. Print media messages are delivered through the printed word, usually in newspapers or magazines, while broadcast media messages are delivered through the airwaves, on television or radio. In direct mail, advertising and other types of messages are delivered through the mail.

Direct mail is a particularly attractive option for small business owners, because it can communicate complete information about a product or service, to almost any conceivable target group, at a relatively low cost. Direct mail can provide the basis for a business, or it can be used to supplement a company's traditional sales efforts. For example, a small business could use direct mail to inform potential customers about its offerings, and then follow up with a phone call or a visit from a salesperson.

Owners of start-up businesses may find direct mail an effective method of creating awareness and interest in a new product, while owners of existing companies may find it useful in generating new business outside their usual customers or geographic area. Another advantage of direct mail is that it is testable, so that entrepreneurs can try out different sales messages on various audiences in order to find the most profitable market for a new product or service.

In the late 1990s and early 2000s, some analysts predicted that the growth of Internet retailing and advertising could lead to a decline in the usefulness of direct mail. A study reported by Debora Toth in Graphic Arts Monthly, however, predicted that direct mail expenditures would grow at an estimated rate of 6% per year from 1998 to 2008. In addition, the study predicted that direct mail's share of total advertising expenditures would remain stable at 11%. Printing company president Rick Powell told Toth:

> The Internet is only enhancing direct mail. Corporations still need to send a campaign based on direct mail in order to drive consumers to their Websites. After the consumer receives a beautifully printed piece, the firm then can follow up with an email message.

In fact, the Internet offers some benefits to direct mail marketers, including easy access to database lists and Websites that automate the direct-mail production process.

Advantages of Direct Mail

Direct mail has several marketing advantages.

- **Laser-like targeting.** Historically, the most important aspect of direct mail has been its ability to target current customers or a highly targeted group of prospects precisely. If a suitable list was available, it also did a good job of targeting new prospects in a business's Primary Trading Area.

- **Communication of information and offers.** A comprehensive direct mail package can communicate the whole story about a product and combine it with a purchase offer. The auto companies used direct mail to target import buyers with a special incentive good for those who owned a competitive import vehicle.

- **Personalization.** Direct mail can be addressed to customers personally and can be tailored to their needs, based on previous transactions and other gathered data.

- **Optimization.** Because of its direct accountability, direct mail can be tested to find the best list, the best offer, and the best timing. Then the winners can be rolled out to a wider audience for optimal results. Since relatively large expenditures are required for mailing to lists of thousands or millions, most direct mailers take advantage of the medium's testing capabilities. Accumulation. Responses (and non-responses) can be added to the database, allowing future mailings to be targeted better.

Disadvantages of Direct Mail

Direct mail also has some disadvantages:

- **Cost.** The cost per thousand will be MUCH higher than almost any other form of mass promotion, although the wastage rate may be much lower. Depending on the package being mailed and the postage costs, direct mail can cost anywhere from less than $1.00 per package to over $5.00. That equates to a CPM of $1000 to more than $5000, which is much higher than alternative media.

- **Inefficiency.** Because of its cost and high CPM, direct mail is too inefficient to use for mass-market advertising.

- **Waste.** Large quantities of paper are thrown away.

- **Alienation.** Some recipients resent being subjected to direct marketing. Their objections may take the form of boycotts or even prohibitory orders against companies whose direct marketing has offended them.

Best Practices

Direct mail is perhaps the most scientific form of marketing communications because of the enormous amount of testing that is done. In direct mail, everything is testing—from the mailing lists to the sales letter to the offer to the envelope copy. This discussion will provide only a brief overview of direct mail practices.

Data Base Development

Whenever Direct Mail is discussed, very quickly the conversation turns to database development. Everyone's database requirements are different. The guiding question should be *What data will be needed about customers in order to carry on a meaningful dialog with them by mail, by phone, or in person?* The data collected should be actionable, not just interesting. List Selection

Mailing List

Many direct mail professionals believe that the single most important factor affecting the direct mail response rate is the quality of the mailing list. Marketers often use a combination of customer lists and purchased lists. Customer lists may be based on previous purchasing behavior. For example, Lands End mails different catalogues to customers who have a history of purchasing women's wear or men's clothing or outerwear. Purchased lists can be compiled to match a variety of criteria a marketer thinks important for maximizing response. For example, an auto manufacturer might have a list of competitive sports car buyers who are women who bought their last vehicle three years ago.

The Mailing Package

Direct mail gives you control over the sales message and allows you to present a great deal of information about a product or service in the sales letter and brochure. The mailing package is limited only by your imagination and budget! In addition to letters, brochures, and testimonials, mailing packages may include product samples, coupons, sweepstakes offers, CDs, advertising specialties, and whatever else someone dreams up.

The Envelope

The outer envelope is a major influence over whether the mailing package will be opened. People often sort their mail over the trashcan. That means you only have only a split second for them to decide whether they'll open your letter or not. Window envelopes look like bills so don't use them. Labels are impersonal. Addresses printed directly onto envelopes give a much more personal touch. Handwritten envelopes, in the past, have had by far the best impact because they are the most personalized of all addressing methods. Test this for yourself, though; for some, hand-written addresses may cause suspicion. Test outer envelope copy. Test instructional copy. Test a provocative statement or graphic. If you're giving away a premium, or have an offer, feature it on the envelope.

Postage

Postage represents both a sizeable cost and a success determinant. There are several options, but many direct mail experts recommend using actual postage stamps because they are much more personalized than postage imprints. The bulk rate is the dumpster rate; the Post Office freely admits that 20% - 30% of all bulk mail gets thrown out for various reasons. After taking the proper steps to get the best list, don't blow it by being cheap on the postage.

Measurability

Direct mail provides a high degree of measurability, which in turn allows for extensive testing. Every element of direct mail can be tested to maximize response and ROI. Lists, offers, and packages can all be tested in one mailing when done properly. You construct a test matrix consisting of individual test cells. Each test cell contains a unique combination of elements being tested and makes up a portion of the overall mailing. After the entire mailing is dropped, you track responses from each test cell to determine the performance of the tested elements.

Repeat Mailings

Repeat mailings take advantage of the product's or service's potential for repeat sales as well as capitalizing on opportunities to sell related goods and services to the same lists. Direct mail programs are generally more than a single mailing. You stage multiple mailings that build on each other to lead the consumer down the purchase funnel and closer to purchase.

For example, Spring Green, a medium-sized lawn services company, executed a three-stage mailing. The first mailing to about half the country was intended to build awareness, generate sales inquiries, provide a gift, and provide the business card for the local franchisee. The second mailing was a direct sales piece that included coupons or other special offers. The third mailing tried to get recipients to buy before it became too late (incentives expired). Franchisees judged the direct mail program to be highly effective, with one franchisee claiming that it accounted for 75% of new sales.

Telemarketing

Telemarketing is a cousin to direct mail, using the telephone rather than the mail to go directly to the target audience in order to generate leads, make sales, or gather marketing information. Telemarketing can be a particularly valuable tool for small businesses in that it offers many of the same benefits of direct contact with customers but saves time and money as compared to personal selling. In fact, experts have estimated that closing a sale through telemarketing usually costs less than one-fifth of what it would cost to send a salesperson to make the sale. Though telemarketing is more expensive than direct mail, it tends to be more efficient in closing sales and thus provides a greater yield on the marketing dollar.

Although telemarketing has been the center of some controversies—ranging from scams run over the phone to a number of legal issues that have been the center of debate at both state and national levels—the industry continues to grow. In fact, the American Telemarketing Association found that spending on telemarketing activities increased from $1 billion to $60 billion between 1981 and 1991. By the mid-1990s, telemarketing accounted for more than $450 billion in annual sales, a figure that is expected to continue to rise through the foreseeable future.

Advantages of Telemarketing

Telemarketing has a number of self-evident advantages over other forms of marketing communications.

- **Targetability.** While not as plentiful as mail lists, targeted telemarketing lists are available for purchase.
- **Conversation.** If the telemarketer can engage in conversation with the consumer, there is an opportunity to explain and persuade
- **Prospecting & selling.** Telemarketing is successfully used in direct sales, prospecting, and appointment setting.
- **Marketing.** Although some businesses operate exclusively by telephone, telemarketing is most often used as part of an overall marketing program to tie together advertising and personal selling

efforts. For example, a company might send introductory information through the mail, then follow-up with a telemarketing call to assess the prospect's interest, and finally send a salesperson to visit.

- **Response Rates.** Research has found that the use of telemarketing in combination with mail significantly increases the response rate.

Disadvantages of Telemarketing

- **Negative Attitudes.** Consumers have become increasingly averse to telemarketing. More of them are using technology to screen out unwanted calls, and putting their numbers on the Do Not Call List.

- **High Cost.** Telemarketing is labor intensive, so the cost to generate enough calls to get a positive response can be substantial compared to other forms of direct response media.

- **Scams.** Unfortunately, telemarketing has been the basis for numerous scams over the years. Federal authorities estimate that con artists using the phone bilk consumers out of least $1 billion a year. Some analysts contend that the figure may even be closer to $10 billion, because many victims shy away from filing complaints. Although these frauds have given the telemarketing industry bad press, the industry considers monitoring vital to maintaining quality control and protecting consumers, so many firms ask employees to sign a release allowing such monitoring.

Sponsorships & Events

Similar to sponsoring media events on television like Sunday Night Football or the Academy Awards, marketers can also sponsor live events to attract their target audiences. As an example, the auto companies sponsor annual auto shows in larger markets, as well as specialty shows where Corvettes or antique cars are on display. Sports venues, concerts, fairs and festivals, air shows, theatres, home & garden shows, museums, and racetracks always attract a multitude of sponsors. Even a snack food company may buy a partial sponsorship of an event where samples of their product can be offered to anyone walking by their display space. The Army participates in event sponsorships, as do builders, remodelers, and dozens of other types of companies.

One of the fastest growing forms of marketing communications, *event marketing* is gaining a serious foothold in the communications toolboxes of businesses all over the world. While the concept may be relatively new to the Saskatchewan market, it is really quite mature, with its roots having been planted over 20 years ago at major U.S. and European events.

Event Audiences

With many thousands of potential event sponsorship opportunities available, marketers can select events that attract consumers in their target market. For example, General Motors was a sponsor of the Texas State Fair (the largest fair in the US), as well as Seattle Sea Fair (boat races), which attracts up to 500,000 visitors over a weekend, an above average percentage of whom were new car/truck buyers. The majority of events, however, do not attract hundreds of thousands or millions of visitors. They attract smaller audiences with an interest in the subject matter of the event, like a boat show or a home and garden show.

Activating Event Sponsorships

Event sponsors begin by buying the rights to conduct certain marketing activities at an event. Events are typically activated in some of these ways:

- **Signage** within the event venue; types of signs, how many, and their locations are negotiated with the seller (rights holder).
- **Product displays** may be set up by manufacturers or retailers to allow consumers to interact with the product—see, touch, feel, smell, or taste. For example, auto manufacturers may set up display areas showing off their vehicles and make them accessible to consumers. The Army or Navy may have a display area at events where representatives can talk to prospective recruits and give out literature. A food company may give out samples.
- **Product specialists or representatives** are often on hand to demonstrate product features and authoritatively answer consumers' questions.
- **Product information** should always be available for consumers to view on interactive kiosks or to take away (brochures, flyers, special offers) or both.

252

- **Activities** within the marketer's display area, such as a rock-climbing wall or a product quiz, can be used to attract attention.

- **Entertainment**, such as music and bands, magicians, photos-with-Batman, and the like are also used a good way to attract attention to a sponsor's venue.

- **Promotional item giveaways** sporting your logo—hats, coffee cups, T-shirts, and other tchotchkes available from advertising premium suppliers are also good reminders once visitors have left the event.

Advantages of Event Sponsorships

Sponsorship of events can provide many benefits to advertisers that are not available in any other form of marketing communication. For example, events can:

- **Reach specific segments** of target markets, for example, boating enthusiasts at a boat show, car enthusiasts at an auto show, hockey enthusiasts at a hockey venue and in the media

- **Provide interactive engagement** between consumers and product. Imagine allowing potential consumers to test drive vehicles, giving them the opportunity to feel the soft leather or smell cookies baking.

- **Interactive and sensory** occasions for consumers to see, touch & feel, smell, and taste products and interact with product specialists

- **Conduct sampling and trial activities** within the event venue, often from a sponsor booth.

- **Connect directly with potential and current customers**, enhancing their experience at the event

- **Public relations opportunities** before, during, and after the event.

- **Consumer experiences** at live events can leave a more lasting impression than exposure to ads in media can.

In addition, surveys of the general population have shown that consumers are more likely to experience good feelings about businesses that contribute to their communities, and as a result, they are more likely to purchase goods and services from those businesses.

Disadvantages of Event Sponsorships

Event sponsorships have a couple of disadvantages you should consider.

- **Audiences are relatively small**, especially when compared to media audiences. A few hundred or a few thousand participants may attend an event, compared to hundreds of thousands in a mass media audience. (Some events do generate large audiences, e.g., 500,000 attendees at the Seattle Sea Fair)
- **Costs can be substantial** in relation to the size of the audience (event attendees and those exposed to media reports). Normally a rights fee must be paid to the event promoter, and there can be significant additional costs to activate the event—tent, literature, product set-ups, on-site personnel, give-away items.

Best Practices

- **Audiences.** Study audience sizes and demographics before making event sponsorship decisions.
- **Interactivity.** Sponsors without a need or a plan to interact with event attendees (e.g., sampling, test drives, entertainment) may be wasting their money.
- **Coordination** with Other Marketing Activities. Event sponsorship activities are most effective when they are coordinated with other marketing communications and promotional activities, as one element of an integrated marketing communications program.
- **Activation.** Signage, on-site sales spiels, literature, and all the rest of your presentation must reflect a unified message and coordinate as well with your other marketing activities.
- **Cost.** When weighing cost vs. benefits, be sure to include the costs for rights, activation, and promotion of the event (or your participation in it).
- **Measurement.** A number of methodologies exist to measure the effectiveness and ROI of event sponsorship. The most basic measures include a count of the number of attendees at the event and the number of attendees who visited your display area. Some companies conduct test vs. control experiments to determine how

much lift was generated among event attendees compared to non-attendees.

WORD-OF-MOUTH MARKETING

Word-of-Mouth Marketing (*WOMM*) is an orchestrated attempt to get a target audience to talk to each other about your product or business. The idea is to create a viral effect where people tell people who tell people who tell people... Most marketers place significant value on positive word-of-mouth, which is achieved by creating products, services, and customer experiences that naturally generate conversation or *buzz*.

WOMM uses a variety of techniques to spread the word, among them free publicity, buzz, blogs, viral spreading of the message, grassroots efforts, social media, ambassador programs, and consumer-generated media. Because of the personal nature of communications between individuals, product information communicated in this way may have an added layer of credibility. Research points out that we are more inclined to believe WOMM than more formal promotion methods. The receiver of word-of-mouth referrals tends to believe that the communicator is speaking honestly and is unlikely to have an ulterior motive.

How do you create buzz, a form of WOMM? How do you generate conversation about your product or business? How do you turn customers into ambassadors? Put your creativity into over drive!

Here is a description of a Vespa Motor Scooters buzz scenario:

Frequent the right cafes around Los Angeles and you might have encountered a gang of sleek, attractive motorbike riders who seem genuinely interested in getting to know you over an iced latte. Compliment them on their Vespa scooters glinting in the brilliant curbside sunlight, and they'll happily pull out a pad and scribble down an address and phone number—not theirs, but that of the local boutique where you can buy your own Vespa, just as (they'll confide) the rap artist Sisqó and the movie queen Sandra Bullock recently did. And that's when the truth hits you: This isn't any spontaneous encounter. Those scooter-riding models are pitch people on the Vespa payroll, and they've been hired to generate some favorable word of mouth for the recently reissued European bikes. (AddMarketing.com, 3/7/11/11)

So, welcome to Buzz. Marketers are taking to the streets, as well as cafés, nightclubs, and the Internet, in large numbers. Vespa importer

Piaggio USA has its biker gang. Hebrew National (hot dogs) is dispatching Mom Squads to fire up backyard barbecues, while Hasbro Games has deputized hundreds of fourth- and fifth-graders as Secret Agents to tantalize their peers with the new POX electronic game. The goal: seek out the trendsetters in each community and subtly push them into talking up a brand to their friends and admirers, orchestrating a tsunami of chatter that will transform a niche product into a mass phenomenon.

Here's another example. Rather than blitzing the airways with 30-second TV commercials for its new Focus subcompact, Ford Motor Company recruited a handful of trendsetters in a few markets and gave each of them a Focus to drive for six months. Their duties? Just be seen with the car and hand out Focus-themed trinkets to anyone who expressed interest. "We weren't looking for celebrities. We were looking for the assistants to celebrities, party planners, disk jockeys—the people who really seemed to influence what was cool," says marketing consultant Julie Roehm.

So how does it work? In a successful buzz campaign, each carefully cultivated recipient of the brand message becomes a carrier, spreading the word to yet more carriers, much as a virus races through a population. Buzz marketing is credited with taking one online brand from 450,000 unique visitors per month to 15 million unique visitors, which led to its acquisition by a NASDAQ company.

Advantages of WOMM/Buzz Marketing

Like other forms of viral communications, Word-of-Mouth and Buzz marketing have advantages and disadvantages, although there are more advantages, as listed here.

- **Source.** When word of mouth comes from a trusted personal source, it can be more persuasive than communications in traditional media
- **Cost.** Compared to advertising and other forms of paid marketing communication, WOMM is very cheap.
- **Viral Potential.** The bigger and better the idea, the more likely it is to go viral. Once that happens, the buzz can generate and engage a large and targeted audience.
- **Publicity.** If it captures the attention and imagination of the press, buzz has the potential to generate a lot of publicity.

- **Global Potential.** Thanks to the Internet, buzz can take a concept global.
- **ROI.** Successful programs are executed at a very low cost, so they have the potential to provide good returns on investment.

Disadvantages of WOMM/Buzz Marketing

Word-of-mouth and buzz also have some disadvantages.

- **Weak Ideas Don't Work.** The strength of the marketing depends on the transmission of enthusiasm among individuals as to the benefits of the product being sold. A weak concept or poorly executed concept may not generate much buzz and will not become viral.
- **Competition.** The presence of competitors within a buzz campaign will reduce its effectiveness.
- **Insufficient Buzz.** If you don't create enough buzz to generate publicity, your effort is futile.
- **Danger of High Pressure.** Hard-core selling among participants (who are working for sales commissions) may alienate rather than entice potential buyers.

PUBLICITY

Advertising is paid communication. Advertisers have control over the message, timing, and placement. To obtain that control, advertisers pay the media a negotiated sum to run the ad or commercial.

Publicity is different. An element of public relations, it is free or nearly free message placement. Publicity results when you suggest or otherwise provide editorial content—an interesting story or important news—to a communications vehicle. If a journalist, editor, or producer thinks your story is newsworthy or of audience interest, it may run free of charge, time or space permitting.

Billions of dollars worth of publicity are stories available for the asking—in newspapers and magazines, on television and radio stations, at websites and blogs—any medium disseminating news or information will give you publicity for the right stories. Media have large amounts of time or space to fill and are always searching for content that will be of interest or value to their audiences.

257

At worst, seeking publicity rarely does harm. For the most part, making a story suggestion to editors or journalists will lead to:

- **No coverage.** The editor may decide not to run your story. In fact, despite the impression you may have gotten from the paragraph above, most publicity requests are rejected. To understand this, and increase your odds of avoiding it, study the next section, on press releases.

- **Mention.** Your product, company, or service may be included in a larger story about your field. Your timely contact with the medium can get attention to your product in a piece already in progress.

- **Focused story.** A complete story may be created from scratch, built around the story angle you suggested or some other but featuring your company, the trend you discovered, or an interview.

The Press Release

The most important tool for submitting stories to journalists is the press release. Simply put, a press release is a news story that presents the most newsworthy aspects of your product, company, or service in a format and language familiar to the journalist. You may have a PR agency that writes and distributes press releases or you may be more personally involved. In any event, you need to understand the ABCs of sending out effective press releases.

With any of your press releases, there are many story angles, but any story must be newsworthy and interesting to the media audience. For example, maybe you are opening a new store or introducing a new product. Maybe you have changed your product. Maybe you have hired some new executives. Maybe you are changing your marketing direction. Maybe your sales have increased significantly. Maybe your business plan provides a good case history. Any of these events can form the basis for a press release and publicity.

The most popular structure for news stories is the inverted pyramid. Unlike ordinary writing that builds fact upon fact to reach a conclusion, the journalistic story begins with the conclusion. As many as possible of the Five W's (Who, What, When, Where, Why) are included in the lead. The two most important—Who and What—must be at the top. Succeeding paragraphs explain and support the lead, with the less important details appearing at the end of the story.

Your press release follows the journalistic pattern of the inverted pyramid. The first paragraph begins with *what* your news is and *whom* it happened to or who did it or is going to do it. Then you say *when* it did or will happen, *where* it was or will be, and *why* it matters. You arrange the rest of your information, including details about the five W's, in descending order of importance. The most important material in the press release appears at the beginning of the story, and the less important material follows, until everything has been said and you quit.

Your press release should also contain a great headline, one that will capture attention and engage a target audience, beginning with the editor who is sifting through a blizzard of hopeful press releases. Your headline must entice the editor to keep reading.

Press Release Selection

Knowing how the press chooses one news release over another will give you an advantage when you write your won. Most large pressrooms get hundreds of news releases a day. Yours competes with all the others that come in at the same time to the same pressroom. Here's what happens to them in a typical selection process.

First, an *assignment editor* determines what is news and what isn't. This person sorts through all incoming releases and either assigns them to editors or discards them. Typically, an assignment editor will sift through press releases the way you go through your mail—over a wastebasket. If a headline doesn't catch the assignment editor's eye, the lead is not likely to be read and the press release goes straight to the trash. Without a catchy headline to grab the editor's attention, followed by a strong lead, the first paragraph won't stand a chance.

Stories That Get Covered

Your best chance of being covered by the local media is to give them what they want. Each medium is looking for specific types of news events.

Newspapers want information that is interesting and informative. They like to educate their readers with timely news and articles that are interesting and educational.

Radio can be a bit more creative in the nature and style of releases. Many radio stations like information that is controversial, funny, or weird.

For example, one of the most popular five minutes of a particular local radio station is the Birthday Scam, in which the DJ's call up an unsuspecting person who is having a birthday and create a combative and hostile conversation full of accusations and lies. The sparks start to fly and so do the ratings!

Television gets excited about stories that include great visuals. Sponsoring a local high school reading contest in which the principal gets dunked in a tub of Kool-Aid will get a TV station's attention.

All media love human-interest stories. They know that people are interested in other people. In fact, the number one topic of talk radio is relationships. If you have a good human-interest story that others would find interesting you're on your way.

Making Stories Newsworthy

The key to getting publicity for your business is to make it newsworthy, be prepared to create news. There are several good ways to do this.

- **Start with hard news.** Are there newsworthy changes occurring in your business? Expansion? New product lines? New or newly promoted executive? Antique car show? Models available to show women's clothing for hapless husbands?

- **Create buzz.** If part of your marketing plan involves creating buzz, use publicity as a way to help generate the buzz. For example, a Detroit area Irish bar & restaurant the held a contest on St. Patrick's Day to see who could keep singing *Danny Boy* the longest. Naturally, the bar stayed open all night. This buzz was spread by substantial coverage on local television stations and other media. Other than the cost of staging the event on site, the buzz and publicity generated were free and of high value; they called a lot of attention to one establishment among thousands in the market.

- **Provide survey results.** Do a customer survey and include controversial questions. Write articles about the results of the survey. Media love survey results.

- **Create Top 10 lists.** Create a top ten list about something in your business. If you're a beautician, write an article titled, Top Ten Most Popular Hairstyles for Women. Top ten lists are very popular; just ask David Letterman.

- **Sponsor an award.** Develop an annual award for someone in the community or a business in your industry. For instance, give an award to a local outstanding teacher who has gone above and beyond the call of duty. If you're a supplier, give an award to the Best business (customer) in the industry you service.
- **Offer surprising facts.** Tell the audience something they don't know about your industry or business. For instance, if you're a recruitment firm, write an article titled, "The Average Starting Salary of an MBA Graduate is 40 percent Higher than Their Pre-MBA Earnings."
- **Additional opportunities include Piggybacking off a national story**, sponsoring a local community service project, holding a memorable event, challenging certain sacred cows, writing an informative story (imagine that!), prove your superiority, and be audacious! (Do some things in marketing that are daring and will generate buzz and publicity. Remember when Richard Branson, CEO of Virgin Airlines appeared in public dressed in a $10,000 white silk bridal gown?)

Distribution of Releases

To send your releases out to the media, you can compile a list of media and contact personnel and send your releases directly to them. You can use a PR release distribution company (like PR Web) that will distribute your release to target industries and locations for a relatively small fee. The cost ranges from nothing to over $100, depending on the number of features you want built into your release.

Advantages of Publicity

Publicity offers some advantages and disadvantages to organizations large and small. The advantages are rather obvious.

- **It's free.** Publicity is free, apart from any expenses you incur in hiring personnel to write or distribute your news releases.
- **Credibility.** It can be argued that news stories in a reputable medium are more credible than advertising.
- **Focused message.** The release communicates what you believe is important to your business.

- **Continuity.** Assuming that you have a publicity plan, you can issue releases at intervals that support your plan.

Disadvantages of Publicity

Publicity does have some disadvantages not present in paid communications.

- **Uncertainty.** Your stories may or may not run, and you can't be sure they won't be altered. These uncertainties can also make it difficult to plan a communications schedule.
- **Lack of control.** Timing and content are controlled by the media.
- **Control of content.** The media may cut or edit your story, for better but also for worse.
- **Futility.** If you have a time-sensitive message to get out, it is dangerous to rely on free publicity as your exclusive communications channel.

MEDIA INTEGRATION

With the growth of media options, especially on the digital side, a perplexing issue has arisen: how to create integrated plans that include traditional, alternative, and digital media. Although some marketers still think they have to choose between traditional and new media, it is not true. Media and communications can and must work together in a complementary and synergistic manner. To that end, the communications role of each must be clearly defined.

Here are some simple examples of how communications and media forms can be planned and orchestrated to complement each other:

- Someone sees or hears an ad, then blogs about it;
- Someone sees a TV commercial, and then purchases the product using a cents-off coupon that came in the mail;
- Someone sees some advertising, and then starts a buzz on Facebook.
- Someone's video on You Tube went viral and ended up on network television

The growing importance of the Integrated Marketing Communications (IMC) philosophy—the ANA's top priority—combined with the rapid growth of digital and other nontraditional media, creates challenges for managing a complex marketing communications plan.

Don't panic. The truth is, smart marketers and media planners have always selected and integrated communications forms and media vehicles. They have always worked with apples and oranges and all kinds of metrics. When all was said and done, more often than not, they made decisions that worked—about outdoor vs. television, radio vs. magazines, direct mail vs. paid Internet search, and advertising vs. event marketing. Your challenge is a matter of degree, not difference.

Analyzing your IMC options does require comparing apples with oranges because the nature of media audiences is different, the metrics for measuring audiences and effectiveness are different, the nature of communications messages is different, and the costs are different. But that has always been true, and it has always been true that the solution is to define the marketing and communications tasks.

Remember what the Cheshire cat said: *If you don't know where you are going, any road will get you there"* Yogi Berra agreed (or misquoted): *If you don't know where you are going, you will wind up somewhere else.* You must know where you're going and have a vision for getting there.

Sometimes media planners spend too much of their time playing around with solutions in search of problems. Trying to figure out what to do with some new media idea or some new technology or gimmick is upside down thinking; trying to retrofit a tactic into a strategy that it doesn't fit, is upside down thinking, not smart planning.

Define the problem or task, then blitz for solutions. If you spend the necessary time figuring out what the tasks are—whether increasing top of mind awareness or generating visits to a website—you will find that prioritizing your communications options to address those tasks is much easier and will produce effective plans.

That is the premise behind Task Matching, a methodology developed by 2020:Marketing Communications LLC to help match tasks to communications forms.

TASK MATCHING: AN IMC PLANNING PROCESS

What kind of planning can evaluate and integrate so many communications options? The answer is that a conventional planning process works just fine if you think strategically and understand your options. For example, while there are many thousands of potential media vehicles, there are only a few dozen forms of communications. Once the right communications forms are selected, tactical evaluation of specific vehicles is greatly simplified.

If a media strategy used magazines as the primary medium, you would not start by evaluating 8,000 different magazines. You would start by focusing on a few. Once the decision has been made to use newsweeklies, the planning task is less daunting, because there are fewer than six to be evaluated. The larger issue is defining communications tasks and needs.

For example, if a rep comes in to sell banners and display ads on a large network of websites, the planner's first job is to determine whether online display advertising is *on strategy*. Other than the visceral satisfaction of using the Internet, what is the role of such advertising? No matter how elegant the banners being presented, the question is, do they fulfill a strategic role? If that's engagement, are there better ways to engage consumers? If it's website traffic, are there better ways to drive traffic? Finally, do Internet display ads and/or banners address the defined task better than what is currently planned? Once decisions like these are decided, the rest will begin to fall in place. Ask yourself continually what are the tasks, what are the communications priorities selected to address them, and why. Don't ask whether it's a good banner or a better billboard. Ask what is the strategic role and effectiveness of each medium.

Those with vested interests in digital media may argue that conventional planning processes do not apply to the Internet. Why not? All media are vying for a share of the same budget. All should be directed at the same goal. To suggest that some are exempt from the processes of reasoned decision argues against the whole idea of integrated planning. All media must be judged on the same basis: the specific benefits they provide in relation to your needs, including what audiences they reach, how they communicate, how effective they are, and how much they cost.

Regardless of whether there are 1000 or 10,000 media vehicles, communications forms should be utilized that best address defined communications tasks in a cost effective manner. If the task is to raise top of mind awareness of a food product, television might receive strong consideration. If the task is to create improved customer relationships, social media may be on the short list.

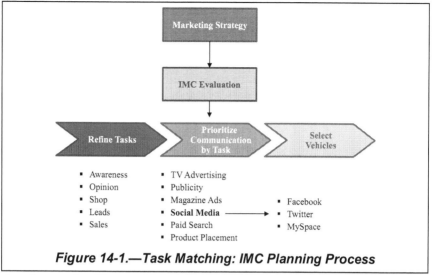

Figure 14-1.—Task Matching: IMC Planning Process

As shown in Figure 14-1, the IMC planning process begins with translating the marketing strategy into media tasks, followed by identification of marketing and communications priorities. Once the tasks are defined, marketing communications alternatives can prioritized for each task and specific vehicles selected.

Is there a role for conventional reach and frequency metrics, impressions, audience composition, and cost efficiencies in implementing this model? Yes, of course, there is a role for conventional media planning and buying metrics when you're using traditional media. Metrics like reach, frequency, and impressions, are used for some digital media, but not for others, either because there are no metrics or because the metrics are simply different.

Many advertisers using display ads on big bundles of websites routinely look at the impressions, reach, and frequency of their package. The numbers come from a variety of Internet audience research companies, including Nielsen NetRatings.

On the other hand, it doesn't make sense to evaluate search programs on the basis of impressions or reach and frequency. Search is not about higher awareness; it is about attracting website visitors. In the example used for Figure 14-1, CRM (Customer Relationship Management) was defined as the highest priority communications task. CRM includes the overall strategy and activities for nurturing customer and prospect relationships. An example of a CRM activity might be to send customers an email advising them of certain specials in advance of a general announcement. Second, social media were identified as a strong option for addressing CRM. Once social media were defined as a media strategy, Facebook, Twitter, and MySpace were recommended vehicles for accomplishing the task.

Figure 14-2 depicts a hypothetical example of how this reasoning works in

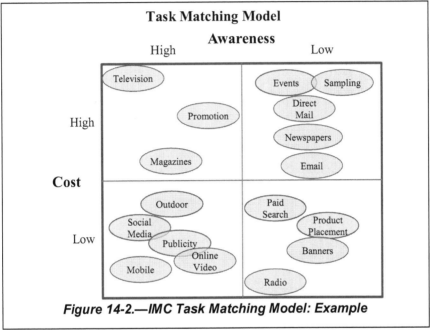

Figure 14-2.—IMC Task Matching Model: Example

the Task Matching Model. The task is defined as *increasing name awareness at low cost*, and any relevant objectives and communications forms may be analyzed, e.g., information vs. involvement, leads vs. costs. Marketing communications options are then plotted on a map to reflect the relative awareness-building potential and cost for each communications option. The model does not make decisions, but it can help you more deliberately evaluate the options. Of course, your plot points may vary from those presented in Figure 14-2.

SUMMARY

As you will recall from the introductory chapters of this book, marketers (clients) see integrated marketing communications as the biggest challenge they face. Agencies have been fired because they didn't understand it or couldn't figure out how to deliver it at a profit.

Marketing and advertising are devoted to satisfying consumer wants and needs better than the competition does. When the consumer is the client/marketer, there is plenty of competition eager to win any business you can't handle.

Media planners play or can play an important role in helping clients achieve more effective marketing communications by removing their blinders. This is no longer a world of automatic advertising. This is a world of putting together the most effective mix of integrated marketing communications. Media planners are already beginning to help manage all of the brand contact points from all forms marketing communications.

You must educate yourself in all the forms of marketing communications that are potential alternatives to advertising. This chapter has given you a view of the strengths, weaknesses, and best practices for various forms of marketing communication.

What types of communication should you propose? You now have the knowledge you need to compare and contrast the contributions of advertising and seven other forms of marketing communications: publicity, word of mouth and buzz, event marketing and sponsorship, telemarketing, direct mail, product placement, and sales promotion.

15. TRADITIONAL MEDIA
Rumors of my death have been greatly exaggerated.

–Mark Twain

Now that you have studied market and media analysis, you understand how to define your target audience and trading area, you can write media objectives, and you are equipped to consider alternative communications forms, you are ready at last to begin selecting media! Chapter 15 will discuss each of the major traditional media: television, radio, newspapers, magazines, and outdoor. Chapter 16 will discuss the Internet.

Chapter 15 provides an overview of some of the strengths and weaknesses and best practices of traditional media with respect to audience, cost, and impact. For example, television's salient characteristics are mass audience, geographic versatility, high cost, intrusiveness, and multi-sensory communication, and ability to generate exposure frequency. How do these characteristics compare to those of other media?

In addition to audience and cost considerations, the communications strengths and weaknesses of each medium must be considered. For example, what is each medium's ability to communicate your unique message and engage your target audiences effectively?

Table 15-1, a subjective analysis from DDB Needham Worldwide and 2020:Marketing Communications, demonstrates the kind of thinking you will learn to do as you work your way through Chapter 15. It presents a list of communications tasks and shows the relative effectiveness of selected media for the performance of each task.

As you just learned in Chapter 14, task definition is where it all begins. Of course, task performance is only one dimension of the medium that will influence your media planning decisions. At minimum, you also have to consider audience and cost.

Table 15-1.—Relative Strength of Media Task Performance

Task	First Choice	Second Choice	Third Choice	Fourth Choice
Bigger than Life	Outdoor	Television	Newspapers	Radio
Demonstration	Television	Magazines	Newspapers	Outdoor
Elegance	Magazines	Television	Outdoor	Radio
Entertainment	Television	Radio	Newspapers	Outdoor
Events	Television	Newspapers	Radio	Magazines
Excitement	Television	Magazines	Radio	Newspapers
Features	Magazines	Newspapers	Television	Outdoor
Humor	Television	Radio	Outdoor	Newspapers
Imagination	Radio	Television	Magazines	Newspapers
Information	Magazines	Newspapers	Television	Outdoor
Leads	Internet	Magazines	Television	Outdoor
News	Newspapers	Television	Radio	Outdoor
One on One	Television	Radio	Magazines	Outdoor
Package ID	Outdoor	Magazines	Television	Newspapers
Personal	Radio	Magazines	Television	Outdoor
Prestige	Magazines	Television	Newspapers	Outdoor
Price	Newspapers	Radio	Television	Outdoor
Product in Use	Television	Magazines	Newspapers	Radio
Quality	Magazines	Television	Outdoor	Newspapers
Recipes	Magazines	Newspapers	Television	Outdoor
Sex Appeal	Magazines	Television	Outdoor	Newspapers
Snob Appeal	Magazines	Newspapers	Television	Outdoor

Adapted from DDB Needham Worldwide brochure & 2020:Marketing Communications LLC

*Question: Do you agree with the first-choice selections
for most effectively communicating the list of tasks—whether elegance or
demonstration of the product or humor?*

TELEVISION

Television is the single most important medium to advertisers and consumers. In 2008, watching television ranked third among all of life's activities in average time spent daily (2.6 hours per day, behind only personal care activities and work), with hours spent remaining unchanged since 2003. While total television viewing levels haven't changed, viewing has become much more fragmented owing to increased viewing options.

In addition, according to BIGresearch's SIMM VII survey, television ranks second in consumer perception of influence on purchase decisions, as shown below:

1. Word of mouth
2. Television
3. Coupons
4. Newspaper inserts
5. Read article

In terms of total advertising expenditures, television continues to be the number one advertising medium in the United States. According to Kantar and Jack Myers, companies that compile and analyze data on competitive ad expenditures, TV spending in 2009 totaled $62 billion with the cable networks receiving the largest share.

Medium	Billions
Network TV	$16
Cable Networks	17
National Spot	13
Syndicated	2
Local/Spot	11
Local Cable	3
Total	**$62**

There are a variety of choices for advertisers to achieve national or local coverage in hundreds of different programs and times of day on the two primary types of television outlets: broadcast and cable. *Broadcast* refers to outlets that distribute programming over the air. *Cable* television distributes programming via cables or satellites. Programming may be broadcast in normal digital, HD, and increasingly in 3D.

National or nearly national television advertising may be purchased on any of the *broadcast networks* (ABC, CBS, FOX, NBC, CW, UPN), the *cable networks* (TBS, Discover, Lifetime, Fox News, SciFi, or nearly a

271

hundred others), or ad hoc *syndicated networks* of individual stations that broadcast programming in syndication (off-network or original).

Federal Communications Commission (FCC) regulations limit the number of network-owned stations as a percentage of total market size. Networks therefore tend to have *owned and operated* stations (*O&Os*) only in the largest media markets, like New York City and Los Angeles, and to rely on affiliated stations to carry their programming in other markets.

For local advertising, commercial time may be purchased on local TV stations (network O&Os, affiliates, or independents) in any of the 210 DMAs. Commercial time also may be purchased on individual local cable systems or on a local network of cable systems called interconnects.

Geographic Coverage

Each broadcast network has 200+ station affiliates in local DMAs throughout the U.S. The geographic coverage of a network program depends on how many affiliates the network has and how many affiliates choose to clear each program.

It is important to understand that local stations decide whether to clear programs fed to them by the networks. Sometimes local stations pre-empt network programs if the station feels the program is inappropriate for the market or decides to run a locally produced program instead of the network show. Depending on the program, therefore, broadcast network commercials may clear in markets representing anywhere from less than 70% to 99% of total U.S. households. Commercials are integrated into the programs by the networks. (Remember: coverage is not viewing.)

Commercials purchased on local stations, of course, *cover* most the DMA where which the station is located. Television stations frequently pre-empt local spots in order to sell the position to an advertiser who is willing to pay a higher price or because the station pre-empted the program for any variety of reasons.

Commercials running in cable network programming may be seen only on systems carrying that network's programming. Approximately 89% of U.S. households get cable or satellite television. About 80% of those receive advertising supported networks, but penetration by network varies widely. Advertisers buying on a large number of networks will have a greater balance of geographic coverage than those buying only a few networks. If you're buying only one or a few networks, you should check to make sure there is sufficient coverage in any of your priority DMAs.

Advertising time may also be purchased on up to 10,000 local cable systems. *Interconnects* are a network of local cable systems that may be used to cover local market areas. Some advertisers choose to buy time on individual cable systems, which is more targeted but less cost efficient if you have to purchase many individual systems. If a trading area comprises targeted zip code clusters within a DMA, of course, you will want to look into buying only the cable system(s) that target the desired area.

Programming

The broadcast and cable television networks feed a huge selection of programming to their affiliates or cable systems. They produce or buy new programs each year, which air as new shows and then reruns. Eventually, the more popular shows go into syndication where local stations and cable operators use them.

Television programming comes from a variety of sources. The broadcast and cable networks produce original news and entertainment programming and may obtain the rights for "Hollywood" movies and specials like the Academy Awards. Independent program developers develop and sell program concepts such as the popular *Wheel of Fortune*, which they sell to individual stations, creating a syndicated network of stations for the program.

While individual television stations primarily run programming fed to them by the networks, they also produce local news and entertainment, which may pre-empt network programming. Even some of the pay cable channels like HBO and Showtime are now producing original programming such as the *Sopranos* and *Rome*. Finally, advertisers may initiate projects for television series or specials that they sponsor, with some commercial time turned over to the network or station to sell.

Having the right programming available is crucial to advertisers because programs generate and segment audiences and provide a context for the advertisers' commercials. Advertisers seek to buy time in individual programs or cable channels that best reach their target audiences, effectively and efficiently. For example, fast food chains buy a selection of programs in primetime and other dayparts. On the other hand, a small food company promoting the use of its products as recipe ingredients may buy spots on the Food Channel, while a golf club manufacturer who wants to reach golfers may buy sponsorships of golf tournaments.

The *syndication* option is sale of the right to broadcast programming to multiple stations without going through a broadcast network. These shows may be off-network reruns or they may be original programs produced for syndication. Some well-known shows produced for syndication include *Jeopardy*, *Wheel of Fortune*, *Jerry Springer*, and *Entertainment Tonight*. Most popular primetime network TV shows also get into syndication, sometimes even before the broadcast network cancels them. For example, *CSI* and *NCIS* are broadcast both on network and in syndication.

Commercial Lengths

Commercial time may be purchased in a variety of commercial lengths (:90, :60, :30, :15, :10) on networks, stations, and cable systems on a daypart or program by program basis. In Chapter 19, you will learn about the intricacies of buying television.

On Demand Television

One of the most important events affecting 21st century media planning was the invention of *on demand* television, which gave consumers more choice and control over viewing and content. In 1999, TiVo changed forever the way television is and will be viewed. TiVo was developed and marketed as a digital video recorder. For the first time, TiVo gave consumers the ability to record wish lists of programs in a variety of ways—episodes in a series, category/genre, keywords, or even by specific actors or directors.

Many would say that TiVo blazed the trail for the DVR industry expanded by the cable and satellite TV companies. Cable's version of DVRs emulated the TiVo model and soon overtook TiVo sales in the mid and later 2000s.

Today, TiVo is attempting to stage its rebirth by providing capabilities not yet available with cable's DVRs. TiVo is evolving to a more advanced home entertainment device, serving as a home multi-media hub, connecting to the Internet to download additional media and port other devices—like PCs, iPods, iPhones, and DVD players.

For example, TiVo can replace the cable box by having the cable company install CABLECARDS, which allows the TiVo device to connect directly to cable service. Further, when connected to the Internet, TiVo allows users to search Internet sites like YouTube, playing the result directly on the television set.

TiVo also has the capability of providing interactive opportunities for both consumers and advertisers. For example, in one promotion with TiVo, Domino's Pizza has begun taking orders from customers who have broadband TiVo service. When the consumer forwards through a Domino's commercial, TiVo flashes a screen that asks customers whether they would like to order a pizza. Consumers answering yes are redirected to a Domino's ordering screen.

Question: What are the most important ways in which TiVo and other DVRs have affected advertising and media?

Other Recent Developments

Other recent developments affecting the quality of the audio/video and viewing experience for consumers and advertisers alike include HD and more recently 3D television. In addition, television sets may be enabled for WiFi viewing to permit watching certain content on the Internet, like movies on Netflix or Hulu.

Advantages of Television

Based on their budget allocations, it is clear that large advertisers—manufacturers, retailers, online companies, and even business-to-business advertisers—believe television is still the most effective communications medium for their objectives—increasing awareness, image, purchase consideration, and intention. As an advertising medium, television (broadcast/cable/syndication) offers certain advertisers many advantages:

- **Mass Reach.** Though the viewing audience is divided among an abundance of viewing alternatives, television reaches almost everyone almost every day.

- **Selective Reach.** A degree of targeting is possible with proper TV program selection. Sports, for example, typically target men, while situation comedies are stronger with women. News programming reaches older consumers while *American Idol* concentrates on younger viewers.

- **Sight, sound, and motion.** Research has always found that persuasion generally increases with number of senses a message engages.

- **Intrusiveness.** Television is intrusive, meaning that if someone is watching, it is more difficult to avoid seeing a commercial when it comes on, compared to, a magazine ad, which is easier to avoid. Intrusiveness helps achieve higher perception of commercial messages

- **Media flexibility.** Television offers a great deal of flexibility. Commercial lengths are available from :10 to :90+ that allow an advertiser to remind quickly or persuade more leisurely. Geographic flexibility allows the medium to be used nationally, regionally, or locally. Television also permits virtually any message timing— morning, afternoon, night, late night, all night.

- **Creative flexibility.** Television invites creative flexibility, lending itself to demonstrations, announcements, slice-of-life executions, problem/solution, and drama. Music, personality, and special effects can create unlimited emotion or highlight rational facts.

- **Purchase funnel impact.** Many studies find television to be cost effective and impactful. Other media rarely challenge TV's superiority, arguing only that they should be part of a media mix.

Disadvantages of Television

Despite its advertiser-perceived superiority of impact and flexibility, television has some practical disadvantages that may negate its use. These are worth considering.

- **High Cost.** To use television effectively (Effective Reach Model or Recency Model) requires a large out-of-pocket investment, which makes it unaffordable for many mid-sized to smaller advertisers. Just 1000 TRPS in primetime network television could cost $25 million.

- **Declining cost effectiveness.** The Association of National Advertisers (ANA) has raised concerns about broadcast television's declining effectiveness and rising costs. ANA cites declining and increasingly fragmented audiences, in an environment of increased clutter (*commercial density*), and commercial zapping in a rising percentage of households with *personal viewing recorders (PVRs)*.

- **Intrusiveness.** The intrusiveness of television is a two-edged sword. On the one hand, intrusiveness increases the likelihood of commercial exposure. On the other hand, it can become annoying with its barrage of seemingly irrelevant messages.

- **Zapping.** TiVo and DVRs are making it easier for consumers to delete commercials at playback. It has been reported that with TiVo, commercials are zapped as much as 80% of the time.

- **Geographic coverage.** Since television stations primarily cover DMAs (large areas), local businesses with smaller trading areas such as targeted zip codes, may have no better option than local cable systems.

RADIO

An amazing 99% of adults say they listen to radio. Consumers did not rank listening to radio as being a top American pastime, though, as they did watching television. Perhaps this is because radio is a background medium, whereas TV enjoys higher levels of attention and involvement.

Radio's attractiveness to advertisers has been declining, partly due to growth in Internet advertising and partly due to softness in the retail sector. Radio attracted less than $15 billion in 2009 advertising expenditures, down 22% vs. 2008. Nearly 80 per cent of total radio spending is done by local businesses, with only about 20 per cent by national advertisers, network and spot combined. Of that amount, the networks generate only about $700,000 in ad revenues. From the perspective of advertisers, obviously, radio is a medium reserved for use by local businesses.

Radio Availabilities

Radio is anything but a homogeneous medium. In addition to dozens of formats, there are now three delivery systems: terrestrial, satellite, and Internet.

Terrestrial Radio

With over 10,000 *broadcast* (*over-the-air*) *terrestrial* radio stations in the U.S. (over a hundred stations in some large DMAs), there is a radio station format for nearly every taste or interest. Of these stations, about 2,000 can broadcast in *high definition* (*HD*) which makes even an AM station sound like FM. Although consumers must buy a special receiver for HD radio, HD radio itself is free. Still, HD radio has not taken off to the extent that its promoters had hoped.

There are approximately 33 radio networks made up of ever-changing combinations of stations. Each network has its own sound and format, e.g., Dial Global Contemporary vs. Premiere Male Focus.

Satellite Radio

In addition to the terrestrial stations, some *non-commercial* forms of radio are stealing some audience from *commercial* radio stations. Satellite penetration has grown to 20% of households in 2010. Initially, XM and Sirius Radio did not accept commercials, but since 2006 and after their merger, some commercial positions have become available, no doubt at the expense of terrestrial radio stations.

Internet Radio

Internet radio presents online listeners with a stream of audio that cannot be paused or replayed, much like terrestrial radio. While it does not offer on-demand audio, some Internet radio sites allow listeners to construct a custom-tailored station that plays specifically selected content. Many online radio services are associated with a corresponding terrestrial radio station or radio network. Internet-only radio stations are independent of traditional broadcasters.

An April 2008 Arbitron survey in the U.S. found that more than one in seven persons aged 25–54 years old listens to online radio each week. Thirteen percent of the population listened to the radio online, compared with 11 percent in 2007.

Naturally, it is possible to buy advertising on Internet radio networks. Companies like TargetSpot deal with both large and small businesses for traditional network or spot radio advertising buys.

Geographic Coverage

Like television, radio advertising may be purchased to cover the total U.S. or individual radio markets (*MSAs*). Network radio commercials will likely not be fully national, as station clearances vary considerably by network. If you're interested in network radio, you should study the station list and clearances by market.

Most radio stations have much smaller geographic coverage areas than television stations. The rule of thumb is that radio stations cover metropolitan area (MSAs), but most won't cover large DMAs effectively because their signals don't go as far as that. Some stations, like WJR-AM, however, do have very wide coverage areas.

Programming

Station Formats

There are over 30 different radio formats in the U.S. that target consumer demographics in the same way television programs do. A radio station format is defined by the way it is programmed, including its unique content and sound. For example, in Detroit, the station with the market's largest audience WJR-AM, a good example of talk radio where the hosts take calls from listeners on political or other newsworthy issues. While WJR has the largest total audience, it skews heavily to older males. Its shows therefore might target investors, but perhaps not Nike buyers.

The top 10 formats include:

Format	# Stations	Format	# Stations
Country	2019	Top 40	502
News/Talk	1324	Sports	497
Oldies	773	Classic Rock	461
Hispanic	703	Adult Standards	405
Adult Contemporary	884	Hot AC	380

Figure 15-1.—Top Ten Radio Station Formats

Stations sometimes switch formats to try to ride listening trends and garner a larger share of the listening audience...which, guess what... justifies a price increase for their spots.

279

Programs

On some stations, advertisers may buy spots in or sponsor specific programs—like the *Handyman Show, Dr. Merkin, Ric Edelman Investments, Rush Limbaugh,* or *Dr. Laura.*

Dayparts

As on television, radio spots are normally sold by dayparts, dividing the day as shown in Table 15-2.

Table 15-2.— Radio Daypart Availabilities

Daypart	Time
Morning Drive Time	6-10 A
Daytime	11 a.m.-3 p.m.
Afternoon Drive Time	3-7P
Night	7P - Midnight

Morning and afternoon drive times provide the largest audiences. You will find detailed discussion of radio buying in Chapter 20.

Advantages of Radio

Radio offers communications advantages for certain advertisers due to its precision, cost economy, and creative functions.

- **Targeting.** Radio formats can target certain demographics and lifestyles—from teens to older adults—more precisely than most other media. Rap stations, for example, appeal to a pre-adult audience with a specific taste in music. Other formats may target Hispanics or African Americans or Asian Americans. Radio music formats in many respects are generational, playing music reminiscent of an era's youth.

- **Cost efficiency.** The cost of radio (CPP) is usually less than 50% of television's CPP. This is especially cost effective if radio's creative is of high quality. However, it must be pointed out that comparing radio CPMs to television CPMs is extremely misleading because of the apples and oranges situation discussed earlier.

- **Tighter geographic targeting.** Radio wastes less audience for advertisers whose trading area is inside the DMA and metro area.

- **Affordability.** A targeted radio schedule on just a few stations is affordable for smaller advertisers.
- **Creative impact.** Radio offers great opportunities to create theatre of the mind. Close your eyes for a moment and imagine that the room is filling with whipped cream. That is what radio can do, though it rarely does. Radio is not for trying to communicate 300 words of copy plus disclaimers. It is about creating imagery, and you should take advantage of that.
- **Imagery transfer.** If a visual idea is planted on television, radio can bring it to life at a fraction of the cost.
- **Research Findings.** The radio industry has conducted research that shows the communications effectiveness of radio, especially when used in combination with other media (see www.RAB.org).

Disadvantages of Radio

Radio's disadvantages lie in communications effectiveness.

- **Advertising exposure.** Because radio is a background medium cluttered with commercials, the audience usually is not paying full attention, reducing the likelihood that commercials are actually exposed and heard. (Note: Attention levels radio vary by format. Music formats typically generate lower attention levels, while news, talk, and sports formats garner higher attention levels.)
- **Non-visual.** If visual images—like logos, packaging, or appetizing foods—need to be communicated literally, radio cannot do it. However, the right kind of creative, using theatre of the mind, may minimize this handicap.
- **Non-intrusiveness.** Lack of intrusiveness combines with commercial clutter and lack of visual sensory appeal to reduce effective exposure to commercials.
- **Commercial positioning.** Radio is between a rock and a hard place. Listeners don't want so many commercial interruptions; advertisers don't want to be positioned inside a string of commercials that reduces communication and commercial recall.

NEWSPAPERS

As newspaper circulation and advertising revenues continue their downward spiral, there is perhaps a bright spot for the industry. For example, Scarborough reported newspaper readership at 55% in 2008, although Nielsen reported that 64% of adults were reached by a newspaper, virtually unchanged from 63% two years earlier.

- 79% of adults employed in white-collar positions read a newspaper in print or online,
- 82% of adults with household incomes of $100,000 or more read a newspaper in print or online,
- 84% of adults who are college graduates or who have advanced degrees read a newspaper in print or online.

The fact that the circulation numbers have remained strong among those aged 65 and above suggests that print continues to be a viable option for senior living communities. Newspaper ad revenues totaled an estimated $34 billion in 2009, compared to $49 billion in 2006. Over 80% of newspaper ad dollars are local.

After a wave of hysteria concerning the demise of the newspaper industry, the gloom and doom appears rightly to have subsided somewhat. In fact, the Newspaper Association of America (NAA) reported findings in mid-November 2009 that indicated continued strong readership. For instance, in an average week:

Newspaper Availabilities

In many ways, newspapers are not your father's ad medium. They represent the ultimately flexible medium where today advertising can take many forms—from display ads of any size and color in the pages of national newspapers like the *Wall Street Journal* or *USA Today* to a local market daily newspaper in any DMA or MSA in the country.

Besides ads in the pages of the newspapers, you can also buy ads in Sunday supplements, freestanding inserts, classifieds or classified display, polybags and sample delivery, or web ads on the newspapers' websites. Many newspapers even offer turnkey direct mail services. Print is evolving, becoming more interactive both in how it is consumed and in how readers engage with advertisers whose ads they see in print.

Geographic Coverage

Newspapers can provide national, regional, and local DMA coverage, as well as zoned and suburban coverage. To generate national attention in newspapers, you can use national newspapers such as the *Wall Street Journal or USA Today* (which offer national, regional, and some major market editions), or you can employ any of a long list of daily newspapers that cover every market in the U.S.

Daily newspapers offer full-run editions throughout their coverage areas. Some large dailies also offer zoned editions (usually on certain days) that target smaller geographic areas within the larger market. In addition, freestanding inserts in newspapers can often be targeted to certain zip codes. Some newspapers also offer targeted direct mail programs that can be used in concert with other newspaper advertising.

Targeted Newspapers

In addition to the general press, there are thousands of free and paid suburban and community newspapers and shoppers as well as special interest newspapers. If you can validate actual readership, you can consider suburban newspapers either for coverage of specific trading areas or for supplemental DMA coverage. An example of a suburban weekly is the *Birmingham Eccentric*, a paid bi-weekly with circulation among consumers who shop in and around Birmingham, MI, one of the most upscale communities in the nation.

Suburban newspapers are represented by a sales rep firm (*USSPI*) that will develop lists of suburban newspapers covering advertisers' priority areas, which are then sold by USSPI at discount rates. USSPI also handles the logistics of issuing insertion orders and billing.

There are also narrowly targeted newspapers, including newspapers for ethnic groups (Hispanic, Asian, African American, Italian, Polish, and as many other ethnicities as you can name), entertainment and nightlife, business, church, college, entertainment, gay, and a large variety of special interests such as yoga.

Ad Positioning Within Newspapers

Ads may run in any section of the paper but advertising clutter makes positioning a concern. Average weekday section readership by gender, shown in Table 15-3, demonstrates the point.

Table 15-3.—Newspaper Readership by Section of Paper

Gender	News	Business	Sports	Entertainment
Male	89%	67%	76%	57%
Female	91	56	48	53

Source: NAA

Question: Based on these data, in which section of the newspaper would you ask for your golf ad to be positioned?

Advantages of Newspapers

Newspapers offer important advantages, especially for local retailers whose target audience is current shoppers.

- *Editorial context.* The editorial/news context of newspapers provides a sense of immediacy, especially important to retailers and other advertisers with newsworthy announcements.

- *Good reach.* Even now, newspapers reach at least 50-60 percent of adults daily, with a higher reach of older, upper-income adults. This can be an important advantage for announcing a new product, promotion, or sale.

- *Shopping comparisons.* When purchasers have decided to buy, they search newspaper ads for price comparisons. For example, once auto buyers have narrowed their choices to two brands and three models, they shop newspaper ads to find the best deals. (*Time* studies)

- *Geographic targeting.* Newspapers offer a wide array of geographic targeting opportunities, ranging from national to regional to local market to retail trading areas. Using zoned editions or inserts dropped in certain zip code clusters, some papers can target local trading areas.

Disadvantages of Newspapers

There are, of course, disadvantages that you must weigh against the advantages of newspaper advertising:

- *Declining quality.* Newspapers' cost problems risk dilution of editorial product quality. Due to cost pressures, some newspapers have reduced the number of reporters and writers, reduced the size of the paper, and eliminated daily distribution.

- *Perceived editorial bias*: The political philosophy of some newspapers may be all too apparent in its pages, alienating the portion of its audience that doesn't share its philosophy.

- *Cost efficiency.* Newspapers are extremely expensive, both in out-of-pocket cost for a large ad or schedule of ads and the high CPM premium. For example, a half page in the *Sunday New York Times* would cost a national advertiser almost $70,000 for 650,000 circulation, a CPM of over $100. Is it worth it?

- *Rate inequities.* For decades, despite the complaints of national advertisers, newspapers have persisted in using rate cards that charge national advertisers at least 100% more for an inch of advertising than a local advertiser pays. This practice, unsurprisingly, has resulted in a smaller book of business from national advertisers and, more surprisingly, the practice has not changed over time.

- *Ad clutter.* Ad clutter is extremely high and, combined with ad stacking, makes it extremely difficult for smaller ads to stand out, be seen, and be read in newspapers.

- *Declining audiences.* Newspaper audiences are declining, for many reasons, including the fact that broadcast media and the Internet have moved to the forefront of the news business. The younger generation's lack of interest also contributes to the decline in newspaper circulation.

- *Production quality.* While production values and color technology have generally improved, the results vary by paper. Production inconsistencies across the country are always a concern.

- *Logistics.* The lack of uniformity in newspaper sizes, layouts, color capabilities, and complex advertising rates makes the medium complex for advertisers to use.

MAGAZINES

Approximately 17,000 magazines in the U.S. serve almost every national and local consumer interest, and need. According to a study conducted by Nielsen Media Research for the TVB, magazines reach about 51% of adults daily.

In 2009, advertisers spent an estimated $14 billion in consumer and business publications, down 22% from 2008. How much of this dip was the result of a soft economy vs. switching to other media? A clue to the cause of the decrease may be found in a survey of advertisers who were asked where the dollars for their increased Internet spending came from. More than any other source, dollars for Internet advertising were diverted from magazines/print. In 2006, 20% of advertisers diverted magazine dollars to the Internet; in 2008, that figure rose to 32%.

Magazines have been slow to climb aboard the digital bandwagon. According to the *Media Guardian/UK* blog, the magazine industry has generally been reticent in experimenting with digital products. However, in 2009, their reluctance may have begun to fade away. Captivated by the charm of the iPhone, Kindle, and I-Pad, publishers began to think more seriously about digital applications.

In December 2009, a project that could be styled iTunes for Magazines was announced. The five major U.S. publishers—Time Inc, Condé Nast, Hearst, Meredith, and Rupert Murdoch's News Corp.— formed an alliance to develop a technological platform and collaborate on advertising and digital sales. The project will open 50 of the top-selling magazines to digital readers, among them *Time, Vanity Fair, New Yorker, Wired, People, Sports Illustrated* and *Esquire.*

In addition, portable devices such as the iPhone or tablets developed by Apple and Hewlett Packard will change reading behavior. According to Time Inc's interim managing director and executive vice-president, John Squires, in an interview with portfolio.com:

> *We're not trying to be the web. What we're trying to do is present a whole experience. Deeper reading. A more emotional connection to your content.*

Magazine Availabilities

Magazines target almost every conceivable demographic and lifestyle/interest category for consumer and business markets. *Standard Rate and Data* (*SRDS*) (available in the business reference section of subscribing libraries), classifies magazines by subject matter and detailed information on editorial content, circulation, and rates. There are separate editions for consumer magazines and business & trade publications.

While magazines prefer to sell ads on a run-of-book basis, with the magazine deciding where in the magazine to put your ad, you can often negotiate preferred positioning on the second or third cover, page one, or within an editorial section relevant to your business.

Magazines also offer many special space units—inserts printed on special papers, micro-encapsulation (smell the coffee), advertorials (sponsored advertising sections on a particular editorial topic—you've seen them; they look like, and often are, special sections of news written by the magazine about the sponsoring company's product or industry).

Geographic Coverage

Contrary to the perception that magazines are only for national advertisers, there are many ways for regional and local advertisers to use magazines.

National Coverage

Most of the consumer and business magazines listed in SRDS provide national coverage. They also offer less than national editions—for different regions of the country or for large markets like New York, Chicago, or Los Angeles. By stopping the presses and printing different advertising versions of the magazine, magazines can provide more geographic flexibility than you might expect.

Local Coverage

In addition to national and regional coverage, magazines can also provide targeted local coverage in specific DMAs. Magazines can be used to target larger local markets in several ways:

Local Editions of National Magazines

Most of the larger national magazines offer regional and local market editions. For example, you could buy a full-page ad in *Time* or *Newsweek* that would appear only in the region or market(s) you ordered. The circulation mailed to subscribers in Buffalo could contain your ad, but not the copies mailed to Indianapolis. Of course, magazines charge a cost efficiency (CPM) premium for the targeting.

Local Magazines

Many cities have local lifestyle, food, entertainment, travel, ethnic, and/or business magazines. These magazines target different audiences with circulations concentrated in individual local market areas. If your market area effectively covers the DMA, local magazines could be a possibility for you.

Media Networks (MNI)

In addition to targeting ads to local markets in individual magazines, you can order ads in a group of magazines targeted to various audiences on a market-by-market basis. Media Networks (MNI)—owned by Time Warner) offers networks of magazines targeted to specific types of consumers within local markets. Some of MNI's networks include:

- **News:** Time, Newsweek, U.S. News, Sports Illustrated
- **Executive:** Business Week, Forbes, Fortune, Inc.
- **Hispanic:** Latina, People Hispanic
- **Home:** House Beautiful, Cooking Light
- **Luxury:** Food & Wine, In Style
- **Lifestyle:** Golf, Golf Digest, Esquire
- **Family:** Parenting, Parents, Family Fun

Advantages of Magazines

Magazines play an important role in the media mix for many advertisers, offering several of the following advantages.

- *Communication.* Magazines can communicate more information than other media to anyone who is paying attention. Whether it is an appetizing portrayal of a food product as a recipe ingredient, information about the performance of a new car, or advice on the latest pharmaceutical discoveries, magazines provide interested readers with information that affects purchase decisions.

* *Long issue life.* Magazines are retained for future reference, providing an opportunity for repeat ad exposure. You can think of this benefit as a *catalogue effect.*

* *Targeting.* Within the universe of thousands of magazines, there are individual magazines that target almost every conceivable consumer or business market/audience—from music or auto or wine enthusiasts to highly specialized trade/business audiences.

* *Context.* A relevant editorial context can enhance interest in a related ad. (Remember context? Food advertising in *Martha Stewart Living* is in a relevant context, but the same food ad in *Car & Driver* is not.) Context is an important element of the engagement model of advertising.

* *Excellent color.* Magazine color enhances creative for products like food, fashion, and travel and for highly graphic executions.

* *Promotion.* Magazines are good for coupon placement and promotional offers.

* *Prestige.* The right magazines may help improve your image, credibility, and stature, especially if undiscovered by your competitors. *Cooking Light* may enhance the appeal of olive oil, while *Road & Track* helps Corvette.

* *Competitive edge.* If your competitors are not using magazines, they could be your niche.

* *Enhanced media mix.* Used in combination with television and the Internet, magazines (or other media) may be able to increase media effectiveness.

Disadvantages of Magazines

There are also disadvantages to be weighed before you plan to purchase advertising in magazines.

* *Selective perception.* Readers can easily skip over ads that are not of interest to them or that make them uncomfortable.

* *Lack of immediacy.* If your message requires immediacy, magazines may not be a good fit. Magazines accumulate their audiences slowly over time; it takes months for a magazine audience to reach 100%.

Magazines also have long lead times for submission of the ads you want them to publish.

- *Cost efficiency.* Small magazines are frequently not cost efficient.

- *Slow to build reach.* In television, a :30 spot reaches 100% of the viewers immediately (except for DVR replays). However, it takes time for magazine audiences to build, although audiences for weekly magazines are usually generated faster than for monthly magazines.

- *Imprecise geographic targeting.* Even though magazines do offer some geographic flexibility, it may be insufficient to blanket your primary trading area.

OUT OF HOME

Out of home media are *place-based media*, which reach outdoor audiences. Aside from certain digital media, perhaps no other medium is poised for more growth than outdoor, which has introduced brilliant digital applications and a much-needed new audience measurement system. It is probably also true that no medium offers more advertising options.

Out-of-home advertising expenditures peaked at over $7 billion in measured media in 2007-2008. Of that, nearly 60% was local advertising and 40% national. About 96% of adults pass by outdoor locations during an average week.

Outdoor Availabilities

Reportedly, about 500,000 outdoor locations are available, covering many different kinds of outdoor units. Out-of-home advertising (or outdoor advertising) is made up of more than 100 categories, including billboards, street furniture, transit, and *alternative* outdoor. Seven of the major categories are posters, billboards, digital, street furniture, transit, alternative, and scented.

Posters

There are 30-sheet posters and 8-sheet posters. At 12 feet high and 24 feet wide, 30-sheets are the second largest of the billboard structures, illuminated or non-illuminated. Located on high-traffic commuter and commercial area surface streets, 30-sheet poster panels are excellent for market coverage, name recognition, and message or product reinforcement. Poster locations can be customized and rotated for specific advertising goals like supermarket coverage, product placement, new product launches, and ethnic and/or demographic targeting.

Figure 15-2.—A 30-Sheet Poster

Eight-sheets are the smallest of the billboard structures. These poster panels, primarily used as a local or regional reinforcement of a message or product, are 5 feet high and 11 feet wide. Positioned just above eye level, they are freestanding units or they are mounted on the sides of buildings. The structures are usually located in residential and commercial areas near convenience stores, gas stations, and restaurants. 8-sheet poster panels are rotated every 30 to 60 days to give the advertiser more exposure and visibility in a specific coverage area.

Billboards

Billboards may be *rotaries* (meaning literally that boards rotate through multiple locations), *permanent bulletins*, or *spectaculars* such as those seen in Times Square. Bulletins are one of the largest outdoor formats with a standard size of 14 feet high by 48 feet wide. Usually illuminated, they are most often seen on freeways throughout the country. Their large format gives them tremendous impact in the outdoor marketplace.

Located primarily on major highways, expressways, or principal arterials, bulletins are located in areas of high-density vehicle traffic. They present excellent visibility, not only because of their large size, but because they allow creative customizing through extensions and embellishments.

Billboards may be located on either side of a highway, they may be set back a great distance or they may be situated close to the road, they may be on an angle, and they may be illuminated for nighttime visibility or they may not be illuminated.

In addition, (for an extra charge naturally), advertisers will often add *extensions* to outdoor bulletins. Extensions are normally fabricated from wood and are placed on the top of the board or sometimes on a side. Companies may put their name atop of the board; the extension could be something like the dolphin leaping out of the water at Sea World. Some advertisers have even attempted to make a board look three-dimensional, as if something is jumping out at you.

Directionals are the bulletins one sees along the highway that tells passersby where to exit for Joe's restaurant or for gas.

Outdoor's big, recent innovation, of course, has been the introduction of bright digital boards where the content can be managed from a central location.

Figure 15-3.—A Creative Billboard

Digital

New digital technology is giving advertisers the ability to provide visual impact as well as to change their outdoor ad messages quickly and efficiently. Digital billboards are updated electronically through a variety of methods. Some are networked, most are operated remotely, and all of them can be updated quickly, sometimes with just the click of a mouse.

A recent study by Arbitron, the media research company, found that nine out of ten passersby notice the advertising copy on digital billboards some or most of the time. Nearly two out of three find digital billboards to be a cool way to advertise, and recall for specific brands hit 50% for some advertisers.

Street Furniture

Street furniture includes signage on benches, shelters, and phone booths. For example, CBS Outdoor offers what it calls a wider canvas, with bus benches intended to deliver street-level impact as well as a creative opportunity brought about by human contact with an interactive ad. Interactive street furniture could make sense for advertisers looking to engage their clients physically, owing to the proximity of the ads to the audience.

Transit

Bus, train, transit, and airport advertising reaches commuters as they wait or ride. For example, car and subway advertising is available in a variety of formats and sizes, including subway platforms (framed one-sheet (46"H x 30"W), two-sheet (46"H x 60"W), and three-sheet (84"H x 42"W) displays located on the platforms at exits, entrances, and waiting areas of train and subway lines. They are used to reach commuters in major markets who are waiting for trains or already on other trains. In addition, transit posters may be purchased within train and bus interiors and dioramas are available inside terminals.

Alternative

Wraps are an exciting alternative form of out of home advertising—furniture wraps, wrapped cars, insides of buses and trains, building wraps...let your imagination run wild. Have you ever seen a skyscraper wrapped with an outdoor message? Or a wrapped VW beetle?

You see them every day—one is pictured at Figure 15-4. Vehicle wraps, fleet graphics, truck graphics, truck wraps—whatever you call them, it isn't as important as what they do! Wraps are a cost-effective way to communicate a company or brand message wherever your potential customers are.

Figure 15-4.—Truck Wrap

Scent Boards

Another outdoor advertising innovation is to add a scent. One restaurant used a high-powered fan at the bottom of its billboard to emit the scent of grilled chicken from 7:00 to 10:00 a.m. and from 4:00 to 7:00 p.m. by blowing air through fragrance-oil-saturated cartridges. Charlotte-based ScentAir provides custom scents and fragrance-delivery systems for hotel lobbies, casino gambling floors, and retail stores.

Geographic Coverage

Outdoor advertising is perhaps the most geographically flexible mass medium available.

National Coverage

Since all outdoor locations are local, national coverage can be achieved by buying the desired type and TRP level of outdoor in every market important to the advertiser. Achieving national coverage usually requires purchasing locations from a variety of outdoor companies who represent locations in your desired markets (e.g., Clear Channel, Lamar, Adams).

Local Coverage

Depending on the availability of outdoor locations, outdoor may be purchased to target individual DMAs, metro areas, counties, or zip codes. Obtaining the desired coverage in a market may require working with multiple vendors. Outdoor locations can be purchased in certain zip codes to focus on retail trading areas. Outdoor directionals can be purchased to reach drivers traveling in a single direction with a message like, "Exit 23 for Jimmy Bill Bob's BBQ."

Advantages of Out of Home

While it is obviously difficult to describe all kinds of outdoor in one assessment, they do share some advantages.

- **Large audience potential.** High reach and frequency—96% of adults pass outdoor locations every week. Frequency is generated among those who pass locations regularly.
- **Measurement system.** The new Eyes On measurement system should provide much better measurement of outdoor audiences and exposure to boards.
- **Simple awareness.** Outdoor can help build awareness of something very simple: a name, an image, a graphic, or a very short slogan of copy.
- **Geographic flexibility.** Outdoor provides a lot of geographic flexibility. Thirty sheet and 8-sheet posters, for example, can be placed in targeted zip codes and neighborhoods.
- **Ethnic group targeting.** Outdoor boards (e.g., 8-sheets) can be purchased in ethnic neighborhoods.
- **Fit in media mix.** In most cases, outdoor is supplemental and complementary to other media activities, not the primary medium.
- **Lighting.** Many boards can be lit or backlit for nighttime viewing.
- **Directionals.** If your business would benefit from directionals for travelers, outdoor fills the bill.

- **Effectiveness.** Research confirms that media programs including outdoor can be very effective when implemented correctly.

Disadvantages of Outdoor

Like other advertising media, outdoor has disadvantages, some of which can be overcome with due diligence and creative development.

- **Glance medium.** At most, an outdoor bulletin or poster receives a glance from passersby. An outdoor board may be exposed for less than a second or up to two seconds. Only a short, simple, visually dominant message can be communicated.

- **Distorted size perception.** Perception of size is based on viewing distance. Outdoor boards may look giant-sized when you are close to them because their physical dimensions are huge. However, the setback—distance of board from exposure point—is often so great that a giant board looks like a postage stamp. This is made worse if too many words or complicated graphics are used on the board.

- **Location, location, location!** Many of the disadvantages of outdoor are related to where the boards are located.

- **Obstructions.** Boards located behind full or partial obstructions can be significant problems. Boards may be hidden by trees, road signs, or structures. You need someone representing the advertiser to *ride the boards* with someone from the outdoor company to make sure your ads are well located and visible.

- **Limited availabilities**. There are few outdoor availabilities in upscale communities. In many affluent areas, zoning does not permit outdoor. Check your locations!

- **Problematic creative.** A lot of outdoor creative is way too complicated to be seen and comprehended in a second or less. Have you seen boards laden with copy you can't read, graphics you don't understand, brand names you can't see? A few words and a relevant impactful graphic are worth their weight in gold.

- **Low CPMs.** The low CPMs touted by reps are misleading when advertising exposure and communication effectiveness are taken into account. It is hoped that the industry's new Eyes On research (see Chapter 5) will shed some light on how outdoor boards are seen and perceived by consumers.

SUMMARY

Traditional media will continue to provide an important channel of communication for advertising. Television, radio, newspapers, and out of home media all have strengths and weaknesses for different kinds of advertisers and communications situations.

All media are good. All media are useful. All media can be used creatively and mixed together effectively. Traditional media should be evaluated in accordance with the Triangle of Effectiveness:

- Audience size and quality
- Communications impact and relevance of ads in the medium
- Cost

Since traditional media will continue to play an important role in your media mixes, Chapter 15 has prepared you with information about each of the five principal forms of traditional media—television, radio, newspapers, magazines, and outdoor. Now that you have learned more about each medium and its advantages and disadvantages with respect to the three selection criteria, you are farther along the road to competent media planning.

16. INTERNET MARKETING

The Internet is like a freight train roaring along while people are laying tracks in front of it. It's not just gaining on those laying tracks; it's gaining on the steel mills.

−Matt Mathis

Internet advertising opportunities are presenting themselves at rates of change previously unknown. While Search remains the granddaddy of Internet advertising, social media, mobile, and Internet video are busy elaborating the future.

The Internet is used to promote both online and offline businesses, local, national and global, and, increasingly, local businesses. Did you know that you could buy an ad on AOL that would appear only in Detroit?

An effective presence on the Internet is essential to the success of almost any business in the 21st century. The right website properly promoted to generate traffic can level the playing field for competitive businesses. A company's web presence can even give it a competitive edge. Chapter 16 will show you how a good website will:

- Provide information about your company, its products, and its services to visitors who are seeking that information when they are seeking it.

- Give your product or business credibility, regardless of its physical facilities (or lack thereof).

- Give you the ability to compete locally, nationally, and globally.

- Allow you to take orders and collect leads 24/7.

- Assist with customer services and support 24/7.

- Save employee time and expense by making operations more efficient.

Chapter 16 will orient you to Internet marketing for both online and offline business. It focuses on the importance of building a world-class presence on the web and tells you how to do it. Other strategies and tactics for using the Internet will be discussed in Chapters 17 and 22.

INTRODUCTION

Research says: 84% of people conduct product information searches on the internet prior to making a purchase. Nuff said?

Clearly, the Internet plays an important role for online, offline, and hybrid businesses that sell directly from their websites (called *e-commerce*) and from their brick and mortar stores. Wireless Internet and broadband permit users to access the Internet from wherever they are. Communities provide wireless service to allow access in their geographic area. The growing penetration of broadband allows users to view videos, including TV programs and movies, and if you can believe it, commercials.

Given these developments, it is clear that the Internet isn't just for large businesses any more. The Internet can help small to midsized companies increase sales significantly through a new online channel of distribution and access to a whole new group of consumers who are actually interested in what the company has to sell. A small local business in a small town can become a national or global marketer on the Internet. What an opportunity!

In addition, the Internet helps increase the efficiency of business operations and customer service by automating certain work and making it available round the clock. Finally, a myriad of digital marketing tools can be used to promote simultaneously both online and offline businesses.

Almost all national retail organizations have a website where anyone can place an order, request information, or obtain customer service. Most are able to accept credit card or Internet payment for instant processing of an order. In fact, some companies accept orders solely from the Internet.

CASE HISTORIES

Three case histories will demonstrate the Internet's marketing role has for three very different kinds of companies.

Office Depot

In addition to e-commerce sales (selling direct from their website), Office Depot has gone a step farther than its competition has and included perks for contract customers. They have linked their website to their ES9000 mainframe, enabling customers to get individualized contract pricing. The closest any competitors have come is storing customers' shipping information. The result was $67 million in sales in a recent year. That doesn't come close to an Internet-only retailer like Amazon.com, but it is a phenomenal success for a traditional company's first year in the Internet market.

Increased sales revenue is not the only benefit that Office Depot's Internet marketing plan has reaped. A new level of efficiency was also achieved. For an online order, an order-entry clerk is not required, and Depot does not have to devote personnel to answering questions or trying to understand precisely what the customer needs—customers can browse through the company's entire catalog of merchandise.

With more online sales, more of the company's resources can support customer services. A salesperson can get out in the field to meet one-on-one with prospective customers. Order-entry clerks can spend more time making sure in-store customers get what they want.

Are customers also benefiting from Office Depot's website? Customer feedback has been overwhelmingly positive, mainly because Internet ordering is an additional service, not a substitute for service. Customers have always been frustrated when they couldn't speak to a "real person." Now when they need to place an order, there is usually no need to wait, and when more clarification or special attention is required, a real person is usually available for customer service.

Cannondale Bicycles

In early 2005, Cannondale Bicycle Corporation, a manufacturer of high-end bicycles, was looking for new ways to engage more directly and interactively with its customers in order to strengthen its brand and help drive sales. Cannondale decided to take advantage of the opportunity presented by the Internet to build on the brand's cult following, gain input for new product development, and promote recreational cycling.

To get started, Cannondale created a company blog operated by "Brad," a pseudo-employee and longtime Cannondale Headshok icon, who would comment about company developments and respond to customer questions. The company saw this as a more personal way to interact with its core customers and provide an alternative to its traditional customer service department. The biking community immediately latched onto the idea and passed around the link, driving traffic to Cannondale's site.

Cannondale also adopted blogging technology to connect externally with its retail partners. The company's e-commerce site allows retailers to order products online and communicate with one another and Cannondale's dealer service group. Cannondale's foray into blogging has been more successful than the company expected, going beyond the intangible benefits of improved customer and retailer relationships to increasing sales and improving the corporate brand.

Laser Eye Surgery Clinic

A laser eye surgery clinic offered the latest technology in LASIK and PRK, two of the most popular procedures for correcting near-sightedness, far-sightedness, and astigmatism. Its website was not coming up high on search engine results, and the owner believed that the website needed a new look to improve conversion (percentage of visitors who actually inquire or buy). Over the course of a year, consultants worked closely with the clinic to achieve dramatically improved search engine results, enhance website content and design, and streamline sales processes. As a result, unique visitors increased over 500% in a year, as first-page listings on Google and Yahoo soared.

ABOUT WEBSITES

A company's website is its face to the world. Once it is found on the Internet among the millions of websites that are there, the website must then convert visitors to leads or sales.

What is a website? This book uses Wikipedia's definition:

A collection of related web pages, images, videos or other digital assets that are addressed relative to a common Uniform Resource Locator (URL), often consisting of only the domain name, or the IP address, and the root path ('/') in an Internet Protocol-based network. A website is hosted on at least one web server, accessible via a network such as the Internet or a private local area network.

A *web page* is a document, typically written in plain text interspersed with formatting instructions of *Hypertext Markup Language (HTML,*

XHTML). A web page may incorporate elements from other websites with suitable markup anchors.

Web pages are accessed and transported with the Hypertext Transfer Protocol (HTTP), which may optionally employ encryption (HTTP Secure, HTTPS) to provide security and privacy for the user of the web page content. The user's application, often a web browser, renders the page content according to its HTML markup instructions onto a display terminal.

All publicly accessible websites collectively constitute the *World Wide Web*, also known as the *Internet*.The pages of a website can usually be accessed from a simple *Uniform Resource Locator* (*URL*), the *homepage*. URLs organize pages into a hierarchy, although hyperlinking among them conveys the site structure and guides the reader's navigation of the site.

Some websites require a subscription to access some or all of their content. Examples of subscription sites include many business sites, parts of many news sites, academic journal sites, gaming sites, message boards, web-based email, services, social networking websites, and sites providing real-time stock market data.

TYPES OF WEBSITES

There are five primary types of website: brochure sites, e-commerce sites, communities, portals, and search engines. Which kind of website a company chooses depends on its marketing strategy and the purpose(s) of its website.

Brochure Sites

Figure 16-1.—Brochure Website

Brochure sites are used by companies that want to provide product information online with the hope that the visitor will ask by email or telephone for more information. Websites for auto companies provide good examples of upper-end brochure sites. Go to Chevy.com, for example, and you can search for information, pictures, and videos about each of Chevy's car and truck models. You can request additional information and brochures, and you can search for dealers in your area.

Go to websites offering business to business and technical products, and you will find brochure sites explaining their offerings while asking for contact information.

If you were looking for a new advertising agency, you might visit websites like jwt.com or campbell-ewald.com. These brochure sites provide information about the agencies and their clients, with contact information for visitors who want to follow up by email or phone.

Also visit Mcdonalds.com, another brochure site, which highlights the McDonald's menu, store locations, and news such as the free Wi-Fi they began offering beginning in January 2010.

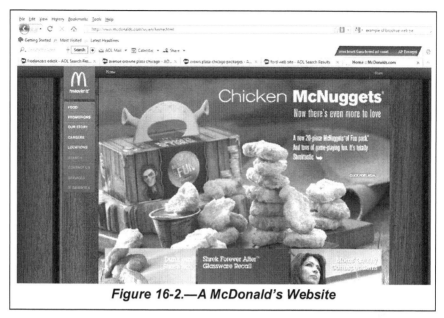

Figure 16-2.—A McDonald's Website

Companies often have multiple websites, each serving a different purpose. The main site might provide an overview of the company and its products or services, while supplemental or specialized sites focus on specific topics. For example, if a company is planning a special promotion, a new website might be developed to explain the promotion and garner consumer response such as entering a contest or sweepstakes.

E-commerce Websites

Unlike brochure sites, the primary purpose of an e-commerce site is to sell goods or services immediately. Amazon, Target, Penney's, QVC, and thousands of others sell directly from their websites. Visitors to e-commerce sites very often are looking for something specific, so it behooves the site owner to help them find it.

Amazon is a great example of an e-commerce site; it sells everything from books and music to electronics and gourmet foods, all of which visitors can find easily by searching keywords on Amazon.

E-Commerce is about conducting business with customers online. E-commerce provides many benefits to small businesses as well as to large firms and organizations.

305

- **Increased customer base and sales.** Marketing over the Internet grows business. Online sales transactions are increasing almost exponentially as more and more consumers are shopping online. Your physical location becomes irrelevant, and your marketing area can extend globally if you wish. The Internet also is being used as a research tool for collecting information about products, services, and retailers prior to visiting their establishments.

- **Stronger customer relationships.** A company's achievement is built around its dealings with customers. The stronger the relationships, the greater the success. e-commerce improves these relationships. It automates the sales process so that customers can get their questions answered in a straightforward manner.

- **Reduced costs.** e-commerce can drive order costs down. Research indicates that the average cost of electronic orders ranges from $10 to $75 per order. By mechanizing the order procedure online, a company can significantly reduce costs. (Parker, 2004).

- **Increased marketing effectiveness.** e-commerce helps companies promote their products more quickly and boost demand by offering all essential information—product as well as design details, metaphors, pricing and delivery information, category and accessibility—in one place where customers can access it at will.

Web Community Sites

The third type of website is the community site. Web communities come in all sizes, shapes, and tones, but their common purpose is to bring together like-minded users. For example, there are communities of websites that specialize in aquariums and fish, women's issues, travel, politics, and even advertising. Some communities may be relevant to certain marketers' businesses.

Portals

Portals, as the name suggests, are sites that serve as gateways to information. A good portal provides information precisely relevant to the visitor's search. For example, if you searched for advertising agencies, search results would likely include some portals with links to advertising agencies.

Search Engines

The last type of website is search engines, probably the most useful tool on the Internet. Without search engines, it would be almost impossible to find anything on a Web that encompasses everything. The three largest search engines are Google, Yahoo!, and Bing (MSN). Chances are, you will not build any new search engines, but it is important to know about them and how they work. Search engines can be effective and relatively inexpensive marketing tools. Search engine marketing is explored later in this chapter.

Building a Website

Before you begin to create your website, make a quality commitment that your web presence will convey to consumers that you are a reputable, important, and viable alternative to your competitors, large or small. Arfter that, it is not especially difficult to build a world-class presence on the World Wide Web with a reasonably small investment. You can spend as much or as little as you want; what you must not do is overlook entirely this tool that will help you compete.

Building a successful website doesn't happen all by itself, however, and whether you create a website yourself or work with outside consultants or an agency, you need to understand the process and best practice. The process begins with benchmarking the competition and defining the website's purpose, then it proceeds through nine steps to establish the site, which will then require continuous improvement:

1. Benchmark the competition
2. Develop an outline of content
3. Design the site
4. Select a hosting service
5. Secure a domain name
6. Optimize the site for the search engines (SEO)
7. Go live
8. Submit the URL to search engines
9. Promote the site
10. Analyze results
11. Continuously improve the site.

Benchmark the Competition

Begin by making a list of your competitors. Include all the most successful companies, whether or not you compete with them in your market area. Study their websites, print copies of the best ones, make notes on their content as well as their look and feel. For each site, study the following:

- Purpose
- Structure
- Business objectives
- Direct sales (e-commerce)
- Target audiences
- Primary selling message
- Support for sales propositions—price, service, incentive
- Content & visuals
- Personality & brand character
- Keywords used to generate traffic
- Strengths & weaknesses

Then ask yourself what opportunities your competitor's site presents.

Define Website Purpose

You know that you want a website that is at least as good as the sites of your competitors. Now that you've studied those, it's time to think about yours. What is its *purpose*? Should it sell directly? Get leads? Give information? Should it be for e-commerce? For customer service?

When you know the purpose of the site, decide whether it should be a brochure site, an e-commerce site, or one of the other types. What is your main selling idea on the site? What products and services should you offer? What competitive advantages can you present? Why should consumers looking for what you sell buy from you rather than the competition? What should your site look like? How should it work? What content can you offer?

Develop Outline

Once you have envisioned the structure and basic content of your site, your initial organization and copywriting begin. Figure out what specific pages you will include and write a rough draft of the copy for each of them. If you are building an e-commerce site, you will have at least six pages:

1. Home Page
2. Products & Services
3. About Us
4. Site Map
5. Privacy Page
6. Ordering/Shopping Cart/Payment

The home page will be the *landing page,* the most important page for visitors who will spend only a few seconds there before deciding whether to look further into your site. Your home page needs a strong headline, good supporting copy, and attractive illustration, as well as clear navigation to other pages.

Developing your outline means deciding for the home page and each of the others what it will say and how it will relate to the other pages. You want to be sure that information your visitors want is available to them, that they can find it, and that it makes sense to them. Outlining is a way to take care of organization before things get too complicated. You will discover that some of your copy begins to draft itself during this process and to suggest accompanying images and navigational pathways.

Design Your Site

After you have a rough draft describing what your website will say, it is time to design how it will look and feel. This is the stage of website development where you choose graphics and illustrations, layout, typography, and links.

You can do this work yourself with low-cost software, which includes templates where you fill in the blanks and provide illustrations. Most major web hosts include software that facilitates your web design.

On the other hand, you may prefer to hire a web designer. If you are not proficient in web design, letting a professional design the site at your direction is recommended. Qualified professional designers have technical, programming, and creative expertise that most of us don't possess, and hiring their services need not be prohibitively expensive. Many web designers are registered on freelance sites such as guru.com and elance.com, and they will bid on your projects. You give the designer your copy and the URLs of websites you benchmarked, along with any specific requests or ideas. The designer will submit the creative product to you for your approval and revision as the design progresses.

Select a Hosting Service

A web hosting service will provide your gateway to the Internet, and it will provide the necessary storage for your website. Two good, inexpensive hosts are 1&1.com and StartLogic.com. Hosting services can cost less than $10.00 per month, usually payable one year in advance. If you have an e-commerce site, you may choose a specialized host at a somewhat higher cost.

Secure Your Domain Name

Your website will have a unique address on the Internet called a *URL* (*Universal Resource Locator*), e.g., www.AdMediaStore.com. You should reserve several or many domain names to prevent competitors from overlapping your business and to have the option to launch related sites in the future. Any web host will do this for you at no or for a nominal cost, or you can search *domain names*). Your domain name should pass three tests:

- Define your product/service using words consumers would use to search for what you offer, so that search engines will index and find you
- Be easy for surfers to remember
- Use no more than 63 characters!

It is likely that at least some of the names you want will have been reserved already by someone else, so you need a good list of alternatives, which can include variations in the suffix. If a domain name with .com at the end is taken, it may be available as.org or .biz.

Optimize for Search

You would like your landing page to be among the top 10 results of an Internet search. This is extremely difficult to accomplish, but being in the first several pages may be achievable.

The major search engines—Google, Yahoo!, Bing, Ask.com—will find your website based on the keywords with which the pages in your website are associated. Connecting your pages to search engines by using the right keywords is a technical process. If you have the technical expertise, you can do this yourself. If not, your web designer might be able to do it for you, or you can hire a Search Engine Optimization (SEO) expert to help you. Some SEO advice includes these best practices.

- Choose keywords that describe your website offerings—and that users would most likely search—and make sure that these words and phrases are amply represented on your pages.
- Create HTML meta tags for each web page. Search engines will also consider tags in their searches.
- Design or modify your copy (if you can without ruining it) so that 5-10% of the words on each page are keywords.
- Use keywords in the links among your pages, e.g., rather than having a user click on a link that says Home Page, use a keyword phrase to identify that link.
- Get other websites to link to your website.

Search engine returns are influenced by the keywords you use, their frequency, and the other pages that link to yours. Do everything you can to maximize those features without compromising the purpose of your site.

Go Live!

Your website has been written and designed. You have a domain name. The site is optimized for search engines to find it. Now it is time to upload the site to your host server. This is something else that you might be able to do yourself, your designer might be able to help you with, or your webmaster can do for you. If your website was created with a web-authoring tool, the HTML version must be uploaded into the host account using the File Transfer Protocol (FTP) function.

Submit the URL

More than 80% of website traffic comes from search engines, so it is vital that the engines be able to find your site when someone enters one of your keywords. Once your website is live, however, it must be registered with the search engines before they will even know it exists, so submit your URL to the engines, especially Google, Yahoo, Bing, AOL, and Ask.com.

You can manually submit your site to search engines or hire someone to do it for you. There are many paid submission services like Addpro.com, which provides manual submission to the most important engines and online submission to 1,500 others. You also should be sure to submit your site (or have it submitted) to online directories like The Open Directory, www.dmoz.com.

Promote Site Use

At last, it is time to lure visitors to your site. Generating qualified visitors (those with the interest and income to purchase) to a website can require more time, effort, and money than any other single aspect of Internet marketing. Marketing tools that will help you generate this traffic are reviewed later in this chapter.

Analyze Results

One of the great things about marketing on the Internet is that almost everything is quantified for analysis. In your CPC programs, it will be easy to tell which keywords are generating clicks (visitors) and which aren't. You can tell which of your ads is pulling best. You can determine your conversion rates by ad and by keyword, so that you know which keywords and ads are most profitable. In addition, the audience data available on your control panel provides an enormous amount of results and diagnostic information to help you improve your performance—either your website structure and content or the site's marketing and promotion.

Improve Conversion

Conversion refers to the percentage of website visitors who take some desired action, such as buying a product or requesting information. It is important to get consumer feedback on your website. You should be asking users about your site's content, ease of navigation and usability, and image. Based on such feedback, you can improve your site's effectiveness in providing leads and sales—at a relatively low cost to you.

INTERNET MARKETING TOOLS

The internet can be used to promote both online and offline businesses. Certain Internet marketing activities, such as pay per click programs, apply primarily to online businesses, while other others, like social media and email, can be used to promote both online and offline businesses. Table 16-1 provides a matrix of some of the tools used by companies marketing online and offline.

Table 16-1.—Internet/Digital Marketing Tools

Internet Marketing Tool	Promote Site	Promote Offline
Search Engine Optimization	X	
Pay per Click (CPC/PPC)	X	
Online Display Ads	X	
Email	X	X
Email Newsletters	X	X
Article Submissions	X	
Links	X	
Social Media	X	X
Mobile Media	X	X
Affiliate Marketing	X	X
Offline Ads	X	X
Press Releases	X	X
Podcasts	X	X
Online Video/Rich Media	X	X
Online Games	X	X
Advertising in Apps	X	X
Advertising Networks	X	
Pop Ups	X	
Pop Unders	X	

The principal purpose of Internet marketing and advertising is to drive traffic to a website(s). Advertisers want to visitors to their brochure sites or e-commerce sites for branding and sales purposes, and may use online and offline methods to generate the traffic. Secondarily, many Internet/digital marketing tools are also used to promote offline businesses. Each of these marketing tools is reviewed here.

Search Engine Optimization (SEO)

SEO's objective is to increase a website's traffic count, which is the source of conversions, sales, and inquiries. This requires ranking high in the results of searches for the keywords in the search query. SEO makes it easier for the search engines to find the site. The site's content is worthy of higher search engine ranking if it is more relevant and competent. The SEO process is often a struggle to rank well for just a few keywords. In return, you can generate free traffic to your website!

If you search your best keywords, you will see the leading sites in the rankings; to obtain traffic for your content, you will need to rank higher than they do. It is not enough simply to submit the site to a million search engine indexes and directories or to add meta tags onto the web pages.

In order to obtain significant website traffic, you must achieve first-page search engine results. To do that, you must build a great content-rich site, submit it properly to search engines and directories, and optimize it.

There are no secret shortcuts to SEO. There are ranking and placement methodologies to follow, for which classroom SEO training may be helpful, as are unique content writing and linking services. Getting good rankings requires education, effort, and—at least in the beginning—expert technical support. Do a search on the key word phrase, *Search Engine Optimization* to see how many candidates would love to help you improve your search engine rankings!

Pay-per-Click Advertising (PPC/CPC)

Pay per Click (PPC) and Cost per Click (CPC) are the same thing: the advertiser pays the search engine only when someone clicks one of the advertiser's key words and is redirected to his website. It is one of the most important and cost efficient ways to generate website traffic (visitors). Google is by far the largest PPC engine, followed by Yahoo!, Bing, and then dozens of others.

The signup process is very simple. To sign up for Google's AdWords program, simply go to adwords.google.com, provide the typical registration information, and select the language and geographic area you want to target (world, countries, U.S., or your specific local market). Follow the prompts to write one or more brief ads that users will see when doing a Google search for one of your keywords, provide a list of the keywords you want, your bid for each, and your monthly budget for clicks to your website. Generally, the higher your bid vs. competitive bidders, the more ad impressions you will get.

For example, suppose that one of your keywords is Edsel. A web surfer asks Google to search for Edsel. When the search results come up, at the top or bottom of the page is your ad: Edsel Owners—parts and service at discount prices. The surfer clicks on your ad and is redirected to your website. You pay Google the amount of your bid per click for Google deliveries on the keyword Edsel.

Google offers several targeting options and is always coming up with new ideas for this type of pay-for-performance advertising. Currently, Google is testing pay-per-sale, where the advertiser would pay Google a fixed amount for a conversion shown on your AdWords pages.

Like everything else, AdWords is not as simple as it seems. You can hire professional assistance to maximize ROI from PPC advertising while you are educating yourself to do it independently. Google offers online training, and so do other PPC search engines.

Online Display Ads

For branding as well as generating website traffic, you can use Internet display advertising—banner ads, small button ads, vertical skyscraper ads, and many other formats. AOL sells ads that look like news stories.

Figure 16-3.—Example of Banner Advertisement

- Banner ad standards have changed over the years to larger sizes, and are continuing to change, in part due to increased resolution of standard monitors and browsers, in part to provide advertisers with more impact for their investments. Posters, fliers, transit cards, tents, scale models are examples of display advertising. Display advertisers use cookie and browser history to determine users' demographics and interests so they can target relevant ads to those browsers.

Email

Although email usage has declined over time as an Internet marketing tool, it is still important for several tasks. The most important use of email is to maintain contact with current customers. Companies may send customers special offers or rewards; some send newsletters to customers.

To prospect for new customers, it is difficult to use email without spamming. To develop a prospect list, companies may attempt to build a database of inquirers, visitors who have joined their mailing list, or those who have requested newsletters.

Another method is to rent a targeted list from a reputable company that has opt-in lists for your target audience. (Opt-in lists include only those who have given their permission to receive your email.) Rented lists will cost between $100 and $500 per thousand addresses, and the list brokers will insist on sending your email themselves, for two reasons: (1) to protect their lists from duplication and (2) to monitor your message content.

The <From> and <Subject> lines are the most important components of your emails. They are what the recipient sees first. The decision to open or delete email is based on what appears in these two components. <From> should be used to brand your company and/or give the name of the sender. <Subject> must entice the recipient to open the email, without being misleading. Writing the subject is an art unto itself. Some criteria are brevity, urgency or timeliness, relevance, and uniqueness.

Avoid overuse of capital letters or symbols. They are cues for spam filters, as are the words FREE and WORK AT HOME anywhere in the email. Even if a capitalized message made it through the filters, it would do you no favor. Writing in caps is like shouting—not good marketing.

While there is no solid evidence as to the best days to mail, some studies have shown them to be Tuesday through Thursday. Data do show that those are the days when most email is sent, and it's not hard to explain. On Monday, everyone is busy with a new workweek; on Friday, they're trying to finish projects or get out of the office early. Run your own tests to see which are the best days for your customers.

Email Newsletters

Email is also useful for distributing newsletters to your customer list and to website visitors who *ask* to receive it. (Do not spam recipients with your unsolicited newsletter. That could get you kicked off your host service and get you blacklisted.) Electronic newsletters are much cheaper than printed newsletters, and they can be extremely effective in driving traffic back to your website as well as for customer retention and sales promotion. A newsletter is a project you can do yourself; you can hire a specialist to write it and handle the distribution for you; or you can use a combination of approaches to prepare and disseminate it.

Article Submissions

Getting articles published by other webmasters is an important SEO technique. The greater your presence on the Internet, the more likely it is that the search engines will include your site in search results. Toward this end, you can provide articles embedded with your URL and keywords to webmasters who have specialized editorial sites related to your business.

Article submission is an effective, low cost method of getting quality incoming, lifetime links to a website. Search engines love links from content-rich pages. Article submissions can improve your search engine ranking as they build your site authority.

There are hundreds of *article directories* where you can submit *articles* for others to read and republish in their newsletters, e-zines, and other online publications. There are also firms that will submit articles for you (for a fee, of course).

Links

Developing links from other websites to yours may also help raise your rankings with the search engines, especially Google, by creating *link popularity*. What is link popularity? It refers to the weighted value of the combined number of inbound links to a particular web page from other web pages as an indicator of page importance.

A web page is deemed more important when more pages link to it. In a sense, a link is a vote cast by one page for another, but the votes are not equal. A vote from a page that high link popularity itself transfers a greater weighted value than a page with lower link popularity.

Backlinks are *incoming* links to a website or web page. Number of backlinks is one indication of the popularity or importance of a website or page used by Google to determine page rank.

Social Media Networks

Social media became a hot medium in the early 21st century as Facebook, YouTube, and Wikipedia claimed nearly a quarter of the world's online time by the middle of 2010 (*NielsenWire*, 6-15-2010). Chapter 17 will cover in detail how social media marketing can assist branding, consumer research, and traffic generation to websites.

Mobile Media

Advertisers are closely watching the mobile phone user segment, which was projected to be an $11 billion business in 2011. The soft economy may have delayed timing somewhat, but cell phone advertising may be the next big advertising media idea. Audiences increasingly use their phones to browse the web and perform other web applications.

Google mobile ad technology is part of Google's platform and allows advertisers, content providers, and developers to capture the mobile opportunity. Using a CPC pricing model, an advertiser can connect with mobile Internet users while they're on the go with Google's mobile ads. With Google mobile ads, you can choose from text or display ads across Google's Search and Content Networks, in mobile applications, and on YouTube Mobile.

Cell phone ads are mostly *small text message, Short Message Service (SMS)*, sent to a downloaded list of recipients. Location-based advertising is also a possibility, taking text messages to another level. With *GPS (Global Positioning System)*, you could track mobile phone users and send timely messages to them. For example, as a coffee shop owner, you could send a message about the day's special to pedestrians passing your store.

In some markets, the most common type of mobile advertising is *mobile web banners* (top of page) or m*obile web posters* (bottom of page). Other markets are dominated by SMS advertising, which as of this writing represents over 90% of mobile ad revenue worldwide. In addition to SMS, cell phones receive the following rapidly-growing forms of advertising:

- Multimedia Message Service (MMS) messages, which may contain images, video, and sound
- Video advertising
- Advertising within mobile games and mobile videos

- Mobile TV ads
- Full-screen interstices (which appear while a requested item of mobile content or mobile web page is loading)
- Audio advertisements that can take the form of a jingle before a voicemail recording or an audio recording played during a telephone-based service such as movie ticketing or directory assistance.

Of the more than 220 million mobile device users, almost 40% are regular text messagers, so the potential audience is significant. Some research has also found that text ads have an average CTR (click-through rate) of around 4%, which is better than the normal web CTR of 1%.

Affiliate Marketing

Many companies that sell goods or services on the Internet use *affiliate marketing* to generate incremental sales at low cost. Affiliate marketing is a revenue sharing venture between a website owner and an online merchant. A website owner will allow placement of advertisements on his websites either to help sell the other merchant's products or to send potential customers to the other merchant's website, in exchange for a share of the profits.

Offline Advertising

When many of the online heavyweights look to increase traffic to their own websites, they look primarily to traditional media, especially television. Ever wonder why? Brick and mortar retailers, small businesses, Yahoo!, Overstock.com, and many others spend millions in television and other media to generate website traffic and new visitors that they hope will convert to orders. The purpose of most offline advertising is to build awareness of the company's URL and give reasons to visit their website.

Press Releases

Similar to article submission, another relatively low cost way of increasing relevant website traffic is to send out press releases that can be posted on the major search engines to help raise your ranking in search engine results. Distribution services like PRWeb.com will distribute releases to both online and offline media outlets at relatively low cost. The hope is that the PR release will become viral, picked up by blogs, newsletters, other online news services, and even offline media.

Podcasting

Podcasting delivers audio content to iPods and other mobile media players on demand so that it can be listened to at the user's convenience. With podcasting, listeners can synch content to their media players and take it with them wherever they go. Since podcasts are typically saved in MP3 format, they can be heard on a variety of receivers. Podcasting can be used for publishing almost any kind of audio, creating an alternative distribution channel for audio content, and allowing publishers to extend the reach of Internet content to times when users aren't even connected.

Rich Media

The term *rich media* was coined to describe a broad range of digital interactive media. Rich media can be downloadable or may be embedded in a webpage. Downloadable rich media can be enjoyed offline with media players such as Real Networks' RealPlayer, Microsoft's Media Player, or Apple's QuickTime. The defining characteristic of rich media is that it exhibits dynamic motion. The animated, interactive presentation file embedded in a web page is rich media. For example, when you go to AOL you will often see an ad with dancers gyrating to attract attention and generate click-throughs to the advertiser's website.

Online Games

Since Sony launched its first PlayStation console in 1995, video gaming has enjoyed a rapid transition from the bedrooms of pubescent boys to that most coveted of locations: the space under the living room TV. The demographics have changed accordingly. Teenage boys have grown into the 18-34 age bracket; their wives and girlfriends regularly join in playing, particularly with social games and mainstream offerings like karaoke. With advertising investment projected to exceed $1 billion in 2010, advertisers see games as a great way to reach this demographic.

The Nintendo Wii has been credited with getting grannies out of their chairs, its motion-sensing controllers limiting the intimidation many non-gamers feel when exposed to outwardly complex controllers for the first time, and allowing such diverse activities as bowling, fishing, and even yoga.

In-game advertising is unique in that gamers actually don't mind seeing real brands and advertising because it adds to the environmental and contextual realism within these increasingly photorealistic virtual worlds. For example, a study by Nielsen Interactive Entertainment found that over 70 percent of gamers responded positively to the presence of real brands and advertising in games, so long as it was contextual.

Advertising in Apps

Apps are supported by advertising, a trade-off most users are happy to accept. Attitudes about advertising in software have changed. You don't expect your desktop software to contain ads (sorry, no pop-ups on Excel or Photoshop, please), but everyone understands that websites are supported by ads. That's true of everything from blogs and reference sites to NYTimes.com and SDTimes.com. Mobile apps—which spread like wildfire from Apple's iPhone to other platforms, like Google's Android and Microsoft's Windows Phone 7—are more akin to websites than to desktop software.

Apple's iAd for Developers program is a way for developers to promote their paid or free apps to millions of iPhone and iPod touch users around the world. Using this advertising program, you can reach the right audience to drive more downloads of your app. Getting started is easy. You only need to create the banner ads and Apple does the rest to get your iAd up and running.

Internet Ad Networks & Exchanges

Internet ad networks and exchanges place display ads and banners for advertisers on networks of websites targeting particular audiences. Doubleclick, AdBrite, and ValueClick are examples of ad networks that sell banners and display ads for websites and cell phones on a CPM, CPC, or PPC (pay per conversion) basis. Advertisers can select target audiences on the basis of demographics, product/service category usage or by keywords. The ad networks pay website owners a fee in exchange for the right to place advertising on their website. This subject will be discussed more fully in Chapter 22.

Pop-Ups & Pop-Unders

Pop-ups are those annoying small windows that open automatically in front of whatever you're trying to see. Pop-ups are a form of online advertising intended to attract web traffic or capture email addresses. They work by spontaneously opening a new web browser window to display advertisements. You have no doubt seen many pop ups while browsing the net—when unrequested ads just pop up! Pop up blockers, of course, reduce available audiences.

A variation on the pop-up window is the *pop-under* advertisement, which opens a new browser window hidden under the active window. Pop-unders do not interrupt the user immediately, becoming visible only when the covering window is closed, making it more difficult to determine which website opened them.

Advertisers may buy pop ups and pop unders from a large number of online vendors.

SUMMARY

The Internet is revolutionizing marketing.

Among its other contributions, the Internet is a great equalizer. Consumers cannot judge the size of your business from your website, which is at the core of Internet marketing.

Chapter 16 began with a discussion of the kinds of websites you can build and described the process of creating one. The second part of the chapter has reviewed an array of digital marketing tools you can use to promote both websites and offline businesses, including search marketing, PPC, display and banners, email, articles, mobile media, affiliate marketing, offline advertising to bring visitors online, PR, rich media, games, apps, ad networks, and pop-ups and pop-unders. These Internet marketing techniques, with their respective promises and pitfalls, are now in your media planning repertoire. Chapter 22 will teach you about buying Internet media. First, though, Chapter 17 will examine the role of social media in free marketing.

17. FREE MARKETING IN SOCIAL MEDIA

Social media allow big companies to act small again.

−Anonymous

Initially used as a way for family and friends to stay in touch and share, social media are now becoming an important marketing tool. Almost every issue of Advertising Age *and* AdWeek *devotes significant space to social media and marketing. Advertising agencies like Campbell Ewald are adding senior social media marketing specialists to their staffs. Public relations professionals monitor social media to identify impending crises or trends in public opinion.*

Nonetheless, there is still some confusion about the marketing role of social media in general, as well as that of specific applications like Twitter, Facebook, and YouTube. In social media, we are not yet sitting in full shade; we are still planting forests.

INTRODUCTION

Social media are those in which the users create the content. They are interactive, regardless of the communication platform. A particularly good definition of Social Media has been offered by Joseph Thornley, CEO of the PR firm Thornley Fallis: *Social media are online communications in which individuals shift fluidly and flexibly between the role of audience and author.* Thornley calls attention to the use of social software that does not require knowledge of coding and that permits flexibility of application—posting, commenting, sharing, and mashing content—to form communities based on common interests.

Another, even simpler, definition comes from Isabella Hilborn on her blog: *Social Media. Any communications format where the users publish the content.* Social media began as a great vehicle for staying in touch with family and friends, networking, sharing information and opinions on blogs, posting photos, and more. They were novel, fun, and sometimes frivolous. Now, however, social media are also a popular, powerful, and ubiquitous marketing communications tool.

Users are free to communicate with their friends using social media, and a friend is not necessarily the person you go out and have a beer with after work. A friend is a person with whom you have a mutually agreed connection on a particular service like Facebook or Twitter. In some instances, a friend in this context can be anyone who chooses to listen to you or to converse with you.

In a business context, social media users usually try to add as many contacts as possible to their *Friends List*. Advertisers can freely contact friends, but they are strongly discouraged from spamming others' friends.

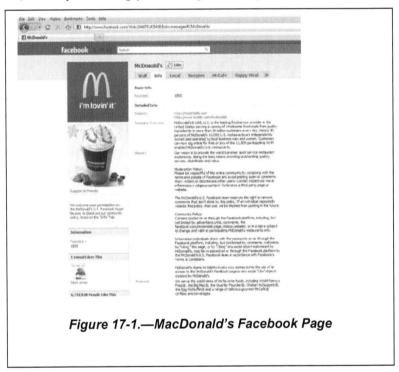

Figure 17-1.—MacDonald's Facebook Page

Figure 17-1 displays an example of a Facebook page for McDonald's, which has *millions* of fans! McDonald's uses its Facebook page to communicate its specials in various geographic markets.

Some of the most popular social media forms and applications are listed below.

- **Blogs**: Blogger, LiveJournal, Open Diary, TypePad, WordPress, Vox, ExpressionEngine, Xandi

- **Micro-blogging/presence applications**: Twitter, Plurk, Tumblr, Jaiku, fmylife

- **Social networking**: Bebo, Facebook, LinkedIn, MySpace, Orkut, Skyrock, Hi5, Ning, Elgg
- **Social network aggregation**: NutshellMail, FriendFeed
- **Events:** Upcoming, Eventful, Meetup.com
- **Wikis:** Wikipedia, PBwiki, Wetpaint
- **Social bookmarking (or social tagging):** Delicious, StumbleUpon, Google Reader, CiteULike
- **Social news:** Digg, Mixx, Reddit, NowPublic
- **Opinion sites:** epinions, Yelp
- **Photo sharing:** Flickr, Zooomr, Photobucket, SmugMug, Picasa
- **Video sharing:** YouTube, Vimeo, sevenload
- **Livecasting:** Ustream.tv, Justin.tv, Stickam
- **Audio and Music Sharing:** imeem, The Hype Machine, Last.fm, ccMixter
- **Media & Entertainment Platforms**: Cisco Eos
- **Virtual worlds:** Second Life, The Sims Online, Forterra
- **Game sharing:** Miniclip, Kongregat
- **Skype:** Some believe, like AIM & chat, Skype is about engagement

SOCIAL MEDIA IN MARKETING

What is social media marketing exactly? Social media marketing is promoting products, a website, or business through social media channels. Its supporters argue that there is no other low-cost promotional method as effective in generating large numbers of website visitors, some of whom become repeat visitors—even to the point of becoming fans or followers of their favorite websites. Whether selling products, providing services, or simply publishing content for ad revenue, social media marketing is a legitimate strategy used by more and more large and small marketers.

Marketing Roles for Social Media

While social media are obviously not a panacea for all marketing ailments, they can play an important role in the mix for many companies—

particularly for product and service branding, generation of website traffic, and soliciting customer insights and feedback.

Branding

Branding is the first place where social can play a marketing role. It has often been said that social media are all about developing relationships with customers or other consumers through relevant, online interactions. This is very consistent with the Advertising Research Foundation's emphasis on advertising and marketing communications planning for consumer engagement.

As discussed in Chapter 9, the ARF defines engagement as *the extent to which a consumer has a meaningful brand experience when exposed to commercial advertising, sponsorship, television contact, or other experience.* If the test of engagement is relevance and context of both message and medium, then social media passes with flying colors.

Social media applications like Twitter and Facebook, used intelligently and creatively, can strengthen the relationship between a brand (advertiser) and its consumers. By definition, creating beneficial two-way communication between marketer and consumer should increase brand loyalty.

As social networking tools continue to increase in popularity, and as marketers figure out how to use these new media innovatively and strategically, marketing and media mixes will include more social media. Facebook and others have already crossed some of the oldest boundaries of conventional advertising.

Absolut Vodka used social media as a branding tool in 2009 when it launched a multichannel campaign using mobile, interactive video, and social networks to promote responsible drinking. Absolut's *Recognize the Moment* campaign gave consumers easy-to-use tips and tools for making responsible decisions. Ostensibly, promoting responsible alcohol consumption is important to Absolut. Commercially, they want consumers to buy their products, but their message of moderation and personal responsibility in the *Recognize the Moment* campaign is presented through various media very much like that of a friend or confidant who alternates with you as the designated driver, or who takes the car keys when you shouldn't drive. Absolut thus endeavors to partner with its consumers in the safe use of its products.

From a media perspective, the very scope of Absolut's campaign is breathtaking. They have developed and produced over 100 videos, all of which are posted on YouTube and have received millions of free views.

Another effective use of social media is demonstrated by Blendtec, a relatively unknown manufacturer of kitchen blenders. Selling for around $400, Blendtec blenders are tough as nails. In fact, the blenders are capable of literally blending two-by-fours and nails. When Blendtec's new marketing director noted this interesting (and scary!) capability, he quickly launched what became a highly acclaimed series of videos, called: *Will it Blend?* Each video demonstrated how Blendtec could blend some unexpected and very tough ingredients. After all, don't we all like to destroy something occasionally?

The videos of mass destruction were distributed online. Blendtec's employees reached out to their personal networks of friends and associates urging them to send Blendtec's videos to their friends. Eventually *Will it Blend* became an Internet phenomenon, generating over 100 million views and still growing. One 2008 video (which blended iPhones) received over 8 million views, and a more recent video (blending a new iPad) received 1.7 million views within 23 hours of being posted on YouTube.

Website Traffic

The second major marketing role of social media is to help drive targeted traffic to advertisers' websites. As explained in Chapter 15, websites play an extremely important role for modern companies, which therefore place a high priority on generating as much targeted website traffic as possible.

The cost of website traffic generated from social media is minimal, because the initial out of pocket cost is so low (primarily overhead, cost of computers, and time). This enables companies to experiment and innovate, to whatever extent they can create new content and marketing initiatives.

What is the most effective way to generate website traffic—through social media or CPC programs? In an effort to answer that question, the research company Marketing Experiments conducted a study to determine whether social media could generate significant free website traffic, compared to Google AdWords, the number one paid search engine. Over a 12-month period, a variety of social media generated 93,207 unique visitors to the test website, at a cost per visitor of less than $0.04. By comparison, over a three-month period, Google AdWords generated only

2,047 total visitors at a cost of $1,250 (See Table 17-1). Based on these data, the research firm concluded that social media yielded a 1,427% greater return on investment compared to Google AdWords.

Table 17-1.—Social Media versus Google AdWords Cost per Visit

Source	Total Visitors	Total Cost	Cost Per Visit
Social Media	93,207	$3,600	$0.04
Google AdWords	2,057	$1,250	$0.61

However, one must take into account that the social media traffic was accumulated for 12 months, whereas the Google traffic was accumulated during a single quarter—this was not exactly an apples-to-apples comparison. Efficacy of the Google keywords was not analyzed and it is not known whether daily budget and cost per click were optimized. It is also probably reasonable to assume that a majority of the AdWords visitors were looking actively for certain products or services, whereas the social media visitor was more likely to be just *surfing*—clicking onto one site after another in search of something interesting.

Although it does appear that social media can make a major contribution to website traffic at a very low cost, therefore, it is probably premature to forego search engines that generate paid-for traffic, because the quality of social media generated traffic is still subject to question.

Most social media sites also offer paid advertising to their members. Similar to the search engines, the advertiser receives a small text ad that is placed on pages where the target audience theoretically—or purportedly— is. For example, if men 18-24 years old were your designated target audience, Facebook would likely place your ad only on pages where registrants' profiles indicate males in that specific age range. Advertising on social media sites is sold on either a CPM or a CPC basis. Obviously, while paid advertising is not required to use social media sites for marketing, if you use advertising, there will be a cost.

Customer Insights & Feedback

The third important marketing role for social media is to obtain customer insights and feedback. Social media can provide brands with valuable feedback on consumer/user likes and dislikes, preferences, suggestions, product opinion, and advertising issues. This kind of consumer feedback can help ensure that the marketer creates the right products at the right time to be in the right distribution channels at the right price—and that all of these factors are communicated in the right, timely manner to interested and engaged customers or general consumers.

If it works, the result should be increased *brand equity* and website traffic. What better way is there to build brand loyalty than to encourage customers to contribute to the design and improvement of their brand? Look at Microsoft's campaign in which happy users end a commercial conversation by saying, *I'm a PC, and Windows 7 was my idea!*

MyStarbucksIdea.com provides an interesting example of using social media to generate new ideas for the company. The site encouraged community members to post their ideas for improving Starbucks. Everyone sees all the posted suggestions, and visitors can vote up the ideas they like. Starbucks ultimately announces what actions they have taken, and that leads to further discussion about the ideas and their merits. It is an ongoing conversation with Starbuck's customers, much as you might have with a friend over coffee in one of Starbucks's shops.

Marketers' Opinions of Social Media

What do leading marketers think are the major benefits of social media and marketing? In 2008, *eMarketer* surveyed several hundred marketing executives to assess their perceptions of the benefits of social media marketing. The findings of the study support the view of social media's marketing roles in branding, website traffic, and customer feedback.

- **Engagement.** Perhaps not surprisingly, 85% of the media executives surveyed by *eMarketer* believed that the primary benefit of social media marketing was *customer engagement,* which is consistent with the focus advocated by ARF.

- **Direct Consumer Communication.** Communicating directly with consumers was important to 65%, who valued quick consumer and customer preferences and issues in real time and regularly.

- **Low Cost.** Low cost was important to 51%. Using social media is almost free, although it can be labor intensive to manage properly. Other costs include computer equipment and any paid advertising you decide to buy on social media websites.

- **Brand Building.** According to 48% of marketers surveyed, brand building was an important benefit. Social media's capacity for engaging consumers and building long-term relationships with them contributes to brand equity and brand loyalty.

- **Market Research.** Market research was rated high by 42%. Social media conversations provide opportunities to collect and monitor consumer preferences and attitudes, competitive intelligence, and opinions on marketing tactics. In addition, social media function as a kind of early warning system for unforeseen problems with product quality, availability, or delivery. Monitoring the voice of the customer is perhaps one of the most important things you can do, and a vehicle that allows them to give you feedback constantly — and thus enables you to fix problems proactively —is an extraordinarily smart investment.

- **Reach.** Reach was most important to 37%. Planned and executed properly, social media can target consumers who are most important to building brand sales—those most likely to buy goods or services. Social media also contribute a multiplier effect. Very large audiences can be built virally, as users pass information about the brand or website to others. This extends the ability of social media to help generate leads and contribute to customer satisfaction and to do it worldwide. There is something amusingly sublime about the way the Internet takes word-of-mouth global.

Cost Effectiveness of Social Media

Are social media cost effective compared to traditional media channels? The formula for cost effectiveness is:

Cost Effectiveness = Cost/Value Received

On the cost side of the equation, out-of–pocket costs are minimal, but time spent managing social media marketing campaigns can be extensive, which some, quite rightly, would consider as a significant cost. Moreover, costs may be incurred for paid advertising.

On the value-received side of the equation are the factors measured in the eMarketer survey, which are harder to assess in monetary terms. However, assuming these are reasonable expectations for social media— improved customer engagement, direct consumer communication, brand building, competitive research, and expanded reach—even the worst case scenario would yield at least some significant value. To receive any value whatsoever at scarcely any cost equals high cost effectiveness.

If you spent $1000 to spread your message virally to thousands of consumers—or hundreds of thousands—and you received some valuable suggestions for improving your product and advertising, and you received a few thousand visitors to your website, what would that be worth to you? Now compare that to traffic from a search engine, which merely redirects to your website visitors who may actually be looking for something else.

Because social media offer so marketing communication opportunities of such importance, the remainder of this chapter will examine their specific forms: blogging, social networking, publishing and news platforms, social bookmarking, and video sharing.

BLOGS & BLOGGING

Nobody knows for sure how many blogs there are or how many bloggers. As of December 2007, the blog search engine Technorati was tracking more than 112,000,000 blogs, according to Wikipedia, but the number changes constantly.

What are Blogs?

Blog is an abbreviation for the word *weblog*, a web-based journal in which a person publishes thoughts and opinions. As one pundit put it, "It is everyone's home on the world wide web and probably the number one venting venue." There are millions of bloggers on every subject imaginable—politics, business and industry, advertising, cooking, interior design and furniture, foods and health, space and science, lawn care, and trucks, auto racing, sports, gossip, and anything else that comes to mind.

Figure 17-2.—Dave's Cupboard Blog Page

Figure 17-2 is a screen shot from Dave's Cupboard, a blog that reviews foods and restaurants and provides links to other food blogs. It is just one example of the millions of blogs.

Dave's Cupboard also sells advertising. Note the Meijer ad in the lower, right-hand corner of the page.

Why Blog?

Blogging is the easiest and quickest avenue for the non-technical to put a message online. Most blog services are free, even for casual or non-demanding professional uses. Individuals and companies publish blogs for marketing or just for fun. Here are a few things you can do with a professional blog:

- **Product Promotion.** Posts can be created as product reviews, articles, or news items. You can link your blog to your corporate or sales websites.
- **Education.** Blogs can be used to educate customers and shareholders with product news, tips, service messages, company news, articles, and announcements.
- **News and Information.** You can disseminate current events with commentary relevant to your product or your brand's values. News events can include new product introductions or arrivals.

Blog Services

Blogging is a highly individualized endeavor for companies, just as it is for individuals. From the corporate or business perspective, it is vitally important to create a blog that is consistent with the company's or brand's objectives and image.

Dozens of blog services are available, making it relatively easy to set up a professional looking blog site. A blog service includes several benefits such as a domain name, hosting, wide selection of design templates, widgets, and professional support. Two of the easiest to use are free: *Wordpress*.com and *Blogger*.com (owned by Google).

When looking for a blog service, you should select one that offers the kind of exposure and capabilities needed to support not only your values and goals but also your level of expertise—or naïveté. Below are some criteria that can be used to help evaluate hosted blog services:

- **Blog Design Tools.** The top blog sites offer an assortment of templates and tools to customize blog entries, including the ability to add photos and sidebar links. Services ought to offer tools for experienced coders as well as non-coders, so that you can compose posts in code or through a text editor.

- **Promotion/Tracking Tool.** A blog service provider may host its own site with a directory or it may facilitate your design and submit it to several directories. A few help you track visitors and referrers, as well as customer questions and comments.

- **Ease of Use.** Because blogs are composed and posted by users who may not be versed in coding, the service must accommodate all levels of expertise. Most providers recognize this need.

- **Technical Help/Support.** Since many blogging sites are free, technical support is limited to online documentation like FAQs and searchable knowledge databases. However, the best sites also post tutorials and a weblog that covers a range of help topics.

Marketing Role of Blogs

Not so long ago, doing online research before making major purchasing decisions—*considered purchase* products like automobiles or appliances or computers or professional services—was something of a new frontier, a hit-or-miss proposition. You might find some objective, evaluative information on-line, or you might not. Today, online research has become not just customary but probably essential. A recent notable trend is the emphasis on the influence of *consumer-generated content* on purchasing decisions.

So, can blogs affect purchase decisions? Well, yes. With Universal Search—the Google invention that returns not only text but also video and graphics—and the emergence of blended search results, blogs have become increasingly common, and their role has become twofold: marketing and SEO.

Primarily, blogs provide a forum for communicating information to consumers and allowing them to interact with the company. This opening of communication channels provides consumers with the candid information they are seeking when researching a product or service.

Many blogs provide product evaluations and reviews, free publicity for the blogger's products. For example, a self-published author can use a blog to invite readers' reviews of the blogger's latest publication. That will generate further interest, which in turn should increase sales.

The SEO benefit lies in a blog's fresh, continually updated content, most of which is consumer generated. Consumer generated content is advantageous, technically, as comments provided by your guests provide the fresh content that search engines view and rank favorably.

Consider this quote from a small business blogger who was asked about the importance of blogging for his business:

Is blogging significant? Blogs have changed my business completely. When I realized what a powerful tool blogs could be for businesses, I dove in headfirst. Patsi and I studied TypePad in depth and taught a teleclass for coaches about how to set up a blog. That turned into a blog about blogging (this blog), then it evolved into an ebook, Build a Better Blog, then it became a TeleSeries called Conversations with Experts (Paul Chaney was our very first guest and since then we've done 62 Conversations!). Next came consulting and training and setting up blogs for clients. A whole new business was born and Patsi and I officially became The Blog Squad and business partners, merging our two businesses into one in July 2006, nearly two years after we started blogging.

Blogs are not my only marketing tool, but a primary one. We have 10+ blogs. Each has a different purpose, whether as a private training system, a private membership blog for clients only, for the public to learn more about blogs, Internet marketing and ezines, or as a way to focus and feature a specific project. Blogs have extended the reach of my business in ways I could never imagine...

How to Start a Blog

You can easily start a blog for personal or business use. It's straightforward and, in a lot of cases, free. There are four steps: select a provider, customize a design template, start posting, and build an audience.

Select a Blogging Provider

Find a blog service provider that meets your needs. The most popular providers include WordPress.com, Blogger, TypePad, and Xanga. They all offer pre-made templates and push-button publishing that don't require a lot of technical know-how.

WordPress has a four-star rating because it is excellent for both amateur and seasoned bloggers, and it is uncomplicated to use. WordPress.com is a free blogging service inspired by the community of users of WordPress.org, who requested an easy to use, hosted blog service. This service is simple—it hosts your blog, submits it to the Goggle blog directory, and monitors your stats. This is an all-inclusive, free blog package (www.wordpress.com). A WordPress landing page is pictured in Figure 17-3.

Figure 17-3.—WordPress Landing Page

For under $10.00 per month, you can get TypePad, a tool rated at three-and-a-half stars. TypePad is good for bloggers who want exposure. It can submit your blog to Google, Technorati, FeedBurner, and others, but if you want to keep it private, TypePad also supports private and password protected blogs. Unlike many of the free blogs, TypePad does not put ads on your site unless you request them. The service is comparable to WordPress, although not free, but it offers few customization features unless you upgrade to their Pro package (www.typepad.com).

Three-star-rated **Blogger** launched in 1999, sold to Google in 2002, and became one of the most popular free blog services. Google ownership makes it easy to sign up for AdSense (Google's program to pay bloggers to run ads), and they automatically submit your blog to the Google blog directory, making your blog available to millions.

Users seem to like Blogger (www.blogger.com) because it is easy but still flexible enough for advanced users who want to build their own templates. Blogger doesn't provide tracking features to monitor your visitors; however, you can purchase separate traffic monitoring programs.

Choose & Customize a Design Template

Once you sign up with a blog provider, you'll have a gallery of ready-made templates to choose from, allowing you to pick a color scheme and layout for your blog. Then add your name, interests, images, and other information you wish to share. For a unique template, find a website that offers enhanced designs, such as PimpMyProfile.com or Pyzam.com.

Start Posting

Once your blog is live, you can begin posting quality content that invites others to join in the conversation that you start. Post often!

Build an Audience

After publishing your blog, submit its URL to the search engines, send the URL to your friends, publish the URL on your website, and post the URL on other social media sites. Add the URL to posts you make on other blogs. Add the URL to your business cards and your other advertising!

Visit similar blogs to build a blogging circle. When you leave comments on those blogs, always add your blog address so those users can visit you too. (Of course, this will not work if your blog is private.)

SOCIAL NETWORKING SITES

Social networking sites are for building relationships among those who share interests or activities. Of the many social networking sites, the four largest are covered in the following discussion: Twitter, Facebook, MySpace, and LinkedIn.

Twitter

Twitter (www.Twitter.com), one of the top 50 sites in worldwide Alexa's traffic estimates, according to Wikipedia, was founded by Jack Dorsey, Biz Stone, and Evan Williams in March 2006, and launched publicly in July 2006. Twitter is a social networking and micro-blogging service that allows users to post their latest updates in *tweets* limited to 140 characters. They can be posted in three ways: web form, text message, or instant message.

The company has been busy adding features to the product, like G-Mail import and search. Twitter also recently launched a new section on its site called *Explore,* which enables external and third party tools to interact with Twitter. There is also a new visualization tool called *Twitter Blocks.*

Twitter as a Marketing Tool

For business marketers, Twitter is another channel to connect and engage current and potential customers with your product or brand. It allows deeper infiltration into the values and lifestyles of interested participants, which can help marketers build customer satisfaction and brand loyalty. When Gary Vaynerchuk, who owns the Wine Library in Springfield, New Jersey, and does a popular video blog called Wine Library TV, used Twitter to promote a one-time, free-shipping offer on wine mail orders, he got 3,000 new customers—all from a single, 140-character tweet!

Kate Kay of ClickZ wrote about Twitter as a marketing tool in December 2008, pointing out that Twitter has proven itself as a marketing tool by attracting big name brands from Ford to Dunkin Donuts to Whole Foods, all of whom are experimenting with Twitter. Before joining Ford Motor Company as its global digital and multimedia communications manager, Scott Monty reportedly had a good following on his personal Twitter account. "I wanted to get down and personal with people," said Monty, who believes Twitter enables that approach better than Facebook, MySpace, or blogs. Getting personal made sense for Ford, which, according to Monty, hopes to "humanize the brand" (ClickZ).

Besides branding, Twitter is also a traffic generation tool. The placement of links within profiles and conversations can direct visitors to specific website(s), and is especially powerful if you are targeting early adopters and influencers.

Twitter's Audience

What is Twitter's audience? Is it really a major factor in the media marketplace? In 2008, Twitter's user base grew by 422%, and by early 2009, it had grown another 1,382%. By June 2009, according to Internet audience research firm *comScore,* Twitter reached 44.5 million users worldwide, 20 million of whom are in the USA. That makes Twitter's audience is about twice as large as the audience generated for an above-average-rated primetime network TV program.

According to Hitwise data, Twitter's demographic profile is quite different from that of Facebook or MySpace. The majority of users are males, they are a little older than the Facebook or MySpace crowd, and they are in careers. A minority are liberals earning over $250,000 per year. Hitwise's Twitter profile can be summarized as follows:

- 63% are males.
- 26% are 35-44 years old.
- 15% of Twitter visitors are in the Stable Career category, comprising young and ethnically diverse singles in big cities like Los Angeles, Philadelphia, and Miami. The Stable Career group tends to work in the arts and entertainment industry, drive small cars, and espouse very liberal political views.
- 12% of Twitter's visitors are Young Cosmopolitans: 40-somethings who are more likely to drive a Prius, earn household incomes over $250,000 per year, and identify with very liberal politics.

According to Hitwise, Twitter is no longer dominated by the 18-24 age group that fed its early growth—middle-aged men are now the key drivers! This is consistent with Twitter moving from the "My cat's been sick" status report to a distribution network and feed reader.

Facebook

Facebook (www.facebook.com) is a *global social networking website* that is operated and privately owned by Facebook, Inc. Users can add friends, send messages and update personal profiles to communicate life changes with family, friends, and colleagues. They also can join Facebook networks organized by city, workplace, school, and region.

While a student at Harvard, Mark Zuckerberg founded Facebook with his college computer science buddies, Eduardo Saverin, Dustin Moskovitz, and Chris Hughes. Initially, Facebook's membership included only Harvard students, but it was gradually expanded to include other Ivy League schools and Stanford University. Later, Facebook was opened to any university student, then to high school students, and, finally, to anyone at least 13 years of age.

Facebook has met with some controversy. It has been blocked intermittently in several countries, including Syria, China, and Iran, although Iran unblocked it in 2009. Facebook has also been banned in many workplaces to prevent employee distraction. Privacy has been a continuing problem: it has been compromised several times and users object to unannounced changes in privacy settings. Facebook is facing several lawsuits from some of Zuckerberg's former classmates who claim that the company stole their source codes and other intellectual property.

Facebook as a Marketing Tool

Facebook represents a potentially important viral marketing opportunity aimed at all age groups. A January 2009 *Compete.com* study ranked Facebook as the most used social network, thus overtaking MySpace in number of worldwide monthly active users. Facebook reportedly had 300 million users worldwide in September 2009, half of whom used Facebook every day. *Compete.com's* Facebook profile can be summarized as follows:

- Potential global audience: 300 million users
- Potential U.S. audience: 150+ million
- Increasingly balanced demographics
- Demographics: skewed towards women (56%), 18-24 year olds, but with most of its recent growth among users 35 and over.

Forty-one percent of 2009 users were 18-24, but the growth rate among the 35-54 demographic was a staggering 276% during the six-month period from April to September 2009, while the growth rate was 194% among the 55+ age group.

Is Facebook Effective?

Dessert Gallery, a Houston-based cafe chain, recently examined the effectiveness of their Facebook presence in a study featured in the March 2010 issue of the *Harvard Business Review*. Based on interviews with more than 1,700 respondents over a three-month period, the Dessert Gallery (DG) found that compared with their typical customers, the company's Facebook fans:

- Made 36% more visits to DG's stores each month.
- Spent 45% more of their eating-out dollars at DG.
- Spent 33% more at DG's stores.
- Had 14% higher emotional attachment to the DG brand.
- Had 41% greater psychological loyalty toward DG.

This study seems to indicate that Facebook fan pages significantly increased sales, word-of-mouth marketing, and customer loyalty among a growing subset of Dessert Gallery customers.

Facebook Costs

Facebook, by almost any measure, is extremely cheap. While the basic service is free, Facebook also offers members the opportunity to place ads on the site. The ads are targeted to specific audiences on Facebook and are priced either on a CPM or CPC basis. Primary costs involve computers, staff time, and any optional advertising or promotion. This is not to say, however, that there isn't a lot of sweat equity involved in the "free" claim. Managing a significant social media program is quite labor intensive.

MySpace

The third major social media site is MySpace (www.myspace.com), another social networking website. Its headquarters are in Beverly Hills, California, where it shares an office building with its current owner, Fox Interactive Media (owned by News Corporation). MySpace was the most popular social networking site in the United States in June 2006, but by April 2009, according to *comScore*, MySpace was overtaken internationally by its main competitor, Facebook.

MySpace vs. Facebook

There may be some confusion about whether MySpace is just another Facebook or vice versa. Although there are some similarities, the two sites look different and function quite differently in ways that you need to understand when you select your marketing tools. Among other differences, the sites have distinct profile presentations, audience demographics, site etiquette, and functionality.

MySpace as a Marketing Tool

Although declining in worldwide number of monthly users, MySpace remains an important marketing tool, especially used in combination with Facebook. Its audience is about 100-125 million total users worldwide, 75 million in the U.S. Regular monthly users are somewhat fewer, estimated at about 65-66 million as of April 2009 in the United States.

Demographically, compared to the U.S. population, MySpace users are more likely to be female and still quite young (26% are 13-17 and 46% are 18-34). MySpace users are also below average in income and college education, probably due to their young age profile (Quantcast).

MySpace can create an additional presence on the web, especially for marketers who cater to MySpace's largely younger audience. Since MySpace is affiliated with MSN, anyone who uses Windows Live is more likely to find your space.

LinkedIn

LinkedIn (www.linkedin.com) is a *business-oriented social networking site* founded in December 2002 and launched in May 2003, primarily for professional networking. As of July 2009, it had more than 43 million registered users spanning 170 industries.

LinkedIn's CEO is Jeff Weiner, previously a Yahoo! Inc. executive. On June 17, 2008, Sequoia Capital, Greylock Partners, and other venture capital firms purchased a 5% stake in the company for $53 million, giving the company a post-money valuation of approximately $1 billion.

The purpose of the LinkedIn site is to allow registered users to maintain contact information about persons they know and trust in business. The members of the list are called Connections. Users can invite anyone (whether a site user or not) to become a Connection. This list of Connections can then be used in a variety of ways.

- A contact network is built up of users' direct connections, the connections of each of their connections (termed second-degree connections) and the connections of second-degree connections (termed third-degree connections). Connections can gain introductions to others through mutual, trusted contacts.
- LinkedIn can be used to find jobs, contacts, customer prospects, and business opportunities recommended by someone in the contact network.
- Employers can list jobs and search for candidates.
- Job seekers can review hiring managers' profiles to discover which of their contacts can introduce them.

Specifically designed and intended for professionals, business owners, entrepreneurs, and corporate executives, LinkedIn is different from other social networking sites. With over 40 million users, the goal is not social communication but business connection.

SOCIAL NEWS SITES

Social news sites are used to discover and share content. The largest of the genre is *Digg,* which will be examined in detail here.

Digg helps users discover and share content from anywhere on the Internet. Users submit links and stories, and they vote and comment on other submitted links and stories. Voting stories up or down is the site's cornerstone function, respectively called *digging* and *burying.*

Many stories are submitted every day, but only the most *Dugg* stories appear on Digg's front page. Digg's popularity has prompted the creation of other social networking sites with story submission and voting systems, such as Reddit. Digg surfaces the best content as voted on by its users. You won't find editors at Digg because it's there to bypass the editorial process. Digg's community collectively determines the value of content.

Everything on Digg—from news to videos to images—is submitted. Once something is submitted, others see it and "Digg" what they like best. If a submission receives enough Diggs, it is promoted to the front page for the millions of Digg visitors to see as soon as they open the site.

Digg's original design was ad free, but as it became more popular, Google AdSense was added, and now banners and display ads are available on the Digg website. Its most important marketing use probably relates to SEO, however. Search engines, especially Google, rely on social media sites to identify quality content. Because users vote on Digg content, it is an easy, self-correcting way to identify popular and filter out less popular content.

Here is an example of how this social networking site was used to generate website traffic.

Soccer Tickets Online *was a new website. Its first goal was to make users aware of the site's existence. The company chose a strategy of link baiting – adding content or features to a website that induces viewers to link to it from other websites – and developed a page called "The best 5 soccer players of all-time." When they submitted it to Digg, the post made the front page and crashed the server. Not a bad start for Soccer Tickets Online!*

PUBLISHING PLATFORMS & COMMUNITIES

Where can a business publish web pages that may entice potential business prospects? Do you Squidoo?

Squidoo is a community website that allows users to create small web pages (called *lenses*) for subjects of interest. The Squidoo website is in the top 500 most visited sites in the world and is in the top 300 most viewed in the United States. Squidoo grew 91% in 2008, and had 900,000 hand-built lenses as of February 1, 2009. Over 400,000 users reportedly visit Squidoo every day. Development on Squidoo started in 2005, and a beta test was launched in October of that year. The site came out of beta testing two months later and reached 100,000 lenses within the first six months.

Squidoo is a user-generated website, the lens concept its primary feature. Lenses are like single-subject blog posts. The site allows content creators to earn revenue from referral links to sites like Amazon.com and eBay. *Lensmasters,* users who create lenses, can be anyone with an interest, not necessarily recognized experts in their subjects.

Squidoo says, "Publish gorgeous web pages about all your favorite things. Squidoo is home to millions of pages of the best content, advice and recommendations online. .."

Figure 17-4 provides an example of a Squidoo lens (website) created for a small company selling rathr unique products (calling itself Rocket MOMS.)

Do you Squidoo?

Figure 17-4.—Rocket Moms' Squidoo Lens

Squidoo is noted for allowing users to create multimedia pages without having to learn HTML. These pages often achieve popularity due to their association with thousands of other Squidoo pages. Figure 17-4 shows an example of a unique Squidoo lens for Rocket Moms, which sells unique toilet seats. Clicking the Buy Now button redirects the visitor to an Amazon website for order placement and fulfillment.

Squidoo employs a unique payment scheme. Five per cent of its revenue goes to charity, 50% goes to the lensmasters, and 45% goes to Squidoo. The lensmasters and Squidoo rely on advertising and affiliate links to create revenue. Nearly half the lensmasters donate their royalties to any of 65 featured charities, ranging from NPR and the American Heart Association to smaller organizations like Chimp Haven and Planet Gumbo. In the month of October 2008 alone, Squidoo donated $80,000 to charity.

Besides being free of charge and easy to do, setting up Squidoo lenses has other benefits for Internet marketers:

- **SEO.** Search engines, especially Google, love Squidoo. Using Squidoo can increase your search engine ranking and the traffic that comes to your site. The more lenses you make, the more your website ranking will improve.

- **Polling.** Squidoo lets you set up polls on your lens that can provide valuable insight into your niche markets. You can ask readers about products they use, get reviews of products they bought, and hear about problems they encountered. You can even ask questions that link to other lenses providing the answers. It's an interactive way to get some great niche insight.

- **Hosting.** A Squidoo lens can host eBay auctions, Amazon books, and YouTube Videos. If someone clicks on your Amazon link, you earn a royalty.

- **Testing.** A Squidoo lens is a good way to test out keyword phrases for popularity and web traffic. Your Squidoo dashboard provides statistics, including number of visits to your lens.

- **Content.** Besides earning money by promoting your affiliate program or eBay shop, you can also earn by being a Squidoo content provider or lensmaster. When Squidoo runs ads on a lens you created, you get a cut of the revenue generated when a reader clicks on the ad.

SOCIAL BOOKMARKING SITES

Social bookmarking is how Internet users share, organize, search, and manage bookmarks of web resources. One of the primary social bookmarking sites is StumbleUpon, an Internet community that allows users to discover and rate web pages, photos, and videos. It has a personalized recommendation engine that uses peer and social networking principles to rate submissions.

StumbleUpon was owned by eBay from May 2007 (when they acquired it for $75,000,000) until April 2009, when two of the founders, backed by investors, bought it back.

Web pages are presented when the user clicks the Stumble! button on the browser's toolbar. StumbleUpon chooses which Web page to display based on the user's ratings of previous pages, ratings by the user's friends, and ratings of users with similar interests. Users can rate any Web page with a thumbs-up or thumbs-down, and clicking the Stumble button resembles surfing the Web, or even surfing regular cable TV. StumbleUpon also allows users to indicate their interests from a list of nearly 500 topics to produce relevant personalized content. One-click blogging is built in as well.

StumbleUpon has approximately 14 million users but the number should be treated with caution, because it counts anyone who has ever registered for the website, not just current, active site users.

StumbleUpon can probably be used best as a tool to increase website traffic. It does not replace search or sites like Digg but is unique due to its collaborative filtering and recommendation engine. StumbleUpon works like Amazon's reader and shopper recommendations, only for web pages, photos, and video.

Sponsored Stumbles can be an alternative to services like AdWords among visitors interested in a topic or category. StumbleUpon's fees are currently $0.05 per click, although it plans to implement a bidding model similar to Google's.

VIDEO SHARING

There are several video sharing websites; however, YouTube is by far the premiere. This discussion will highlight YouTube's features as a model of video sharing applications to advertising and marketing.

What is YouTube? It is a video-sharing website (www.youtube.com) where users can view, upload, and share videos. Three former PayPal employees created YouTube in February 2005 as a venture-funded technology startup, primarily with $11.5 million investments from Sequoia Capital between November 2005 and April 2006. In November 2006, YouTube, LLC was bought by Google, Inc. for $1.65 billion, and it is now operated as a Google subsidiary.

The company uses *Adobe Flash video technology* to display user-generated video content, including movie clips, TV clips, and music videos, as well as amateur content including video blogs and short original videos. Most of the content on YouTube has been uploaded by individuals, although media corporations (CBS and the BBC among them) offer some material as part of the YouTube partnership program.

Unregistered users can watch videos, while registered users can upload an unlimited number. Videos considered potentially offensive are available only to registered users over the age of 18. Videos containing pornography or material encouraging criminal conduct are prohibited by YouTube's defamation rule. The accounts of registered users are called *channels.*

YouTube as a Marketing Tool

YouTube has become an extremely popular marketing tool for individuals, companies, organizations, and even politicians. Certain videos go viral, catching the attention of national or even international press, exponentially increasing exposure. YouTube has developed a large audience to whom it offers an effective communications tool that anybody can use, no doubt disconcerting the traditional over-the-air television networks.

According to data published by Internet researcher, *comScore*, Google received about 6.4 billion video views in January 2009—a staggering 43% of all videos viewed on the Internet—and YouTube accounts for 99% of Google's video views. YouTube says viewers are watching hundreds of millions of videos every day on the website and uploading hundreds of thousands. Every minute of every day, ten hours of video are being uploaded to YouTube!

YouTube's user base is broad in age range, 18-55, evenly divided between males and females, and spanning all geographic regions. Fifty-one percent of users go to YouTube at least weekly, and 52% of 18-34 year-olds share videos often with friends and colleagues. With such a large and diverse user base, YouTube offers something for everyone (YouTube).

YouTube and Advertisers

Advertisers are looking for more cost-effective alternatives to commercial television—alternatives that provide the communications benefits and impact of video such as sight, sound, and motion, but more targeted and much less expensive.

Consequently, more and more companies are using YouTube as a marketing tool where video clips can be hosted and viewed without charge. Some diehard Internet users reportedly have stopped watching TV altogether, preferring to watch YouTube or other Internet sites. Given its vast and growing popularity, YouTube is an irresistible free showcase. As an indicator of its potential media value, some videos have generated over 50 million views. If you bought 50 million impressions on one of the commercial broadcast networks, you could spend $700,000 or more!

The Obama Girl's 3-minute, 18-second video reportedly generated an estimated 3.4 million views, worth around $68,000 on network television... plus a huge volume of free publicity in the mass media.

There is also a *cascading effect*. The more a video is viewed, the greater its popularity, the nearer it gets to the top page—the home page, which draws the top views. Once the clip is uploaded, you are given some code that you can use to embed the video into your own blog or website. You can also increase views by putting the video link in your email signatures, your other social network pages like Facebook, and any other websites you maintain.

Increasing Video Audience

In order to increase the audience gravitating to a video, YouTube offers some reporting features and insights that can be extremely helpful.

- **Content sharing.** YouTube has sharing options like those found on blogs and social networking sites. Users can share videos with the popular social networking sites, including Twitter. You also can send them to your YouTube friends or email contacts; you may embed content for a single video, a playlist, or a channel.

- **Social activities update feeds.** While not as comprehensive as Facebook or other feed activity updates, with the release of *realtime updates,* YouTube seems to be going in that direction. This feature and other recent enhancements may indicate that other tracking capabilities will be along shortly.

- **Effectiveness feedback.** One of the challenges of social media is the difficulty of measuring its effectiveness. Understanding how the market responds can help video publishers hone in on relevant content to grow their businesses and increase sales. Besides feedback from video ratings and user comments, YouTube offers Insight Statistics and Data.available.

- **Insight.** YouTube's reporting function helps you understand views, viewer demographics, popularity, and community.

- **Community**. The community tab on Insight reports YouTube users' interactions with your video contents, providing ratings, comments, and favoriting. This information can make the content you publish in the future more relevant and targeted.

- **Hot Spots.** Hot Spots helps you understand the attention paid to one of your videos compared to other videos of similar length. Learning where you are losing user interest can guide appropriate adjustments for future improvement.

No other social networking site provides these kinds of data at no cost. Let's hope they continue building on these useful reporting features!

Going Viral

Going viral is the name of the game on YouTube. There are no guarantees, but you can give yourself some advantages.

- Make sure you have a good, professional (but not slick) video that your target audience will want to watch. Engage them with content that is funny, entertaining, or informative!
- Email the video to your company's lists and others meeting your demographic target.
- Post the YouTube video on your blog.
- Email the video to your site's email list.
- Post the video on social networking sites.
- Post the video to relevant message boards on You Tube. To embed You Tube videos into message board posts, you must find a video that has something to do with the subject the thread is talking about (taking care to avoid spam that could get you banned).

SUMMARY

Social media is an excellent no-fee or low-cost marketing communications strategy. Chapter 17 has examined the strategic role of social media marketing and reviewed the most popular social media sites.

The world is dominated—at least for the moment—by the social media phenomenon, or explosion. From Facebook to Twitter to YouTube, these new tools help thousands interact each day, around the globe and around the clock. As you explore the opportunity, however, don't abandon other options. Your outreach to older consumers will require older methods, at least for a while longer. Statistics have shown that youngsters still constitute the bulk of the social media fan base.

Bear in mind that a high quality, highly professional social media website requires a lot of work. If you intend to build a brand and a name through social media, you must invest in quality at the outset and continuous updating during its life.

Remember the "social" in social media. It is imperative that you remain sensitive to your audience. According to virtually all of the experts, the law of reciprocity will apply. You must reply to users' queries and satisfy their curiosity promptly. The very essence of social media is near-instantaneous response or dialogue; if you let it lapse, your competition will surely take full advantage your customers' loss of confidence.

It is essential to stay abreast of new sites, particularly competitive ones, and adjust your own as necessary to remain in fashion. If you are not adaptive and proactive then you are in trouble. The very nature of social media is constant change and reinvention.

18. STRATEGIC MEDIA PLANNING

If you don't know where you are going,
you will wind up somewhere else.

−Yogi Berra

Strategy is the art and science of planning and marshalling resources for their most efficient and effective use. The first seventeen chapters of this book have given you the knowledge to begin to devise strategy. Chapter 18 will take you through the process of developing a strategic media plan.

You now understand media terminology and concepts including audience, cost, and impact. You have learned how to compare media options using basic math. You understand important marketing considerations affecting the development of a media plan, including target audience, geography, timing, and budgeting. You know when to consider various marketing communications options such as advertising, publicity, direct marketing, WOMM, and social media, and you are acquainted with the major traditional advertising media.

In this chapter, you will apply all that to developing media strategy:

1. *Determine the IMC/media implications of the marketing situation, objectives, and strategies. (Chapter 8)*

2. *Define the most important marketing problems or opportunities.*

3. *Identify the marketing task(s) you must address to achieve your marketing objectives.*

4. *Adopt a working theory of how marketing communications will work for your brands. (see Chapter 9)*

5. *Develop communications & media objectives and strategies for an integrated marketing communications plan, including:*

   • *Assessing available marketing communications and media options (Chapters 15-17)*

   • *Creating and evaluating alternative scenarios until you discover a strategy that accomplishes your objectives within your constraints.*

   • *Preparing a schedule describing ad appearance in each medium you selected.*

   • *Summarizing your plan in a calendar and a budget.*

- *Evaluation and measurement of your plan vs. its objectives*
- *Test marketing and implementation*

This guide should provide a roadmap for accomplishment of a professional media plan. To speed you on your journey, recognizing that objective information looks different when you need it, core content from previous chapters has been brought together here with the relevant strategic advice. By the end of Chapter 18, you will be equipped to incorporate Media Planning & Buying *into your own media plan development, and you will be ready to learn about media negotiation and media buying.*

INTRODUCTION
The New Media Planning

Media planning is ever more complex, creative, and challenging. Reach and frequency are still important tools, but increasingly, the ways consumers feel about your message and interact with it carry equal weight. Taking advantage of the one-on-one promise of the Internet requires a departure from the paradigms of traditional media, but every form of marketing communication has its own paradigm. Each plays a unique role, and your job is to capitalize on it.

As media guru Erwin Ephron puts it:

The new media planning is about picking combinations of media (and permutations of media, where sequence of exposure is important). This increases relevant media choice from a manageable few hundred to an unruly few hundred thousand. It also means comparing apples with oranges...

The complexity of the media world can be overwhelming. How on earth can all of these media be integrated into a cohesive, synergistic plan?

Integrated Marketing Communications and the explosion of new media environments have changed the role of the media planner. You are no longer just somebody who develops broadcast media plans; you are the point person for managing a variety of communications forms, old and new, that are having an impact on your brand.

Step by Step Media Planning Process

An integrated, strategic media plan is built step by step. The steps are:

1. Situation Analysis
2. Problem & Opportunity Statement
3. Marketing Communications Task Definition
4. Communications Model Selection
5. Media Objectives Establishment
6. Media Strategy Formulation (IMC)
7. Tactical Planning
8. Test Marketing
9. Implementation Planning

Each of these steps will be explained here. This advice, presented with information from previous chapters, should provide adequate guidance for development of a professional media plan.

STEP 1. MARKETING SITUATION ANALYSIS

During this phase of the planning process, you *must* immerse yourself in the company's marketing plan and other relevant business and consumer research, including syndicated studies like SMRB and MRI. If a competent marketing plan doesn't exist, piece together the relevant information—marketing objectives, sales and market share, consumers, creative strategy—from wherever you can find it. You can do this by constructing a list of key issues and questions, conducting research on your own with syndicated research sources, and having conversations with the client and the rest of the marketing team.

Effective media plans are marketing driven, meaning that the media plan must be an extension of the marketing plan. A media plan disconnected from the goals and intentions of the marketing plan through inadequate understanding of target markets or geographic potential, or selecting media on the basis of how COOL something sounds, will fall short of expectations and deliver a disappointing ROI.

The purpose of advertising and integrated marketing communications, remember, is to help move the advertiser's business forward. For example, your plan might target an emerging market segment that could provide incremental sales, it might help to protect the advertiser's business in high brand development (BDI) markets, or it might simply remind impulse buyers just prior to purchase to buy this advertiser's product.

Whatever their purpose, marketing plans, or your equivalent database, wherever you find the data, should include at least the following basic information. See Table 18-1 for additional considerations.

- **Marketing goals and objectives** define what is to be achieved by the marketing plan, e.g., what levels of sales, market share, distribution, competitive penetration, awareness, sales leads, website visits—or other measures. *There has to be a goal. If there is no goal, there is no plan.*

- **Sales data for industry and relevant brands**, ideally by geographic market areas, will help you decide how to allocate your budgets geographically.

- **Consumer definitions and *data*** beyond what may be found in syndicated research sources like SMRB or MRI help to understand consumer groups on a deeper level, e.g., purchase decision-making processes. Advertisers often conduct their own proprietary research to obtain these data.

- **Competitive marketing strategies and activity** are crucial to understanding the brand's competitive situation. How much do competitors spend? What media do they use? What is their creative? How will their activity affect your brand and planning?

- **Planned marketing activities** such as new product introductions or promotions must be understood in advance, so that they can be planned and integrated intelligently into the overall media plan.

- **Creative strategy and executions** can significantly affect media planning decisions. Since the role of media is to deliver the message to the target audience, media need to support creative intent. For example, :15 second TV commercials running with high frequency may be used to increase brand name awareness if creative executions are designed to emphasize the brand name.

- **The budget** may be fixed by the advertiser or you may be asked for your recommendation. Either way, there is never enough money to do what you really want to, so your task as is to make each dollar work like two or three.

Table 18-1.—Situation Analysis: Factors Affecting Media Planning

Factors Affecting Media Planning	Potential Media Implications
Marketing Objectives & Strategies	Task, Objectives, Strategy
Geographic Business Analysis	Objectives, Strategy, Tactics
Competitive Analysis	Objectives, Strategy, Tactics, Budget
Seasonal Purchase Behavior	Objectives, Strategy, Tactics
Results of Past Marketing Efforts	Strategy, Tactics
SWOT Analysis	Task Definition, Objectives, Strategy
"One" Most Important Problem	Task Definition, Objectives, Strategy
"One" most Important Opportunity	Task Definition, Objectives, Strategy
Industry Trends	Task, Objectives, Strategy
Brand Performance/Trends	Task, Objectives, Strategy
Awareness, Consideration Levels	Task, Objectives, Strategy
Image	Task, Objectives
New Product Introductions	Task, Objectives, Strategy, Tactics
Planned Promotion or Events	Task, Objectives, Strategy, Tactics
Pricing Changes	Tactics
Current Marketing Mix	Task, Objectives, Strategy, Tactics
Consumer Characteristics	Objectives, Strategy, Tactics
Consumer Behavior	Task, Objectives, Strategy, Tactics
Budgets	Objectives, Strategy, Tactics

Question: Table 18-1 shows <u>where</u> the
influence of media planning factors is likely to be felt.
<u>How</u> might each of those factors affect media planning?

STEP 2. STATEMENT OF THE PROBLEM

Based on the marketing plan and other information, you must identify the most important problem or opportunity that can be affected by marketing communications. If the number one problem inhibiting sales is top of mind awareness, your media plan should be built to increase top of mind awareness. Other problems might include the following:

- Low brand name awareness
- Low brand familiarity
- Low top of mind awareness
- Good awareness, low purchase consideration
- Good purchase consideration, low purchase intention

- Good purchase intention, low actual purchase
- Low trial rates
- Too few sales leads
- Low repurchase or frequency of purchase
- Low quality image
- Doesn't support self image
- Inadequate distribution
- Overwhelming competitive marketing activity
- Negative consumer product perceptions lag reality

Examples of opportunities might include:

- Competitors' inventory shortages or distribution difficulties
- Competitive product recalls
- Demonstrably superior product
- Hot new product
- High CDI/high BDI markets showing opportunity for growth
- Great new advertising campaign
- Favorable publicity (product awards, consumer enthusiasm)

STEP 3. TASK DEFINITION

Look at your Problem/Opportunity Statement. What is the number one marketing task that your media plan should address? Are there second and third place priorities? Your task statement should address those priorities, should be quantitative, and should specify time frames for performance.

While we cannot address here the untold number of marketing tasks suggested by countless situation analyses, here are five examples to illustrate how different kinds of tasks address different problems.

Problem: Low Name Awareness
Task Definition: Increase brand name awareness from 10% to 40% by 2011.

There are different kinds of awareness. Total Awareness is an aided measure of whether the consumer has ever heard of a brand ("Have you ever heard of Ford?)" Top of Mind Awareness is deeper and more correlated with share of market, e.g., "When you think of buying a new car, what brand comes to your mind first?" Familiarity requires a degree of product knowledge. Brand Name Awareness is an aided or unaided measure of whether consumers know or recognize the brand name. If consumers don't know the name of the product or what it looks like on the shelf (or wherever it is sold), that single problem would likely result in lower sales. So, if you and your team believe that low brand name awareness is the biggest obstacle to consumer purchase, it must be solved in order to move the business forward.

Problem: Leads
Task Definition: Generate 50% more qualified sales leads among target audience during first quarter.

Suppose your client is very successful in closing sales among interested prospects but is running low on good leads. If the company is generating too few leads and that deficiency is inhibiting sales, you have to increase the number of quality leads, perhaps by identifying those who have expressed interest or requested additional information in response to a story, magazine ad, or website visit.

Problem: Low Market Development
Task Definition: Improve Top of Mind Awareness by 50% Among Upscale Hispanics within six months.

Recognizing that your share of market is below average in an important market segment defines a priority problem. If research into the potential causes for this market share shortfall showed an especially low share among Hispanics (or other ethnic market segments), who are also a long-term market of interest, your task is to raise top of mind awareness among Hispanics.

Opportunity: Vulnerable Competitor
Task Definition: Provide product samples to 100,000 Brand X customers by the end of next month.

Consider that a competitor appears vulnerable to your demonstrably superior product. (Or maybe a competitor is vulnerable because of low awareness or purchase consideration, spotty distribution, poor reception of a new product, decreased marketing budget, or supply difficulty due to low inventory.) If your problem is how to take advantage of this vulnerability, your task might be tempting their customers with samples of your product. You could mail samples, insert coupons in newspapers for distribution to subscribers in zip codes with a high incidence of competitive purchasers, or set up in-store or event sampling.

Opportunity: Successful New Product Introduction
Task Definition: Generate 30% trial within three months following product launch.

When new products are initially introduced to consumers, there is no pre-existing awareness, no purchase consideration, and no intention to purchase. There is no image. Zip. To create sales for a new product, you must generate trial *(initial purchase), followed by* repurchase *and* frequency of purchase. *The media plan plays an important role in generating initial trial and repurchase. New product introductions typically utilize a mix of advertising, promotions containing trial offers such as coupons, publicity, direct mail, Internet advertising and search, social media, WOMM, and more.*

Because properly defining tasks and objectives is hard work and a little risky, some organizations resist defining objectives precisely. When you encounter a wild, free-flowing marketing objective, the best way to counteract it to ask a couple of non-combative questions: *What is the one thing you would like to accomplish next year? How will you know if you accomplished it?*

The answer may be something like: *Have our core buyers buy more. For example, if they each bought one more pair of sandals next year, we would have surpassed our business goals.* Ah, now we're getting somewhere, because the question you then ask yourself is, *How can I help them accomplish this?* If you're feeling ambitious, you may also follow up with, *Is there a second thing you would like to accomplish?* The response may be, *Well, I'm glad you asked, I would like to identify a new market for sandals, as well.*

Once the primary marketing tasks are defined, the next step is to define the specific objectives for the IMC/Media plan (i.e., media objectives.) Before proceeding to discussion of media objectives, however, it is essential to distinguish among objectives, strategies, and tactics.

Objectives state what you want to accomplish. *Strategies* describe globally how you will achieve the objectives. *Tactics* are all the specific things you do to execute a strategy ("the plan").

Think of them this way: your *objective* is to get to Paris. Your *strategy* is to fly. Your *tactics* are to drive to the airport, park in the remote lot, shuttle to the terminal, walk to Gate X, board Delta Flight 123 at 8:35 EST on April 16, return on Delta 456 at 6:35 AM on April 30, and retrace your steps back to your car and hence home. Obviously, tactics can be the hard part, and without problem-specific task definitions, you will be helpless.

STEP 4. MEDIA MODEL SELECTION

How do advertising media work? Chapter 9 introduced several competing models of how media work. Before developing your media plan, you must decide whether Recency applies to your planning situation or whether Effective Reach applies better. How important is SOV as a planning model? The Purchase Funnel? Engagement? These decisions will have a significant effect on how you develop the media plan.

You will recall that Engagement is the choice of the Advertising Research Foundation, with media context and interaction being especially important. The studies by Calder that were cited in Chapter 9 demonstrated that media context affected response to ads. His suggestion that it would be smart to adjust ads to media content (make different TV commercials for an action/adventure programs or for American Idol) is called the *Congruence Hypothesis.*

STEP 5. ESTABLISH MEDIA OBJECTIVES

After conducting due diligence by studying the marketing situation analysis and marketing objectives, internalizing the brand's primary problems and opportunities, defining the key task(s) of the media plan, and embracing a communications philosophy that suits your present needs, the next step is to define your media objectives.

Here's a useless media objective: *Drive consumer engagement within the target audience, increase exposure with new vertical segments, and utilize high value offers to drive up purchase intent.* Based on that, what would you recommend as media objectives? How would you measure progress?

Sound media objectives are always explicit about the following, the first three of which we will consider at length.

- Whom to reach and the relative importance of each target
- Where to advertise geographically with what emphasis
- When to advertise and with what emphasis
- How much to advertise
- How to extend creative impact

Who: Target Audience Objectives

The first step in developing media objectives is to define your target audience. Who are you trying to reach, and with what emphasis for each target group?

Target audiences may be defined in a variety of ways, including demographics (e.g., all adults, men aged 25-54, women in $50K+

households, children aged 6-11), psychographics, purchase behavior, purchase influence, emerging market groups, and all the rest that were covered in earlier chapters.

Target Definition

Chapter 10 explored several ways to define target audiences for marketing and media selection. One key task of the media planner is to define target audiences in ways that are both consistent with the marketing plan and relatable to media audience databases. In many cases, especially if the target is defined in lifestyle terms, there is no syndicated audience information to rely upon. However, most of us are not brain dead: if the target is interested in cooking, we can assume that print or broadcast media that focus on cooking should at least be considered and evaluated in relation to one another.

Audience Valuation/Weighting

If a target group is defined incorrectly or inaccurately, or if the target group is too small to make the needed contribution to accomplishing the marketing objectives, media plan effectiveness will suffer. What are the target audience priorities then? Who is the primary target audience, and who is secondary or tertiary?

If mothers are the primary target for a cookie and children 6-11 are the secondary target, then most of spending and media weight should be directed to mothers, with a smaller percentage directed to kids. When there are multiple targets, with what relative emphasis should each be reached?

When you're considering emphasis, it is important to keep in mind that target definition is not necessarily an up or down decision. Defining the target in narrow terms can miss the bulk of the market. For example, referring to Table 18-2, you could target women 18-34 because they account for 30% of purchases, more than any other demographic shown. If you did, though, you would be ignoring 70% of the market, including men, who together consume more than the highest-using women!

Table 18-2.—Audience Weighting

Demographic	% Potential Sales
Women 18-34	30
Women 35-49	20
Women 50+	10
Men 18-34	20
Men 35-49	15
Men 50+	5

*Question: On the basis of sales potential, should
any spending/media weight be given to
older female or male audiences?*

Reach & Frequency Goals

Typically, target audience objectives define the reach and frequency or effective reach objectives for each target group identified in your target audience definitions. Like most things in advertising, there is no single gauge to the right reach and frequency levels because so many variables are involved. (Besides, if advertising were like accounting, it wouldn't be as much fun!)

Reach Objectives

You will recall that Reach is defined as the net percentage of a target universe that is exposed to one or more media vehicles one or more times. Given your budget and your communications goals, what percentage of the target should you plan to reach in an average month, week, or day?

Some students of media believe that reach should be emphasized over frequency (remember, as reach goes up, frequency goes down and vice versa because TRPS = Reach x Frequency). Although most situations will require you to strike a balance between reach and frequency, there are times when you just need to reach as much of the target group as possible.

- **Recency Planning.** If you are implementing Recency Planning, your media plan will seek to maximize daily or weekly reach of near-term shoppers in order to remind them to buy your brand when they go to the store tomorrow.

- **Promotions.** Introduction of a promotional offer, especially one that is so compelling that one exposure is all it takes, will emphasize reach. Imagine a car company offering a $15,000 rebate, a deal so sweet that everybody deserves an opportunity to see the message.

• **Product presentations.** Reach matters more at the introduction of a product or service of very high interest, something that purchasers have been waiting for, like a next generation Apple iPod or iPad or a car that parks itself!

• **Awareness.** If your communications task is to <u>maintain</u> (reinforce) awareness or consideration levels, reach could be more important than frequency. A simple reminder may be all that is necessary to reinforce the message. (However, if you are trying to <u>increase</u> awareness or consideration, you might opt to settle for lower reach and higher frequency).

• **Cost constraints.** Budget restrictions may make the decision in favor of reach if you cannot afford to buy meaningful frequency.

Frequency Objectives

Whenever repeating a message again and again is important to getting the consumer's attention in a cluttered media environment, gaining top of mind awareness, or targeting the competition, you may choose to emphasize frequency over reach. It bears repeating, however, that since reach and frequency are inversely related, an increase in frequency will reduce reach.

The following demonstrates the planner's dilemma. With 150 TRPS, is it better to reach almost everyone once or half of them three times?

Table 18-3.—Reach vs. Frequency: The Media Planner's Dilemma

	Reach Emphasis	Frequency Emphasis
Reach	93%	50%
Frequency	1.6	3.0
TRPS	150	150

You may be able to beat the math to by using more cost efficient media to generate more TRPS. For example, if media with lower CPMs were substituted for the higher CPM media (e.g., add late night programming, reduce primetime programming), TRPS would increase and reach and/or frequency could be further increased.

Situations when frequency could be emphasized over reach do occur:

• When the task is to build awareness, consideration, or some other metric in a competitive marketplace. (Most marketplaces are!)

- When you need to break through the media/message clutter in a competitive product category.
- When a complicated message needs higher repetition so that consumers will eventually comprehend the story.
- When not everyone in an audience sees or hears a message the first or second or even the third time it appears.

If you subscribe to the Effective Reach/Effective Frequency theory, you want to reach the maximum percentage of the target with an effective level of frequency. Although the ANA's report concluded that 3-10 exposures were optimum, there are so many extenuating circumstances for that any formula can be hard to justify.

Regardless of the specific numbers, the principle of effective frequency is one you must deal with for almost every media plan. Setting exposure goals is good. Being too literal with the numbers is not good.

Impact/Engagement

Depending on the planning situation, you may have an objective that states the desired communications effect as: *Engage the target audience...* If one of your media objectives is engagement, then your strategy must spell out how you intend actually to engage the target with media.

Where: Geographic Objectives

Think back to Chapter 11. Is the U.S. a *homogeneous* market for any product or service? Are BDIs, CDIs, demographics, and lifestyle profiles the same everywhere? Is Boston like Fresno? Is Houston like Dallas? Is France like the Ukraine? Is Delaware like Mississippi? Of course not. Politicians running for office figured this out a long time ago. It's amazing that so many national advertisers plan as if the USA were one giant homogeneous market.

As you have learned, industry and brand sales volume, CDIs, BDIs, distribution, trade relationships, sales force effectiveness, competitive activity, consumer demographics and psychographics, and other important marketing variables differ widely from one market to another. Does that mean that marketing problems and opportunities are essentially local because they vary by geographic market area? If so, do media plans have to take into account different local marketing situations? Of course.

Furthermore, to the consumer all advertising is local. The consumer sees an ad and doesn't know or care whether it came from a national TV network or a local station, a national or local print vehicle. If advertisers care, that's because of *their* egos and perceptions—not the consumer's.

Geographic Priorities

Referring back to Chapter 11, and as suggested above, one of the most important media decisions is to decide *where to advertise* and with what *degree of emphasis*. How should precious resources be allocated to different markets? To what extent should dollars be spent in national media to reach everyone everywhere? Should media dollars be focused in certain markets to defend current business? Should advertising be concentrated where there is stiff competition but good opportunity for sales growth? Should dollars be concentrated in markets where the market is strong but the brand's market development is weak? Should dollars be concentrated in highly cost efficient markets to the potential exclusion of highly cost inefficient markets like San Francisco? Here are some specific issues to ponder:

- Do per capita industry sales rates vary by geographic market area? Almost certainly. For example, Texas is a great market for pickups, but the New York DMA is not.

- Do per capita sales rates vary significantly by market? Probably.

- Is the Brand's market development level (BDI) consistent with the total market (CDI) or does it lag or surpass the CDI on a market-by-market basis?

- How heavy is competitive activity on a market-by-market basis? Remember, competitors also adjust their media weights by market.

- Do national media provide uneven TRP delivery by market? Yes. It is not uncommon for 100 national TRPS to deliver 70 TRPS in New York and 130 TRPS in Abilene.

- Do media cost efficiencies (CPM) vary by market, making some markets more cost effective than others (if marketing variables are the same)? Yes.

- Do consumer demographics and lifestyles vary by market, affecting what consumers buy? Yes.

- Do trade and distribution situations vary by market? Of course.

364

Examples of Geographic Objectives

Geographic media objectives can take many forms. The following discussion presents four examples of important geographic concepts and related media objectives.

Geographic objective 1: Support the current business (sales).

One of the most common spending objectives is to support or defend current business by allocating resources in relation to sales. In other words, if a market represents 5% of sales it would receive 5% of the budget. The marketing objective/strategy leading to such a media objective would likely express the need to protect, support, or defend the current business.

Table 18-4 provides an example of relating sales to media budget allocation. By calculating the percentage of total company or brand sales by geographic market, the budget allocation is created: percentage of sales by market = percentage of total budget as shown below:

Table 18-4.—Support the Current Business

Region	Sales (MM)	% USA Sales	% Budget
East	$50,000	50.0	50.0
South	30,000	30.0	30.0
West	20,000	20.0	20.0
Total	$100,000	100.0	100.0

In the support-the-current-business approach, management may be concerned that while current sales are supported, sales potential is not. Therefore, a somewhat different spending objective is to support the business in relation to sales potential rather than existing sales.

Geographic objective 2: Support the business in relation to sales potential.

This *Fish Where the Fish Are* philosophy is intended to grow the business wherever conditions appear to be most favorable—where the category sells at a high rate (high CDI), where there is good brand development (BDI), where the brand has excellent distribution and good awareness, and a strong sales organization. Many companies also weight sales not only to represent today's sales rates but also sales potential. For example, in Table 18-5, without considering future sales potential, Market A would receive just 40% of the budget based on sales, but when the potential is factored in Market A receives 50% of the total budget.

Table 18-5.—Spend in Relation to Sales Potential

Region	% Sales	Potential Index	Adj. Sales	Adjusted % Budget
East	50.0	75	$35,000	35.0
South	30.0	140	42,000	42.0
West	20.0	115	23,000	22.0
Total	100.0	100	$100,000	100.0

Similarly, a marketer may feel that certain markets could be *harvested* if business conditions in the market were ripe because of industry trends, high CDI, sales momentum, or competitive vulnerability.

Geographic objective 3: Harvest High Opportunity Markets

Harvesting high opportunity markets may require targeting additional marketing spending into the harvest markets that are ripe for incremental sales and market share with a relatively modest investment.

In order to identify opportunity markets, planners can screen candidate markets (DMAs) against a set of criteria such as these:

- Minimum Market size = 1% or more of U.S. industry sales: market should be large enough to make a difference
- Category Development Index (CDI) = 125+: above average consumption of product category in market
- Brand Development Index (BDI) = 125+: above average brand performance in market
- 10% + annual sales growth: brand has positive sales momentum
- Excellent distribution and trade relationships: prerequisite to growth
- Excellent media efficiencies: will enhance ROI

Not every market qualifies as an opportunity of growth market. In other markets, a brand's business situation may be more desperate. Many brands underperform in terms of sales and market share in important, high potential markets (high CDI, low BDI situations).

Geographic objective 4: Support Market Development in Key Markets.

To fix important but weak markets usually requires a long-term commitment from management to support the needed investment. Fixing problems in development markets may also require a lot more than more additional advertising and marketing communication. The underlying problem must be defined first. Business may be lagging the national

366

average for a number of reasons: lower or lost distribution, increased competition, lower consumer awareness or, a deficient sales force.

To address these marketing problems requires that the media planner and marketing team accurately identify the problems negatively affecting sales and then plan and implement strategies that will help solve the problems.

In order to identify the most important development markets, you can screen candidate markets (DMAs) against a set of criteria such as these:

- Minimum Market size = 1% or more of U.S. industry sales: market should be large enough to make a difference
- Category Development Index (CDI) = 125+: above average consumption of product category in market
- Declining sales volume
- Brand Development Index (BDI) <80: below average brand performance in market
- Distribution and trade relationships may be deficient
- Excellent media efficiencies: will enhance ROI

Successful market development matters to a company's long-term sales and share growth. For example, when Leo Burnett originally got the Keebler business, the media department quickly analyzed Keebler and industry sales by product category and discovered that Keebler's business was weak (low BDI) in large, high CDI markets like New York, Philadelphia, and Boston. It was strong (high BDI) in small Midwestern markets where industry cookie/cracker consumption was the lowest (low CDI). Not good.

Strategically, it became clear that if Keebler was going to grow its business and market share, it must do so in the large, high consumption markets. Keebler management approved the agency's recommendations and implemented a variety of marketing initiatives in the low CDI markets, ranging from increased ad spending to a shakeup in their sales force.

When: Timing Objectives

Timing can be everything, as you learned in Chapter 12. This third media objective is sometimes the most important because it defines when to reach consumers with sales messages.

Timing Considerations

Many important issues affect the timing of advertising and other marketing communications.

- Sales seasonality for product category vs. the brand. Should advertising be timed to correspond to category or brand sales seasonality? Advertising in relation to sales seasonality means that if 10% of sales were in October, then 10% of the advertising budget would be spent in October.

- For a particular product category, what is the relationship between when customers buy and when they make the decision to buy? For considered purchases, the decision making process may take 6 months or longer, beginning with awareness, research, and analysis, and ending with retail visits when consumers are seeking the best price just prior to consummating a purchase. Spending in relation to sales may not be a good strategy for considered purchase products like cars, because the decision to buy and the actual purchase take place at different times.

- For impulse purchases, good timing could mean being in front of the consumer just prior to purchase.

- Recency planning involves scheduling advertising to maximize daily reach of consumers who will be making a purchase that day. Recency is a form of reminder advertising.

- What are the relative budget allocation risks for spending too much of the budget on new product introduction vs. too little?

- How much will be spent on individual promotions vs. ongoing brand equity and other marketing tasks?

- What is the effect of competitive activity on how advertising should be scheduled?

- What needs are there to support new product introductions, promotions, or other major announcements?

- Should timing be altered to accommodate specific creative executions or a new campaign?

Examples of Timing Objectives

Timing objectives for marketing communications define the best time to reach target consumers in order to achieve maximum sales and ROI. Here are three examples of timing objectives.

Timing objective 1: Allocate advertising dollars, seasonally, in relation to sales.

Allocating dollars in relation to seasonal sales means that if 10% of the sales occur in January, 10% of the budget should be spent in January. The philosophy of advertising in relation to industry or brand sales can also be applied to smaller time frames. Here is an example of an objective intended to gain a higher share of Saturday sales:

Timing objective 2: Concentrate dollars from Wednesday-Friday in order to reach the target audience prior to the highest usage day—Saturday.

Clearly, a company with that objective believes that advertising and communications have immediate results and wants to use advertising to spike sales on the highest sales day, Saturday. (You may want to try to determine diplomatically whether there is an objective basis for this goal.) For those embracing Recency Planning, the timing objective might be articulated this way:

Timing objective 3: Maximize daily reach of the target audience.

This objective would extend reach at the expense of frequency. You will recall that under Recency theory, it would be preferable to reach 50% once daily rather than 25% twice.

STEP 6. DEVELOP MEDIA STRATEGIES

Media objectives define the Who, Where, When, and How Much of the communications plan. Once the objectives are formulated, the next step is to develop media strategies.

Media strategies describe how, in general, the objectives will be met. For example, if the target audience is adult males who frequently engage in do it yourself projects around the house (audience objective), what type of communications medium or media mix would most effectively reach and communicate with that target (strategy)?

Media strategies should describe:

- The mix of communications that will address the marketing task and media objectives, e.g., advertising vs. promotion, with rationale & supporting data
- Proposed media classes & mix, with rationale & supporting data
- Geographic mix of media, market weighting, with rationale & supporting data
- Scheduling & timing, with rationale & supporting data
- Other strategies, with rationale & supporting data

Task Matching: Determining the IMC Mix

The first step in developing the media strategy is to select the forms of marketing communications that should be included in the marketing communications plan and at what budget level. (Review Chapters 14-17 for discussions of alternative forms of marketing communications.)

As already discussed, selection of communications forms should be based on the marketing and communications tasks to be addressed. The Task Matching Model developed by 2020:Marketing Communications LLC can help planners match communications forms to tasks.

For the most part the concept of matching the task to the best communications options is not be rocket science. Here are several questions to ponder:

- If the task is to **raise top of mind awareness**, what are the most cost effective communications options?
- If the task is to **convince consumers** that your new product is far better than the old product, what are your best options?
- If the task is to **gain leads** for the sales force, what are your best options?
- If the task is to **generate more website visits**, what are your best options?
- If the task is to **generate immediate sales**, what are your best options?

The Task Matching Model can be used to identify the forms of marketing communications that best address the priority tasks. Figure 14-2 provided a hypothetical example of a planner's analysis of marketing communications forms addressing the task of awareness at low cost. The model permits the pairing of any two communications needs such as information vs. involvement (Figure 18-1), leads vs. conversion, awareness vs. cost efficiency, and so on.

Figure 18-1 provides hypothetical analysis for an engagement task based on communicating information and audience involvement.

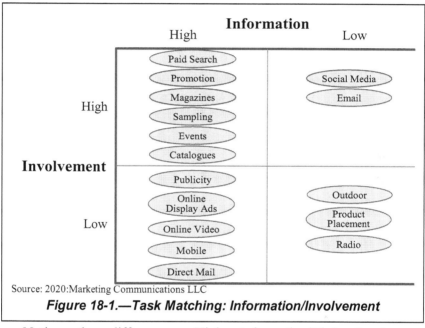

Source: 2020:Marketing Communications LLC

Figure 18-1.—Task Matching: Information/Involvement

Notice the differences. High Information/High Involvement communications forms include magazines, search, website, social media, and event marketing.

The Task Matching tool can help reduce arbitrary decisions and improve the effectiveness of your marketing communications plan. What remains is defining the role and rationale for each communications form. All your communications must work together in a complementary, synergistic manner, focusing on a common creative platform.

Figure 18-2 is a graphic example of how one marketer allocated the firm's marketing communications budget. Advertising received the majority of spending, followed by search and non-traditional media (Word of Mouth and Event Marketing). The marketer wanted to raise awareness and trial of a considered purchase product. The role of the advertising was to improve top of mind awareness; the role of search was to generate inquiries and leads. Event marketing was used to let potential customers experience what the product is like—to see, touch, feel, smell, and play with the product. Word of Mouth generated buzz and free publicity.

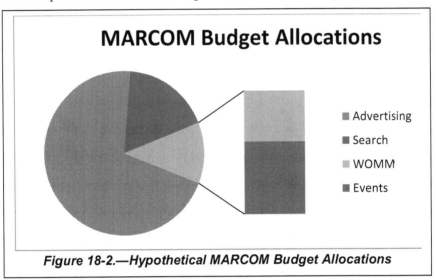

Figure 18-2.—Hypothetical MARCOM Budget Allocations

The preceding discussion has focused on the big picture of selecting an overall mix of communications forms. The following discussion narrows the focus to advertising media.

Media Selection

The next step is to develop a media strategy for the advertising portion of the marketing communications plan. Strategies must be developed that, based on your marketing situation and objectives, address the following questions:

- Which media classes do you recommend for what purposes? Why?
- Will you use a single primary medium or a media mix? Why?
- How will media be used geographically?
- How will media be scheduled? Why?
- Are there other proposed strategies? What? Why?

The media strategy must define and describe which media classes are recommended to most cost effectively reach and communicate the message to the target audience(s). To review: the major media classes include television, radio, magazines, newspapers, out of home, the Internet, direct mail, and other digital or non-traditional classes. In order to select the media classes for your media plan, you must evaluate the alternatives and compare them on the dimensions of impact, audience, cost, and cost effectiveness (see Chapters 5-7).

Impact

A good place to begin the inter-media selection process is to consider each media class in terms of its effectiveness in addressing the marketing task and communicating the message (Chapter 7). This first stage of media selection is more subjective than quantitative. While there are many studies purporting to prove that a particular medium communicates more effectively than other media, there is no definitive evidence. For example, the Television Advertising Bureau (TVB) commissions Nielsen Media Research bi-annually to measure media usage and consumer perceptions of advertising in the major media. The Radio Advertising Bureau and the Magazine Publishers' Association, the Outdoor Advertising Association, and the Internet Advertising Bureau, of course, have their own studies supporting their effectiveness and impact.

Audience

Audience analysis of each media class and the types of media within each class will require use of syndicated research studies from MRI, SMRB, Nielsen, Arbitron, and so on. How can audiences be segmented by each medium in relation to the target audience (see Chapter 10)? What are the reach and frequency patterns?

Cost

What are the cost parameters for each medium in terms of unit cost benchmarks, CPMs and CPPs? Considering audience, cost, and impact, which media classes appear to be most cost effective?

Media Priorities

Once you have identified and prioritized the media classes, you must then focus on determining the most cost-effective forms within those media types. As shown in the following table, all media offer unique genres. For example, if you have selected television, should play an important role in your media plan, you have to decide what kind of television. Television audiences and costs vary by daypart, so your plan must have precise budgets dedicated to the dayparts you want to buy.

Table 18-6.—Media Genres Within Media Types

Medium	Geographic	Sold by	Examples
Television	Network/Local	Dayparts	Daytime, Prime, Late Night, Early News
Radio	Network/Local	Formats	News/Talk, Various Music
Magazines	National/Regional/ Local	Editorial Formats	Food, News, Business, Cars, Home, Ethnic
Outdoor	Market by Market	Type of Unit	Posters, Bulletins, Digital, Street Furniture
Newspapers	Market by Market	Dailies or Suburban	Morning, Evening, Sunday, Other
Internet	Global to Local	Varied	Search, Display, Email, Video, Social Networks

While evaluating potential impact of available media may be a judgment call, determining allocations among media genres is typically much more quantitative. For example, if you are working with a $1 million budget for national television, you have to figure out the most cost effective allocation of that $1 million. Table 18-7 gives an example of how a professional media planner might compare the results of alternative budget allocations by television daypart.

Table 18-7.—Hypothetical $1 Million Budget: Target Women 25-54

Daypart	Plan I	Plan II	Plan III	Plan IV
M-F Day	100%	50%	33%	—
Prime	—	50	33	100%
Late Nite	—	—	33	—
TRPS	110	74	65	36
Reach	60%	61%	63%	30%
Avg. Freq.	1.8	1.2	1.0	1.0
4+ Freq.	30%	20%	16%	7%
CPP	$9000	$18,500	$16,000	$28,000

Table 18-7 shows the projected results of spending $1 million in network television in different dayparts. Plan I spends the entire budget in daytime television (serials, game shows, comedies, network reruns). Plan II splits the budget evenly between daytime and primetime, while Plan III allocates the dollars among three dayparts, and Plan IV goes for broke by spending the entire budget in primetime shows.

According to these estimates, Plan 1 will deliver the most TRPS, higher average exposure frequency, and higher effective frequency. At the other end of the spectrum, because primetime costs so much more (CPP) than daytime or late night, Plan IV will deliver less than half of the gross exposure (TRPS), as well as significantly lower reach, average frequency, and effective frequency than Plans I-III.

What about impact or engagement? To consider the communications value of each option, you can assign effectiveness weights to the unadjusted TRPS. Refer back to Chapters 7 and 15 for help with this.

Single Medium vs. Media Mix

A key element of the media selection strategy is the decision to use a single or primary medium or whether to use a *media mix* instead. The answer depends on several variables, including the cost of the alternatives, which will weigh heavily in the decision.

Arguments for Using a Single Medium

The arguments for using a single media class such as television or newspapers include these:

1. A single medium may be the most cost efficient way to reach a particular target audience.
2. The budget is adequate to use only one medium effectively.
3. A particular media type includes tactical opportunities that are especially important, e.g., bonus circulation, free ads, and special editions or content.
4. The need for continuity, frequency, or consumer engagement may require focus in one medium.
5. Achieving more visibility vs. a key competitor may require focus in one medium.

Arguments for a Media Mix

There are equally good arguments for using a media mix:

1. Multiple media classes create synergistic effects.
2. It may be important to use media that play complementary communications roles, e.g., television to create brand name awareness, radio to provide targeted frequency, magazines to explain the product benefits and search to generate website visits and sales leads.
3. A media mix will extend your reach. Using more media classes increases reach (at the expense of frequency), while using few media increase more added frequency than reach.
4. A media mix can flatten the frequency distribution and increase effective reach. For example, if television were the single medium being used, most exposure would occur among heavy TV viewers. The addition of other media will usually help to balance these frequency patterns. For example, magazines or radio or newspapers are ways to reach light TV viewers.

Role of Media Mix Models

Some advertisers use *media mix models* to help them determine what their media mix should be at a certain budget level. Media mix models are computer simulations estimating audience delivery, such as gross impressions, reach and frequency, and frequency distributions for almost any target group for which there is data.

Some models allow you to inject effectiveness weights and other parameters. For example, if you give a higher effectiveness weight to one media class than another, the calculations will provide both unadjusted and adjusted data.

TELMAR is a leading worldwide supplier of media modeling and many other simple and complex data analyses. TELMAR capitalizes on Nielsen, MRI SMRB, and other data sources. Advertisers must be subscribers to the data services to use them. Table 18-8 shows the kind of analysis that a media simulation model might produce.

Some advertisers think media mix models are a useful tool in improving media effectiveness. However, this can be argued either way. Some advertisers like to quantify (even if the purpose is simply to quantify), while other advertisers are skeptical of the validity of results. Others believe that media mix modeling is useful as additional information to be used only with a full understanding of its limitations. Some of the limitations of multimedia mix modeling include:

- Inter-media audience data are not comparable;
- Different methodologies are used to measure audiences;
- Ad units are not comparable (a page versus a :30 TV commercial),
- Involvement and communication with audiences is different by medium, and
- Media effectiveness weights are largely subjective. (Garbage in, garbage out.)

Nevertheless, media mix modeling is common. Table 18-8 is a hypothetical comparison of the unadjusted performance of three $10 million plans. In this case, Media Mix 3 was the winner. Can you see why?

Table 18-8.—$10 Million Media Mix Analysis

Outcome	Media Mix 1	Media Mix 2	Media Mix 3
Television % Spend	100%	70%%	60%
Magazines % Spend	–	30%	25%
Radio % Spend	–	–	15%
Reach	90%	93%	94%
Avg. Frequency	7.8	8.6	9.1
Frequency 5+	27%	31%	33%
TRPS	500	600	750
Effective TRPS	**350**	**400**	**450**

Some media planners just run with the numbers, which is not a good thing. Good planners always understand what the data actually mean and what their limitations are.

Geographic Media Strategies

Geographic media strategies translate geographic media objectives into a media weight and geographic budget allocation strategy. How much spending in national, regional, local, micro markets? How many TRPS in Los Angeles vs. San Francisco?

For example, a geographic media strategy might establish a base of network television and Internet search supplemented by local market spot television and radio in strategic markets or DMAs. Another media strategy might focus all media spending exclusively on several key markets, especially if dollars are too limited for national advertising. A third example might allocate the budget for a DMA among broad coverage of the DMA and each of the several retail trading areas within the DMA.

Fortunately, most advertising media offer good geographic flexibility. Media can be planned to reach national, regional, local market, and sometimes micro-markets. Table 18-9 provides an overview of the geographic flexibility offered by a variety of media.

Table 18-9.—Geographic Flexibility of Media Types

Medium	National	Regional	Metro/DMA	Zip Clusters
Broadcast TV	Network	Some	Spot	No
Cable TV	Network	Some	Interconnects	Systems
Magazines	Natl Editions	Yes	Largest Markets	No
Daily Newspapers	No	No	Yes	Yes
Radio	Networks	Limited	Yes	No
Out of Home	No	No	Yes	Yes
Internet	Yes	Yes	Yes	Yes
Direct Mail	Yes	Yes	Yes	Yes

National Advertising Coverage

If the advertiser is a national marketer, an important issue is how much advertising should be placed in national media vs. regional or local media where marketing problems or opportunities exist. National media, such as network or cable television networks, magazines, can reach audiences throughout the country. National media usually have lower CPMs than local media, but their audiences are uneven by market, they don't emphasize markets of more importance, etc. On the other hand, national media offer the benefit of better ad positioning and simplicity of buying.

Regional Advertising Coverage

If a company primarily does business in a region of the country (like the Southeast, Northeast, West Coast, etc.), they may choose regional availabilities from national media. Some media can be used to cover large regions of the country, excluding the rest of the country. For example, television networks sometimes have regional feeds available for sale, the majority of magazines sell a variety of regional editions.

DMA Advertising Coverage

As you have already learned, the most common local market definition is the DMA (because television has dominated media usage for decades). Plentiful advertising media can be purchased to saturate individual DMAs with media weight. For example, local television and radio stations, newspapers, outdoor, direct mail, in store advertising, and even some national and local magazines can be used to target buyers in individual DMAs and with the flexibility to vary TRP levels by market.

Targeting Retail Trading Areas

Some companies with customers or sales in a small area will find that even DMAs are too big and expensive to target, making the use of spot television or radio not cost effective. For example, a target audience may be highly concentrated in a few zip codes within a DMA. Or a local retailer may draw 75% of its customers (and resulting sales) from a three-mile radius, which can be defined by zip codes or even block groups.

Since advertisers pay for exposure in 100% of the DMA, if the advertiser's market resides in 5% of the DMA, DMA targeting would not be cost effective, just as national advertising would not be cost effective if their business was in only 20 of the 211 DMAs. While media opportunities are not as plentiful and the CPMs will be higher, there are many ways to target micro-markets with traditional media.

Advertising can be purchased on individual cable TV systems that cover individual communities within the DMA. Newspapers often offer zoned editions and the ability to drop freestanding supplements or samples in selected zip codes. Direct mail can be targeted down to the block level. Outdoor bulletins, posters, spectaculars, street furniture, and more can be targeted to small geographic areas or ethnic neighborhoods. Email and Internet search can also be targeted to local trading areas; rather than generating keyword clicks from all over the country, an advertiser can tell Google or Yahoo to show their ads only to viewers within a defined geographic area.

In addition, guerrilla media such as flyers, newsletters, seminars, in store advertising can be additional options for those needing to target small retail trading areas or zip codes.

Geographic Weighting

Because the relative marketing importance of individual market areas (regions, DMAs, micro-markets) varies widely, planners usually want to provide proportional media weights. This may take the form of increased or reduced TRPs in the same media or different media included in or deleted from market schedules. For example, you may decide to add 500 television TRPS or 1200 radio TRPS to the media schedule in Orlando.

Your task is to figure out the best way of weighting markets in relation to some measures of marketing importance or competitive activity. For example, you may decide that Orlando should receive 1000 TRPS but Miami should receive only 500.

Table 18-10 depicts a determination of national vs. local media weights and plan expenditures. In this example, TRP goals are established by market area on the basis of CDI. TRP goals are then established for each Area, ranging from 2000 TRPS for the highest CDI to 500 TRPS for the lowest CDI.

This planner established a base level of 500 network television TRPS. To determine how many TRPS are needed to bring the national level up to Area needs, the network TRP delivery is subtracted from the TRP goals. Costs for the resulting spot TRPS are determined and added to the network allocations. In this (atypical) allocation, the total $25 million budget went to network ($10 million) and spot ($15 million).

Table 18-10.—Determination of National vs. Local Budgets

Area	% Sales	CDI	TRP Goal	Network Delivery	Net Cost*	Spot Needed	Cost	Total Cost
A	40.0	200	2000	500	$2500	1500	$8000	$10500
B	25.0	150	1500	500	2000	1000	6000	8000
C	15.0	100	1000	500	1000	500	1000	2000
D	20.0	50	500	500	5000	—	—	5000
Total	100	100		500	$10,000		$15000	$25000

*Pro rata network cost by area.

Timing & Scheduling

It is extremely important that the advertising (or other communications) reach the target audience at the right time to influence them. You studied this concept in chapter 12 and encountered it again earlier in this chapter (see Timing Objectives). There are two important media planning issues to consider: (1) allocation of media weight and spending throughout the year, and (2) scheduling that media weight for greatest impact.

Timing

Timing refers to the most strategically effective allocation of advertising dollars through planning period. On average, 8.3% of sales would be expected to occur in each month of the year (100%/12 months = 8.3%). However, each month's percentage of annual sales is actually higher or lower than that.

A brand's seasonal sales percentages may also deviate from industry sales patterns. Some companies or brands, especially retailers, find that up to 50% or more of annual sales occur between Thanksgiving and Christmas. These facts raise questions:

- Should advertising/communication be allocated when sales occur?
- Should media spending lead sales? If so, by how long?

The following discussion will provide some food for thought about timing according to the consumer's purchase decision-making process, product category, and budgets.

- **Considered purchase** products are those that consumers research and deliberate about prior to making their final purchase decision. Examples of considered purchase products/services include cars & trucks, cameras, a new lap top computer, new office equipment, insurance, travel to a particular destination, and so on. For such products, the decision making process occurs over a period of time; consumers are paying extra attention to advertising for the products, talking to friends and relatives, doing research on the Internet, and maybe visiting retailers to see, touch, and feel the merchandise. From a timing point of view, when should considered purchase advertisers advertise?

- **Impulse purchases** include things like cookies. On Wednesday, the kids see some TV commercials for Keebies and point them out to mom, who is going to the supermarket on Thursday to do grocery shopping for the week. Since the purchase of cookies doesn't require too much analysis, mom puts Keebies on her shopping list and purchases the brand the next day. In this case, it was important to advertise close to when sales actually occur.

- **Promotions**, such as an auto manufacturer's Spring Sales Event, means purchase incentives will be available briefly, and new promotion creative has been developed to support it. Should the auto company kick off its Spring Event advertising the day the promotion starts—or should timing of the advertising lead the promotion? (Keep in mind that nobody even knows about the promotional offers until they have "seen" several ads announcing and explaining the offer.)

- **Christmas!** Some brands and retailers generate 50% or more of their annual sales between Thanksgiving and Christmas. In the extreme situation of Christmas/holiday sales, the advertiser has a very short window in which his entire year will make or break. Should a holiday-dependent advertiser begin advertising at Thanksgiving or should advertising start earlier or later? (Note: if a brand/retailer has little awareness or consideration by Thanksgiving, and it takes time to build (even with good creative and heavy media weight), does the late advertiser risk missing the market? Should the advertiser have begun advertising for the Christmas surge in October? Or with a limited budget, is it more prudent to wait until the cash register starts ringing more often?

- **New product introductions** are more complicated because there are many tasks to address. First, awareness and trial must be quickly generated. Repurchase must be stimulated. Frequency of purchase may call for reminders. Typically, advertisers front-load their media scheduling, spending between 40-60% of the budget during the first month or two. At the same time, there must be sufficient media to stimulate repurchase following the initial, heavy launch.

Scheduling Patterns

In addition to figuring out how to allocate budgets throughout the year, month, or day, you must also determine the most effective *scheduling pattern* for the advertising. Scheduling alternatives include continuity scheduling, flighting, and pulsing.

Continuity Scheduling

A *continuity* advertising schedule refers to one where the advertising and communication are scheduled relatively evenly through the year. For example, an advertiser with 2400 annual TRPs would schedule them at an average rate of 200 per month, roughly 50 TRPs per week.

Continuity scheduling might run 25 TRPS per week for 52 weeks, as at any TRP level. If there are other considerations such as sales seasonality to consider, weekly TRP levels can be adjusted so that in certain weeks TRP levels are higher vs. lower in other weeks.

Recency Planning advocates continuity scheduling to provide the highest possible daily reach, reminding tomorrow's shoppers to buy the advertised brand. Opponents of continuity scheduling argue that the TRP levels are never high enough to break through the clutter and be noticed, an opinion supported by Zielskie's early research.

Advantages of continuity scheduling are:

• Consistency of advertising week in week out,
• Recency: daily/weekly reminders to buy, and
• Coverage of the entire purchase cycle,

Disadvantages of continuity scheduling are:

• Lack of impact as compared with frequency,
• Difficulty breaking through the clutter?
• Difficulty building awareness with weekly/monthly reach, and
• Levels are lower.

Flighting

The second type of scheduling pattern is called *flighting* (or *bursting*). Flighting is intermittent periods of advertising alternating with periods of none. If a total plan consisted of 2600 TRPS for the year, it could be scheduled evenly at 50 per week continuity, it could be scheduled in bursts of 100 per week for 26 weeks, or it might vary TRP levels during the flight periods. Of course, flights may also have heavier or lighter media weights at particular times to support seasonal sales, promotions, new product introductions, or competitive initiatives.

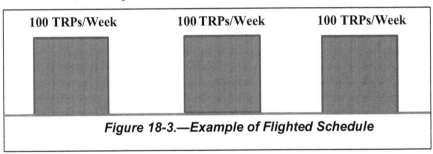

Figure 18-3.—Example of Flighted Schedule

Flighting or bursting runs the same number of TRPS at higher levels for fewer weeks. Flighting advocates believe that this scheduling pattern ultimately will result in somewhat higher awareness, because the higher frequency during advertising periods makes the advertising more memorable. It is more likely to break through the clutter and to be seen more often than the competition's advertising. The trade-off is that sharp memory decay may occur during the periods when there is no advertising.

Advantages of flighting are:

- Effective Frequency approach—minimum frequency needed to be effective,
- Dominate competitors for a while,
- Break through the clutter at least for a short time, and
- Little waste since advertising is concentrated during the best part of the purchasing cycle.

Disadvantages of flighting are:

- No advertising between flights; top of mind awareness may decline when not advertising, and
- Competitors will be advertising when you are not.

Pulsing

The third basic type of scheduling is called *Pulsing*. Because it combines the principles of both continuity and flighting, some believe that Pulsing provides the best of both worlds. The heavy periods are strong enough to break through the clutter, while the steady lower levels help to prevent the memory decay that occurs when there is no advertising at all.

The strategy in Figure 18-5 combines flighting and continuous scheduling by using a low level of advertising all year round with heavy advertising during certain periods. Product categories that are sold year round but experience a surge in seasonal or holiday sales are good candidates for pulsing. For instance, deodorant sprays that are sold heavily during the summer months would receive more attention then.

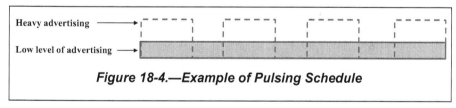

Figure 18-4.—Example of Pulsing Schedule

In pulsing, the theory is that the heavy ups will spike awareness (or whatever metric is being used), which does not occur in continuity scheduling. It is also assumed that the reduced levels between heavy ups are adequate to maintain the awareness generated during the heavy up period. On the other hand, although pulsing provides both continuity and heavy ups, it may not deliver a sufficiently powerful TRP level to satisfy advocates of Effective Reach.

Advantages of pulsing are:

- Combines some advantages of both continuity and flighting,
- Covers different market situations, and
- Supports Recency and Effective Reach to a degree.

Disadvantages of pulsing are:

- Continuity levels may not provide enough weekly reach to implement Recency, and
- Frequency levels during heavy up periods may not be adequate to support Effective Reach.

STEP 7. DEVISE TACTICAL PLAN

The sixth step in the media planning process is elaboration of the tactical plan. The Media Plan—the Action Plan—provides details of the media & spending plan, including which media vehicles you will use and why; timing, dates and scheduling; costs and budget recaps; plan performance in service of the objectives; and decision dates.

In addition to identifying recommended media vehicles, audiences and costs, the Tactical Plan includes a flow chart showing the scheduling of media activity, including reach and frequency. The flow chart should allow someone quickly to see the entire plan for a company, brand, or task.

The above flow chart at Figure 16-5 shows much of the media plan's detail. Two flights of late night network television are scheduled in January and March, with spot television in February. Oprah's magazine has four-color page insertions scheduled in January and March, while "Fit for Life" is scheduled for February. In addition, the plan utilizes continuous paid search in Google and Bing as well as in social media, Twitter and Facebook.

The tactical plan also contains analyses and details for other elements of the plan. A variety of tables showing analyses of alternative media vehicles, budget, recaps, and performance reports back up the flow chart.

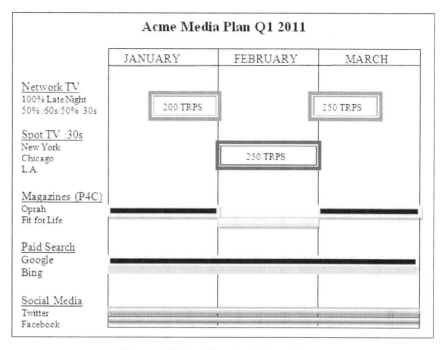

Figure 18-5.—Tactical Flow Chart

Table 18-11 provides an example of a budget recap for each market.

Table 18-11.—Key Market Summary FY 2011

DMA	% US HH	% US Sales	Spot TV TRPS	Spot TV Cost	Spot Radio TRPS	Spot Radio Cost	Total Cost
New York	6.8	7.7	2000	$4,140	1500	$1500	$5640
L.A.	5.0	6.0	2500	5500	2000	1600	7100
Chicago	3.1	4.2	2000	2100	1500	400	2500
Seattle	1.6	3.0	1500	450	1000	154	604
Dallas/FW	2.1	2.8	1500	950	1000	218	1168
Tampa/SP	1.5	2.0	1000	350	500	71	421
Total	20.1	25.7	—	$13,490	—	$3943	$17433

Table 18-12 shows a simple comparison of business magazines that were considered for the tactical plan.

Table 18-12.—Comparison of Business Magazines

Magazine	Circulation (000)	Cost P4C (000)	Target Imps (000)	CPM Imps.	Recom-mended
Forbes	900	114	1200	95.00	X
Fortune	930	160	700	228.57	
Bus. Week	900	112	1000	112.00	X
Inc.	700	108	600	180.00	
Entrepreneur	612	83	1100	90.90	X

Advertisers are extremely interested in how their dollars are being spent, so every media plan will include a series of budget recaps and analyses that the advertiser wants to see. Table 18-13 is what a simple budget recap might look like. All such necessary budget summaries should be included in the Tactical Plan section.

Table 18-13—Quarterly Budget Recap by Medium

Medium	1st Q	2nd Q	3rd Q	4th Q	Total	% Total
Network TV	700	1300	1000	1500	4500	69.2
Network Radio	—	100	—	—	100	1.5
Magazines	100	100	150	300	650	10.0
Internet Search	250	300	300	400	1250	19.8
Email	1050	1800	1450	2200	6500	100.0
% Total	16.2	27.7	22.3	33.8	100.0	—

Finally, since the media objectives laid out the reach and frequency objectives for each target group, it is appropriate to include the performance of the recommended plan. An example of a performance summary is shown below in Table 18-14.

Table 18-14.—Plan Performance

Medium	R/F Objective	Plan R/F	Clicks Obj.	Plan Clicks
Network TV	90/10	88/9		
Network Radio	50/5	45/4		
Magazines	60/3	63/4		
Internet Search			200,000	210,000
Email			55,000	60,000

STEP 8. TEST THE PLAN

If the purpose of the media plan is to introduce a new product, a new campaign, or a new media approach, the company may wish to reduce its risk by first test marketing the new product or idea. Given that the vast majority of new products fail, committing huge dollars to a national launch (including costs for manufacturing and infrastructure, staffing, and marketing) is a risk most companies are not willing to take.

Test marketing is a simulation of a national introduction. To contain costs, test marketing is usually conducted in a limited number of smaller markets. While a national launch might cost $50 million (theoretically), it may cost only a few million to implement a test market plan.

Sometimes companies will test alternative launch strategies to determine which spending level, creative approach, pricing, or media strategy will yield the best results.

Test Market Selection

Philosophies vary on how to select test markets. The best practice is to attempt to create a microcosm testing universe by selecting geographically dispersed test and control markets with the right kind of distribution available as well as demographics with category development and brand development profiles similar to the U.S. as a whole. Smaller markets like Peoria, Illinois, are popular because they are demographically typical and small enough to be affordable.

How many test markets are needed? The answer depends on how many variables are being tested (more variables, more markets). Your results will be more credible as your samples grow larger and come from more markets. As a rule of thumb, you should have at least 4-6 test markets and two control markets against which you can compare results. Frequently, test market results vary by market. If the test failed in one market, it would be good to know that it was successful in three others!

Test Market Translation

Once the test markets have been selected, the theoretical national media plan must be translated to the test markets. The translation must simulate what would happen if the national plan were executed.

For example, if the national plan called for 1000 TRPS in primetime television, 1000 TRPS on local stations would be purchased in primetime television in the test markets. If magazines were part of the national plan, test market editions of the same magazines would be purchased. If flights were used in the national plan, the same scheduling patterns would be tested.

Adjusting test market plans is sometimes necessary to offset problems that arise in translation. For example, the in-program primetime spots that would run in national programs may run during station breaks in local test markets, reducing commercial recall. To make the test plan comparable to the network plan, 10-20% more TRPS may need to be added to the translation.

The length of time a brand stays in test market is variable. An average might be 6-9 months, but a company may terminate earlier if it looks like the test is either a home run or a disaster.

Test Market Measurement

Companies typically do field research in test markets to measure awareness, trial, intent to purchase, repurchase rates, product satisfaction, image, reactions to advertising, sales, and market share. Once all of the measurements are in, the company projects the results to a national level, and after studying the test market results, makes a decision about whether to launch nationally.

Test Marketing Risks

Imprecise or unpredictable results are always a major concern. The advertiser wants as much confidence as possible that if the product were launched nationally, the launch would results at least as good as the test. In addition, competition will learn about the new product, will probably monitor its progress, and may even take steps to foil the test by heavying up their own advertising, conducting price promotion, or engaging in trade promotion for better in-store positioning and displays.

STEP 9. OBTAIN AUTHORIZATIONS

The last page of your Tactical Plan addresses timetables and next steps. You should ask for the order or approvals, including the decision dates that must be met, to execute the plan. It might look like this:

Next Steps

Approval	Deadline
Approval of media strategy and plan	3/15
Authorization to buy network TV @ $5MM	4/1
Place orders for magazines @ $2.5MM	4/15
Agreement on Google keywords	5/1

Figure 18-6.—Last Page of Tactical Plan: Sample

SUMMARY

In Chapter 18, you have followed detailed instructions for building a media strategy. Table 18-5 provides a summary of the process for developing a strategic media plan. The companion workbook has several media planning exercises.

Table 18-15.—Media Plan Development Process: Summary

Step	Goal	Planner Tasks
1	Situation Analysis	Identify factors affecting media planning
2	Problem Statement	What marketing issues will be addressed?
3	Task Definition	What is the overriding objective of the plan?
4	Model Selection	What are the communications principles upon which the plan will be based?
5	Objectives Establishment	Audience, reach, geography, frequency
6	Strategy Development	Communications & media mix, national/local media use/scheduling
7.	Tactical Planning	Media vehicles, timing, geographic schedules, budget recaps, plan performance
8.	Test Marketing & Implementation	Timetables, measurements, authorizations

SECTION IV: MEDIA BUYING

As has already been discussed, from the buyer's vantage point, there are two distinct functions—media planning and media buying—that must be optimized. Both functions are equally important to the success of the media plan.

The rubber meets the road when the media plan is translated into reality. The plan calls for 5000 TRPs, but how many TRPs can actually be purchased at market prices? The plan calls for digital outdoor bulletins at certain high traffic locations, but are they still available? Can they be purchased within the budget?

The literature on media planning has neglected the second function, failing to address the strategies and challenges of effective media buying that claims hundreds of billions of dollars. The last section of this book aims to remedy that deficiency.

You will be introduced to the nature of media negotiations first, in Chapter 19, then examine broadcast, print, and Internet media buying in the next three chapters. Finally, in Chapter 23, you will have a chance to consider some unconventional techniques and channels for stretching your media-buying dollars to hit your communications targets.

Chapter 19   Media Negotiations
Chapter 20   Broadcast Media Buying
Chapter 21   Print Media Buying
Chapter 22   Internet Media Buying
Chapter 23   Guerilla Media Buying

19. MEDIA NEGOTIATIONS

In business, you don't get what you deserve,
You get what you negotiate.

–Chester L. Karrass
Leading author & consultant on effective negotiations

Agencies and media buying firms are often hired and fired on the basis of their ability to negotiate media buys "better than anyone else." That's understandable when you consider that you're bargaining with the client's money.

A brilliant media plan is only a plan. The media strategy and plan are somewhat theoretical concepts until they are executed. Are the desired media available? Can the buy be negotiated within the available budget? Can we likely to be able to buy more or less than expected? Which geographic markets are soft and which are tight? Can we get the ads positioned where we want them? Can we get the desired weight or TRPS in the desired weeks?

Media availabilities can be a perishable commodity. Pricing can be variable, too, depending on the prevailing conditions of supply and demand.

Media vehicle availabilities, costs, and other variables cannot always be known until the buyer begins negotiating with media sellers. For example, a media plan might include four commercials in the Super Bowl at an estimated cost of $2.7 million each. When negotiations begin, you might find that only three spots are left and the firm price is $3 million each. Will the client be satisfied with only three spots? Can paying $300,000 more per spot be justified? That's $900,000 total additional cost for the three ads, but still under the $10.8 million allocated for the Super Bowl.

When you try to bring the media plan to life, you'll find that sometimes the devil in the details. You'll learn in Chapter 19 that the buyer's challenge is to figure out how to negotiate the specifics of the media plan most effectively, protecting your budget while meeting or exceeding your communications goals. Figure 19-1 depicts your balancing act.

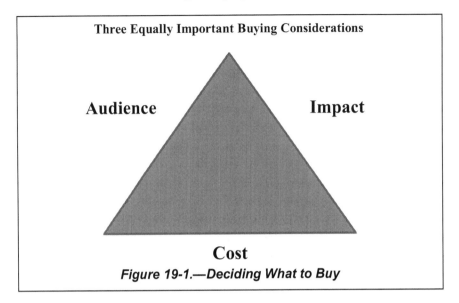

Three Equally Important Buying Considerations

Audience   **Impact**

Cost

Figure 19-1.—Deciding What to Buy

INTRODUCTION

Make no mistake about it. Agencies and media buyers get paid to win—to win in negotiations. What makes it interesting is that the sellers also get paid to win. To win, you must know what *media value* you want or need. You must have the right negotiating strategy, and you must be able and willing to say, NO, to the seller. You must know what your *walk away point* is.

Media buying is the process of negotiating all of the particulars of a media plan with media sellers who may be employed by the medium or who may be professional reps hired by the media to represent them in sales negotiations. Media buyers select broadcast stations and programs, times, websites, magazines, newspapers, online activities, outdoor locations, or anything else the media plan calls for. Buyers negotiate the price and all other terms and conditions of purchase with the sellers: number of media units (commercials or ads) and estimated audience, scheduling, timing, ad positioning within vehicles, value-added and promotional add-ons, research to be conducted, in store merchandising programs, and anything else important to the advertiser.

When deciding what to buy at what price and on what specific terms, you have to evaluate audience sizes and demographics, psychographics, pricing, and cost efficiencies for each alternative media vehicle in relation to the target audience definition. That's what you were doing when you developed your media strategy.

If your plan says to reach adventurous men 25-54 with 100 TRPS in primetime action programming during a particular week, you will attempt to negotiate the purchase of airtime during programming that effectively reaches that target. You will contact the networks or stations to determine what action programs are available for the desired week(s).

If there is commercial inventory available within the desired program types, you will ask each network/station to submit a proposal that includes their specific programs, dates, asking prices, and terms for your other criteria. Then you will analyze the proposals they submit and negotiate with each until the best deal is reached.

THE ART OF NEGOTIATION

The art of negotiation is the process by which two or more parties with different needs and goals work to find a mutually acceptable deal. Because negotiating is an interpersonal process and each negotiating situation is different, each negotiation is influenced by each party's skills, attitudes, and style.

Perhaps because negotiation is an interpersonal process, there are many false notions about how negotiators should behave to achieve their goals. Figure 19-2 illustrates some of the myths about negotiators.

Buying Myths

- Tough negotiators get what they want.
- Honey works better than vinegar.
- We really beat 'em up!
- It's all about Friends & Favors.
- It's all about Clout!!!
- It's all about our superior negotiation skills.
- My relationships get me better deals.
- Buy locally for better rates. Forget the reps.
- You *have* to buy our station; we're #1!
- Local rating books identify the right programming for your audience.
- We bought more TRPS or spots than they did, so we're better.
- A Rating is a Rating is a Rating!

Figure 19-2.—Buying Myths

For example, the myth that tough negotiators get what they want comes from the styles and behavior among some immature buyers who assume that shouting and threatening will induce a seller to sweeten a deal. Other agencies are notorious in their new business claims—selling their media buying effectiveness on the premise that their buyers have good relationships with the local reps or that their buyers beat up the reps.

Another problem is the belief among many buyers that *a rating is a rating is a rating*. This assumes that TRPS deliver equal communication value, a major fallacy.

Negotiating can be regarded as an unpleasant task because it implies conflict, but negotiating need not be characterized by bad behavior or hard feelings. Understanding more about the negotiation process will allow you to manage your negotiations with confidence, increasing your chance for outcomes that will be satisfactory all around.

Negotiating expert Chester Karrass captures the challenge of effective media negotiations in the title of his book: *In Business, You Don't Get What You Deserve, You Get What You Negotiate.* In media buying, you only get what you negotiate.

You may think negotiation applies only to the purchase of broadcast media. While it is true that broadcast media buys are always negotiated, print and Internet buys are also highly negotiable. You must think outside the box to maximize value through professional negotiation.

Here is how a buyer-seller negotiation could start:

SELLER: *This is a great TV program developed by the same folks who did "Survivor." And the station is going to promote it as its #1 show. It is sure to do at least a 25 share and a 15 rating.*

BUYER: *You must be joking, Bill! Everybody and his brother are doing reality knockoffs. If the show is lucky, it will do a 20 share and a 10 rating. And I don't think it is worth more than $110 per point! What are you willing to guarantee?*

SELLER: *We feel so good about this show that we are willing to guarantee a 15 rating.*

BUYER: *Well, I still think you are dreaming, but we might consider buying in if you will provide bonus spots in "NCIS" that would double any audience shortfall.*

TO BE CONTINUED...

This example is typical, in that sellers and buyers are always trying to convince each other of their divergent points of view about the *value* of a media package.

SUCCESSFUL MEDIA NEGOTIATIONS

To conduct a winning negotiation, you must have a winning negotiation strategy. If you conduct negotiations by the seat of your pants, you will likely be the loser in the professional relationship, if not the negotiation. Here are the Top Ten rules of effective negotiation that have proven highly effective with sellers of media.

1. Be Prepared

In any media negotiation, information, knowledge, and facts are power. If you have not done your homework, you will probably not achieve the outcome you might have. What information do you need? What are the supply and demand conditions? Is the market soft with a lot of inventory available, or is the market tight with a scarcity of good availabilities? Do you understand the market's dynamics—the client's business, demographics, and psychographics? What are the competitive advantages and disadvantages of each medium about which you will be negotiating, in terms of audiences, audience cumes, cost efficiencies, ad placement policies? What—beyond money—does the seller want?

2. Know What you Want

In order to negotiate a media buy effectively you must first begin with the end in mind. What objectives must be met by the buy in terms of audience delivery, cost efficiency, website visits, quality, media audiences adjusted for communication variables like positioning, timing, or whatever your priorities are. Your buying objectives, of course, must be realistic based on the market conditions you have identified in step number one.

3. Create a Negotiating Strategy

To get what you want in a negotiation, you must have a *winning negotiating strategy*. If you wing it, you will likely fall short. A negotiating strategy includes elements like these:

- **Know what you want**: media value you must get vs. what you would like to get (content, CPM, TRPS, positioning, etc.)
- **Know when to walk away**
- **Have back up plans:** Be prepared to walk away from any negotiation and execute Plan B, Plan C, etc. with another sellers
- **Use the budget as leverage**: e.g., winner takes all

Negotiation occurs when you have something the media want (your prestige and your budget) and they have something you want (access to consumers). You need each other. Successful negotiations are usually a win for both parties.

For example, if a seller (or more likely the seller's management) rejects a buyer's offer based on a significantly lower out of pocket cost, the buyer is still free to make a counter offer, altering the buy's content or conditions slightly, or by offering the seller a slightly greater share of the total budget.

Don't be a naïve buyer. The rule is to have a plan to win. But understand that a seller isn't going to hand over $100,000 worth of media just because you are a nice person. You need a well thought out plan.

4. Create Bargaining Leverage

Why should a seller give you what you want?

Building or creating bargaining power is a critical element of your negotiating strategy. Think: why would a seller give you what you want (which may not be perceived to be in their best interest)? Awarding the entire buy and budget to one or two sellers (out of the many pitching for your business) would be a significant incentive. Your bargaining leverage could be, *Winner (or very few winners) takes all (or a substantial portion)*. Such an approach would be very enticing to a seller looking to strike a big deal. Of course, if that deal would not meet your tactical objectives, you'd need to find some other leverage.

5. Always Have a Plan B

What do you do if a seller will not give you what you want?

Your negotiations strategy should always include a Plan B. If Plan A fails, you need a fallback position. For example, if you are negotiating for rate reductions with a media rep (who does not agree to your terms), you should be prepared to walk away and execute an alternative arrangement. For example, if one key seller can't or won't agree to your drop dead terms, go to Plan B (following by Plan C, D, and E if necessary). As an example, Plan B might involve buying schedules on the second and third ranked stations in a market rather than the highest priced top ranked station.

6. Get a Breakdown of Costs

Sellers sometimes resist providing specific cost breakdowns for their proposals. You need that information. For example, in television, you need to see the audience, unit pricing and cost efficiency for each spot. That will show you quickly which spots are overpriced and which are attractively priced. If you have the details of the sellers' proposals, you can restructure them more to your liking.

7. Shut Up!

Provide essential information and feedback, but don't offer more information than you have to. Anything you say might be used against you. Essential information—like your target audience, markets, timing, desired positioning, and promotions—you should freely communicate. You also need to provide feedback to competing sellers concerning their competitive positions after each round of the negotiations. On the other hand, it would be foolish to share budgets, TRP goals, client preferences, or other information that would give the seller a negotiating advantage.

8. Be Skeptical

Be skeptical. *Caveat emptor!* Each party will present information favorable to them, and leave out what isn't. The seller might say, *We can't do that without losing money*...then later take the deal. The buyer might say, *I don't have the money to do that*...only to come up with the money later. Or, the seller might say that his or her proposal will deliver 100 million impressions, but when it is objectively researched and analyzed, you find that it might deliver 50 million impressions at best.

9. Never Agree on Anything Unclear

It should go without saying, but it doesn't. Don't agree to something you take for granted or don't understand, hoping to come back later and get clarification. You should never be in the position of saying, *But I thought....* Get it in writing one way or another—confirm proposals or terms by email or memo, and make sure you understand them.

10. Watch Out for Monopoly Money!

In media, you deal with funny money—CPMs, CPPs, manipulated unit pricing, incomprehensible discount schedules, fixed costs, rotators, premiums, and audience guarantees (based on what measurement?). Always be clear on how audience performance and value are measured— know the audience or research source, whether the measurement is for the whole schedule or individual media vehicles. *Caveat Emptor.*

11. Be Aware of Human Obstacles to Negotiations

Egos and emotions frequently blow negotiations—for no good reason and to the detriment of both buyers and sellers.

It is amazing how many professionals believe that the most effective negotiators behave like obnoxious jerks. They believe that abusive behavior yields good results. It is not only uncivil and unprofessional, it blows far more deals than it closes. If you are confrontational, you will have a fight on your hands. If you are emotional and not rational, you will lose. If you are dishonest, you will ruin your career. Just be professional.

SUMMARY

A great broadcast buyer once said to me, "Some buyers try to get what they want with vinegar, while others use a little honey." What's your style?

The terms and conditions of all media buys are negotiated in varying degrees. Sometimes negotiations will focus on price or cost efficiency.

Sometimes the issue will relate more to the content of a buy. Sometimes positioning and competitive separation are the overriding issues.

In order to conduct an effective negotiation, smart buyers (and sellers) begin with a negotiations strategy firmly in mind. Creating a win-win negotiating strategy is critical, as is developing some negotiations leverage (such as giving a particular seller all or most of the budget in exchange for the desired concessions from the seller. Buyers must always have a Plan B and be prepared to walk away from a negotiation if it is clear that it won't work.

Buyers and sellers must also overcome the barriers to a successful negotiation by avoiding confrontation, playing the blame game, letting emotions get in the way, and the other rather childish behaviors that adults in which adults can play.

Good media negotiators are worth their weight in gold and will always be in high demand.

20. BROADCAST MEDIA BUYING
Buy communication, not TRPS.

—Ronald Geskey, Media Director, Author

TRPS are not communication. TRPS are a pre-requisite to communication. Good buyers negotiate elements into their buys that enhance the likelihood of communication and consumer engagement.

The art of media negotiations discussed in Chapter 19 certainly applies to buying broadcast media, but the broadcast media buyer must pay attention to additional, specific considerations peculiar to broadcast. Chapter 20 will address those considerations for television (broadcast and cable) and radio. The chapter will cover buying issues that television and radio share, as well as unique concerns pertaining to each medium.

The lowest cost per point doesn't necessarily translate to the best media buy. If you thought of broadcast media inventory as a commodity, you might focus on getting the most TRPS at the lowest possible cost, regardless of programming or other qualitative considerations. The challenge, however, is to negotiate media buys that engage your target audience(s) for best communication.

Effective media buying is more than trying to negotiate the most TRPS at the lowest possible price. Anyone can buy a cheap media schedule; it takes a professional to negotiate real communication.

This chapter will look into some respects in which the buyer can make a real difference. Chapter 20 will begin by discussing the broadcast marketplace in general and then shift to specific discussions of buying television and radio advertising time.

THE BROADCAST MARKETPLACE

Broadcast media—television and radio—are bought and sold more like stocks or commodities than other media are. In order to buy broadcast media, it is important to understand how the media marketplace functions.

Supply and Demand

Broadcast media prices (CPM or CPP) are always a function of supply and demand, as you learned in Chapter 2. The seller (network or station) always wants to sell at the highest possible price, and the buyer always wants to buy at the lowest possible price. At some point, the buyer and seller come together on the price and all the other terms and conditions of an order, and you have a buy.

Since the supply of commercial inventory in the broadcast media is constant, advertiser demand is the key variable. The seller with a ton of unsold commercial inventory is more likely to agree to a lower price and additional requests made by the buyer—selection of choice programs or commercial positioning, for example.

A seller that doesn't have enough inventory to meet advertiser demand will hold out for higher prices. If buyers and sellers cannot agree on pricing, the buyer who feels that there is more supply than demand will walk away and wait for a better time.

Ad spending is affected by general business and economic outlook as well as events like presidential elections or the Olympics, which can absorb billions of dollars in commercial inventory. Elections where politicians now spend billions of dollars reduce supply, driving up prices for other advertisers. In addition, over the long term, shifts in advertising budgets from one medium to another—from broadcast television or radio to Internet applications—can be expected to affect demand and pricing.

The dynamics of supply and demand also work at the micro level. Individual TV programs that are in high demand sell for higher CPMs, while programs that nobody wants sell at bargain basement prices.

The Super Bowl is a good example of supply and demand at work on the micro level. The 2010 and 2011 Super Bowls generated a 46+ ratings (based on households), which made them among the highest rated programs in US history.

(Note: It is a myth that the Super Bowl is the highest rated program in history. The final episode of *M.A.S.H* in 1983 generated a 60.2 household rating. An episode of *Dallas* in 1980 received a 53 rating. The final episode of *The Fugitive* in 1967 got a 49.9 rating However, partly due to population growth, the Super Bowl generated more individual viewers.

But the network's price of $3 million per :30 commercial ($65,000 CPP) made the Super Bowl a very expensive buy compared to good primetime programs purchased at around $20,000 CPP. Nonetheless, the network was able to sell out its Super Bowl advertising at $3 million because advertisers were willing pay a 300% cost premium price just to be in the Super Bowl.

Question: Was Super Bowl advertising worth its cost?

Timing Can Be Everything!

Timing can be everything. The first step in buying time is determining exactly when to buy. Media are perishable commodities. An unsold time slot or ad page in yesterday's TV or radio program has zero value. On the other hand, if you want to buy more audience than is available, prices go up dramatically and quickly. Both buyers and sellers are constantly trying to forecast supply and demand—and the consequences for pricing.

Because the price of broadcast media is driven by supply and demand, it is important to understand that supply and demand conditions can change very quickly. You must buy precisely when optimum programming and pricing can be negotiated. Like commodities buyers, media buyers (and sellers) are constantly trying to predict the market in order to determine whether to buy now or wait a little longer.

Here is an example of how quickly market conditions and pricing can change. A large agency bought a primetime TV schedule in New York for a major client. A week later, the client decided that media weight levels in New York should be increased. By then, prices for the same programs had increased 75-110% because new money coming into the market increased demand. The supply and demand dynamic drives pricing for television and radio networks and stations, dayparts and individual programs.

Long Term Buying

An advertiser who believes prices are likely to rise through the year or who wants to leverage the budget (to get more value per dollar) might make a long term buy (e.g., for 52 weeks). Many large advertisers believe they will be able to get more of the programming they want to reach their target audiences at a lower price by participating in the *upfront market*— which normally occurs in the April–June period each year.

It is called the upfront market because the broadcast and cable networks sell commercial time well ahead of the new TV season. For example, it was estimated that for the 2008-2009 television season, advertisers invested $9.1 billion to $9.2 billion with the broadcast networks and another $8.6 billion on the cable networks.

However, in addition to normal market forces of advertiser budget reductions and future business forecasts, lower prices also resulted from the economic downturn and predictions that the writers' strike would eliminate programming needed to generate audiences. So, advertisers reduced their budgets, causing prices to fall further.

Typically, TV networks will sell about 75 percent of their commercial inventory in the upfront market. In this instance, the percentages were as high as 80 to 85 percent.

However, it is important to note that advertisers placing 52-week orders during the upfront market can usually cancel some of their commitment before their specific cancellation dates. In spot, cancellation requires only two weeks' notice.

A seeming contradiction is that the increase in demand for commercial time in the 2008-2009 season was partly fueled by the lower ratings for prime-time series. To reach the same number of viewers in broadcast TV, advertisers had to buy more spots.

"It's totally counterintuitive," says Michael Nathanson, a media analyst at Sanford C. Bernstein & Company in New York, "but the harder it is to find audiences, or barrels of oil, the fiercer the frenzy to pay more to acquire them." In other words, the better-than-expected results for this upfront market were probably at least partly the result of advertisers wanting to hedge their bets against rising prices later in the season.

Short Term Buying

After the upfront buying is done, the networks still have unsold commercial inventory that they offer in the *scatter market*. Scatter market is the term used to describe the short-term buying that advertisers do quarterly or as needed.

When advertisers expect prices to be coming down, they invest less in the upfront market, waiting to buy in the scatter market where they compete with advertisers who need flexibility because they are unsure of their timing needs. In contrast to those who believed that the best prices were available in the upfront market, they believe that they will be able to do as well or even better in the scatter market. What's more, these advertisers believe, the flexibility they gain trumps any cost penalty.

THE BUYING PROCESS

After calculating how much to invest in long term vs. short term buys, you have to actually do it. How does a professional buyer actually make a broadcast media buy with a network or station? What does it look like? Here's a twelve-step process.

1. Study/Know the Market

Make sure you are fully informed about the markets, including stations' strengths and weaknesses, program trends, supply and demand conditions, upcoming marketing and media opportunities, and pricing trends.

2. Study Buy Specs

The media planner will issue specifications (*buy specs*) with the information needed to negotiate the buy—budgets, target audience definitions, daypart mix, timing, desired commercial positioning and value added, audience guarantees, reach and frequency goals, and any special instructions. Study them carefully and review them with the planner if necessary. These specs will shape many of your buying decisions.

3. Develop a Negotiating Strategy

Everything is negotiable: programming, positioning, and price. As you learned in Chapter 19, to achieve the desired results the buyer must develop a sound negotiating strategy and plan before entering negotiations.

Decide in advance what you want to accomplish in the negotiation in terms of audience, impact, and pricing/efficiency. Establish your priorities. For example, will you or won't you buy a station that can't promise to avoid scheduling your commercials in pods with competitors? What are you willing to give or concede in exchange for what you want? What is your back-up plan?

4. Request Avails

Once all your homework is done (Steps 1-3), call each network or station's sales representative and request their *avails* based on your buy specs. Networks or stations need guidance if they are to submit a relevant proposal, and most of that guidance is contained in the buy specs. Each bidder will put together a proposal based on the budget you provide.

5. Analyze Proposals/Options

You will receive detailed proposals from the networks/stations. Evaluate them using audience and cost efficiency analyses, and do reach and frequency analyses on the best alternatives.

6. Provide Feedback to Sellers

Let bidders know where they stand, so that they can make their proposals more competitive. Be sure to provide each station with a factual analysis of its submission compared with competitive submissions—*Your primetime CPP is 30% higher than the average of the other submissions* begins a conversation about improving the proposal.

7. Continue Back-and-Forth Negotiations

Most sellers will revise their proposals several times based on your feedback. A seller's CPP that was $500 in the original proposal, then $450 in the first revision, might be $400 in the second revision. Your objective is to find the bottom of the market. Continue the process of feedback and revision until you believe you have reached the bottom line.

8. Construct the Optimum Buy

Once you have the seller's bottom line, construct the plan you want to buy. Maybe you have decided to give all your business to one television station if they will fulfill your requests. Maybe you want to cherry-pick inventory from two or three stations. Figure it out and put it together.

9. Place Orders

Based on your best buy constructs, place orders that include all the terms and conditions on the selected broadcast outlets. Keep in mind that sellers may make counter offers, so be prepared, and have Plan B close at hand.

10. Communicate Decisions to Sellers

After your offers have been accepted, provide feedback to the reps whose stations you didn't buy. This is partly courtesy, partly education for later. The reps have to explain to their managements why they didn't get a piece of the buy, and you hope your future negotiations will be more favorable.

11. Issue Buy Reports

Once all of the details of the buy are in order, issue a schedule and analysis of what you have purchased for the client and others who need to know what the schedule is.

12. Manage the Buy

You still aren't finished when your offers are accepted. Now you must monitor audience performance and cost efficiency against changing market prices. Negotiate make-goods and changes in the buy—programming and prices—as appropriate. If market conditions change, be prepared to renegotiate!

The buyer develops initial projections of audience and cost efficiency performance—projected TRP delivery and costs during the buy time frame—before orders are placed. After the buy has been completed and the schedule has run, a post-buy analysis should be performed that compares estimated audience and cost efficiency of actual delivery. If delivery is below projections, you have grounds for negotiating reduced cost or a *make good* package to bring the buy up to mutually agreed TRP levels.

HOW TO BUY TELEVISION

Frustrated with a spot TV buy, a client once remarked, "Any moron can buy cheap TV schedules. Even I could. What we need are TV buys that help drive our message home."

It's true. Anybody can buy cheap spots in programs no other advertiser wants to buy. Anybody can let a station run spots wherever the station wants to schedule them. Anybody can allow the station to schedule a spot in the 15th position in a commercial pod. Anybody can buy cheap. But not everybody can buy good. Or better. Or best.

All buyers, consciously or unconsciously, enter negotiations to buy television (or radio) schedules with different philosophies about what is important and effective. Some buyers want to buy as cheaply as possible. Other buyers are more concerned with quality than cost. Who is right? Let's look at buying philosophies on a spectrum.

Buying Philosophy

Tonnage or Quality? What is the overall buying philosophy? You must decide where you want to be on the spectrum shown in Figure 20-1. The difference is between buying maximum TRPS (tonnage) vs. communication potential (quality), where the buyer is concerned about the specific programs and commercial positioning.

There is not a simple answer to what kind of commercial inventory you should buy, because it depends on the needs of the advertiser. A direct response advertiser may maximize ROI with tonnage. A car company, concerned with the context if its advertising, may be willing to pay a cost efficiency premium to be positioned in high involvement programs delivering the right audience.

As the following illustration shows, different media buying philosophies can result in paying the lowest CPMs for *tonnage* (low-demand inventory) or paying a premium price for higher quality (high demand inventory).

Media Buying Philosophies

Tonnage		Quality
Lowest Demand Inventory		High Demand Inventory
Lowest Priced Dayparts		Higher Priced Dayparts
Lowest Ratings		Higher Ratings
Unmeasured Audiences		Measured Audiences
Overnight/Late Late Night		No Overnight/Late Late Night
Run of Schedule		Specific Programs
Untargeted programming		Selective programming
Weakest stations		Stronger Stations
Gratuitous sex/violence		No Gratuitous sex/violence
Last Minute/Distress		Last Minute/Distress
Pre-empted by Other Advertisers		Fixed Schedules
No Audience Guarantees		Audience Guarantees
No Promotion/Merchandising		Value Added Opportunities

Figure 20-1.—Contrasting Media Buying Philosophies

Commercial inventory in high supply or hard to sell goes for less, and vice versa. Popular primetime programs with higher ratings will sell at a significantly higher CPM or CPP because they are in higher demand among advertisers.

The other side of the coin is the buying opportunity for advertisers who don't believe they need to be in the highest rated shows, or who will take the risk of waiting until the last minute to buy unsold inventory at much lower prices. Keep in mind that there is no relationship between rating size and commercial recall.

Television Advertising Expenditures

The size of TV investments seems to suggest that the death of television is indeed greatly exaggerated—for the near future, anyway! While it is true that network TV's share of ad dollars has declined, cable's share has increased.

Despite the grumbling about declining TV effectiveness, television is still the number one advertising medium in the U.S., gobbling up $66 billion of TV spending in 2009, according to competitive expenditure reports from Kantar.

Table 20-1.—2009 TV Advertising Expenditures

Medium	$Billions
Network TV	$16
Cable Networks	17
Syndicated	2
Local Spot	11
Local Cable	3
Total	$62

Source: Kantar, 2020

Among life's activities, watching television still ranks third in average daily time spent (2.6 hours per day, behind only personal care activities and work), and those hours spent remain unchanged from 2003 to 2007. Television's influence on purchase decisions continues second only to word of mouth, as shown in Table 20-2.

Table 20-2.—Influence on Purchasing Decisions

Communication	Influence
Word of mouth	#1
TV	#2
Coupons	#3
Newspaper inserts	#4

Source:BIGresearch SIMM VII Survey

Television: the Players

Although television viewing and perceived influence levels haven't changed much, viewing has become much more fragmented. There are six broadcast television networks, approximately 800 television stations, more than 80 cable networks, and thousands of individual cable systems operating in the U.S. Television advertising may be purchased from the networks for near national coverage or from individual TV stations or from cable systems to cover individual DMAs or neighborhoods within DMAs.

Figure 20-2 summarizes the broadcast and cable television outlets available in the U.S. marketplace, according to 2020:Marketing Communications LLC.

Television: the Players

Networks
- ↗ Broadcast: ABC, CBS, NBC, FOX
- ↗ Cable: 80+ networks, e.g., A&E, CNN, Discovery, FNN,

O&Os
- ↗ Owned and operated by a television network

Affiliates
- ↗ Independently owned but affiliated with network & broadcasts their programming

Independents
- ↗ Independently owned & programmed

Public
- ↗ Public service programming (not commercial)

Cable
- ↗ Interconnects and individual cable systems in communities

Figure 20-2.—US Broadcast & Cable Television Outlets

Television Advertising Availabilities

Television provides a great deal of flexibility for advertisers, as you learned in Chapter 15. They can run their advertising where and when they want to, in almost any commercial length or daypart, and in the specific programs that best reach their target audiences.

Geographic Coverage

You may purchase advertising to achieve national or regional market coverage via national broadcast networks or cable TV networks. National or local advertisers may purchase time on local TV stations or cable systems to reach consumers in particular DMAs. You may purchase commercial time on individual cable TV systems targeting specific communities or retail trading areas.

Network commercials normally clear in markets representing up to 99% of U.S. TV households. Commercials in cable programming will be seen on those systems carrying the network. Local spot TV commercials will cover the DMA and beyond.

Commercial Lengths

Although the :30 commercial is the basic unit of sale for both networks and stations, :60s are usually available at twice the :30 rate, while :10s, :15s, and :20s are usually be sold at 50-70% of the :30 rate. In 2007, 55% of commercials on network TV were :30s, compared to 77% in spot television.

Dayparts

Television is programmed and sold by daypart: *early morning, daytime, early fringe, prime access, primetime, late night, weekend, and sports*. Because audience sizes and demographics, as well as supply and demand, vary so dramatically by daypart, pricing and cost efficiencies follow suit. For example, on network television, a household rating point in primetime costs up to $25,000, but a household rating point in daytime is closer to $8,000.

Television dayparts are normally separate profit centers. Consequently, networks and stations develop programming for and manage sales separately by daypart. Daypart planning results in programs geared to women during the day, including popular soap operas and talk shows. Late afternoon is programmed toward children, while primetime is programmed for a variety of audiences through action/adventure, sports, comedies, and reality shows.

Programs

Even though TV buys are normally budgeted and negotiated by daypart, advertisers target TV audiences by selecting the *right programs* within the selected dayparts.

Television programs attract different kinds of audiences, which vary in size, demographics, viewer interests, viewer involvement, attention levels, and costs.

Television: What to Negotiate For

The most cost effective television buys result from negotiating the most favorable terms possible for audience, impact, and cost. You must make sure the buy reaches the right audience and maximizes effective communication with the target, at the lowest possible price. Each of the three considerations is examined here.

Question: You are making a television buy. What should you negotiate for to make your buy cost effective?

Audience

From the broadcaster's standpoint, audiences and ratings are money. What is one rating point worth? To broadcasters, an average increase of one single rating point during primetime is worth an estimated $250 million in annual advertising revenues (combined networks and stations). On the other hand, a loss of a rating point could likewise result in $250 million in lost revenues. Financial stakes like this explain why television networks and stations are so desperately focused on rating performance

One of the top priorities of the media buyer is to look for ways to identify, negotiate, and deliver more audience (TRPs), especially a more interested audience.

The following discussion explores ways buyers can enhance the quality of audience delivery in network, cable, and spot media buys. Some of these buying tactics are completely controlled by the buyer, while others must be negotiated with the sellers. Review Chapter 2 for the definition and measurement of media audiences so heavily relied upon by media buyers on which to base buying decisions.

Caution: For purposes of negotiation, media buyers and sales representatives often look at television audiences and ratings as if they were 100% accurate, haggling over a difference of a fraction of a rating point. The reality is that ratings are simply a measure of *TV set tuning, not viewing.* Of course, like political polls, TV ratings are also subject to statistical error based on sample sizes and other methodology issues.

Equally important to understand is that ratings do not measure exposure to commercials. Ratings are merely the result of Nielsen's monitoring of TV set tuning among a sample of households hooked up to an audimeter. Household members are supposed to indicate on a device when they enter the room.

Advertisers have long been critical of Nielsen's TV audience measurement because the traditional average audience rating applied to programs but not commercials. Nielsen is now delivering *commercial ratings* that count the audience tuned in when a commercial is aired, as well as accounting for DVR usage. Viewers in the room may also be talking, multi-tasking, reading, or playing with the kids. On average, commercial ratings are about 3% less than average audience ratings.

While Nielsen's commercial ratings are a step in the right direction, they do little toward measuring the actual audience exposed to a commercial. That is because commercial exposure is affected by viewer behavior while watching TV—channel surfing, talking, leaving the room, multi-tasking on the computer, reading, playing with the kids. Viewer attentiveness and involvement are important.

Program Selection

Buyers seek out those programs that they believe do the best job of efficiently and effectively reaching the advertiser's target audience.

TV Programs
Example of Audience Profiles
Index of Ratings vs. U.S. Average

	Prog. A	Prog. B	Prog. C
Adult Rating	8.0	10.2	7.6
Rating Index			
18-24	80	100	120
$50+K HHI	135	110	90
Some College	140	120	100
Married	110	90	75
Black	90	100	120
Suburban	130	105	80

Source: 2020:Marketing Communications LLC (shown for example only)

Figure 20-3.—Sample TV Audience Profile

TV programs generate audiences of varying sizes, characteristics, and viewing behavior. Nielsen Media Research provides the most recent data on audience size, but they may be inadequate to determine whether a program is a good fit with a specialized target market because Nielsen can only report basic demographics, primarily gender and age.

For better descriptions of media audience appropriateness for a given advertiser, tap additional audience research sources. For example, as you learned earlier in this book, SMRB and Simmons can provide much deeper insight into TV audiences by viewer attitudes and psychographics, purchase behavior and purchase intentions. Scarborough and The Media Audit are additional sources that provide much more detailed audience data on a near national as well as a local market basis.

Gaining Audience Insight			
Lifestyle Indicator	**Vehicle A**	**Vehicle B**	**Vehicle C**
Own BMW	120	135	125
Tent Camping	220	180	115
3+ Children	70	65	80
HHI $150+	150	200	210
Graduate Degree	135	120	115
Listen to Hip Hop	70	60	50

Source: 2020:Marketing Communications LLC

Figure 20-4.—Supplemental Audience Data: Sample

The alternative is to let the station run your spots in a rotation wherever and whenever they want (*ROS: Run of Schedule*). Stations like to sell ROS packages because it gives them scheduling flexibility—and the ability to dispose of their low demand inventory.

Under Valued Programs

One of the most important ways to buy more audience for the budget is to identify and buy undervalued programs, e.g., good programs with a low CPP. For example, in the 2009 television season, there was over a 100% difference in CPP paid by buyers for top network programs.

Good buyers will uncover program opportunities that deliver more audience for the money. By loading buys with under-valued shows, you can generate more audience. Consider the following list of hypothetical primetime programs and how they are priced for their ratings and CPPs. These wide disparities in pricing versus delivery are not unrealistic.

Table 20-3.—Finding Undervalued Programs

Program	Cost/:30	Rating	Target CPP
Student Warriors	$200,500	10.0	$20,050
Y Files	150,000	12.0	12,500
90 Minutes	70,000	2.5	18,000
Found!	142,500	15.0	9,500

Question: If your budget were $600,000 for a four-week period, which of the above programs would you buy?

Question: How many :30s would you buy in each purchased program?

419

Bonus Spots

Bonus spots are free spots added to a buy in order to increase audience delivery and make the buy more cost efficient. If the price of a proposal is too high, buyers will attempt to negotiate bonus spots. Sellers may offer bonus spots to make a package more cost efficient. Keep in mind that bonus spots usually represent commercial inventory the network station has difficulty selling.

Opportunistic Buying

Many buyers hold a portion of their budget in reserve for buying opportunities. For example, networks and stations frequently offer unsold inventory at large discounts on short notice. It is common to receive a call at 4:00 PM Friday saying that there is a spot available in Sunday's game for less than half of the going price.

Billboards

Billboards are typically 5-second IDs that networks and stations use to begin or end a break in the programming, e.g., "Brought to you by the Chevrolet Malibu, Motor Trend Car of the Year." You may be able to negotiate billboards into your buy, gaining additional audience exposure.

Growth Programs

Emphasize programming that you believe is low risk—with a lot of upside audience growth potential (as opposed to losing audience). Buying into TV shows is a little like buying stocks. You hope that the audience will grow, but it may not, depending on many factors outside your control. You must forecast the future audience performance of television programs included in the schedule.

Forecast Conservatively

Regardless whether buying network or spot, buyers must forecast the *actual future performance* of a buy (Rating = Share x HUTS). Buyers use historical audience trends for programs under consideration as well as competitive programs. Most buyers will buy based on conservative forecasts of future audience. It is always better to get more than expected rather than have to explain to a client why your buy fell short!

Station Websites

Station website audiences are growing, and they can represent an opportunity to increase audience exposure. You may be able to negotiate advertising exposure on their website as a bonus for placing an order.

Cross Platform Opportunities

Media conglomerates and groups often own or are owned by a larger media conglomerate. This opens the opportunity of creating cross platform deals that provide audience and promotion in a variety of outlets. For example, an advertising schedule on ABC could be combined with a Disney promotion and magazine exposure. (This subject was discussed in detail in Chapter 23.)

Audience Guarantees

Buyers often negotiate audience delivery guarantees with networks or stations so that if a buy doesn't deliver the promised audience, the advertiser receives a credit or bonus spots to make up for it. The difficulty is for buyer and seller to agree on the level of guaranteed audience.

Specific Programs vs. Rotators vs. ROS

On network TV, advertisers buy into specific programs that target their audience efficiently and effectively. However, on a local market basis, stations also offer advertisers rotators or run of schedule options. *Rotators* are spot packages where the advertiser's commercial is rotated evenly through a list of programs. *Run of Schedule* (*ROS*) means that the advertiser's spot may run, at the station's discretion, anywhere in the daypart where the station has an opening. Rotators and ROS spots are sold at lower prices, but you relinquish control over the audience reached and the program context.

In Program vs. Between Shows

On a local market basis media, buyers have to decide whether to buy spots to run within programs during commercial breaks or between programs, at a lower price but when channel surfing increases. Not surprisingly, research has found higher recall of in-program commercials.

Preemptions & Make-goods

There are situations—such as presidential addresses, specials programming like the Academy Awards, or sporting events—that may cause the network or station to pre-empt your spot(s). When this occurs, the advertiser may take a credit for the missed spot or may decide to take replacement spots (make good). This presents an opportunity to either take the credit to use later for an opportunistic buy or to accept a make-good only if it offers a large bonus relative to the original spot.

Television Impact

Are all TRPS created equal?

Media buyers who buy tonnage believe that all TRPS are equal value. Buyers who consider communications effectiveness do not believe that GRPS are equally effective. In addition to improving a television buy by negotiating more or better audience exposure, buyers can also negotiate improvements in the communications effectiveness of television buys.

TRPS (and GRPS) are measures of gross media vehicle audience, which has little to do with the communication of advertising messages. TRPS do not answer the important questions. Is the audience paying attention? Will viewers see the commercial? Will they recall it?

Specifically in television, a variety of media related factors affect overall communications effectiveness. Some of the questions facing buyers include:

- Is cable TV as effective as broadcast TV?
- Does program involvement affect commercial recall?
- Are higher rated programs more effective than lower rated ones?
- Are there differences in viewer attention levels by program?
- How does commercial positioning affect commercial recall?
- How does the proximity of competitive commercials affect recall?
- How does commercial length affect recall?

Broadcast vs. Cable TV

Whether to buy or exclude cable TV from a broadcast buy has long been debated. In the early days of cable TV, Ted Turner had a heck of a time convincing advertisers to spend money on WTBS, Turner's superstation and the first foray into cable. Today, network cable TV is gaining share from the broadcast networks and often competitive with local broadcast.

At issue is whether there is a difference in effectiveness between broadcast and cable programs. This question naturally has inspired a lot of research sponsored by the cable TV industry wanting to prove the effectiveness of advertising on cable TV. This led to the "One World" study, which found that viewers select programs to watch, not stations or cable systems. The key differentiator was the program, not where it originated. Further, SMRB's analysis of the attention levels paid to cable versus broadcast programming showed little difference.

Broadcast vs. Cable TV Attention Levels

Medium	% Fully Attentive
Broadcast TV	21-60%
Cable TV	26-50%

Source: SMRB

In fact, due to its growth in penetration, cable television schedules can now provide high reach and frequency levels competitive with broadcast. Consequently, if the price is right, buyers may sometimes find that an all cable schedule is preferable to a schedule including broadcast television.

Size of Rating

A second issue that has plagued media buyers for years is whether higher rated shows have more communications value than lower rated shows, thus justifying a higher price. A meta-analysis of studies on rating size relative to commercial recall finds that there is probably no significant difference in commercial recall by rating size.

Table 20-4.—Index of Commercial Recall by Rating Size

Year	Source	Ratings		
		High Recall	Medium Recall	Low Recall
1961	Needham	122	89	—
1968	Hooper	139	104	84
1974-77	G&R	97	99	106
1977-81	G&R	94	105	100
1999	Zenith	105	96	100
1999	Western Intl	64	105	1009

If there is no evidence that higher rated spots are more effective than lower rated spots, it makes little sense to pay a premium price for higher ratings. At the same time, it is not prudent to buy extremely low rated spots if the audiences are too small to be statistically valid.

Program Involvement

Several studies have found a relationship between program involvement and advertising response. The conclusion from the studies is that the higher the viewer's involvement with the program, the higher the response rate, as shown in the Table 20-5.

Table 20-5.—Viewer Response by Program Involvement

Measure	Low	Average	High
Unaided Recall	18.4%	21.0%	22.2%
Aided Recall	34.0	48.0	54.0
Copy Credibility	24.0	37.0	41.0
Purchase Interest	13.2	15.7	18.0
Pre/Post Behavior Change	6.4	12.6	18.0

Source: Various Studies

Commercials are recalled at higher levels and generate higher response in purchase interest and behavior change in higher involvement programming than programming that does not require high viewer engagement, such as situation comedies or game shows, which have lower viewer attention levels. Therefore, in addition to audience, buyers should consider program involvement when selecting programming.

Commercial Positioning

Commercial positioning is extremely important, and you should attempt to negotiate for advantageous commercial positioning. Where a commercial is physically positioned within (or between) programs has a major effect on its communications effectiveness. Commercials lost in a sea of clutter, one lost in a commercial pod, or worse, one near a competitive spot, perform relatively poorly.

Position in Pod

Figure 20-5, using data based on a five-commercial pod, shows major differences in unaided commercial recall according to positioning within the pod. The lesson: as a condition of ordering, require the first position for the majority of the schedule. If you can't get it, walk away.)

Commercial Recall by Pod Position

Pod Position	Recall Index
First	125
Second	116
Third	84
Fourth	67
Fifth	104

Source:CAB/Nielsen Media Research

Figure 20-5.—Commercial Recall by Position in Pod

Clutter in Commercial Break

It is not surprising that the higher the clutter, the lower the effectiveness of a commercial (Figure 20-6). As shown in the following

424

table, commercial recall in a break with few competitive commercials is almost twice as high as in a break with 10 commercials. Make sure you understand which pods you will be in; walk away from pods with too many commercials.

Recall vs. Clutter in Commercial Break

# Commercials In Break	Recall Index
1-3	157
4-6	117
7-9	86
10+	79

Source: CAB/Nielsen Media Research, 2000

Figure 20-6.—Recall vs. Clutter in Commercial Break

Proximity to Competitive Messages

It should come as no surprise that the closer a commercial is to competitive commercials, the lower its recall. Advertising research company Gallup & Robinson has found that a competitive commercial in the same pod may significantly reduce commercial recall because consumers get confused over which commercial was for which advertiser. Other research has found that the presence of competitive commercials in the same pod can reduce recall by 30%.

These findings have led some major advertisers like General Motors to require at least 15-minute separation in order to qualify for any of their business. Stations that refused lost GM business.

Recall by Length of Commercial

Networks and stations offer long form commercial positions (:30s, :60s) as well as short form commercials (:10s and :15s). The longer commercials have higher recall, but when cost is factored in, shorter form commercials enjoy higher recall per dollar. However, they may be deficient in communicating the selling message, which requires more time.

Table 20-6.—Recall Index vs. Commercial Length

Length	Recall Index	Cost Index	Efficiency Index
:60	132	200	66
:30	100	100	100
:15	73	50	140
:10	56	40-50	110+

Source: G&R

Value Added

Finally, TV buys can often be made more effective when the buyer negotiates a no-charge value added package. Such a package may consist of bonus spots (extra free spots), billboards, turnkey promotions, tickets to sports or entertainment venues (that could be used for promotions), or trade/sales persons incentives like a golf outing.

Negotiating the most cost effective media buy involves a lot more than trying to get sellers to cut their prices. Greater ROI improvements can be made by improving program selection, commercial positioning, value added, and other non-price advantages.

Television Pricing

Simultaneous with audience and impact enhancements to a television media buy, the cost must also be negotiated with the seller. Ultimately, pricing will be determined by the parties' perceived supply and demand conditions. Remember that the goal of the seller is to sell at the highest possible price, while the buyer's objective is to buy at the lowest price.

The buyer has determined what programming and audience criteria the network or station needs to satisfy, along with commercial positioning requirements. Now it's time to make an offer based on the competitive bidding situation.

At this point, the question is what will you have to pay to get what you want. If one seller will sell you want you want (audience and communications enhancements) at a $1000 CPP, you can use that competitive offer with higher priced sellers to see if they are willing to reduce their prices to get a piece at the business. This process, if done properly, will eventually find the bottom of the market.

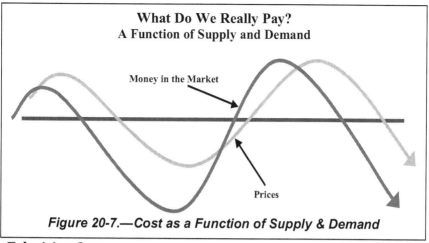

What Do We Really Pay?
A Function of Supply and Demand

Money in the Market

Prices

Figure 20-7.—Cost as a Function of Supply & Demand

Television Costs

What does it cost to advertise on television? Television costs are typically expressed in CPM or CPP for a :30 commercial by daypart for the relevant demographic by quarter. CPPs may be based on network television with national coverage or any of the 212 DMAs in the U.S.

The following table shows comparative CPPs for network and local market spots. Estimates are based on Adults 25-54 in the fourth quarter and reflect an average mix of programs; actual CPPs will vary depending on actual programs purchased, timing, and similar factors.

Television Cost Per Point (CPP) Adults 25-54, 4th Quarter 2009			
	Prime Time	Daytime	Early News
Network TV	$40,000	$9,000	$18,500
New York	5,234	1,267	1,723
Chicago	2,613	863	1,361
Phoenix	807	540	447
Omaha	126	107	120
Glendive, MT	7	5	5
Source: Media Market Guide, 2020 estimates			

Figure 20-8.—CPP for Network vs. Local Spot TV

Rate Cards

Even though actual pricing is negotiated simultaneously with other terms of a buy, TV networks and stations do maintain rate cards detailing the prices for each program. After orders are placed, the buyer receives a confirmation that includes spot-by-spot costs. Rate card prices are still important because they are used for billing purposes and for establishing the value of pre-empted spots and make goods.

Local stations' rate cards are sometimes more complicated. Stations offer advertisers a menu of rate alternatives. Keep in mind that rates and other terms are still negotiable with any station who wants your business. Figure 20-9 shows an array of primetime costs as of 2009, and a discussion of rate card options follows.

What do Prime Time Network Spots Cost?

Program	Cost/:30	HH Rating	CPP
House	$260,000	8.0	$32,500
Desperate Housewives	319,000	10.7	29,813
CSI	262,000	12.8	20,469
NCIS	122,000	11.3	10,796
The Mentalist	97,000	10.0	9,700

Source: Based on 2009 season reports from advertisers, Advertising Age, 2020 estimates.

Figure 20-9.—Cost of Prime Time Spots

Pre-emptible Rate

Pre-emptible rates are low, but your spot isn't guaranteed. When stations offer spots on a pre-emptible basis, this means that if another advertiser is willing to pay a higher price, your spot will be pre-empted.

Fixed Rate

The fixed rate is a premium rate not subject to preemption by a higher rate advertiser because it is the highest rate. You pay it to ensure that your spot runs as planned.

Rotator / Run of Schedule (ROS)

Stations offer reduced rates to advertisers that allows the station to rotate commercials through an agreed upon list of programs. The lowest rates are available to advertisers that don't care when or where their spots run and buy ROS. Giving station the right to rotate spots through their programming in exchange for a theoretically lower rate, you forfeit the flexibility to select specific programs that you believe are more focused on your target audience.

It is true that the best spot is the spot that runs, but you should be cautious about agreeing to rate schemes that benefit stations at the expense of your ability to select the right programs or that make it impossible to get guarantees on commercial positioning or other preferences.

HOW TO BUY RADIO

Radio differs from television in many ways—other than its obvious lack of video! In contrast to television, which is used primarily by national advertisers, radio is used primarily by local retailers, who account for about 80% of radio ad expenditures.

2008 Radio Advertising Expenditures

Medium	Billions $
Network	$0.7
National Spot	3.4
Local Spot	14.6
Total	18.7

Figure 20-10.—2008 Radio Ad Expenditures

While the broadcast and cable networks dominate the television business, dozens of diversified radio networks represent less than 5% of radio revenues. National advertisers account for only about 20% of ad spending in radio compared to 75% of the television ad spend.

Radio Availabilities

Like television, radio provides a great deal of flexibility for national or local advertisers, with a variety of stations and audience segmentation possibilities, geographic coverage, commercial lengths, dayparts, sponsorships, and timing.

Geographic Coverage

Similar to television, radio advertising may be purchased on networks with semi-national coverage or on major stations that cover metro areas. In addition, there are thousands of local stations in smaller towns, often without reported ratings, which can be used to focus on specific suburban areas or smaller towns within the DMA.

While there are some powerful AM radio stations (like WGN/Chicago or WJR/Detroit) that can be heard across a 200-mile radius, most radio stations cover much smaller geographic areas than television does. The rule of thumb would be that radio stations cover metropolitan areas (*SMSAs*), but most won't effectively cover large DMAs because their signals don't go as far out as TV signals do.

Radio Stations

The first important way radio differs from television is in the size of its distribution system. Not including satellite and online radio (which to date carry little advertising), there are over 10,000 radio stations (mostly small) for buyers to choose from. That averages out to about 50 stations per DMA—though large DMAs can have 100 stations or more. The result is that radio audiences are extremely fragmented, compared to television, and average ratings are very small. In addition, satellite and online radio are stealing audience from commercial radio stations, which further fragments radio advertising. (Note: Satellite penetration had grown to 12.5% and Internet radio penetration had grown to 15.6% by 2007.)

Commercial Lengths

While various commercial lengths may be purchased, the :60 commercial is the basic unit of sale. However, many stations charge 80 per cent of the minute rate for a :30 (stations typically want to discourage :30s because they create the perception of even more commercial clutter). Advertisers also resist paying 80% of the price for 50% of the time (in television :30s are 50% of the :60 cost).

Audience

Unlike television's mass appeal, radio is a more personal medium. In television, audiences are segmented by program types and individual programs—NHL hockey, food, home shopping, action-adventure, soap opera, situation comedy, reality. In radio, audiences are segmented by stations' *programming formats*. Radio stations target audience niches in specific geographic areas using programming formats that they hope will attract large audiences. To appeal to baby boomers, a station might focus on news/talk or sports programming which attracts an older audience, while another station might use a format that appeals to teens and young adults. Sometimes broadcasters change formats in attempts to carve out better audience niches for themselves.

When buying radio, it is important to understand the psychographics—interests and tastes—of the target audience. The buyer must match target psychographics with radio stations' audiences, For example, is the target a classical music buff? News/talk addict? Conservative or liberal? Lover of music from the 60s? Rap enthusiast?

Dayparts

Spot announcements in radio are normally priced and sold by daypart. For example, the following table shows that, on average, about 20% of Persons 12+ is listening to radio in all dayparts except nighttime. Therefore, if the total average listening audience in morning drive is 20%, that "20" is divided up among all of the stations in the market generating some audience. A strong station with a 10% share of audience would have a 2 rating among persons 12+ (Rating = PUR x Station Share).

Table 20-7.—Total Radio Audience Size by Daypart

Daypart	Time	P12+ PUR
Morning Drive	6A-10A	20%
Daytime	10A-3P	20
Afternoon Drive	3P-7P	20
Nighttime	7P – Mid	7
Source: Arbitron, Spring 2007 Persons Using Radio (% demo group); PURs vary by demographic groups. Visit www.arbitron.com for detailed data		

While stations like to sell spots based on average audience ratings for the whole daypart, obviously, audiences will vary from hour to hour especially in markets with a significant car commute to and from work. Good buyers study audience flow by hour to help negotiate a schedule that delivers an above average audience. For example, a station's average 6-10 AM rating is the average of its ratings at 6-7, 7-8, 8-9, and 9-10 AM.

Like TV stations, radio stations also like to sell ROS schedules that allow the station to slot your spots where they want. ROS gives stations more scheduling flexibility and allows them to save their best availabilities for favored advertisers. Unless the buyer is following a tonnage philosophy, buying ROS spots may not be to the buyer's advantage.

Radio Sponsorship Opportunities

Besides spot announcements, some stations also offer sponsorships. Examples include sponsorships of professional or college sports teams, news programs, or even segments of talk shows. For example, WGN-AM Radio in Chicago owns the radio broadcasting rights for the Chicago Cubs and Chicago Bears games. The station sells sponsorships of these sports franchises to national and larger local advertisers.

Sponsorships are sold in shares. For example, advertisers may buy a one-quarter, one-half, or a full sponsorship entitling the sponsor to a proportionate number of spots. The larger the sponsorship, the more spots and value added the advertiser receives.

Larger sponsorships typically include commercial time, billboards, on-air mentions, competitive exclusivity, stadium signage, advertising in program guides, and on-site promotion (product displays) in the venue.

Buying sponsorships often requires a higher CPM or CPP than buying spot participations. You must make a judgment about how much of a cost efficiency premium a sponsorship is worth. Buying sponsorships often becomes emotional; a good buyer must maintain a rational perspective on the realistic value and cost effectiveness of a sponsorship.

Radio Station Formats

With over 10,000 stations in the U.S. and over a hundred stations in some large markets, there is a radio station format for nearly every taste. Every station attempts to deliver a format creatively in a way that will give it a competitive advantage in the market and attract a sufficiently large number of listeners. On-air talent plays a major role in differentiating station formats, as talent may have a loyal following.

There are over 30 different radio formats in the United States. Stations sometimes switch formats to try to ride trends and garner a larger share of an audience so they can increase the price of their spots. Here are the top 10 formats.

Top 10 Radio Formats

Format	# Stations
Country	2019
News/Talk	1224
Oldies	773
Hispanic	703
Adult Contemporary	884
Top 40	502
Sports	497
Classic Rock	461
Adult Standards	405
Hot AC	380

Figure 20-11.—Radio Formats

Radio stations attract specific audiences by utilizing a proven format or sound to attract certain types of listeners. Here are the top formats:

- **Active Rock.** Music intended to be loud, such as hard rock, metal, and heavy metal.

- **Adult Album Alternative (AAA).** Plays mostly current music, appealing more to adults than to teenagers.

- **Adult Alternative.** Current hits, either single releases or popular album tracks, which tend to appeal to adults more than to teenagers, with play lists drawn from rock, pop, country-rock, folk-rock, and blues releases.

- **Adult Contemporary (AC).** Popular and rock music released during the past fifteen or twenty years, plus a limited selection of older material and current hits, designed for general listeners.

- **Album Oriented Rock (AOR).** To be distinguished from Top 40 stations of the past, which played primarily singles. AOR stations thrived between the late 60's and the 80's, during the heyday of FM Rock Radio.

- **Alternative Rock.** Rock music stylistically derivative of the Seattle grunge bands of the late 80's, and to some extent, the punk/new wave artists of the late 70's, not the classic rock artists of the 60's and 70's. These stations aim primarily at teenage audiences and feature mostly current single releases and popular album cuts. Since the Alternative Rock peak of the mid-90s, many alternative rock bands (and stations) have evolved in the direction of modern rock, or in some cases, hard rock.

433

- **Classic Rock.** Rock music released during the 60's, 70's and 80's. These stations recreate the sound of Album Oriented Rock stations of that period (although often with a much more limited playlist) and appeal mainly to adults rather than to teenagers. Some Classic Rock stations play some current releases stylistically consistent with the station's sound.

- **Contemporary Hit Radio (CHR).** Current popular music, whether singles or album cuts. With singles remaining on the charts for 30-40 weeks or longer, current refers to music released within the last year. A more accurate description for CHR would be Current Hit Radio. This format is the descendent of the Top 40 stations popular from the 50s through the 80s.

- **Ethnic/International.** Traditional or popular music of a particular ethnic group, nation, or region, aimed at listeners from the featured group or place. Compare to World Music.

- **Hot Adult Contemporary (Hot AC).** Commercial popular and rock music released during the past fifteen or twenty years, more lively than the music played on the average Adult Contemporary station but still designed to appeal to general listeners rather than listeners interested in hearing current releases.

- **Lite Adult Contemporary (Lite AC).** Particularly easygoing popular and rock music released during the past fifteen or twenty years, designed to appeal to general listeners. This format is the descendent of the not-quite-extinct Easy Listening format.

- **Modern Rock.** Mostly current rock music performed by artists who have become prominent during the past five to ten years. Stylistically, the music tends to fall between Rock and Alternative Rock. See Alternative Rock, Rock.

- **Oldies.** Popular, rock and roll, and rock music released during the golden era of hit music, roughly 1955-1975. The term Oldies is actually a misnomer; a more accurate name for this format would be Golden Hits, as music from the post-1975 period may qualify as old but will rarely qualify as gold.

- **Rock.** Mostly current rock music, single releases or album cuts. Due to the diversity within rock music, the play lists of different rock stations will tend to fall within different stylistic ranges. See Modern Rock, Alternative Rock, Active Rock, Rock AC.

- **Smooth Jazz.** Easy-going popular music with a jazzy feel, designed to set a mood rather than to invite critical listening. Smooth Jazz is often set to a medium-tempo or Hip-Hop beat.

- **Talk.** Hosts discussing current events and other topics, often in the context of a particular political ideology. Talk programs frequently feature in-studio guests and calls from members of the public, representing varying degrees of expertise. Health, medical, and financial topics are especially popular.

- **Urban.** Music such as rap, hip-hop, R&B, and soul in styles that are descendents of rhythm & blues music of past decades. The mix favored by any given station depends in large part upon the age of the station's audience. Many Urban stations that appeal to adults rather than to teenagers include soul/R&B hits dating back twenty years or longer, and are sometimes characterized as Urban AC.

- **World Music.** Music that evokes one or more regions of the world though not necessarily performed by musicians from those regions or aimed solely at listeners from those regions. Compare to Ethnic/International Music.

Radio: What to Negotiate For

Like television, there are three equally important buying considerations in buying commercial time on radio: audience, impact, and cost. The remainder of this chapter will review these.

Audience

Survey says: "99% of adults listen to radio." However, even though nearly everyone listens to radio, most radio stations' audiences are extremely small. It would be almost impossible to reach 99% of adults with even a heavy radio schedule.

As discussed in Chapter 4, network and local market radio audiences are measured by Arbitron, a large media and marketing research company. Using a recruited panel of diary keepers, Arbitron measures network and local market radio audiences. Arbitron measures ratings, shares, and listeners by station and time period, trends, and limited demographics. You should be wary of sample sizes, especially for stations with small audiences, where more error affects reported ratings and impressions.

435

Radio Ratings

Because there are so many radio stations, and because there are relatively few listeners at any given time, radio audience ratings are usually quite small compared to TV ratings. A higher rated drive time spot may have a rating below 1.0. To generate acceptable reach and frequency, you will probably need schedules on several stations, as one station's cumulative audience may be less than 10% of your target audience.

Demographics

Radio stations with variety in their program formats do have distinctive demographic profiles. Table 20-8 compares share of audience for five radio formats. Note that Country has only a 3% share among adults 65+, while News/Talk garners 42% of their listening.

Table 20-8.—Share of Audience by Format

Format	P 12+	M 25-64	W 25-64	P 65+
Country	10%	8%	11%	3%
News/Talk	17	20	8	42
Oldies	6	6	6	5
Hispanic	11	13	12	7
Adult Contemporary	14	10	21	11

Source: Arbitron, Radio Today

As important as understanding the demographics of a station's audience is understanding their interests and tastes. Radio formats, uniquely executed by individual stations, paint a more insightful portrait of the listener than demographics do. Each format appeals to a different kind of listener based on something other than basic demographics: love of classical music, love of conservative talk shows, love of 60s music...

Besides the simple demographics provided by Arbitron, data from Scarborough and The Media Audit can support a deeper analysis of radio station audiences, including more complete demographics, purchase behavior, and some psychographics.

Average vs. Cume Ratings

Average ratings in radio are statistically similar to television ratings [Rating = Share x People Using Radio (PUR)]. For example, during morning drive time in a major market, 25% of adults are listening to the radio in the car, at home, or at work, and 5% of them are tuned to WXMR, that station would enjoy an adult rating of 1.25 (25% PUR x 5% share =

1.25% rating. Most stations' average drive time ratings are less than 1.0 (25% PUR/50 stations = .5).

Cume ratings are the cumulative percentage of a demographic group that listens to a station over time, for example one week. Cume ratings are important to because they define each station's total audience potential. If you want to reach 50% of a target, but a station's cume is only 15%, you must add enough more stations to achieve your goal of 50% reach.

Because every radio station programs a unique format and sound, a successful station develops loyal listeners who choose that station most of the time. To reach a station's total cumulative audience, of course, requires a heavy schedule in multiple dayparts. The following table demonstrates weekly cume ratings for the top rated stations in Detroit, according to Media Audit. WWJ-AM, a major news station, could reach 15% of the adults in this market. If your goal were higher than 15%, additional stations would be required.

Table 20-9.—Total Cume Ratings %

Top Stations	Adults 18+	Adults 25-54	Index*
WWJ-AM	15%	14%	93
WKQI-FM	14	14	100
WJR-AM	12	10	83
WNIC-FM	11	14	127
WRIF-FM	11	15	136
WYCD-FM	10	12	120
WJLB-FM	10	10	100
WDVD-FM	9	11	122
WOMC-FM	8	7	88
WDRQ-FM	7	11	157
WHTD-FM	8	9	113
WMXD-FM	8	8	100
WCSX-FM	7	10	143
WDTW-FM	6	8	133
WVMV-FM	7	NA	NA

Source: MG Media/Media Audit, Oct.-Dec. 2007   *Index of A25-54 viewing to total adults 18+

Cume ratings can help buyers determine which and how many stations are needed to meet reach and frequency goals. In the analysis shown in Table 20-10, if 1000 TRPS were purchased on one station with a target cume of 15%, reach would be 15% and the average listener would be reached an average of 66.7 times. Need higher reach? Buy more stations.

Table 20-10.—Comparison of Radio Plans

Statistic	Plan I	Plan II	Plan III
# Stations Bought	1	3	6
TRPS	1000	1000	1000
% Reach	15%	30%	45%
Avg. Frequency	66.7	33.3	22.2

Source: 2020

Audience Guarantees

It is nearly impossible to conduct an accurate post buy analysis of a radio schedule, because audiences during most of the year are not measured. (There are four 4-week surveys in the top 100 markets and two annual surveys in the bottom 100 markets.) In addition, stations regularly use promotional tactics during ratings measurement periods to hype audience sizes. In markets surveyed only twice a year, nonetheless, you can negotiate audience guarantees based on the next ratings report.

Radio Impact

Most of the media research to date on radio, besides audience measurement, has been designed to prove radio's communications effectiveness to national advertisers—why radio should be included as part of the media mix. Although little has been done at the tactical level to help guide buyers toward more cost effective decisions, available research suggests that impact considerations should be taken into account when negotiating radio buys and making purchase decisions.

What is the Role of Radio in the Media Plan?

The first impact question is why you have radio in the media plan. What is the communications role of radio?

Is radio included in the media plan simply to add frequency against a segment of the target? Is radio to reinforce imagery created in television advertising? To extend the awareness of music or jingles? To enhance the advertiser's image by leveraging the credibility and stature of certain radio celebrities? To execute a new creative concept using theatre of the mind? To generate traffic for a retailer?

The answers to questions like these can affect such decisions as which stations you purchase and how many, the formats you choose, and the personalities you want to enhance your advertiser's message.

Commercial Positioning

Secondly, like television, where and how radio commercials are positioned in a station's commercial string has a major effect on effectiveness (heard/recalled).

Many stations, hungry to build audience, run commercial free for an extended time, and then run a mega-block of commercials. Listeners no doubt like the commercial free listening. Advertisers hate the commercial blocks because they reduce commercial recall and communication. (The television research reviewed earlier indicates that there is an advantage to being in the first position, but a huge disadvantage in commercial recall for advertisers in the middle or later positions in a commercial chain.)

You have two basic remedies: One, don't buy stations that run long commercial strings unless they guarantee that your spot will be in first position. Two, reduce the expenditure to a cost effective level. If you estimate a loss of 70% of commercial audience due to positioning, agree to pay a maximum of 30% of the negotiated rate. Stations will resist, but there are a lot of stations in the sea.

Based on the television research cited earlier, do not allow stations to run your spots near competitors' spots (require at least 15 minute separation), as this also diminishes your commercial recall.

Attention Levels

Radio is often referred to as a *background medium,* as you learned in Chapter 9, with implications for impact (see also Chapter 15). It has been portrayed as a background medium because listeners are usually physically or mentally occupied with other things and not listening attentively. Obviously, if attention levels are low, chances of commercial exposure and communication are greatly reduced.

Early research by Motivation Analysis, Inc. found that, on average, only 20% of radio listeners paid full attention—not good news for advertisers. However, the research also found that attention levels were much higher for some station formats (news and talk) than for others (classic or easy listening). While the data are limited, the findings are common sense, and you should incorporate attentiveness judgments into your decisions about which stations are the most cost effective.

Value Added

Beyond advertising, radio stations often create and execute *turnkey promotion* and merchandising programs at no additional cost to the advertiser. Naturally, the larger the buy in dollars, the more the station can afford to do. Many stations even have promotion staff to help advertisers maximize the value of the combined advertising and promotion package.

Examples of promotion/merchandising packages can include:

- On air talent testimonials/use talent in commercials
- Traffic building promotions, promoted on air
- Remotes from the advertiser's place of business
- On air giveaways of advertiser merchandise
- Tickets for sporting or other events
- Hosting clients or sales reps at a dinner/event
- Bonus spots
- Signage at entertainment venues
- Ads on station websites
- Ads in programs and partner media

Stations use value added programs as a carrot to sell advertising schedules. Smart advertisers are not lured into buying schedules on stations that make no sense for them (wrong audience, excessive cost), but station merchandising and promotion are great if you are going to buy the station anyway or if you need a tiebreaker.

Importance of Great Radio Creative

Having great advertising creative is critical for optimizing the success of any advertiser in any medium. Radio is no exception, especially since radio creative needs to overcome the medium's limitations (low attention levels, commercial positioning, and lack of multi sensory communication).

The Radio Advertising Bureau (RAB), whose role is promoting and selling radio as an advertising medium, believes that the creative is a problem in selling radio. The RAB sponsors creative competitions with generous awards to those who produce great examples of radio creative.

While buyers obviously are not personally responsible for creating radio commercials, you can collaborate with planners and creative staff to overcome the medium's limitations.

Radio Costs

Advertiser demand for radio has been declining for several years. If demand for radio continues to be soft, you should be able to negotiate extremely attractive packages containing prime availabilities, impact enhancements, and reduced prices. Of course, conditions will vary significantly by market and by station.

Radio Rate Cards

Radio networks and stations have rate cards that specify what the stations' theoretical rates are for spot participations, programs, and sponsorships. However, like television networks and stations, radio's rate cards may not have much relationship to the actual prices paid by advertisers. Why? Because, like television, actual radio prices are a function of supply and demand.

If a radio station has a glut of unsold inventory, any measured audience spots will sell, if they sell, at very low unit prices. On the other hand, certain leading stations may be nearly sold out and able to command higher prices because advertisers want to be on the station at any price.

Compared to television rate cards, the out of pocket cost of :60 announcements on radio is usually extremely low. Spots may range in price from less than $5.00 each to $150.00, up to over $1000 for a major market station, compared to thousands of dollars for a primetime television :30 in a medium sized market.

Question: Are such cheap spots too good a bargain to pass up?

What is a Radio Spot Worth?

Is the opportunity to buy a package of spots for $3.00 per :60 just too good to pass up? The answer is, a spot with no audience is worth zero. A spot with measured audience is worth something, but how much depends on size of audience, whether the audience fits the advertiser's target, and how the CPM/CPP compares with that of competitive stations.

If the CPP of a $3.00 spot is estimated at $15.00, compared to a CPP of $10.00 on other stations (same daypart, commercial length, etc.), the $3.00 spots would be a bad deal. On the other hand, $1000 spots with a $7.50 CPP would be a good deal. Furthermore, if there were no other buyers for those cheap spots, the station would likely take whatever it could get—maybe $1.50!

Naïve advertisers are often duped into buying a big package of cheap spots thinking that they have just bought a saturation advertising campaign. *Caveat-Emptor.* The out of pocket cost of a spot is not a good measurement of the spot's value.

What Does Radio Actually Cost?

The following table provides estimated CPPs for several demographics in the top 10 Metro Survey Areas in the U.S. These data are available for each of the 200 radio MSAs. What observations about radio costs can you draw from this comparison? The cost of reaching men vs. women? Teens vs. 18-24 year olds? 35-64 year old listeners?

Table 20-11.—CPP for Top 10 Radio Markets (:60s, Top 10 Markets)

Demographic	AM Drive	PM Drive	Daytime	Night
Men	$4468	$5666	$4717	$2386
Women	4967	6304	4747	2676
Teens	2600	2774	4996	1138
A 18-24	6658	6575	5983	1784
A 35-64	4409	5608	4620	2734

Planners use these data to calculate estimated costs for a radio schedule. Buyers use the data to benchmark CPPs from stations' proposals against market averages.

A MEDIA NEGOTIATION EXAMPLE

Following is some realistic dialogue between a media buyer who wants to purchase a broadcast schedule and a media sales rep who wants to dispose of some of the station's unsold time. What are their negotiation strategies? What, exactly, does each party want?

BUYER: *Hi, Sally, this is Bill Buyer from the Tiger Company. I'm calling for avails for a buy we have coming up in Detroit for ACME.*

SELLER: *Hi, Bill. We're a little tight on inventory right now, but we will bend over backwards to help ACME.*

BUYER: *Interesting that you should say that. It seems like some of the other stations have plenty of inventory, they say, sales are soft. Anyway, let me give you the specs.*

◆ *Market is Detroit*
◆ *Timing is June 1 to July 15*
◆ *Target audience is men 18-49*
◆ *Daypart mix is 50 percent primetime and 50 percent late night*
◆ *Programming wise, we prefer drama and action adventure shows like "CSI" and "NCIS" for this target.*
◆ *No Run of Schedule, we want to be in-program in higher involvement shows.*

◆ *We will need **audience guarantees**. If the buy under delivers men 18-49 TRPS, we will take make goods to bring the buy up to agreed TRP delivery*

◆ *We would want a **Value Added** package, consisting of on air promotion funded by the station, submitted for approval.*

◆ *Finally, **commercial positioning**. We want to be first in the pod and no competitive commercials in our pods.*

SELLER: *Phew! OK, Bill, I'll see what we can do. But I think my management will have a real problem with giving you all of our best shows at a competitive price, and they will choke on your requests for audience guarantees, value added, and first position in the pod. **By the way, what's the budget?***

BUYER: *Sally, I can't release that number right now. I need to see plans and pricing first. Why don't you let me look at a plan for $50,000 and another for $100,000? Depending on what happens I can be happy buying five stations or one station.*

SELLER: *Well, OK. What are your TRP goals?*

BUYER: *I don't want to disadvantage you by giving you that number either! Just give me your best plan and prices and we'll see how the TRPS shake out for you and the other stations. Can you get the plans to me first thing in the morning?*

SELLER: *(Next day). Hi, Bill, did you have a chance to look at my plans? How do we look?*

BUYER: *Sally, it looks like your cost per point for men 18-49 is about 30 per cent higher than the next three stations. Can you sweeten the pot, and are you OK with our commercial positioning requirements?*

SELLER: *Bill, we are close to the bottom line. I don't think you are taking into consideration the high quality of our plan. You have cherry picked our best programs and that will hurt us with other advertisers. Anyway, let me talk to our sales manager again to see if there is anything we can do.*

SELLER: *(Later) Bill, good news. We can add two more CSIs and two NCISs. How does that sound?*

BUYER: *Well, in all honesty, that only adds about 10 per cent more TRPS, which means you're still at a competitive disadvantage. The other stations have added bonus spots into their plans as well. If you can get me another five units in our prime shows, and if you can deliver the commercial positioning we need, I would agree to give you the whole budget...$150,000...if you can deliver what we want.*

BOTH: *(To be continued until negotiations are complete & orders placed)*

443

SUMMARY

Broadcast media buying is a specialized subset of the media negotiation skills and goals studied in Chapter 19. Chapter 20 has showed you the specific processes that negotiate execution of media plans with sellers of network or local market television and radio stations. After negotiations are completed, you ultimately purchase and contract for the plan's TRPS by daypart, and then continue to be responsible for managing and maintaining the buys.

Based on media availabilities, broadcast buyers negotiate on topics uniquely broadcast related to optimize three equally important aspects of any radio or television advertising buy: audience, impact, and cost. In this chapter you have seen how negotiations occur in a broadcast marketplace regulated by the forces of supply and demand, where timing matters. Supply and demand conditions affect the degree to which you can optimize all three of your values in the commodities market of broadcast media.

21. BUYING PRINT MEDIA

It is so hard to be a writer these days
when everything has been written.

–Anonymous
Found in Egyptian writings dating 5000 BC

Buying print media is different from buying broadcast media. The nature of the medium is different. Magazines, newspapers, and out of home are used for different reasons, and the analysis and evaluation process is different. For these and other reasons, print media negotiations differ from broadcast media negotiations.

The terms of broadcast media buys have always been negotiated between buyers and sellers in the general manner set forth in Chapter 19. The unique process of buying print media is the subject of Chapter 21.

BUYING NEWSPAPERS

Print media have always published rate cards showing their rates in detail, as shown in Figure 21-1. Historically, print media regarded their rate cards as sacrosanct and refused to make deals violating them. However, in recent years business has been tough for print media—both newspapers and magazines—which have experienced declining circulation and share of market. Some print media face near extinction at the digital hands of the Internet, and the media-buying world has changed. Print media are now more likely to negotiate the terms of media buys.

Print Rate Cards

Figure 21-1 is an example of a hypothetical rate card for a print advertising medium. Notice that rates change according to size of ad, frequency of insertion, and coloration.

Large advertisers (like General Motors) with big print budgets changed print media rate cards forever when they consolidated their brands' (Chevrolet, Cadillac, Buick, GMAC) print budgets and asked every major magazine and newspaper for much larger discounts and more favorable treatment in exchange for a corporate schedule guarantee.

445

Rate Card Example

Four Color

	Open	4 Insertions	8 Insertions	12 Insertions
1 Page	$100,960	$88,840	$85,830	$82,790
2/3 Page	75,380	66,350	64,090	61,800
1/2 Page	60,570	53,310	51,490	49,670
1/3 Page	39,030	34,350	33,200	32,010
2nd Cover Spread	226,140	199,000	192,210	185,420
3rd Cover	102,980	90,540	87,520	84,440
4th Cover	133,260	117,270	113,270	109,270

Two Color — Black and One Color

	Open	4 Insertions	8 Insertions	12 Insertions
1 Page	$85,830	$75,530	$72,940	$70,370
2/3 Page	64,090	56,410	54,480	52,540
1/2 Page	51,490	45,340	43,800	42,240
1/3 Page	33,200	29,230	28,220	27,230

Black and White

	Open	4 Insertions	8 Insertions	12 Insertions
1 Page	$68,640	$60,430	$58,360	$56,300
2/3 Page	51,270	45,130	43,600	42,040
1/2 Page	41,200	36,270	35,020	33,780
1/3 Page	26,540	23,370	22,580	21,790

Figure 21-1.—Rate Card Sample

These advertisers created a win-win for themselves and the print media. They wanted large rate concessions and the media wanted more money and commitment—and knew that they would be shut out if they continued to be rigid about their rate cards.

The following discussion covers other buying considerations for the major print media—newspapers, magazines, and out of home.

Newspapers

Newspapers offer the whole array of advertising options discussed in Chapter 15. National, local daily, suburban, lifestyle, ethnic, and college newspapers offer a wide array of advertising availabilities. Ads may be of any size and shape, black and white or color, the quality of which has improved greatly in recent years. Ads may run in a variety of ways.

Run of paper (*ROP*) advertising means that the newspaper decides where your ad runs on a space available basis; you can request section or page positioning, but you get no guarantees. You also may order the ad to run in a particular section such as sports or business, or on page one in some newspapers. Other choices include Sunday supplements, freestanding inserts, polybags & sampling, newspaper websites, comics, and classified or display classified.

Geographic Targeting

Daily newspapers offer full-run editions in their coverage areas. Many also offer zoned editions, usually on certain days, which target specific geographic areas within the market. From a pure geographic targeting standpoint, newspapers serving one particular suburban area or community provide maximum targeting. However, especially if the paper is distributed free, you should satisfy yourself that the editorial product is capable of generating a quality audience that will read the paper with a high level of attention and interest. Freestanding inserts in newspapers can be targeted to specified zip codes. Suburban or community newspapers, of course, cover their particular communities.

Section of Newspaper

An important buying issue relates to where your ad should appear within the newspaper. Ads may run in any section of the paper, and newspapers want the flexibility to run an ad where they have an open spot in their layout. This is not always in the advertiser's interest. Table 21-1 shows average weekday readership by gender for various sections.

Table 21-1.—*Weekday Newspaper Readership by Section by Gender*

Readership by Section of Newspaper

	News	Business	Sports	Entertainment
Men	89%	67%	76%	57%
Women	91%	56%	48%	53%

Your ad's position within the newspaper is important. Page three in main news is probably the best position in the paper because virtually every reader will turn to it. The only readership advantage to positioning in a particular section is a tie-in of content.

Newspaper Costs

A rate card is the publication's statement of advertising rates. It may also detail deadlines, demographics, policies, additional fees, and artwork requirements. The smaller the publication, the less information may be available in the rate card.

Some newspapers have complex rate cards describing all their discount programs. Some even have rate cards for particular categories of advertising, with rates presented by retail display, classified, display classified, business, the higher national ad rates.

Rate cards help you understand what kinds of ad sizes, discounts, and other advertising the publication offers. You can use them to compare rates based on circulation before you buy advertising space. Many newspapers post their rates online at their websites.

Calculating Display Ad Rates

To calculate the rates for a display ad, determine the number of column inches in the ad by multiplying the number of columns wide by the number of inches deep. For example, an ad 3 columns by 12 inches deep totals 36 column inches (3 x 12). If the *open rate* (without discounts) is $8.00 per column inch, a 36-column-inch ad @ $8.00 per inch costs $288. Display Advertising Mechanical Measurements

There may be some variation in the way different publications measure ad space. Here are the definitions of column inch, standard advertising unit, and pica:

- **Column inch**. Display's primary space measurement, generally one column wide x one inch deep, may vary by publication.

- **Standard Advertising Unit (SAU)**. Ad size format daily newspapers will accept; standard created to facilitate placement for large advertisers in many different newspapers.

- **Pica**. Typographic unit of measurement = 1/6" (0.166"); 6 picas = 1" (or 0.996"); also 1 pica = 12 points.

Newspaper Audience Information

Scarborough and The Media Audit (see Chapter 5) provide syndicated local market audience data. Many newspapers also conduct their own audience and media effectiveness studies. Your rep should provide this information to you.

Circulation Guarantees

Newspapers normally base their rates on a defined level of circulation called a *rate base*. If a newspaper falls below its rate base, it owes you a credit or make-goods to offset your loss of circulation. An 8% shortfall in rate base circulation is worth an 8% price reduction.

Buying Process

- Before placing an insertion order for an ad, be sure you understand the terms and conditions of advertising with the newspaper. If there is a conflict between the insertion order and the rate card, the rate card is probably going to be the deciding factor.

- If you're interested in advertising within a particular publication, check its website or call the office and ask for a copy of the current rate card. Many newspapers and magazines post their rate cards online in a PDF format, but this does not mean the prices on the rate card are fixed. Most sales representatives will offer special rates for first-time advertisers, as well as other discounts.

- As newspaper ad revenues remain soft, newspaper rates are increasingly negotiable for off-rate-card deals.

- Try to negotiate a significantly better price! Understand that negotiations are a two-way street, and you will stand a better chance of getting price and other concessions if you are able to offer the newspaper something it wants—like a commitment for increased volume of business. The perfect example is the GM advertising deal with which this chapter began.

BUYING MAGAZINES

There are approximately 17,000 magazines in the U.S. serving almost every consumer and business interest and need, including magazines in business, home, travel, and other categories distributed exclusively in local markets. In 2006, advertisers spent about $19 billion in magazines, up almost 25% from 2002. According to a study conducted by Nielsen Media Research for the TVB, magazines reach about 51% of adults daily.

Magazine Availabilities

Magazines target almost every conceivable demographic and lifestyle and interest category for both consumer and business markets. *Standard Rate and Data (SRDS)*, likely to be available in your library, classifies magazines by subject matter and detailed information on each magazine's editorial content, circulation, and rates, with separate editions for consumer magazines and business and trade publications.

While magazines prefer to sell *run-of-book* ads (they decide where in the magazine to put your ad), you can often negotiate special positioning on a cover, page one, or within some relevant editorial content. Magazines also offer special space units—inserts printed on special paper, micro-encapsulation (smell the coffee), or advertorials.

Magazine Costs

Like newspapers, magazines publish rate cards detailing their rates and discount structures for different ad sizes, colorations, special editorial editions, and geographic editions. Magazine rate cards also usually include basic circulation data, closing dates for when they need ad materials for a particular issue, as well as mechanical specifications (e.g., page size).

Magazines like to stick with the rates on their cards, so you will need to use creative negotiating tactics if you are to obtain concessions. There are some tips below that may help.

Magazine Audience Information

The two primary sources of magazine audience information are Media Mark Research (MRI) and Simmons Market Research Bureau (SMRB). Both studies are large sample (25,000+) annual surveys of consumers and provide single-source data on consumer behavior, demographics, and media exposure in hundreds of market segments. Want to know who bought a Toyota Camry? How many there were, their demographics and psychographics? Whether they read *People* magazine?

In addition, some magazines commission their own readership studies if they are not measured by MRI or SMRB—or if they don't like the results! If you do not otherwise have access to the data, magazine reps will provide it for all the competitive magazines in their category. If you have additional questions, you can request a special analysis or some cross tabs.

Circulation Guarantees

Like newspapers, magazines have a circulation rate base—the circulation they guarantee at a given page rate. If they guarantee 1,000,000 circulation but deliver only 500,000, they owe you a 50% rebate. Check their circulation audit statements from ABC or BPA. Be leery of unaudited publications that provide only sworn publisher statements.

Magazine Ad Recall by Type of Ad

The average recall of ads in magazines varies by size, coloration, and positioning. Table 21-2 shows the average ad recall with cost indices by position compared to the average page (index = 100).

Table 21-2.—Index of Magazine Ad Recall by Type of Unit

Position	Recall Index	Cost Index
Full Page	100	100
Inside Front Cover	112	100
3rd Cover	100	100
Back Cover	115	120+
Multi Page Unit	117	400
Spread	112	<200
Fractional Page	81	40

Some space units yield an ad recall bonus in relation to costs, while others do not. For example, the average ad on the inside front cover generates 12% more recall per dollar (Recall Index: 112), whereas two-page *spreads* also typically get 12% higher recall but at nearly double the cost (Cost Index<200). That is not to say that spreads are bad, but you need to be aware of the facts so you can have an intelligent conversation about your options. Otherwise, the creative idea—the need for more space to tell the story—and the need to project a leadership image may trump media considerations.

Assuming you can negotiate no cost premium for the second cover, you should receive at least a 12% bonus in ad recall. Multi-page units are not efficient for ad recall, but they still may be worth the premium if you have a complex story. Spreads are not efficient for recall, while fractional pages are, as measured by the Recall Index/Cost Index ratio.

Buying Process

The process for buying ads in magazines is similar to that described for newspapers.

Contract

Be sure you understand the terms and conditions of advertising with the magazine, especially as it relates to the amount of advertising you must run in order to obtain the contract rate. If you fall short of your volume commitment, you will be short rated on your previous ads within the contract year.

Insertion Order

Issue an insertion order to the magazine along with creative/production materials for each ad. Magazine ad rates have become increasingly negotiable for off rate card deals. Try to negotiate a significantly better price! Understand that negotiations are a two way street; you will stand a better chance of getting price and other concessions if you are able to offer the newspaper something it wants—like a certain volume of business. Remember, General Motors's off-card deals included not only newspapers but magazines.

PRINT NEGOTIATING TIPS

Historically print media—newspapers and magazines—were able to sell advertising at rate card prices. In today's world, however, print media will often make concessions to get your business—reduced rates and special discounts, preferred ad positioning, value added promotions, or merchandising. The following tips will help you negotiate successfully with print media.

1. Don't Ask, Don't Get

Many media planners and buyers are still under the impression that print media will not negotiate the terms of a buy. Many will if you present a win-win scenario. What are you willing give to get the deal you want?

Print media do not broadcast or publish in their rate cards what they might be willing to do to get a nice piece of business. Since print media can add and subtract pages on the basis of their sales, it is not as supply-and-demand sensitive as broadcast. Moreover, newspaper sales and many magazine sales are soft. Always remember the power of the dollar: you have money, and they want it. As long as that is true and you have a good Plan B in your pocket to use as leverage, there are opportunities to negotiate lower prices and added value.

2. Caveat Emptor

Ask questions. Ask reps what the circulation is and whether it is audited, what the rate base circulation is, how many readers they have according to what research, what are the demographics of the readers, what the publication's editorial purpose is, what research they have, what their page opening rates are. Asking the rep good questions will help establish your credibility and let the rep know you are a knowledgeable buyer. Get this kind of information before you give the rep information on your target audience.

3. Create Leverage the GM Way

Go to the publications you are interested in using. Tell them you will increase your financial commitment to them IF they will give you a deep enough off-card discount. Make sure they know that you are looking for media who want a win-win relationship, and you will look elsewhere if they are not interested. Be prepared to walk away.

4. Study the Publication's Ads

Look at the publication in order to see how many *house ads* they run promoting themselves and how many public service ads. If they have a lot of non-revenue-producing ads, it may indicate that they are having trouble selling advertising. Buy low.

5. Always Have a Plan B

If you are unable to negotiate the right deal with a particular publication, move on. Let the publication know you are taking your money somewhere else; you don't have to say where or when. If that brings no response, use your money to buy other media that are equally cost effective and suitable for your purposes.

6. Use Their Rate Card

When discussing rates with a magazine or newspaper that has a complex rate card, it is a good tactic to base your rate reduction rationale on some element of their card. For example, if you are planning to run 3-6 times, ask for the 12x rate. If they offer special rates to realtors or car dealers, ask for the dealer rate since you, too, are a dealer (just not a car dealer). Print media like to stay on their card; find a way to let them.

7. Ask for New Advertiser Discounts

Even the *New York Times* offers certain new advertisers deep discounts—60-70%—based on an agreed level of commitment.

8. Negotiate Value Added

Print media will provide additional value at no added cost—reprints and point of sale, mailings to customers, copies of the publication to distribute at your place of business. Ask them to conduct a sweepstakes or contest. See if they will host a golf outing for your clients. Be creative, but stick to things that fit your strategy!

9. Negotiate for Website Exposure

Newspaper and magazine websites are growing in popularity. Ask that they give you links, ads, and mentions on their website as part of a value added package.

10. Ask for Two Ads for the Price of One

Never forget: the newspaper business is soft. You might be able to get two ads for the price of one if you give the paper a commitment and some scheduling flexibility on the free ads.

11. Negotiate Ad Positioning

Where your ad appears in the publication may or may not be a big deal to you, but you should check out any research, especially *Starch Adnorm* studies, that could indicate whether certain positions would provide an advantage. In newspapers, for example, main news, especially page 3, may be the best position for most advertisers. If positioning is a deal breaker for you, say so!

OUT OF HOME

Out-of-home (outdoor) advertising expenditures have been relatively stable at about $6 billion for the past few years. Of that, nearly 60% is local advertising with 40% national advertising. About 96% of adults will pass by outdoor locations during the average week.

Availabilities

There are around 500,000 outdoor locations available, including many different kinds of outdoor units:

- **Billboards.** 30-sheet posters, 8-sheet posters, permanent bulletins, and spectacular and electronic/digital units
- **Street Furniture.** Benches, shelters, phone booths, etc.
- **Transit.** Bus, train, transit, airport
- **Alternative.** Outdoor & furniture wraps, wrapped cars, inside buses & trains

Audience Measurement

The Traffic Audit Bureau for Media Measurement Inc. (TAB) was established in 1933 as a non-profit organization whose historical mission has been to audit the circulation of out-of-home media in the United States. Recently TAB's role has been expanded to lead and/or support other major outdoor industry research initiatives.

Governed by a tripartite board of advertisers, agencies, and media companies, TAB is an independent auditor for traffic circulation. In Canada, the Canadian Outdoor Measurement Bureau (COMB) was formed in 1965 as a non-profit organization independently operated by representatives of advertisers, advertising agencies, and the Canadian out-of-home advertising industry. COMB is charged with the verifying traffic circulation for the benefit of the industry and its users (Chen 1999).

Buying Process

Here is the process for buying outdoor advertising:

1. Study the market's supply and demand situation, how much outdoor is available, and other aspects of the analysis you have learned to do.

2. Call the outdoor companies or reps selling outdoor in your market area—Clear Channel, Lamar, 3M, Gannett—if there are competing outdoor companies. (One company may own the wholemarket.)

3. Give the reps your buying specs, as you would for a broadcast buy.

4. Evaluate submissions in terms of audience delivery and CPMs.

5. Negotiate a better deal using as leverage that you may spend your money in other media.

6. Ride the boards before you make a final commitment. Drive around the market area with the outdoor sales rep, visually checking location quality. Look for problems like obstructions from buildings, trees, other outdoor boards, or boards are set back so far from the road that they resemble postage stamps not billboards. If your board is piggybacking with another board, make sure the other one is not for adult or other vendors or products your consumers might find objectionable. If you find problems, wait for the outdoor company to find alternate locations before you enter into a contract.

SUMMARY

Print media have worked hard over several decades to establish their rate cards as the medium's bottom line prices. This chapter has explained that it is often possible nevertheless to negotiate lower rates and obtain preferential positioning and value added if a publication wants additional revenue without additional printing costs.

Magazines, newspapers, and outdoor companies that are facing deadlines with open space in their inventories would rather sell at a deep discount than generate no revenue. Chapter 23 offers a more detailed discussion of this phenomenon.

If you follow the negotiation tips Chapter 21 has given you and the more general ones in Chapter 19, you will succeed in saving client dollars while increasing client visibility by advertising in print.

22. Buying Internet Advertising

Give a person a fish and you feed them for a day; teach that person to use the Internet and they won't bother you for weeks.

−Author Unknown

With traditional media like television, media planners have always taken the lead. Planners look at questions like target audiences, geographic issues, supply and demand, timing, alternative media, daypart values, and available opportunities.

Internet buying is different. Supply and demand questions are formulated differently, opportunities are unlimited, and results are more readily measurable.. Innovations in means and methods are continuous. Online media buying requires specialized knowledge of its complexities, and launching a successful online advertising campaign grows ever more challenging. With the Internet, buyers take the lead. Unlike traditional media, there are few standards or consistencies in Internet advertising, and online ad campaigns may require the development of the media plan before the ad creative can begin. Like traditional media, though perhaps to a greater degree, there are esoteric languages and complicated technical processes associated with Internet ad buying. Chapter 22 will introduce you to those; continued study and experience will build competence.

In no other aspect of media planning and buying is there so much change, so continuous and so rapid. This chapter therefore cannot be taken as the last word on most of its topics. It is intended as your orientation to the principal forms of early 21st century Internet advertising; their targeting, pricing, and purchasing methods; and creative concepts and strategies. Chapter 22 presents one principle of Internet advertising that is almost certainly permanent: test, test, test!

Forms of Internet Advertising

Internet advertising takes the many forms as shown in Table 22-1, which demonstrates that keyword search has rapidly become dominant, overtaking display ads by 2006. This chapter will examine these two primary forms of Internet advertising: keyword search and display.

459

Table 22-1.—Internet Spending Trends by Type

	2002	2006	2008
Keyword Search	15%	40%	41%
Display/banners	29	21	21
Sponsorship	18	4	3
Classified	15	20	17
All Other	23	14	14

Keyword search is both a form of advertising and also a targeting method for attracting engaged, interested audiences. In the discussion that follows, it will be obvious that in this as in other respects, Internet advertising is *sui generis.*

METHODS OF TARGETING INTERNET ADS

More than any other advertising medium, the Internet offers the ability to target and engage highly specific audiences who are interested in the advertiser's message. That makes targeting especially important for Internet advertising. There are three important targeting methods: keyword search, contextual targeting, and behavioral targeting.

Keyword Search

As suggested in Table 22-1, the most important method of targeting interested audiences is via *keyword search.* Advertisers select keywords or phrases that they expect their target audience to query for information about products or services like theirs. Typically, advertisers develop long lists of possible keywords or phrases. For example, to bring *interested surfers* to its Malibu web pages, Chevrolet might utilize keywords like *Chevrolet Malibu, mid-sized cars,* or *Motor Trend Car of the Year.* Keywords are used in two important and inter-related ways: in organic search and paid search.

Organic Search

Organic search results are listings that appear on search engine results pages because of their relevance to the search terms, as opposed to their being advertisements. Organic search results are the basic listings that are displayed when an Internet surfer conducts a search. These listings are *free to the advertiser*, so advertisers devote a lot of time and money to optimizing their websites and marketing so that search engines will find and display their listings on the *first page of search results.*

Figure 22-1 is a typical example of first page, organic, search results. These particular results are displayed by Google in response to the term, *advertising media.*

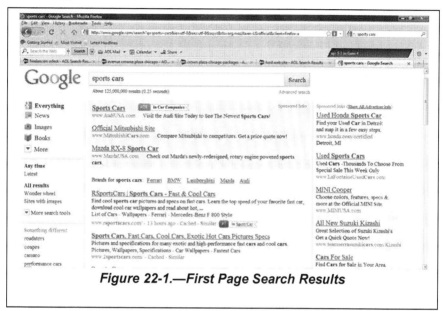

Figure 22-1.—First Page Search Results

Search engines may return thousands or even millions of results. If you are the first, second or third result, you have a decent chance of a click-through to your website. On the other hand, if your result is the hundredth, thousandth, or millionth on the list of search results, your ad isn't going to be seen by many searchers, if any. Consequently, your listing will not generate traffic to your website.

How do advertisers help search engines find their sites? They integrate their keywords into the copy on their web pages. This is part of tuning a website to generate optimum search engine results. The process is called *Search Engine Optimization (SEO),* and it is one of several factors affecting search engines' indexing of websites. Gaining a high ranking in search listings is easier said than done, but it is critically important. Look at the AOL data in Table 22-2: *ninety-two per cent of AOL users clicked on first-page results, while only 1% clicked on page-four results.*

Table 22-2.—*Search Page Result vs. Website Visits*

Search Page	% of Visits
1	92%
2	4
3	2
4	1

Source: AOL Research

Question: Why is achieving a page-one ranking important?

Paid Search

In contrast to organic search, *paid search* is an Internet advertising model used on websites where advertisers pay their host only when their ad is clicked. With search engines, advertisers typically bid on keyword phrases relevant to their target market. Content sites commonly charge a fixed price per click rather than use a bidding system.

Most serious search advertisers utilize paid search to generate additional *interested traffic* to their websites beyond what is achieved from organic search. *Paid ads* are shown in the search results of search engines like Google, Yahoo, Bing, and dozens of other search engines. Ads shown on these pages appear above, below, and alongside the organic search results and attract highly targeted audiences defined by consumer interest. Who would be attracted by the keyword phrase *Affordable Violins?* Who would be attracted by the keywords, *Gourmet Cheeses*?

The CPC/PPC advertising model is open to abuse through *click fraud.* Click fraud occurs when a person, automated script, or computer program imitates a legitimate user by clicking on an ad for no other reason than to generate a charge per click. For example, an unscrupulous person or seller could simply sit in front of his/her computer and rack up hundreds of fraudulent clicks, which would then be billed to an unsuspecting advertiser. Although Google and others have implemented automated systems to guard against abusive clicks by competitors or corrupt web developers, click fraud is the subject of some controversy and increasing litigation, because the advertising networks are its key beneficiary.

Contextual Targeting

Contextual targeting matches ads with content or with specific keywords on websites within a particular content network such as Google. The search engine's contextual advertising system scans the content of a website (e.g., Google); analyzes the content, theme, and links for websites in the network; and returns specific ads to the landing page based on what the user is viewing. For example, the search engine's contextual system might serve Chevrolet's Malibu ad on automotive websites that provide editorial reviews of new cars or that mention Malibu. Of course, other auto-related ads would also be sent to those sites.

Keyword and contextual advertising are not necessarily mutually exclusive. Some search engines use both methods simultaneously to serve advertisers' messages to selected audiences.

Behavioral Targeting

Behavioral targeting allows advertisers to expose their creative to web surfers selected on the basis of what sites they visit and what they do there. As might be expected, behavioral targeting raises *privacy concerns* among web users and advocacy groups. The industry is trying to contain this controversy by providing education, applying constraints that protect personally identifiable information, and seeking user permission to collect data about individual Internet user behavior.

The industry will take some trouble to protect behavioral targeting because of its value to advertisers. To display content to the users most likely to be interested in it, advertisers want to be able to target based on *website visits, keywords or content,* and *redirects.*

Website Visits

The most common form of behavioral targeting is based on websites and pages visited. Behavioral segments are developed by aggregating users who have gone to specific websites with targeted content. For example, an auto shoppers segment might be based on visits to auto manufacturer sites, Edmunds.com, and/or Kelley Blue Book. Users thus identified can be re-targeted when they visit general sites. For example, individuals who have visited the above types of automotive sites could be re-targeted with ads on sites about auto financing, insurance, or auto accessories.

Keywords/Content Read

Another form of behavioral targeting is based on keywords searched or content read, which is just what it sounds like. You can construct an audience of web surfers who have searched for *low calorie chocolate* or who have read copy on other sites that sell low calorie chocolate treats.

Re-Directs

Finally, by placing a simple code on one or more of your web pages, you can create segments of surfers who have visited *your* website or competitive websites. These can be further sorted by home page visits, content page visits, or order page visits, creating an opportunity to develop specific messages for each group. This tactic is often called *redirecting*.

Advertising networks such as Value Click, Tribal Fusion, Burst, and Specific Media claim they can enhance behavioral targeting because they serve many advertisers across many sites. Incorporating demographic data, they offer even richer portraits of audiences, for example, *Internet users seen on football sites are more likely to be males*.

BUYING KEYWORD SEARCH ADVERTISING

Keyword search, which you first encountered in Chapter 6 where its pricing structures (CPC, CPM, cost per action) were introduced, is the largest category of Internet advertising. This chapter's more detailed discussion of keyword purchasing will use the CPC structure as the model for buying keyword search advertising.

Buying search advertising is much different from buying time or space in broadcast or print media. When negotiating traditional media buys, buyers usually negotiate with human beings (sellers). However, advertisers buying CPC schedules typically interface with a computer system that provides information on competitive bids and projected click-throughs based on a specified budget and keywords. (Large-enough advertisers can arrange to speak with live sales persons at the search engines.)

Keyword Selection

Visitors will find your website—or not—depending on the specific keywords or phrases you have designated for your search campaign. Your keywords should be those most likely to be queried for your business.

To select keywords for your campaign:

1. Develop an initial list of keywords and phrases that you believe your target audience will search.
2. Use the search engines' keyword finder tools to expand your list.
3. Search the keywords/phrases to find your competitors' keywords and see how they fare in the search engine results.
4. Factor in CPC costs (see below).
5. Once your campaign is live, track its performance daily.
6. Eliminate low performing keywords.

Cost of Keywords

You place a bid on each of your desired keywords. In general, the higher the bid the higher your ranking in search results where the text ad appears along with other ads. Bids for keywords on some search engines can be as low as $.01 per click or as high as several dollars per click. The more popular the search term with advertisers, the higher the price will be. Part of the challenge is to determine how much to pay for a keyword and how much budget to allocate to generate a profit.

For example, let's assume that you bid $.60 on the keyword *cell phone*. If 100,000 users searched that term on Google, they would have the *opportunity* to see your ad on Google's results page (although they may not notice it). If 1500 people clicked on your ad (1.5% CTR), they would be redirected to your website. You would pay Google for the 1500 clicks at your bid price of $.60 per click, $900.

(Google's AdWords online bidding platform allows Google to offer similar bidding opportunities for banner ads, video, radio, and even television via its alliance with EchoStar satellite television.)

The cost of clicks on keywords ranges from $.01 to several dollars per click, depending on the popularity of the word among searchers and competition for its use among bidders. If there are few or no other bidders for a keyword, a click may cost as little as $.01 (although there may be very few clicks at that rate, as a keyword so unpopular isn't likely to be searched often.) On the other hand, if a lot of advertisers bid on a popular keyword, the cost per click will rise.

The size of the bid affects the position or ranking of an ad in search results. The highest bid will be in the top position where more users will have the opportunity to see and click the ad. Page one rankings have the greatest chance of exposure and clicks (remember Table 22-2). Therefore, a bid of $.50 on a keyword may result in first position, or it may bring a second page or even lower ranking, depending on the other bids. In general, the higher the bid the higher the ranking.

Many advertisers automatically authorize the lowest allowable bid, a practice that may be counterproductive. If you bid $.01 on a keyword on which other advertisers bid $1.00, your ad's ranking in the search results will be very low and therefore will likely generate very few, if any, clicks.

The final purchase consideration is daily budget: the higher the budget, the higher the frequency with which your ad will be served when one of your keywords is searched. If you have a click budget of $1.00 per day your ad will not be served very often; but if your daily budget is $10.00, your ad could be served ten times as often.

Keyword Analysis

Analyzing keyword performance continuously and making adjustments in keywords, bids, and budgets is crucial to achieving a good ROI, and the search engines give you the kinds of data and analysis you need for that. Table 22-3 is a summary of keyword performance based on selected metrics—impressions, click through rate (CTR), number of clicks, cost per click, conversions, and cost per conversion. (You can review Internet metrics in Chapters 5 and 16.)

Table 22-3.—Puzzle of Buying Keywords, May 2011

Search Term	Imps (M)	CTR %	# Clicks	Cost/ Click	Total Cost	Conversions (%)		Cost/ Conversion
A	10000	5.5	500	$1.00	$500.00	50	(10.0)	$10.00
B	50000	1.0	500	0.75	350.00	10	(2.0)	35.00
C	100000	2.0	2000	1.20	2400.00	1500	(1.5)	80.00
D	200000	1.0	2000	0.50	1000.00	10	(0.5)	400.00

Studying Table 22-3, you will note that in May 2011, Keyword A was the most cost efficient with a cost per conversion of $10.00. However, it generated only 50 conversions, not enough to support a business. In contrast, Keyword D generated the most impressions at the lowest CPC, but its low conversion rate resulted in the highest cost per conversion.

Question: If you were armed with the data in Table 22-3 and you had a $5,000 budget, which keywords would you bid on and how much would you allocate to each?

CREATIVE—THE ADS

Assuming that you have selected keywords that your targeted audience is querying, the ad they see in the search results will determine whether interested surfers click on it and are redirected to your website. Like traditional creative, ads developed for the Internet keywords can vary substantially in their ability to generate clicks, so it is important to use effective ads. The following example of a CPC search ad is targeted to searchers selected for their interest in a new, low cost computer.

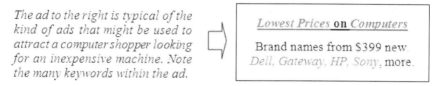

The ad to the right is typical of the kind of ads that might be used to attract a computer shopper looking for an inexpensive machine. Note the many keywords within the ad.

Lowest Prices **on Computers**

Brand names from $399 new. Dell, Gateway, HP, Sony, more.

Figure 22-2.—Strategic Use of Keywords in Internet Ad

Text ads accepted by CPC search engines are usually extremely short, so make every word count. You must capture the target's attention with an ad relevant to the search or query. The elements of an effective text ad on a CPC engine like Google include:

- **Headline**. Five words or less, including the keyword. A discount wine merchant directing an ad to wine aficionados using the search term *fine wines* might say, *Fine Wines, Low Prices*.

- **Supporting Copy.** Up to 10 words further describing the offering

- **Website Address.** Landing page/web address to which clickers will be redirected.

Caution: It is a mistake to write an ad that simply maximizes click-throughs. Since you are paying the same amount for every click, whether it is from a quality prospect or an indifferent browser, the ad should discourage casual surfers. For example, if you are selling a $70.00 book that contains valuable information not available elsewhere, put the price of the book in the ad to screen out low-potential clickers.

Question: Does the following ad meet the above criteria for headline, supporting copy, and website address?

> **Buy Fine Wines**
> Fine Wines at Lowest Prices.
> Expertly Screened, $0 Shipping.
> **www.TastyWinesDirect.com**

Question: Who would be most likely to click on this ad?

Advertisers plan and implement their CPC programs in a variety of ways, some more effective than others. Following are two general approaches: the *Shotgun* approach and the *Ad Group* approach.

Shotgun Approach: An advertiser using the shotgun approach to keyword selection and ad creation develops a long list of diverse keywords, then writes an ad (or two) to appear in search results for this generic list.

Ad Group Approach: Google recommends setting up several different *ad groups* within your CPC campaign, with each ad group directed to a different market segment. If you were a computer retailer, you could develop ad groups for different segments of the total market, as shown in the following hypothetical example

Table 22-4.—Hypothetical Ad Group Scheme

Element	Ad Group 1	Ad Group 2	Ad Group 3
Target	Serious/Professional	Gamers	Price Shoppers
Heading	Professional Grade	Game Speed	PCs From $200
Keywords	Powerful computer Business computer Advanced computer	Gaming computer Fast computer Graphics	Cheap computer Budget computer

The Ad Group Strategy of Table 22-4 shows three different ads targeted to three different targets using keywords appropriate to each target.

Question: Would shotgun or ad group be the most effective way to generate website visitors interested in new computer purchases? Why?

BUYING BANNERS & DISPLAY ADS

As alternatives or supplements to paid search, advertisers can buy *banners* or *display ads*, measured in *pixels* rather than inches, on most of the millions of websites that sell or trade ad space.

Display Advertising Options

Display ads are usually static, meaning that they do not include special movement effects or video (*rich media*). The many forms of rich media—tear backs, moving characters, floating ads, and all the video options—are beyond the scope of this text, but independent study is worth your while.

The regular creative options for Internet display advertising use the ad units standardized by IAB, which measures in pixels (dots of light) rather than inches. For example, a Leaderboard is 728x90 pixels, a short, wide rectangular shape.

Leaderboard (728x90 pixels)

The *Interactive Advertising Bureau* (*IAB*) has established the following standard ad sizes, ranked by the percentage of ad impressions each claimed in 2008. Leaderboards' ad impressions were down from 2006, while medium rectangle ads increased by 25%.

Table 22-5.—Ad Impressions by Most Popular Pixel Sizes

Standard Ads (pixels)	% Ad Impressions 2006	2008
Leaderboards (728x90)	31%	26%
Medium rectangles (300x250)	20	25
Full Banner (468x60)	15	16
Wide Skyscraper (160x600)	13	3
Skyscraper (180x150)	5	3
Large Rectangle (336x280)	2	3

Pricing

Pricing may be per click (CPC) or per thousand (CPM) impressions, more commonly the latter. Regardless, it is important that ad impressions be *target audience* impressions. The CPM impressions on a home page might be lower than on a special page, but the mass audience may result in a very high out of pocket cost when compared with a higher CPM for a section or page that zeroes in on your target audience.

To determine cost, especially on large websites, you have to determine where on the seller's website your ad should be positioned to reach and engage your target audience. If you were a travel company advertising on AOL, you might want your ad on a page in their travel section with a lot of destination guides and travel information.

Buying Banners & Display Ads

Websites on which ads may appear can be selected using contextual or behavioral targeting methodologies. Buyers may negotiate directly with individual website owners, Internet ad networks (media sales firms that represent thousands of website owners), or Internet Service Providers (ISPs) like AOL or Yahoo or ad exchanges. Each of these potential sellers is reviewed here.

Individual Website owners

In you are interested in highly targeted websites, such as those selling micro widgets, only a few sites may meet your needs, and you can deal directly with their owners. To identify potential sites, search the keywords you are interested in and make a list of the websites that look promising. Visit the sites and gather any information available about their advertising options. Then call or email site owners, sales representatives, or the network sales departments. Give them your buy specs, including timing, target audience, type of ad, and so on. Ask them for proposals. Compare the proposals you receive, negotiate further, and decide which to buy.

Service Providers

Like buying directly from individual website owners, advertisers can buy Internet advertising directly from service providers. For example, AOL offers a large variety of static displays, rich media, and video ads targeted to visitors on AOL's pages. Since April 2010, AOL has offered ad placement through a self-serve desk.

Prospective advertisers can gather information about a site's advertising opportunities by clicking on *Advertise with Us*. Large buyers may negotiate directly with sales reps for ads on AOL, Yahoo!, or other mega sites; smaller buyers may negotiate online or by telephone.

Advertising Networks

A third option, more suited to larger advertisers, is to work with one or more of the major online advertising networks. An online *advertising network* (or *ad network*) is a company that connects advertisers to host sites. Its key function is to acquire ad space from site owners and match it with advertiser demand. Online ad networks are similar to television or print ad networks, but the term is increasingly used to refer to online.

If your buy is extensive and you plan to reach your target through contextual or behavioral targeting, you will need to utilize ad networks that can make competitive proposals, including firms like Advertising.com, Google Display Network, Value Click, Microsoft Media Network, and Yahoo Network Plus. Here are two examples of ad networks that sell billions of dollars worth of advertising.

Advertising.com

The largest Internet ad network is *Advertising.com*, which claims to reach almost all Internet users on a daily basis with their member websites. If Advertising.com were pitching you for business, they would tell you:

- They conduct up to 10 billion transactions per day.
- They have been comScore's leading ad network for 6 years.
- They reach 91% of all US Internet users.
- They deliver target audiences. Their targeting systems deliver precisely the audience an advertiser wants at the scale it needs. While other networks may reach a potential customer once a month, they reach that until you get the results you need.
- Their technology includes AdLearn, an optimization and bid management system.
- They offer "the most comprehensive, flexible and accurate targeting options imaginable, and it'll show in your results. Not to get too technical, but its awesomeness is truly breathtaking…"

Google

Google is unique because its Adwords platform (for text ads) allows display advertisers to select keywords, maximum CPCs, and budgets. It also offers advertisers a free display ad builder tool to use within the Adwords system. Therefore, for advertisers who do not have professional display ads ready to run, Google makes it easy to create one using a Google template, uploading pictures and graphics, and revising at will.

Just like on Google Search, where text ads are matched to users' queries, the Google Display Network helps reach the right audience by automatically matching your ads to what users are reading online. Your ad group's keywords determine where your ads are displayed on the Display Network. Therefore, each ad group should have several keywords related to one another but varying within the theme. The closer the relationship between the keyword and your product, the more likely it is that your ad will find the right audience. Aim for about 5 to 15 keywords per ad group.

Ad Exchanges

Ad exchanges broker online advertising by bringing publishers and advertisers together to participate in auctions for ad space. Some examples of ad exchanges are Right Media Exchange (Yahoo!), DoubleClick Ad Exchange (Google), AdECN (Microsoft), and Contextweb Ad Exchange.

An ad exchange is a marketplace—set up like a NASDAQ for online ads—where publishers and advertisers can find and execute advertising transactions. Ideally, exchanges provide a system of controls to keep the community safe from harmful, objectionable content and create an open development structure that encourages innovation in the industry.

Similar to an Ad Network, an ad exchange represents a roster of websites. However, ad exchanges often have much lower entry requirements or even none at all, so there tend to be not only more sites but also more variable quality from more diverse content niches.

An ad exchange provides a platform where publishers, advertisers, and ad networks can buy and sell ad space using real-time bidding. Each impression is bid on separately and automatically to get the advertiser or ad network the lowest price available for the ad inventory they want to buy, and to get publishers the highest price offered for ad space they want to sell. The large ad inventory brings prices that are very attractive to advertisers while still offering publishers a way to monetize inventory they could not otherwise sell.

TEST, TEST, TEST

One of the biggest advantages of the Internet as an advertising medium is the ability to test and optimize almost everything, including creative, keywords, timing, targeting, and placement. *Testing* should measure *one variable at a time* systematically. Does ad performance vary by keyword? By headline? This is easily measured because Google will rotate different ads against the same list of keywords, so by changing only the headline in alternative ads, you can test headlines to find out which best generates impressions, clicks, or conversions. Then you can (if you want to) test alternative copy with the same headlines or test new keywords.

Creative testing can focus on the headline (see previous paragraph), ad themes, positioning, or copy. Is it more effective to include price or not to include price in your copy? Is it more effective to use a Buy Now statement or not? Is it more effective to include a promotional offer?

Given a set of keywords for a campaign or ad group, you can test the effectiveness of ads on CTR and conversions, and make running changes in your ad copy by keyword. Alternatively, with constant ad copy, the effectiveness of various keywords can be measured in impressions and CTR/visitors. By placing the appropriate code on your website, you can also track conversions and cost per conversion. Such data can help you continuously optimize the website traffic, conversions, and ROI of your Internet advertising campaigns.

SUMMARY

Buying advertising on the Internet is unlike buying time or space in other media, and your first task as an Internet buyer is to become expert in the particular form of advertising you want to purchase. Chapter 22 has introduced you in depth to the principal forms—display and search.

Targeting in traditional media is still a blunt instrument, but using the Internet, you can select your audience with precision, based on keyword search, contextual targeting, or behavioral targeting, all capable of being defined in detail. Keyword search matches ads to user curiosity, contextual targeting matches ads to website content, and behavioral targeting matches ads to user history.

Chapter 22 has explored how Internet advertising is typically bought and sold online, in an auction format, using one or more different pricing models: CPM Impressions, Cost per Click, or Cost per Action. You can buy from site owners or ISPs, through ad exchanges or ad networks, negotiating with sales representatives or making automated arrangements with computer programs.

Determining the cost effectiveness and ROI of Internet advertising is typically also much easier than determining similar metrics for traditional media. You can and must test the power of your creative, and you can and must measure the results of your campaign, in ways that are only possible on the Internet.

23. GUERILLA MEDIA BUYING

*Guerrilla media buying tactics can often
give every media dollar the impact of two.*

–Ron Geskey

Tight Budget? No Problem!

Advertisers can often extend their media buying power by shopping in unconventional ways, using guerrilla media buying techniques. Like the leveraging strategies presented earlier, certain guerilla techniques can get you a lot more advertising time and space for your money. Such techniques may be of special interest to smaller advertisers, although there is no reason that larger advertisers cannot benefit from them.

Chapter 23 will introduce you to cost saving techniques like cross platform buying, remnant buying, online auctions and bidding platforms, pay per inquiry, pay per sale, and media barter. Skillful use of these techniques can increase the power of your media budget.

CROSS PLATFORM BUYS

You have learned to buy individual media types—broadcast, print, and Internet. Large media conglomerates own an assortment of media properties that can be packaged to extend value for buyers and sellers. Sometimes it makes sense to negotiate a *cross platform buy* with a media conglomerate. Here are three examples.

Time Warner owns broadcast television and cable networks, cable systems, magazines (*Time*, *Sports Illustrated*), online services (AOL), book publishing, movie and television program production, music, entertainment venues, and even retail outlets. A large advertiser could negotiate a package deal with Time Warner to utilize several of their properties at significant cost savings.

Viacom owns television networks and stations, radio stations, outdoor companies, book publishing, movie and program production, entertainment venues, and retail outlets. You could set up product displays in Viacom's entertainment and retail venues supported with broadcast advertising or outdoor. You might also negotiate product placement in a Viacom movie or TV production.

Disney owns ABC, all the ESPN properties, television and radio stations, publishing, movie and television production, Disney World and Disney Land, music, and retail stores. A major promotion could offer trips to Disney World or Disney Land and communicate the promotion on some of Disney's media outlets, with related product placement in Disney movie or TV productions.

NBC, CBS, and Comcast are other media conglomerates worth investigating for cross platform advertising.

MEDIA REMNANTS

The basis of remnant space advertising is that media companies rarely sell all their advertising space. Their unsold ad space or time, called *remnant space*, can often be bought at steep discounts.

Like unsold airline seats or hotel rooms, advertising time and space are perishable; if not sold, they are lost or given away for public service or another non-revenue producing filler. Instead of taking a loss for unsold airtime or ad space, therefore, media outlets will often take far less than their usual retail fees to unload their remnant space. This means you can buy what is typically expensive media for much, much less than normal.

How best to use remnant space to your advertising advantage depends upon the medium.

Newspaper Remnant Space

Newspapers, because they are published daily and have a fixed format, offer frequent remnant space opportunities. One negotiating factor, especially important with newspapers, is your willingness to accept smaller remnant ads, because those may be what they need to fill out the paper. It also helps to have a good working relationship with your ad sales rep, who can let you know when remnant space is available.

Many firms offer to find newspaper remnants for you. Rather than going directly to newspapers yourself to seek remnant space, or if you are seeking space in many markets, you can work with firms that specialize in matching remnant buyers and sellers. Media Resources is a newspaper and online remnant supplier that reportedly maintains a database of over 1,300 newspapers across the country, and you can identify others with a brief search of *newspaper advertising remnants*).

Magazine Remnant Space

There are significant opportunities to buy remnant space in national and local magazines. National magazines print regional editions and sell regional ads. If they fail to sell all the regional ads (which is not uncommon), or if they sell an odd number, their unsold inventory could be your opportunity.

Even smaller magazines offer remnant advertising. Their editorial content is based partly upon the amount of advertising sold. Sometimes advertisers back out, go with smaller ads, or miss a deadline; sometimes the magazine ends up with extra content. Both create opportunity for you.

Similar to newspapers, if you are interested in magazine remnants, let your magazine sales reps know. The cleanest way to buy remnant space is from the magazine or its sales organization.

Alternatively, you can work with a company like PrintAdvertising.com, which compiles remnant opportunities for buyers and sellers. Remember, though, that all such firms work on commission, so *caveat emptor*!

Radio Remnant Time

Radio is ripe for remnant buys because, unlike print media, which can be expanded and contracted to a certain extent as needed, radio advertising is finite; there are a fixed number of spots in one hour. Thus, getting that unsold time at fire sale prices is certainly doable. Discounts can range from 25% to 75% off retail prices.

An easy way to get remnant radio time is to buy regular time at low negotiated prices. When you are ready to place the order, make it contingent on an equal number of free remnant spots.

Television Remnant Time

The ever-expanding proliferation of television options—network, cable, or satellite—is good news for the frugal TV buyer because it makes plenty of TV remnant space available at a fraction of the normal price. An agency veteran handling smaller and mid-sized clients said of television:

Not really a big deal to big companies. They often do tons of TV advertising and have huge budgets to accomplish such. However, it's a big deal for my clients—those companies of the small to mid-size. Why? Because there's a perception among advertisers and consumers that you're successful if you can afford to advertise on TV.

If remnant space makes sense to you, make yourself easy to work with. Because these ads come up at the last minute, media companies often just offer them to their larger advertisers, because those advertisers have ready budgets, ad departments that can create ads in a jiffy, and managers who can make decisions about as fast. If you want these sorts of opportunities to come your way, then you have to let your ad rep know you are interested and ready, earmark some money, and have ads approved and ready to go.

Online Remnants

Most big companies' online remnant advertising is sold to ad networks such as BurstMedia, which in turn offers remnant advertising to member publishers. Banner companies also buy publishers' remnant ads. The rate can be less than $1 CPM for banner ads that usually go for $5 CPM.

Remnant space is not easy to use because it is so last minute, but it can stretch your advertising dollar. If the opportunity arises, be prepared to grab it; it will certainly be cheap.

ONLINE MEDIA AUCTIONS & BIDDING PLATFORMS

Advertising auctions and ad bidding platforms are beginning to take off after a number of false starts. A lot of their inventory is remnants.

Bid4Spots.com

Bid4Spots.com is an online marketplace for radio stations to sell their unsold commercial inventory easily and confidentially. It's a weekly reverse auction where radio stations (sellers) do the bidding for the advertiser's (buyer's) budget, and spots selling for the lowest CPM win.

Mediabids.com

Mediabids.com is already the largest online auction house for print media. Advertisers can bid on available newspaper and magazine ad inventory or can initiate their own auction by making a bid for media not currently listed on the exchange.

If you're interested in bidding, select the market and circulation area, editorial focus, type of publication, and price point you want. Mediabids.com then provides the availabilities, along with a brief *media kit* on each of their media sponsors.

MediaBuys.com

MediaBuys.com positions itself as an online *media buying club.* To members, MediaBuys.com claims to offer pre-discounted inventory at 10-60% off rate card prices in all media (claims 3,500 availabilities), including television, radio, magazines, and newspapers.

MediaBuys.com offers media planning and even creative assistance at $100 per hour. If the ad inventory you want is not in their ad bank, you can fill out a quote form and receive media space estimates from what they refer to as thousands of competing media sources. They then offer to serve as your intermediary in bidding and purchasing.

RemnantRadio.com

Also called SoftWaveRadio.com, this bidding house solicits last minute inventory from radio stations. It promises buyers that they can buy spot radio that meets their requirements for markets, formats, and demographics, at a price they choose.

NOVEL PAYMENT MODELS

Per Inquiry

Per-inquiry advertising is rather simple and straightforward. Whereas with conventional direct response advertising, you risk spending money without a guaranteed cost per response, with per inquiry, you are guaranteed to pay only a fixed, pre-negotiated cost per response. Under this plan, a PI (per inquiry) firm would air your company's existing lead-generating commercial(s) on television networks, cable systems, and radio stations at a mutually agreed upon, guaranteed fixed cost per lead. If your company does not have an existing commercial, the firms can produce professional, customized commercials to be used to generate lead flow for your company. Obviously, the attractive part of utilizing per inquiry advertising is that your risk will be substantially reduced.

If your company has aired a direct response commercial, you have incurred a specific cost per lead. If you spent $10,000 on a radio campaign and received a thousand (1,000) leads, your cost per lead would have been $10. The per inquiry firm would air that same commercial at a mutually agreed upon fixed cost per lead that would be approximately 20% less than the cost per lead of your conventional media buy.

Pay per Sale Advertising

Online Advertising

Google and a few others are testing a new online advertising payment model—pay per sale, a major development in which payment is based solely on qualifying sales. In a pay per sale agreement, the advertiser *only* pays for sales generated by the destination site, based on an agreed commission rate.

Paying per sale is often seen as the payment model most favorable to advertisers and least favorable to publishers. In such an agreement, the publisher must not only be concerned with the quality and quantity of audience, but also quality of creative units and destination site.

If possible, publishers avoid sales-based agreements, preferring to stick to the CPM model. However, some publishers, facing weak ad sales, have little choice but to accept sales-based agreements to utilize remnant space—especially with Google as a competitor.

For advertisers, pay per sale has some unique advantages. There are fewer concerns about whether conversions are legitimate and whether traffic is incentivized or of low quality.

Direct Response Opportunities

Other companies in the direct response advertising industries offer various forms of *pay per action* payment models using traditional advertising media.

Bartering for Media

What is Barter?

A different way to buy media is to trade something you have for it. Barter is a simple transaction that trades products, goods, or services for other products, goods or services. Frequently no money is exchanged, or it is based on part trade, part cash. For example, a restaurant could trade meals for tickets to sporting events where clients could be entertained. An electronics manufacturer could trade unsold phones for advertising space in a trade publication specializing in the wireless industry.

Barter works best when you have a warehouse full of stuff you want to get rid of. Bartering problem or unsold inventories for advertising time and space can be a great guerilla media-buying strategy. If somebody is willing to trade desirable advertising time or space for something you have and don't need, a win-win is possible.

Barter price valuations are often based on the retail prices of the items being traded. Therefore, if you have $1000 (retail price) in merchandise or services and the merchandise cost you $500, you could theoretically barter for $1000 worth of advertising at $500.

How Barter Works

With barter, you can sometimes attract new cash customers who are also looking to barter. If you can trade $2,000 worth of tires (cost $1000) from inventory for $2000 worth of billboard exposure on a prime expressway, you might generate thousands of dollars in incremental cash sales. You could trade $3,000 worth of fax machines from inventory for newscast radio advertising that could generate thousands of dollars in new fax machine sales. You could trade $300 worth of pizzas for a mailing of 10,000 special offer coupons to homes in your area that will generate cash sales of hundreds of additional pizzas.

On a smaller scale, if you buy a 10" display ad in your strong local paper, you probably won't hurt effectiveness by cutting it down to an 8" ad. The same readers will still see you every week. Now, take that 20% savings and buy advertising in a strong local coupon mailer, multiplying your advertising's reach without increasing your budget...then barter for the coupon mailer. Don't be afraid to create variability in your budget and then play with it.

Direct Barter vs. Trade Exchanges

There are two ways to trade your products or services for media: go directly to someone who would be interested in trading with you or go through a trade exchange. First, you can contact media individually about a possible barter agreement. For example, if you own or represent a nice restaurant, a radio station might trade some time (that they probably wouldn't sell anyway) for business lunches to wine and dine some important media buyers.

Alternatively, you can work through a large trade exchange that has relationships with media and other types of companies. If you choose to work with a trade exchange, you will have to pay a fee to join and leave a percentage of your transactions on their table.

Caveat Emptor

If you pursue barter as a way to buy media, you have to be extremely careful in your dealings with a trade exchange. You must make sure they offer inventory that you want to buy, when you want it and where you want it. You must work through all of the numbers as if you were making a cash buy from media outlets.

SPONSOR A CALL FOR PROPOSALS

Sponsor a *call for proposals* to generate ideas and get media competing with each other. Develop a plan and guidelines that define what you want in a proposal. Like a buying spec sheet, this document will set forth your objectives for activity, target market, timing, budget, creative guidelines, and rationale.

Next, request competitive media to develop *turnkey* (ready to implement) media and promotion ideas for you. Media who wish to compete for your business will develop ideas, prepare proposal packages with costs, and submit them to you. Once you have seen all the submissions, develop a short list to make interactive presentations and field questions, then make your offers in order of preference. Buy one.

SUMMARY

Chapter 19 defined media buying and discussed the art of negotiation. Chapters 20-22 examined unique considerations for buying broadcast, print, and Internet media. Chapter 23 has introduced you to nonconventional—or guerrilla—media buying techniques and channels that complete your media buying repertoire. Do not underestimate the value of this last array of resources.

Cross platform buys with integrated media conglomerates open new integrated advertising and promotional opportunities and bring cost savings by creating integrated programs across a conglomerate's media properties. Media remnants of unsold time or space may be purchased for 50-80% below rate card prices if you are prepared when opportunity knocks. Online media auctions permit advertisers to bid, and barter can make sense if you have excess inventory. Other guerilla techniques to conserve budgets and increase media exposure include contracting with specialized intermediate agencies that get paid per inquiry or per sale (no results, no cost to you) and sponsoring RFPs that capitalize on inherent media egos and competition.

The unconventional media buying channels will bring you more bang for your client's buck. Media buyers are like other professionals: some are comfortable only on the beaten path, while others are willing to get out of the box in a quest for even better solutions. Every buyer's mission is to negotiate optimum media buys; your advantage will lie in the extra effort to use unconventional media tactics and channels.

SECTION V: FUTURE MEDIA

Nobody knows the future. Nobody can predict the future of advertising media. Anything can happen in a field already changing at breathtaking speed. An example is Apple's announcement of its iPhone replacement, which eliminated AT&T's exclusive rights to iPhone, stunned many consumers and marketers.

Population characteristics, metrics, and markets are changing, and media technologies for communicating with each other and with our markets are changing even faster.

Stay tuned. (Be sure to fasten your safety harness.)

24. THE FUTURE
The future of advertising is digital.

–Bill Gates

What is the future of advertising?

Future ads will be engineered to obtain audience information, with mined data immediately fueling message customization. The billboard at the street corner is watching you. A camera is embedded in the billboard, and a computer analyzes the passing public. It tells the advertiser how many persons walked in front of the screen, how many turned to face the ad, and how long each looked at it. It reads gender with 85% accuracy, and projects different ads to men and women.

Plans are underway to detect age differences and identify family groups. This intuitive digital advertisement exists, courtesy of Quividi, a French marketing technology firm. Consumer data is a valuable commodity that will influence businesses and their initiatives ever more as it becomes more comprehensive and more readily available.

It's already happening on the web. Internet services and media companies like Yahoo, AOL, and Google understand that effective contextualization of ad messages requires continuous accumulation and use of individual data.

Static ads are no longer enough to engage an audience besieged by a phalanx of signs. Holosonic, a US technology company has developed the Audio Spotlight, a system that fires a beam of sound into a small area from a distance of more than 60 feet. The effect, the company claims, is to startle and entertain pedestrians without being audible to anyone outside the zone. Can we expect 3-D soap packets, and jingles beamed into our heads as we commute to work?

THE FUTURE

Building on the Revolution described in Chapter 2, advertising will simply advance what marketers have always advocated: (1) ultra-targeted campaigns using messages customized to the interests of the audience, and (2) initiatives that build widespread buzz and natural viral recommendations among user networks and a broad general market.

487

The most significant change will be the improvement of both strategies with new technologies that enhance the *visibility, portability, and impact.* Ad campaigns will become desirable interruptions that preempt consumer needs with their exceeding relevance.

The success of viral videos online suggests a new advertising paradigm that depends on *user-generated media.* Businesses will come to understand how audience participation shapes their brands and messages. Campaigns will create avenues for consumer involvement; absolute control by the advertiser will be seen as neither necessary nor feasible.

Reverse engineer the future, and you'll see that businesses and entrepreneurs should start now to keep abreast of developments in technology and social channels that will help them understand their audiences. Consumers will always be attracted to messages that are highly relevant and interactively intriguing. Learn how to give them that.

WHY THE FUTURE OF ADVERTISING IS NOW

Booz Allen Hamilton identified five predictions for marketing, advertising, and media.

1. Momentum away from traditional media will accelerate as marketers move from impressions to relevance.

2. Consumers will move from captive to interactive as they get more information, more personalized content, and more control over their media consumption, causing traditional media to decline.

3. Digital video will usher in new advertising models as growth in broadband penetration improves video quality.

4. What matters is what will be measured, including consumer engagement and brand relevance measures.

5. Marketers will go to consumers directly, using their own proprietary research and their own entertainment assets, working with media on integrated cross-media platform opportunities.

Future of Advertising Agencies

The old model of developing traditional creative and buying media is obsolete. During the past century and a half, marketers have turned to agencies for both strategic and tactical support. These relationships evolved in response to changes in consumer behavior, technology and communications advances, and changes in agency relationships. Today, as technology becomes a key driver for marketing, we find that agencies have not kept up. To grow stronger, agencies must evolve faster and more dramatically than ever before, while new competition from consultants and technology firms arises to challenge their seat in the value chain.

No one is sure what the new agency business model should or will be, but the chairmen of two of the largest global agency holding companies, WPP and Publicis, advocate the role of *surrounding a problem or opportunity with multiple integrated solutions*. This is consistent with this book's vision of Integrated Marketing Communications.

Forrester Research recently polled 106 interactive marketers, and found only 22% believed their interactive shop could lead their brand, while just 24% thought traditional agencies could effectively head up their digital activity. This is not good news for agencies who have traditionally led their brands.

To reassert their leadership with clients, agencies must learn to deliver integrated marketing and digital media solutions effectively and efficiently, or they will die. WPP and Publicis advocate a *performance-based or profit sharing agency compensation plan* that will motivate the best possible work.

The Future of Television

Relax, advertisers, the :30 TV commercial is not going the way of the dinosaur quite yet. Future TV advertising, however, will be much more targeted, relevant, and interactive.

Targeted means *addressable*, with individualized messages capable of being sent simultaneously. Based on their profiles, part of a TV audience might receive a commercial for a new Corvette, while truck enthusiasts would receive a commercial for a shiny new full size pickup. Cable Systems Corp. is already rolling out technology that was used by the Army in targeting four different ads to different categories of viewers.

Relevance means that consumers more often will see TV commercials only for products that matter to them. Theoretically, the truck guy won't see commercials for Corvettes.

Interactive means that the promise of iTV is just around the corner. You've waited all day to come home and relax. Now you're finally sitting on the couch with your feet propped up on the coffee table (as Mom told you not to do) watching your favorite football team. Life is good. Then a little *i* pops up on your screen. What's that? It's interactive television!

You've seen commercials for Clorox and Purina Puppy Chow. Now you can see those commercials and get coupons at the same time. The interactive screen gives you options to accept or decline an advertiser's special offer. After seeing a Pizza Hut commercial, you want to order a pizza? Go ahead.

With iTV, you also can play along with game shows, vote in live polls, learn trivia tidbits, get game stats, and purchase items just by pushing a button on your remote control. You think control of the remote is a battle now? You ain't seen nuthin' yet!

Some skeptics aren't buying the smart iTV concept, although recent numbers disprove the claims that there's no market for iTV. For example, during a Melissa Etheridge concert, 46 percent of viewers clicked through to learn more about a CDnow.com discount.

WebTV is doing its best to speed up the switch. They recently introduced their new click-to-video ads. When WebTV subscribers click on a banner ad, they view a full-screen, full-motion commercial for the advertiser's product and then go to that company's Website.

Advertisers can submit their current banner ads and TV commercials, and WebTV Networks will convert their materials to the new advertising product. Some of the current click-to-video advertisers are Ford, Maytag, Hewlett-Packard, and Volvo Cars of North America.

Future of Radio

Today you get radio over the air, via satellite, through cable, on PDAs, and by cell phone. Over the air, terrestrial radio is in big trouble as advertising expenditures plummet. HD radio doesn't look like it will save the medium. The only bright spot is that ad expenditure for online radio is growing, but it is still a small percentage of the total.

In order to survive, terrestrial radio will probably have to converge with other forms of broadcasting and create more unique and thematic content, while enhancing current strengths with the power of new media technologies. Future radio will offer more interactive formats, allowing listeners themselves to host and DJ. Tools and programming space for audiences to create, edit, and compile their own audio-based programming would provide interactivity, like iTV.

Will interruptive commercials vanish? Give them up! Future radio advertising calls for a new branding experience that already makes it easier for commercials to break through the extraordinary clutter in radio.

Podcasting could increase relevance with very specific kinds of music, news, or commentary instead of the current content that has to appeal to as large an audience as possible. New radio will have to have a strong focus or theme.

Perhaps radio's future is also tied to the ever-more-indispensible cell phone. The cell phone is extremely portable and could be heir to the transistor radio, which revitalized radio in the 1960s. The convergence of wireless technology, content, and small size could make the cell phone just the thing for radio at the beach, especially if satellite programming and streaming Internet radio were part of the package.

Future of Magazines

Magazines in general can be expected to survive the Internet. As to individual magazines, it will be survival of the fittest. General interest magazines will not survive, newsweeklies probably won't. Magazines serving niche audiences can survive in a combination of print and online. However, readers may be expected to pay more as publishers cease their drive to generate more (expensive) circulation just for ad sales.

Print and online magazines will likely be *separate products*, each with its own business model and profit accountability. The business press will become more adept at using the web.

Magazines will be multi-platform. Readers will access content in different channels and in different ways. Print will still play a flagship role for most magazine enterprises, but there will be a continued drive to expand existing channels including print magazines and newsletters, digital magazines and e-newsletters, mobile, Websites, blogs, podcasts, virtual events, and video.

Research Brief reported a recent study entitled *Going Mobile: How Publishers Are Preparing for the Burgeoning Digital Market*, which stated that 70 percent of publishers are paying more attention to the mobile market this year than last. More specifically, 42 percent of consumer magazines and 45 percent of business publishers are formatting websites for mobile viewing.

The challenge will be to determine how to reach readers in all platforms efficiently while staying loyal to the brand and to core competencies. Don't underestimate the challenge. Digital media require significant investment in hardware, services, and specialized personnel.

Future of Newspapers

In the mid 1990s, newspapers saw themselves in the paper business rather than the news business. Newspapers did not invest heavily in digital ventures to create additional channels for providing locally relevant content. Now, saddled with huge costs and debt, and revenues that have declined 40% over the past four years, newspapers are in a death spiral, and content is getting thinner and thinner as audiences get smaller and smaller. The Detroit *News and Free Press* has reduced home delivery to three days a week, while attempting to sell subscribers Internet access to the daily newspaper.

Like a restaurant in financial difficulty that reduces food quality or portion size, and ends up losing its customer base, newspapers may also be on the route to a self-fulfilling prophesy. As they struggle to cut costs by eliminating reporters and writers and distribution, they risk further loss of their already declining customer base.

Newspapers have obviously lost their original raison d'être, because they cannot deliver news anymore. Television, radio, and the Internet report news instantly and constantly; newspapers report today's news tomorrow, with no update until the day after tomorrow.

Newspapers must redefine their role to survive in a world of digital media. For example, should printed newspapers focus only on local news and information not available elsewhere? Should they morph into commentary, offering thoughtful and in-depth content like the *Wall Street Journal* does? Editorially, the Achilles heel for newspapers has been the perception of liberal political bias that has contributed to loss of readers and doesn't bode well for its future survival as an instrument of commentary.

If newspapers develop separate products for print and Internet, how will they complement each other? What will readers buy?

Many believe that Newspapers have always been the dinosaurs of the communications industry. For example, although they never figured out why they couldn't generate more national advertising revenues, they continued the self-destructive practice of charging 100%+ rate premiums to national advertisers who even supplied them with ready to print materials. If you go to the Newspaper Advertising Association (NAA) website to learn their insights into the future of newspapers, you may find an article, but you can access it only if you are an NAA member. Collecting $1.50 is apparently more important to the NAA than educating buyers about newspapers.

Future of Internet Advertising

Trying to predict the future of the Internet is like trying to predict the future of technology and the next big idea that nobody has thought of yet. However, it is probably safe to say that the short- and intermediate-term future of Internet advertising will likely see the continuation and growth of trends already underway: convergence of the Internet with virtually all other media; greater interaction between buyers and sellers; proliferation of wireless mobile applications, social media networks, and video-gaming; and improved search technology.

Content: Content and who pays for it are major issues for online and traditional media alike. A recent Forrester Research report stated that 80% of U.S. consumers would not pay for online content. Another survey by BCG showed that most respondents would pay a maximum of $3 per month for online paid subscriptions. What this means is that brands must be built through endless supply of content and free distribution systems.

Social Media: A survey by VerticalResponse, Inc. found that 68% of small businesses plan to increase social media marketing. In the future, your own content will spread on multiple locations more rapidly than you can imagine. That is why your website content needs to be nested in as many content aggregation sites as possible. Social media, RSS/blog directories, and influential websites should be your main target. Why is this important? Picture this: If you have a video on your website that is not on YouTube, YouTube's viewers will not bother searching for it because they simply do not need to. For them, YouTube already represents the total number of videos available on their topic of interest. The *Thank You Economy* by Gary Vaynerchuk (March 2011) provides a compelling argument for the ROI of social media/marketing.

Video: Online video will keep growing. It is interactive, memorable, widely accessible, cheap to create, and highly shareable. That is why entrepreneurs and business owners are willing to invest even more in video. Pre-roll ads will continue to dominate online video advertising. No innovations from Hulu, YouTube, or Vivaki will prove as effective as a :15 or :30 coupled with a companion ad.

SEO: Historically, SEO has focused on improving website traffic by rising in the search results. Some now believe that *conversion rate optimization* will dominate SEO in the future. Still the most under-utilized and highest ROI, conversion rate optimization will reach more awareness, and brands will focus on improving conversion over time. Consider that if website traffic is constant and the conversion rate increases by 20%, sales increase by 20% with almost no incremental expense.

Future of Outdoor

What is the future of outdoor advertising? Part of the answer to the question is obvious and part is maybe not so obvious.

The development and introduction of digital outdoor boards saved the outdoor industry. The obvious future involves the expansion of high definition, bright LED digital-video billboards. Advertiser demand has exceeded the supply of digital boards, which are now being deployed in larger numbers in the largest DMAs and in premiere highway exposure.

Since changes in advertising copy can be made instantly on any or all of these boards, they also offer high flexibility and the ability to talk differently to different customers in different locations. A gas station could instantly change its advertised price per gallon, a restaurant could change its menu feature, or a car company could change its featured vehicle.

Perhaps we have just entered the era of greater customization of outdoor boards. Back in 2007, Mini Cooper tested a campaign that brought outdoor customization to a whole new level. Since Mini owners often customize their vehicles down to a fine point, Mini wondered if they could deliver personalized messages that owners would receive as they passed by their local billboard. Mini requested participation from owners who supplied personal information that was loaded onto an RFID- (Radio Frequency Identification) enabled key fob that test subjects attached to their key chains. As participants cruised past a specific billboard, a reader within the board identified that person' key fob, and an individualized statement was posted on the board.

Now, in 2010, IBM UK is taking this idea a step farther and working on a technology to turn digital billboards into RFID readers. They are capitalizing on the fact that most credit cards and mobile phones now have built-in RFID chips that house all of your personal information. The idea is similar to Mini's; a reader inside the board will identify you, perhaps by name, and deliver an advertisement personal to you.

IBM says that this technology would benefit both consumers (from being bombarded with irrelevant messages) and advertisers who could improve advertising effectiveness and ROI. For example, a grocery chain could use this technology to serve up ads for the products that you most frequently purchase or showcase deals at the store where you frequently shop. An airline could serve communications to a specific consumer who makes frequent trips to a particular city, touting their rates compared to those of their competitors.

Obviously, there is major concern that this technology is a heavy-duty invasion of privacy. Do consumers really want brands to be able to see what kind of toilet paper they buy and then post it on a digital billboard? It will probably be awhile before we see this technology rolled out in a form usable by marketers without being overly invasive.

Finally, is outdoor going to be an interactive medium? Starting in March 2011, European wireless operator Orange will run a campaign in London and New York that will allow consumers waiting at a bus stop to hold a Smartphone near an Orange poster to download their app over WiFi. Other companies are beginning to offer similar interactive outdoor opportunities.

Virtual Screens

Several agency networks are working to develop *virtual media* using technologies that recognize faces, expressions, gestures, and sometimes even individuals. This technology can be used for sophisticated outdoor boards that spot consumers who are paying attention to them, and the retail applications are enormous.

Imagine looking in a store window at a poster/mirror-like device that can show you what you would look like in a new Gucci gown. American Eagle Outfitters used the technology to allow children to stand in front of a digital screen and try on a virtual outfit.

Many consumers will get their first look at the technology with Microsoft's motion sensor gaming device called Kinect (November 2011 introduction).

When you began your tour of Media Planning & Buying for the 21st Century, you knew you were entering a wonderful world. As the century unfolds and media development races forward, that world becomes more and more wonderful and exciting. Welcome to the race.

SUMMARY

Most of the future of advertising hasn't been invented yet. Chapter 24 has provided some predictions, some obvious, some perhaps not so obvious, some fantastic. The most important driver of change in the 21st century is consumer control over media and message consumption. We haven't even scratched the surface of learning how to engage consumers with media buys and messages.

Other factors shaping the future include technology and the changing face of America. Amazing new technologies create new and better ways to communicate; convergence of television and the Internet opens new horizons; the long awaited promise of interactive media is coming true. America's demographic and geographic shifts will redefine target audiences and advertising priorities.

There are more questions than answers, none more important than this: how can we plan and execute Integrated Marketing Communications? How do advertising and marketing communications works? How do we develop meaningful metrics for evaluating ROI? These questions will not go away. They are becoming more important. Will it be you who comes up with some answers?

Finally, it is believed that the winners in the 21st century will be those who are the first to learn, and experiment with new technologies before they are widely adopted.

GLOSSARY

AA – Average Audience rating. The average number or percentage of homes of persons viewing during the average minute.

ABC – Audit Bureau of Circulation. Audits the circulation figures claimed by print media

Adjacency – Commercial is positioned next to a program or between programs.

ADS – Alternative Delivery System to wired cable such as satellite

Adstock – Research that found that advertising has residual effects

Addressable Media – Precisely targeted media

Arbitron – Leading media research company that measures radio audiences and performs custom research.

Audience – Persons exposed to an advertising medium

AQH – Average Quarter Hour rating.

Behavioral Targeting – Targets surfers based on their behavior when visiting websites

Bandwidth – Capacity of communication line to carry information.

Bonus Spot – A free spot from network/station.

Barter – Trading goods or services for media time or space

Billboard – A brief sponsor-identifying announcement (e.g., "Brought to you by...")

Blog – Short for Web Log. Online journal or newsletter, frequently updated.

Business-to-Business – Communication by one business to other businesses

Business to Consumer – Communication from business to end consumers

BPA – Business Publications Audit. Company that verifies the circulation of business and trade publications.

Broadband – Transmission frequency that supports wide frequency range.

B/W – Black and white print ads.

C3 Ratings – Ratings based on commercial audience, adjusted for DVR playbacks

Cable TV – Television programming distributed to subscribing households though cables.

Circulation – In print media, the number of copies printed and distributed.

Clearance – Station's agreement to clear a network program.

Click-through Rate – Percentage of internet impressions who click thru to web site.

Closing Date – Date by which advertiser must contractually commit for print ad space.

Communications Planners – Those who plan integrated marketing communications program usually s involving forms beyond advertising

Consumer Promotion – Purchase incentives such as coupons, rebates, sweepstakes

Continuity Scheduling – Relatively consistent scheduling of advertising across years

Contextual Targeting – Matches ad with content or key words on websites

Convergence – the coming together of two or more things, like television and the internet

Consumer Control – New technologies have given consumers increased control over their media consumption through on demand, DVRs, etc.

Conversion Rate – Percentage of website visitors take action, such as purchasing

Cost per Acquisition – Payment model paying "X" per sales or inquiry.

Cost per Click – In paid Internet search, the amount advertisers agree to pay for a click through to their website.

497

Cost per Point –Broadcast cost to reach 1% of a universe such as total US households.
Coverage – Area in which media vehicles are distributed; potential audience
CPC – Abbreviation for Cost per Click.
CPM – Cost per Thousand circulation or impressions. CPM = Cost/Audience x 1000. Used to compare the cost efficiency of media vehicles.
CPP – Abbreviation for Cost per Point.
Cross Media Platform - A media property, service, story, or experience distributed across media platforms using a variety of media forms.
CTR - Click-through rate (%)
Cume – Cumulative audience, e.g., 1 issue might reach 5% of a target while 4 issues might cume to 10% of the target.
Custom Publishing – Usually a company publishing magazine/newsletter on demand.
Customer Relationship Management (CRM) – Communications programs intended to nurture relationship between company and customers
Digital Outdoor Board – High impact digital/electronic board permitting running copy changes.
Direct Marketing – Any marketing activity that sells direct to the consumer via print ads, broadcast, direct mail, telemarketing, internet, etc.
DMA – Designated Market Area (Nielsen defines 211 different DMAs).
Effective Research – Media theory that audience must be reached with frequency
Engagement – Trying to get consumers involved in the brand message
DSL – Digital Subscriber Line, filters out noise, connects at higher speed.
E-Commerce - Trade conducted on the Internet.
Email - Electronic mail, commonly called email or e-mail, is a method of exchanging digital messages from an author to one or more recipients.
Experian-Simmons – A large marketing and media research firm.
Experiential Marketing – Multi dimensional marketing—engages consumers with experiences, actions, emotion, increase engagement, e.g. event sponsorships
Eyes On – New outdoor audience measurement methodology that attempts to more accurately measure exposure to outdoor locations
Fixed Position – a broadcast spot purchased to run in a particular program and time. Not subject to normal pre-emption policies.
Flighting – Running advertising in a series of bursts
Fragmentation – Audiences divided into more pieces due to proliferation of media choices
Frequency – The average number of times an audience is reached by media vehicles.
FTP – File Transfer Protocol, method to move files to a server.
Gas Station TV – TV monitors at certain gas stations containing programming & ads
GRP – Gross Rating Point, equal to reaching 1% of a universe.
HUTS/PUTS – Percentage of households or persons watching TV or listening to radio at a particular day/time.
Impressions – Number of gross (duplicated) exposures to one or more media vehicles.
Infomercial - a long (more than two minutes) commercial providing extensive product/service description and sales information, usually direct response.
Internet Ad Network – Represent site owners to advertisers for purpose of selling display advertising & banners.

Interactive Media – Media that allow two-way communication, e.g., interactive TV, social media

Internet Ad Exchanges - A marketplace for buying and selling internet impressions

Intra Media Comparison – Comparing media vehicles in the same class

Inter Media Comparison – Comparing classes of media, e.g., television vs. radio

Keywords – Words internet visitors use to describe what they are looking for

MARCOM – Marketing Communications (all forms)

Marketing Services Media – Media beyond traditional advertising such as trade & consumer promotion, product placement, event marketing, direct marketing, etc.

Media Audit – Media & market research for top markets in US

Media Buying – The process of negotiating media purchases

Mediamark (MRI) – A leading single source marketing/media research company.

Media Mix – the combination of different media being used, e.g., TV & magazines

Media Planner – Someone who develops media plans

Media Planning – The process of strategically developing a marketing focused media plan

Mobile Marketing – Marketing using a mobile device such as a cell phone

MPA – Magazine Publishers Association, a trade organization promoting magazines.

Multi Media - Media and content that uses a combination of different content forms.

NAA – Newspaper Advertising Association, a trade organization promoting the use of newspapers.

National Rating – Rating based on a total US universe.

Network Affiliate – Station that is part of a network such as ABC, CBS, Fox, NBC and carries network programming.

Nielsen Media Research – The leading media research company that measures network and local market television audiences (ratings).

Open Rate – In print the highest rate against which discounts are based. Usually applies if very few insertions are planned.

Opt In – Individuals who request to be included on certain e-mail lists to receive a newsletter or other information.

Opt Out – Individuals request that their name and e-mail address be eliminated from an e-mail list. :"Do not send me more e-mails!"

P4C/P2C/PB/W – abbreviation for coloration of ads: page four-color, page two color, page black and white.

Paid Inclusion – Pay search engine to include URL near the top of their listings.

Pay per Action – Ad payment model where a website visitor must not only click on the URL link but must also make a purchase or request information (take an action).

Pay per Click (PPC) – Same as Cost per Click.

Piggyback – Two spots run back to back in network or spot positions.

Podcasting – Delivers audio to iPods & other mobile media players

Pod Position – TV commercial's position in a string of commercials, e.g., 1st vs. last

Poster (outdoor) – Outdoor board found on main streets in metro areas, smaller than a bulletin, usually printed on paper.

Press Release – News story sent to media in order to obtain publicity

Product Placement – Product exposure obtained by using product in movie or TV show.

Publicity – Information used to affect people's perceptions

Proliferation (media) – Rapid growth in media options and choices.

Pulsing – Continuous advertising scheduling combined with periodic heavy up periods

PVR – Personal Video Recorder, also DVR

Primary Reader – Persons & their families who purchased a publication.

Purchase Funnel – Stages consumers go through from awareness to eventual purchase

RAB – Radio Advertising Bureau, a trade organization promoting the use of radio for advertising.

Radio Format – Classification of radio stations by the type of programming broadcast, e.g., news and talk format vs. top 40 music format.

Rate Base – Guaranteed circulation for a given advertising rate.

Rate Card – A document produced by media that details their advertising rates, discount structures, materials requirements, etc.

Rating – Percentage of a universe viewing or listening to a media vehicle at a particular time.

Rating = Share x HUTS – Formula for calculating or projecting a rating.

Reach – The number or percentage of different target audience persons exposed 1+ times to media vehicles carrying ad message; also called net reach

Recency – Media theory which advocates maximizing daily/weekly reach

Re-Directs - A page which has no content itself, but sends the reader to another article, page, etc.

Remnants – unsold advertising time or space that can often be purchased at a large discount

Rich Media – Advanced technology used in Internet ads to create special effects, streaming video, interactive features.

Roadblocking - a scheduling technique where a brand's commercial airs at approximately the same time on all three networks or on all stations in a given market.

ROI – Return on Investment.

ROP – Run of paper; print publication places ad where they have open space.

ROS/ROP – Run of Schedule or Run of Paper, broadcast or print media run commercial/ad where it suits them.

Rotary Bulletin – Large outdoor board that rotates through a variety of locations. Usually cheaper than permanent bulletin in prime location.

Sales Promotion – incentives given to the trade or consumers

Scarborough – Media and marketing research in top 70 markets

Scatter – Short term broadcast buys made after up front market is over.

Search Engine Marketing (SEM) – Also called paid search. Involves bidding on keywords. When users search the keywords, your ad may be displayed by the search engine. Users who click on your ad are redirected to your website.

Search Engine Optimization (SEO) – Process of improving visibility of website to the search engines.

Share – The percentage of audience currently viewing/listening who are tuned to a particular program.

Share of Voice – An advertiser's share of total advertising expenditures.

Shouting - TYPING IN ALL CAPITAL LETTERS IS CONSIDERED SHOUTING IN ONLINE COMMUNICATIONS. Avoid this unless you really mean to shout.

Slotting Fees – Special fees chains may charge marketers in exchange for distribution and shelf space.

SMSA – Standard Metropolitan Statistical Area ("metro area").

Spam - to send a message (usually an advertisement) to many discussion groups (bulletin boards, mailing lists, etc.

Sponsorship – Placement of multiple messages on a media property, broadcast, print, website in order to build an association with the property

Standard Rate & Data Service(SRDS) – Source for media rates

Social Media – Media functioning through social interaction, e.g., Facebook.

Spill In - the amount of programming viewed within a market area to stations that are licensed to an adjacent market (DMA).

Street Furniture – out of home advertising on benches and other "furniture."

TAB -Traffic Audit Bureau (outdoor) audits vehicle and vehicle traffic which flows by out of home advertising locations.

Sweeps - the four 4-week periods when all TV markets are measured by Nielsen and Arbitron for station viewing and demographic information. Sweep months are February, May, July and November

Task Matching – Process of matching communication tasks with communications forms

Telemarketing – Marketing by telephone, inbound and outbound

Test Marketing – The process of testing a plan in a limited number of test markets. Used to reduce risk of launching plan without testing it first.

Thumbnail Media Planner – Source for media data and costs

TRP = Target Rating Point (1% of a target universe).

TVB – Television Bureau of Advertising, an industry organization that promotes the use of television for advertising.

Trade Promotion – Allowances given to the trade in exchange for distribution, displays,, etc.

Traffic Audit Bureau (TAB) – Obtains counts vehicle and passenger traffic to use in outdoor audience measurements

Unique Visitor –Unique IP addresses visiting website for first time.

Upfront Market – Long term buys usually made in late spring.

URL – Uniform Resource Locator, identifies a website address

Virtual Screens - Allows user to create virtual images, e.g., in a store window you could see yourself with a new suit of clothes

Waste Circulation – Audiences reached who are not part of target market.

Zapping – Changing channels during commercials or fast forwarded through commercials in recorded programs

WEB MEDIA RESOURCES

URL	Description
aaaa.org	American Association of Advert. Agencies
aaf.org	American Advertising Federation
adage.com	Advertising Age magazine
adweek.com	Adweek Magazine
ana.net	Association of National Advertisers
arbitron.com	Arbitron Research
arf.org	Advertising Research Foundation
buyyellow.com	Yellow Pages Association
cab.org	Cable Advertising Bureau
census.gov	U.S. Census Bureau
claritas.com	Prizm and other segmentation services
conferenceboard.org	Consumer confidence data
experian.com	Experian/Simmons Market Research Bureau
gfkmri.com	Mediamark Research (new site)
iab.org	Internet Advertising Bureau
iaaglobal.org	International Advertising Association
jackmyers.com	Jack Myers Consulting (media/IMC)
marketingpower.com	American Marketing Association
mediaaudit.com	Syndicated marketing/media research
medialifemagazine.com	Media Life Magazine
mediapost.com	Media Post Magazine
mediaweek.com	Mediaweek Magazine
mediabuyerplanner.com	Media Planner/Buyer Online Magazine
mpa.org	Magazine Publishers Association
mri-plus.com	Magazine data and costs
naa.org	Newspaper Advertising Association
nielsen.com	Nielsen Media Research/Ratings
oaab.org	Outdoor Advertising Association
rab.org	Radio Advertising Bureau
scarbough.com	Syndicated marketing/media research
srds.com	Standard Rate & Data Service
sqad.com	Broadcast media costs
the-dma.org	Direct Marketing Association
thumbnailmediaplanner.com	Statistics and costs for all major media
tvb.org	Television Bureau of Advertising
warc.com	World Advertising Research
zapit.com	Broadcast & Cable ratings

BIBLIOGRAPHY

BOOKS & SECTIONS

Aaker, David, *Managing Brand Equity*, Free Press, 1991

Abratt, R. , and P. S. Grober. "The Evaluation of Sports Sponsorship" *International Journal of Advertising* 8 (1989): 351-62.

Association of National Advertisers, *How Much to Spend on Advertising*, 1969

Azzaro, Marian, *Strategic Media Decisions*, The Copy Workshop, 2009

Baker, David. *Share of Voice and Other Vital Metrics*, 2007

Battelle, John, *The Search, How Google and its Rivals Rewrote the Rules of Business and Transformed Our Culture,* Portfolio, 2005

Bonner, Kaitlin , "The Next Wave of Marketing: Relevancy to Personalization?" www.Mullen.com, September 2010

Broadbent, Simon, *Advertising Effects: More than Short Term*, NTC Publishers, 1993

Calder, Bobby J., *Kellogg on Advertising Media*, John Wiley, 2008

Cappo, Joe, *The Future of Advertising*, Advertising Age, 2003

Claritas, *PRIZM, The Integrated Marketing Solution.*

Clear Channel Outdoor, "TAB's Eyes On Methodology," www.clearchanneloutdoor.com, 2011

Covey, Stephen. *The Seven Habits of Highly Successful People*. Free Press, 2004

Cronin, Mary, *Doing Business on the Internet, How the Electronic Highway is Transforming American Companies,* VNR, 1994

Cutlip & Center, *Effective Public Relations*, Prentice Hall,

Davis, John, *Magic Numbers for Consumer Marketing, Prentice hall,* 2005

Donnelly, William, *Planning Media, Strategy and Imagination*, Prentice Hall, 1996

Ephron, Erwin, "Recency," Ephron on Media Newsletter, 1998

Farris, Paul W.,et.al., *Marketing Metrics: 50+ Metrics Every Executive Should Master*, Prentice Hall, 2010

Garreau, Joel, *The Nine Nations of North America*, Avon, 1981

George, David, the ABC of SEO, *Search Engine Optimization Strategies*, Lulu Press, 2005

Geskey, Ronald D., *David vs. Goliath: Guerrilla Media Buying for Small Business, a New Way to Win*, 2007

Geskey, Ronald D. *Free Marketing in Social Media: 500 Tactics and Best Practices*, 2010

Geskey, Ronald D., *How to Really Buy Spot* TV, AdMediaStore.com, ed. 2, 2009

Geskey, Ronald D. *Media 101*, AdMediaStore.com, ed. 2, 2007

Geskey, Ronald D, 2011 *Thumbnail Media Planner*, 2020:Marketing Communications LLC 2011.

Geskey, Ronald D. *Strategic Media Planning*, 2020:Marketing Communications LLC 2007.

Geskey, Ronald D., *Recency Planning: Revisited*, AdMediaStore.com, 2005

Geskey, Ronald D., *Effective Reach: Revisited*, AdMediaStore.com, 2005

Hall, Robert, *Media Math*, NTC Business Books, 1987

Jaffe, Joseph, Life After the 30-Second Spot, Adweek, 2005

Karrass,Chester, *In Business You Don't Get What You Deserve, You Get What You Negotiate*, Stanford Street Press, 1996

Katz, Helen, The Media Handbook, 3rd ed., Routledge, 2010

Kernak, Al., *PuttiTng Your Business Online*, Self Published, Ed. 2, 2005

Bibliography

Knowledge Networks/SRI, "Engagement for Advertising Effectiveness," Spring 2006, www.knowledgenetworks.com

Clancy, Kevin and Shulman, Robert, *The Marketing Revolution*, A Radical Manifesto, Harper Business, 1991

Kobs, Jim. *Profitable Direct Marketing*. 2nd ed. NTC Business Books, 1992.

Lewis, Herschell Gordon. *Direct Marketing Strategies and Tactics*. Dartnell, 1992.

McKenna, Shawn, *The Complete Guide to Regional Marketing*, Irwin, 1992

Miller, Rachel. "Getting Big Results from a Small Spend." *Marketing.* September 7, 2000.

"Mobile Marketing Guide", *Advertising Age*, 2010

Naples, John, *Effective Frequency*, Association of National Advertisers (ANA), 1979

Plummer, Joe, et.al., The *Online Advertising Playbook*, John Wiley, 2007

Rasiel, Ethan, *The McKinsey Way*, McGraw Hill, 1998

Samli, A. *Up Against the Retail Giants*, Thomson, 2004

Schultz, Don & Barnes, Beth, *Strategic Advertising Campaigns*, 4th ed. Lincolnwood, IL: NTC Publishing. 1998

Schultz, Patti and and Kitchen, *The Evolution of Integrated Marketing Communications*: The Customer Driven Marketplace, 2011

Schultz, Don & Tannenbaum, Stanley I. . *Essentials of Advertising Strategy*. Lincolnwood, IL: NTC Publishing, 1998

Schmitt, Bernd, *Experiential Marketing*, Free Press, 1999

Scott, David, *The New Rules of Marketing and PR*, John Wiley, 2007

Sewell, Carl, *Customers for Life*, Double Day.

Sissors, J. and Baron, R. *Advertising Media Planning*, 7th Ed, McGraw Hill, 2010

507

"Social Media Buyers Guide," Internet Advertising Bureau (IAB). 2010

Stone, Bob. *Successful Direct Marketing Methods.* 4th ed. NTC Business Books, 1989.

Surmanek, Jim, *Introduction to Advertising Media*, NTC Books, 1993

Various authors, "The Digital Issue," Advertising Age, Feb. 28, 2011

Thornley, Joseph, *What Is Social Media? Published 2008,* www.thornleyfallis.ca

Vaynerchuck, Gary, *The Thank You Economy*, HarperBusiness, 2011

Volmer, Christopher, *Always On, Advertising, Marketing, and Media in an Era of Consumer Control*, Booz Allen Hamilton, McGraw Hill, 2008

Wells, Moriarity & Burnett, *Advertising Principles & Practice*, Prentice Hall, 2009

Wall Street Journal

Online sources

INDEX

Adstock, 162
Advertising, 85270
    Expenditures, 22, 24
    Messages, 4
Affiliate marketing, 313, 319
African American Market, 65, 197
Arbitron, 51, 89, 106
ARF Response Model, 154
Article Submissions, 313, 317
Asian Market, 65, 198
Association of National Advertisers
    (ANA), 42, 55, 160
Auctions, media, 474, 480
Audience Concepts, Ch., 5
    Attentiveness, 153
    Advertising Audience, 88, 152
    Average Issue Audience,   98
    Broadcast Audience
      GRPS
      HUTS/PUTS, 91-92
      Rating, AA   89
      C3 rating,
      Rating, TA 90
      Share of Audience,
      TRPS
    Circulation, 86
    Coverage, 85-87
    Sales response, 153
    Vehicle Exposure, 152
    Effective Reach, 97, 158
Banner Ads, 480
Barter for media, 484
Behavioral targeting, 473
Blogs, 332
Blogger, 337
Boomers, 64, 192
Branded entertainment, 244
Brand development index, 217, 369
Broadcast Buying, Ch. 18
    Audience guarantees, 411, 423
    Billboards, 422

Broadcast Buying continued
    Fixed rate, 409
    Commercial positioning, 441
    Guerrilla media buying, Ch. 23
    Long term buying, 409
    Makegoods, 440
    Opportunistic buying, 422
    Pre-emptible rate, 418
    Pre-emptions, 411
    Competitive proximity, 415
    Cable television, 7, 425
    Program selection, 275, 420
      Rotators, 423
      Run of schedule (ROS), 421
      Scatter, 410
      Supply & Demand, 116, 118, 397
      Timing, Ch. 12
      Tonnage vs. quality, 414
      Undervalued programming, 421
      Value added, 428, 434
      Websites, stations, 410, 422
Budgets, 235
    Advertising/Sales Ratio, 233
    Allocation of budget, 236
    Methods of Development, 229
    Share of voice vs. share of market
173
    Task Method, 234
Business to Business, 206
Buyers, Media, 485
    Network negotiators, 34
    Outdoor, 34
    Spot (TV/Radio), 34
    Internet, 35
Buzz, 254, 261
Cannondale bicycles, 301
Category development index, 217, 368
Caveat-emptor, preface, 443
Changing face of America, 64
Children as targets, 197
Convergence, 8, 59, 495

Considered purchases, 199, 370
Contextual targeting, 201, 465
Costs, Media, Ch. 6
Cost per point (CPP), 124
Cost per thousand (CPM), 122
Magazines, 121, 276, 452
Newspapers, 450
Online, 22
Costs, Media continued
Out of home, 280
Radio, 120, 442
Television, 117, 429
Cross platform buys, 485
Data merge, 109
Demographics, 184
Designated market area (DMA), 209
Digg, 347
Direct Mail, 245
Direct marketing, 245
Display ads, internet, 322, 461
Display ads, print media, 98
Ebbinghaus, 160,
Effective reach, 97, 158
Email, 316
Engagement, 180
Event marketing, 35, 251
Facebook, 342
Future of media, 474
Frequency distribution, 164
Gay market, 198
Generational targeting, 195
Hispanic market, 196
Geographic market definitions, Ch. 11
County size, 200
Designated market area, 209
Metro survey area (MSA), 200
National, 204, 214
Regional, 215
Retail trading area, 213, 382
Geographic Planning, 211
Market Analysis, 211
Size of market, 211
Geographic Analysis, 216
BDI, 217
Geographic Analysis continued
CDI, 217
Competitive situation, 219
Market analysis, 216
Media Efficiency,
Philosophies, marketing, 200
Size of market, 216
Trade situation, 219
Spending strategies, 215
Globalization, 66
Hispanic Market, 118, 148
Hulu, 8, 275
Keywords, 466
Impact, (Ch. 7)
Context, 181, 288
Engagement, 176
Inter media effectiveness, 129
Intra media effectiveness 129
Residue, 163, 172
Integrated Marketing, Tools, Ch. 14
Cross platform buying, 423
Integration, 265
Philosophy of,
Advertising, 239
Custom publishing, 20
Direct marketing, 245
Event marketing, 251
In-store, 382- 398
Mobile, 52, 493
Publicity, 260
Product placement, 246
Sales promotion, 244
Social media, Ch. 17
Sponsorships, 245, 434
Task Matching, 266, 373
Telemarketing, 250
Internet Bureau of Adv. (IAB), 471
Internet Marketing
Ad Networks, 321
Affiliate marketing, 313, 319
Article submissions, 317
Brochure sites, 304
Build website, 307
Conversion, 302
Cost per Click Advertising, 304

Internet Marketing continued
E-Commerce sites, 305
Email advertising, 316
Games, 320
Marketing tools, 316
Mobile marketing, 52, 413
Newsletters, email, 317
Pay per Click Advertising, 304
Podcasting, 320
Portals, 306
Press releases, 320
Rich media, 320
Search engines, 307
Search Eng. Optimization, 303
Social media, Ch. 17
Social news sites, 332
Squidoo, 336
Websites, about, 304
Web community sites, 306
Laser Eye Surgery Case, 302
Linked In, 343
Links, 311, 317
Magazines, 24, 86, 285, 452, 493
Magazine Publishers (MPA), 132
MARCOM Expenditures, 20
Marketing, Ch. 8
Concept, 139
Objectives, 143
Plan, 138, 145
Strategy, 144
Math, media, (Ch.4)
Averages, 73
Percentages, 73
Indexing, 77
Formulas, 80
Weighting, 79
Media Planning & Strategy
Addressable, 61
Alternative, 9, 52
Audience fragmentation, 52, 64
Buying, 14, Ch. 19-23
Buying services, 29
Campbell Ewald, 46
Categories, 6
Communications models, Ch. 9
Consumers in control, 40

Media Planning & Strategy continued
Context, 181
Convergence, 8, 59
Costs, Ch. 6
CPM, 124
Cost per Point (CPP), 124
Efficiency, 123
Creative (the new creative),
Definition of Media, 5
Departments, agency, 27
Digital, 8
Effectiveness, 127
Fragmentation, 52
Inter-media comparisons, 129
Intra-media comparisons, 129
Jobs, Ch. 1-2
Marketing services media, 9
Media Planning, 12, 65, 135, Ch. 18
Messenger, media as, 4, Ch. 7
Mix, 68, 380
Mobile, 318
Out of Home, media, 290, 457
Problems & Opportunities, Ch. 8,
357, 361
Models, communication, Ch. 9
Objectives, 141, 365
Overload, 5
Proliferation, 52, 479
Return on Investment, 10, 78, 369
Revolution, Ch. 3
Role of, 68
Strategies, 12, 372
Tactical plan, 388
Selection, 81, 129,185, 374
Sales, 14, 30, 398
Purchase Funnel, 176
Quintile Analysis, 165
Strategies, 372
Technology, impact of, Ch. 3
Testing/test market, 390
Timing of, Ch. 12
Trends, 212
Planning, (Ch. 18)
Planning Process, 343
Scheduling, 227, 385
McLuhan, Marshall, 127

Minorities, marketing to, 64
Mobile marketing, 318
MySpace, 342
Naples, John, 160
Negotiations, media, (Ch. 19)
  Art of, 387
  Myths, 388
  Process, 387
  Network Television, 33, 429
Neuroscience, 113
Newspapers, 23, 86, 284, 453
  Newspaper Advertising Association
    (NAA), 521
  Audience, 57, 109, 284
  Costs, 446
  Measurement, 109
Nielsen Media Research, 65, 87, 103,
132, 420
Nielsen Net Ratings, 102,110
One World Study, 420
Out of Home, media, 290, 457
Per Inquiry pricing, 481
Per sale pricing, 482
Podcasting, 320
Promotion, sales, 244
  Consumer, 21
  Cross, 242
  Trade, 10, 21, 388
Problems & Opportunities, Ch. 8, 357,
361
Project Canoe, 62
Publishing, custom, 21
Search, organic 462
Per Inquiry pricing, 481
Per sale pricing, 482
Podcasting, 320
Promotion, sales, 244
  Consumer, 21
  Cross, 242
  Trade, 10, 21, 388
Publicity, 260
Publishing, custom, 21
Psychographics, 185
Radio, 275
  Audiences, 438

Radio continued
  Audience Measurement, 107
  Buying, 431
  Costs, 120, 431
  Dayparts, 270, 421
  Station formats, 281, 434
Recency planning, 97, 168
Re-directs, 466
Remnants, media, 484
Residue, 172
Rich media, 134
Sales reps, media, 14, 30, 398
Schultz, Louis M., 3
SEO, 303
Scarborough Research, 108
Scheduling, options, 227, 385
Search Engine Optimization, 46, 311,
Search Engine Optimization con'd, 314
Search Marketing, 322
Share of Voice, 174
Simmons-Experian, 107, 152, 184
Social Media, Ch. 17
  Blogs, 332
  Facebook, 340
  My Space, 342
  LinkedIn, 343
  Digg, 344
  Squidoo, 343
  Stumble Upon, 347
  Twitter, 338
  Video sharing sites, 348
  You Tube, 262, 348,
Sponsorships, 24, 1343, 443
Super Bowl, 408
Target Audiences 183
  Baby Boomers, 63, 191
  Business to business, 206, 294
  Consumer behavior, 195
  Customers v Prospects,
  Decision makers, 190
  Demographics, 184, 426
  Emerging markets, 67, 193
  Ethnic, 63, 286, 424
  Gay, 194
  Generational, 191

Target Audiences continued
Gen X, 196
Gen Y, 196,
Gen Z, 197
Geographic location, Ch. 11
Psychographics, 189
Purchase influencers, 197
Product users, 192
Target rating points (TRPS), 94, 419
Telemarketing, 34, 250
TELMAR, 379
Testing, 392
Television, 271
Audiences, 103
Audience measurement, 103
Bureau TV Advertising (TVB), 375
Buying, TV, Ch. 20
Cable, 24, 273, 423, 425
Costs, 117
Interactive, 7, 69, 492
Television continued
Network, 19, 177, 41
Interactive, 61
Timing issues, Ch. 12
VAI (outdoor), 109
Video, Internet, 351, 496
Virtual screens, 497
Websites, types of, 304
Word of Mouth (WOMM), 255
Word Press, 337

Made in the USA
Charleston, SC
04 May 2011